Rick Bayless

Mexico

One Plate at a Time

RICK BAYLESS WITH
JEANMARIE BROWNSON AND
DEANN GROEN BAYLESS

COLOR PHOTOGRAPHS BY GENTL & HYERS
MEXICAN LOCATION PHOTOGRAPHS BY JAMES BAIGRIE
GLOSSARY PHOTOGRAPHS BY JAMES ISBERNER
ILLUSTRATIONS BY JOHN SANDFORD

Scribner
New York London Toronto Sydney Singapore

To DGB

SCRIBNER
1230 Avenue of the Americas
New York, NY 10020

DESIGNED BY BARBARA M. BACHMAN
SET IN SCALA AND MATRIX

Manufactured in the United States of America

5   7   9   10   8   6   4

Library of Congress Cataloging-in-Publication Data

Bayless, Rick.
Rick Bayless Mexico one plate at a time /
Rick Bayless, with Jeanmarie Brownson and
Deann Groen Bayless ;
color photographs by Gentl & Hyers ;
Mexican location photographs by James Baigrie.
p. cm.
Includes index.
1. Cookery, Mexican. I. Title: Mexico one plate at a time.
II. Brownson, JeanMarie. III. Bayless, Deann Groen. IV. Title.
TX716.M4 B29523 2000
641.5972—dc21
00-058327

ISBN 0-684-84186-X

For information regarding special discounts for bulk purchases,
please contact Simon & Schuster Special Sales at 1-800-456-6798
or business@simonandschuster.com

ACKNOWLEDGMENTS

• • • • • • • • • • • • • • • • • • •

BECAUSE THIS BOOK'S DEVELOPMENT PARALLELED THE RATHER TIGHT PRO-duction schedule of our Public Television series, *Mexico One Plate at a Time with Rick Bayless*, I have a dedicated and very accomplished team to thank for its completion.

Deann Groen Bayless, who for more than twenty years has shared struggles, triumphs, parenthood, loving embraces and a passion for Mexico with me, continues to be the best "producer" I know, keeping me honest, on track and on my toes. JeanMarie Brownson, a partner in several endeavors, brings clarity and an enormous depth of knowledge to our recipes, scrutinizing them for ease in an American kitchen, availability of ingredients (or alternatives), the easiest and best cooking techniques, you name it. Kirsten West supplied months of research in our collection of Spanish-language cookbooks from Mexico (presently numbering over 500, dating from the early 1800s to the present), followed by months of testing and retesting and, yes, retesting. Without her dedication and love for Mexico and its food, these recipes wouldn't be nearly so finely honed. All the writing in the book—for better and worse—is mine.

Though this book has been written with the same amount of love and care as our others, the impetus for its writing is (joyfully) our Public Television series. Manny Valdes, my partner whose brainstorm spawned our prepared foods company, has had unmatched dedication to the show as he led the team raising the funds for production. Carlos Cata, another partner, has supported every move we've made with typical Carlos gusto.

Chris Gyoury's remarkable directorial vision has captured on the small screen the same spirit I always strive to catch with words. The generous-spirited Dana Popoff kept the grueling pressure of production under control, a feat achievable only because of the care and professionalism of the crew. Rocio Barajas worked tirelessly for months to unearth just the right Mexican location to shoot the perfect soft taco or street-side corn-on-the-cob or plate of *mole*.

I'd also like to acknowledge the enthusiasm with which Chicago's Public Television Station, WTTW, embraced our project. Special thanks go to Marie Considine, Mary Beth Hughes and Fred Schneider. The National Pork Producers Council was first to give a finan-cial vote of confidence to the television production. Without them, and the enthusiasm of generous folks at All-Clad, Geyser Peak Winery, Weber Stephen Products and Sargento Cheese, the show—and the book—would never have happened.

Maria Guarnaschelli, my editor, believed in me—unproven, unknown—seventeen years ago when she signed my first book, *Authentic Mexican*. I am honored and privileged to still be working with such an intuitive, knowledgeable and thoughtful editor.

Doe Coover, my agent, is more a family member, I feel, than a business associate. My mother is no more concerned about my well-being—and the well-being of my writing—than Doe.

Most people know that I have an enormous dedication to Deann and my joined-at-the-hip restaurants, Frontera Grill and Topolobampo (445 North Clark Street, Chicago, Illinois 60610; 312-661-1434; FronteraKitchens.com). I'd still be supervising every dish to this day if it weren't for my enthusiastic, talented and devoted co-workers. Tracey Vowell has spent the last ten years honing her cooking skills here and has helped us further develop the "Frontera Style" with honest refinement and incomparable local organic produce, much of it from her own garden. Carlos Alferez, besides bringing me to a deeper love for his home-land's finest handcrafted tequilas, has the ability to engender in our staff the spirit of Mexican hospitality. Laura Cid Pfeiffer's desserts intertwine her Mexico City/Cordon Bleu sophistication with childhood memories of sweet treats at Grandma's knee in Puebla and Monterey. They are supported by the rest of our remarkable management staff: Ruben Beltrán, Elizabeth Bolger, Larry Butcher, Brian Enyart, Sandi Gerchow, Brad Ilic, Richard James, Pat Schloeman and Mark Segura.

Many people contributed to the production of this book and its beauty. Barbara Bachman has created another design for us that gives visual life to my words. Andrea Gentl and Marty Hyers, working with stylists Michael Pederson and Helen Crowther, created photographs of finished dishes that tell as much as the recipes. James Baigrie, who did the location photography, so shared my vision that we often found ourselves photographing the same things. James Isberner added his camera's perspective to the appendix. John Sandford, ever fresh in his approach, created yet a new style for this book's illustrations. Susan Moldow and Roz Lippel, at Scribner, were unsparing in their support.

Steve Siegelman, working together with Casey McCabe, helped shape our television shows and my words within them. I know that Steve's and Casey's words are filtered all through this book. Olivia Wu's words are here, too, I know. Dear friend that she is, Olivia helped me form introductions when deadlines and exhaustion got far too close.

And Fern Berman and Robin Insley have joined insight with determination to let folks everywhere know about this book.

Lastly, a special thanks goes to Jennifer Fite and Fabiola Guerrero de James. As my assistant and our restaurant's publicist, Jennifer has micromanaged my impossible schedule, unraveling tangled details, organizing the unorganizable, all the while remaining unswervingly positive, and has been a treasured friend. Fabiola has helped take care of our daughter since she was nine months old; words cannot express my gratitude for the sisterly love she has offered Lanie. Helping to nurture a world of beauty and diversity for Lanie and her generation is, quite simply, the reason I do the work I do.

Contents

INTRODUCTION

SEVERAL WEEKS AGO I WAS STRUCK BY WHAT I HEARD A FRIEND SAYING. SHE was decrying blunders she'd found on a couple of new restaurant menus: An Italian one, featuring Roman food, had a section of risottos, and an Asian one offered a spicy, chile-infused Cantonese vegetable dish. Most of us know, she assumed, that risottos are the hallmark of northern—not Roman—Italian cooking, and that Sichuan—not Cantonese—food is the spicy regional Chinese cuisine. What's remarkable is that our knowledge of these basic regional distinctions has come over a few short years as we've digested cookbooks, food magazines and authentic restaurant meals.

But when it comes to Mexican cooking, the cooking of our next-door neighbor, most of us aren't even familiar with the everyday classics found in Mexican kitchens all through the country—the *moles, ceviches, adobos* and *barbacoas*—let alone all the nuances and specialties of Mexico's regional cuisines. We're still at the "spaghetti-and-meatballs stage"— which is how I describe our knowledge of Italian food just twenty-five years ago.

So I wrote this book to help us take the first steps toward real Mexican cooking—steps that parallel the progress we've made in our understanding of real Italian or Chinese cooking. I've dedicated these pages to a celebration of classic (rather than regional) Mexican cuisine, dishes that make all Mexican mouths water.

But don't think that means you'll find great recipes for fajitas, burritos, nachos, taco salads and the like. Those are Mexican-American dishes. And, quite frankly, they seem simplistic in comparison to most of the classic cooking across the border, like long-simmered, complexly spiced red *mole* with braised turkey; tender, aromatic pork in banana leaves; and fish baked with tomatoes, jalapeños and olives.

Though the book is organized like a traditional cookbook, from starters and light fare to main dishes and dessert, each of the classic dishes is presented as a mini-chapter with three parts. First, there is an introduction that I hope will prepare you for the full experience of the dish, from flavor to history and culture. Following is the absolute best recipe (in some cases more than one) that my twenty-five years of testing has produced.

But food—even a classic dish—is a dynamic, evolving creation, so in most of these mini-chapters, I've included a contemporary spin on the classic, one that I think captures the spirit of the original while offering a twenty-first century element or two.

The final installment is a Q&A: questions we asked during our extensive testing, followed by the answers we discovered. You'll learn precisely why we wrote the recipes the way we did, why we made certain choices. I hope this section provides insight about how and why these classic dishes work, and, as importantly, how to cook.

My passion for Mexican cuisine aside, I wrote this book for another reason: I want to engage as many people as I can in sharing fresh, honest food. Until the fairly recent past, our species has lived in small, relatively self-sustaining communities, sharing daily life with the same handful of folks in more or less the same place from birth to death. Without a second thought, we nourished ourselves with locally grown, seasonal foods. All that has changed, and the ties that bound us to our families, communities, terrain, seasons and food have in many cases weakened. I think that it is safe to say that a sense of disconnection, or disenfranchisement, permeates many lives. Just as we've had to learn to substitute planned physical exercise for the healthy exertion most of our ancestors experienced in everyday life, so, I believe, to be completely healthy, do we have to exercise our connection to the world we live in. Food provides the perfect medium for that. Here's my simple six-step "exercise" regimen:

1. *Cook with minimally processed, natural ingredients.* Choosing natural ingredients keeps me connected to my essential dependence (along with all other living creatures) on the fruit of the land. Choosing ingredients that are organically raised insures supporting producers who care about the health of the earth, many of whom run small family operations that are vital to their communities. Also, organic products are not genetically modified (a powerful new technology that has not been sufficiently tested or regulated to ensure its long-term efficacy or safety).

2. *Grow something.* Growing anything—from sprouts on the windowsill to a few pots of chiles to a big garden—keeps me connected to the life-affirming process of regeneration.

3. *Shop at farmers' markets.* Farmers' markets not only offer the freshest local, seasonal food, they offer me a connection to the triumphs and struggles of those who partner with nature to provide our sustenance.

4. *Plan occasional celebration meals around local seasonal foods.* Whether it's the local strawberries that last three weeks in spring or the cold-storage parsnips and potatoes during the winter, celebrating the season offers me a connection to the rhythms of the seasons and the different seasonal needs of my body.

5. *Schedule at least one special meal each week with people I care about.* Planning a special meal, especially one in which everyone (even the kids) contributes something, offers me a connection to others, with nurturance at the center. I do my best to make this special meal a time that no one wants to end by encouraging great conversation, playing games, doing anything that keeps us all connected. Special meals help me reinforce the distinction between simple, lean, everyday eating and pull-out-the-stops celebratory fare. Without both on a regular basis, life is out of balance.

6. *Regularly prepare ethnic dishes, cultivate friends who can share their ethnic traditions, or support restaurants that offer honest, fresh ethnic food.* Relishing food from traditions that are not my own offers me the connection to a world of cultures, to my place in all humanity. My explorations can be as exotic as, say, a trip to Asia, or as easy as a quick excursion to Chicago's Chinatown.

Starters, Snacks and Light Meals

Guacamole

 Was there ever a fruit as sensual as an avocado? So rough-hewn, dare-to-touch-me masculine on the outside, so yielding, inviting, soft spring green and feminine inside? Writers have proclaimed that the avocado, tomato and chile are among Mexico's gifts to the world. And they name guacamole, where all three come together, as a perfect work of art.

It's no wonder that this perfect fruit begs to be mashed to enhance its melting, naturally spreadable quality. Early Spanish settlers called guacamole "the butter of the poor." The Aztecs recognized its possibilities when they coined the word "guacamole": "guaca" for avocado and "mole" for sauce.

Mashed avocado invites you to add flavors—think flavored butters here. Yet, considering how perfect it is in itself, the challenge is to exercise restraint. There are Mexican purists who stop at a sprinkle of salt on their avocado mash and call that guacamole. But I think you can employ a little creativity, setting some limits: no mayonnaise or sour cream. Avocado flesh by itself has an unctuous quality and subtle flavor—no need to dilute it. As for the add-ins, these flavor pinpoints seem more welcome when the guacamole is intended for chips. On the Mexican side of the border, guacamole's role is more as a salsa, something you spread on a taco. A smooth version blended with tomatillos can be a delicious drizzle over practically anything edible.

The second recipe here, the contemporary one, produces guacamole that is boosted with roasted poblanos, roasted tomatoes and roasted garlic. Roasting heightens sweetness, yielding a deeper-flavored guacamole. Though this contemporary version is good in and of itself, it is a perfect sauce for salmon steaks or grilled chicken. Whether you choose traditional or contemporary, feel free to pare these recipes down or add to them. They're yours to make your own.

TRADITIONAL BENCHMARK: In my opinion, the best guacamole is a simple one—one that glamorizes the flavor of really delicious avocados, plain and simple. That starts with hand-mashing thoroughly ripe avocados to a chunky-smooth texture, then underscoring the avocado's natural richness with a little tang from lime juice, perhaps a little perfumy cilantro, maybe some crunchy onion and a hint of hot green chile. And tomato, too, might go in to boost the flavors with sweetness—though that's not always necessary.

WHEN TO THINK OF THESE RECIPES: Guacamole is tremendously versatile. It almost defines the phrase "casual party food," but it's so simple to make that there's nothing to keep you from whipping up a batch for Wednesday night dinner, to spoon, say, onto a simple soft taco or over grilled chicken or fish. Guacamole in a warm corn tortilla is a favorite (if not totally balanced) lunch of mine.

ADVICE FOR AMERICAN COOKS: Decent avocados are quite readily available, but they're not always ripe. You may have to buy them a few days before you need them to ensure that they'll be soft-ripe.

Above: Buying vegetables
Right: Grilled meat taco stalls, Oaxaca market

Classic Guacamole

GUACAMOLE CLÁSICO

Makes about 2½ cups, serving 6 as
an appetizer, 8 to 10 as a nibble

Fresh hot green chiles to taste (about 2 serranos or 1 jalapeño),
    stemmed
½ medium white onion, finely chopped (about ⅓ cup),
    plus a little extra for garnish
6 ounces (1 medium round or 2 plum) tomatoes (you want
    these ripe, though absolute red ripeness isn't as important
    here as it is, say, for chopped tomato salsa)
¼ cup coarsely chopped fresh cilantro, plus a little extra
    for garnish
3 medium-large (about 1¼ pounds total) ripe avocados
Salt
1 to 2 tablespoons fresh lime juice
A few slices of radish for garnish (optional)

TRADITIONAL

1. ROASTING THE CHILES. Lay the chiles in a small ungreased skillet set over medium heat. Turn them every minute or so until they have softened (they'll darken in spots), 5 to 10 minutes. Mash them into a coarse puree, using a mortar, or finely chop them. Place in a large bowl.

2. MORE FLAVORINGS. Scoop the chopped onion into a strainer and rinse under cold water; shake off excess water and add to the bowl with the chiles. Chop the tomatoes into small bits—skin, seeds and all is my preference. You should have a scant cup. Add to the bowl along with the cilantro.

3. THE AVOCADOS. To cut an avocado in half, you have to negotiate the large egg-shaped pit in the middle. Make a cut down the length of 1 avocado straight through to the pit. Continue cutting all the way around the pit until you wind up where you started. Twist the two halves in opposite directions and pull them apart. Scoop out the pit (the *hueso*, or bone, in Spanish) with a spoon. Then scoop out the avocado flesh from the skin and add to the bowl. Do the same with the

remaining avocados. Use an old-fashioned potato masher or the back of a large spoon to mash the avocado flesh into a coarse pulp, mixing in the other ingredients as you go.

4. SEASONING THE GUACAMOLE. Taste the guacamole and season with salt, usually a scant teaspoon, then add some of the lime juice and taste again. Continue seasoning with lime until the guacamole has enough zip for you. Cover with plastic wrap, placing it directly on the surface, and refrigerate until you're ready to serve.

5. SERVING. Unless you're serving guacamole dolloped on tacos or the like, the classic way to present it to your guests is in a Mexican lava-rock mortar (*molcajete*), sprinkled with chopped onion and cilantro. Sliced radish, if you have it, looks pretty here, and to the Mexican eye completes the very popular, patriotic red-white-and-green motif.

WORKING AHEAD: Guacamole is good when freshly made, but, in my opinion, it tastes even better when the flavors are allowed to mingle for about half an hour before serving. If well chilled, it'll keep for several hours. After that, the flavors get out of balance and the avocado starts to turn brown.

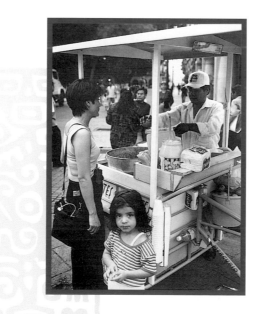

Buying roasted corn-on-the-cob

Roasted Poblano Guacamole with garlic and parsley

GUACAMOLE DE CHILE POBLANO ASADO

Makes 2½ cups, serving 6 as an appetizer,
8 to 10 as a nibble

2 medium (about 6 ounces total) fresh poblano chiles
6 ounces (1 medium round or 2 plum) ripe tomatoes
2 garlic cloves, unpeeled
3 tablespoons chopped fresh flat-leaf parsley
3 medium-large (about 1¼ pounds total) ripe avocados
Salt
1 to 2 tablespoons fresh lime juice
2 tablespoons grated Mexican queso añejo or
    other dry grating cheese, such as Romano or Parmesan
A few slices of radish for garnish

1.   THE POBLANOS, TOMATOES AND GARLIC. Lay the poblanos, tomatoes and garlic on a baking sheet and set 4 inches below a very hot broiler. Roast, turning every couple of minutes, until the chiles and tomatoes are soft, blistered and blackened in spots and the garlic is soft, 12 to 13 minutes. Place the chiles in a bowl, cover with a towel and let stand for 5 minutes, then wipe off the blackened skin. Pull or cut out the stems, seed pods and seeds; rinse quickly to remove any stray seeds and bits of char. When the tomatoes are cool, peel off and discard their skins. Slip the papery skins off the garlic. In a mortar or with a food processor, make a coarse puree of the roasted garlic and poblanos (with both mortar and processor, it's best to start with the garlic, then add the poblanos); place in a large bowl. Chop the roasted tomatoes (for this recipe, it's best not to use any of the juice from the baking sheet) and add to the poblano mixture along with the parsley.

2.   FINISHING THE GUACAMOLE. Cut the avocados lengthwise in half around the pit, twist the halves apart and remove the pits. Scoop out the flesh into the bowl with the flavorings. Using a potato masher or the back of a large spoon, coarsely mash everything together. Taste and season with salt, usually a scant teaspoon,

then add enough lime juice to enliven all the flavors. Cover with plastic wrap, placing it directly on the surface, and refrigerate until you're ready to eat.

To serve, scoop into a decorative bowl or Mexican mortar, sprinkle with the *queso añejo* and stud with radish slices.

WORKING AHEAD: The roasted poblanos, tomatoes and garlic can be prepared a day or so in advance, but don't puree them until you are ready to make the guacamole. It will keep for several hours tightly covered in the refrigerator; add the cheese and radish slices at the last moment.

PREPARATIONS FOR ROASTED POBLANO GUACAMOLE (PAGE 6)

Questions and Answers from Our Testing

What kinds of avocados work best? There are many varieties of avocados in the U.S. commercial market. I've tried most all of them, as well as a good number of the regional varieties found in Mexico. My learning: Choose the widely available pebbly-feeling Hass (often called simply "California avocado" in the market), the one whose skin changes from emerald green to brown-black as it ripens. It accounts for about 80 percent of the California commercial crop (which accounts for 90 percent of the total U.S. crop), and it has several things going for it. First, a Hass avocado has richness that translates to luscious, thick guacamole. Second, it holds beautifully for several days in the refrigerator once it's ripe. Third, it oxidizes (read: it browns) more slowly than other varieties. And, last, it has amazingly good, concentrated flavor that hints at herbs like anise. Hass avocados are available most of the year, though they're iffy in late fall.

In Mexico, I look for the small fig-sized avocados called *criollos*, the ones usually collected from the wild, with large pits and much more intense flavor than a ripe Hass avocado. You won't find those in the United States, though, so make a mental note for your next trip to Mexico. Here you'll find the always-green-skinned Fuertes (the second in commercial volume), Bacons, Pinkertons, Zutanos and the like—most of these are hybrids from the Mexican and Guatemalan avocado species. The availability of these varieties is more spotty than the Hass (they're most abundant from late fall to winter), and their flavor is less intense. What is commonly called the Florida avocado comes from a third species, the Caribbean one, that produces large fruit with a low oil content (25 to 50 percent less than most California avocados). With its bright, sweet flavor, it is wonderful cut into cubes or slices in salads, but it makes a watery, simple-tasting guacamole. The Caribbean avocados are at their peak during the winter months.

How does avocado ripeness affect guacamole flavor? A curious fact: Avocados do not ripen on the tree. It's not until they're picked and given the right conditions that the flesh will begin to soften and the flavor more fully blossom. If you buy avocados that are hard, allow several days for them to soften on the countertop (some folks claim that putting them in a closed bag speeds softening). They're ripe to most people's taste when they give fairly easily under firm pressure. But, as with the ripeness of bananas, every eater has a preference—some like light green, barely ripe flavors; others like the rich, dark complexity of very soft flesh. I think that, by everyone's standards, flesh that won't mash into a smoothish paste isn't ripe enough. Conversely, brown flesh with a pit rattling around inside is past the prime. Refrigerating ripe avocados, except the Hass variety, risks the flesh darkening. Refrigerated ripe Hass avocados will keep perfectly for 4 or 5 days.

HOW DO YOU ACHIEVE THE BEST-FLAVORED GUACAMOLE? Most cooks make gua-camole with chopped fresh hot green chiles like serrano. Here I've asked you to roast those chiles. Roasted chiles add sweetness and underscore the richer flavors of the avocado. Using white onions and rinsing them under cold water before stirring them in ensures a crisp onion flavor that will not dominate the avocado. Work in the flavorings a little at a time until the guacamole tastes really good to you. I have given volume measures of each flavoring ingredient (1/3 cup chopped white onion, for instance), to let you know the quan-tities that are usually right for me. Guacamole tastes harmonious when all the flavorings are finely chopped.

HOW LONG DOES GUACAMOLE KEEP AND WHAT IS THE BEST WAY TO HOLD IT? Though in some places it's the fashion to make guacamole tableside, serving it the second everything's together doesn't give time for the flavors to meld. That takes about 30 min-utes. Any avocado will easily last that long without discoloring, but guacamole made with Hass avocados will stay beautiful for several hours. Refrigerate guacamole to keep it from becoming runny, covered with good plastic wrap placed directly on the surface (Saran Wrap is the least permeable, ensuring the least amount of discoloration). The acid of lime juice also slows discoloration, but too much lime juice can make your guacamole memo-rable for all the wrong reasons.

Ceviche (Lime-Marinated Seafood)

Ceviche: tender morsels of the freshest fish marinated in fresh lime juice, with flecks of sweet tomato, biting chile, odoriferous cilantro. *Ceviche* is as much a place as a dish, though, and the place is far from home. In the shade or full sun, it's casual, spirited beach food. Food that makes folks feel the thick, salty-smelling coastal air with just one bite of its bracing freshness.

Ceviche isn't native to Mexico, even though it's been a daily offering there for so many centuries—since the Spaniards or Portuguese brought limes to this land back in the mid–sixteenth century—that I doubt there's a Mexican who wouldn't defend it as one of his own. The researchers, of course, view it from the unglamorous angle of food preservation: small pieces of fresh fish or seafood gently pickled in lime juice to preserve the freshness of the catch a little longer. The citric acid of the juice actually changes the look and texture of the fish, turning translucent raw flesh into the firm, near-flaky opacity of "cooked" fish.

Mexican *ceviche*, which is unlike those with South American pedigrees, comes in two rather distinct styles, both marked with Mexican national flavors (tomato, chile, cilantro). At one end of the continuum, *ceviche* is a sauceless mélange that's perfect piled on crispy tortillas or saltines (yes, saltines) as a snack. At the other end: saucy with spicy, ketchupy tanginess, served in a cup with crispy tortillas or saltines on the side. And while both styles of *ceviche* are typically created from very fresh *raw* fish (a challenge for the landlocked or squeamish), shrimp, crab, lobster and squid are typically *cooked* before making their way into the marinade—reassuring for many, I imagine.

I've written recipes for three *ceviches* here, two traditional and one contemporary. The first is the sauceless style, made with cubed raw fish. I've kept it to simple perfection, throwing in a few olives and some diced avocado for special interest. The second focuses on cooked shrimp in a saucy mix of lime juice, ketchup and Mexican hot sauce. Cucumber or jícama and avocado spark the imagination here. Of course, feel free to substitute the drained marinated fish from the sauceless variety for the cooked lime-tossed shrimp of the saucy version, and vice versa. The rules are what you make them.

While salmon isn't common in Mexico, it's easy to get here. And it's usually very fresh.

So I've developed a contemporary version of *ceviche* for my American audience that half-pickles the cubed fish in punchy lime and mellow orange, then mixes in classic salmon accompaniments (capers and red onion) along with the very Mexican roasted green chile and cilantro. Elegant, cross-cultural, delicious.

TRADITIONAL BENCHMARK: Whether finished saucy (with ketchup and hot sauce) or not, the best Mexican *ceviches* I've eaten epitomize freshness—fish, vegetables, herbs, lime—shot through with a well-balanced zing, and a medley of textures that brings you back for bite after bite. The fish is softly tender and juicy, not mushy, mealy, raw or dryish. And the *ceviche*'s lime, while something of a swaggert by nature, never leads me to think of "sour" to the exclusion of all else.

WHEN TO THINK OF THESE RECIPES: For most of us, making a dish that requires very fresh fish—or even fish at all—means we're putting some effort into dinner. So I think about making it for a casual gathering when there's something to celebrate—perhaps something as simple as a lovely summer evening in the backyard. *Ceviche* is the epitome of refreshment in warm weather.

ADVICE FOR AMERICAN COOKS: Finding fresh fish is the only challenge in *ceviche* making. Start your search at the most reputable, popular seafood market. Always smell fish for *ceviche* before you buy it: It should have a clean, nonfishy, almost briny, just-from-the-sea smell. The eyes of the freshest whole fish are generally clear, the flesh is firm (if scales are still attached, they should be *firmly* attached) and gills are bright red. Very fresh fillets have a translucency about them. Ask for sushi/sashimi quality (the highest-grade, freshest fish, intended for eating raw) if that is an option your vendor offers.

SHRIMP C*EVICHE* "COCKTAIL" (PAGE 16)

Classic *Ceviche*

CEVICHE CLÁSICO

1 pound fresh, skinless snapper, bass, halibut or other ocean fish fillets
  (the fish I listed I like because they have a large flake or meaty
  texture), cut into ½-inch cubes or slightly smaller
About 1½ cups fresh lime juice
1 medium white onion, chopped into ¼-inch pieces
1 pound (2 medium-large round or 6 to 8 plum) ripe tomatoes,
  chopped into ¼-inch pieces
Fresh hot green chiles to taste (roughly 2 to 3 serranos or
  1 to 2 jalapeños), stemmed, seeded and finely chopped
⅓ cup chopped fresh cilantro, plus a few leaves for garnish
⅓ cup chopped pitted green olives (choose manzanillos for
  a typical Mexican flavor)
1 to 2 tablespoons olive oil, preferably extra-virgin (optional,
  but recommended to give a glistening appearance)
Salt
3 tablespoons fresh orange juice
  OR ½ teaspoon sugar
1 large or 2 small ripe avocados, peeled, pitted and diced
Tostadas or tortilla chips, store-bought or homemade (page 136),
  or saltine crackers for serving

TRADITIONAL

1. **MARINATING THE FISH.** In a 1½-quart glass or stainless steel bowl, combine
   the fish, lime juice and onion. You'll need enough juice to cover the fish and allow
   it to float somewhat freely; too little juice means unevenly "cooked" fish. Cover
   and refrigerate for about 4 hours, until a cube of fish no longer looks raw when
   broken open. Pour into a colander and drain off the lime juice.
2. **THE FLAVORINGS.** In a large bowl, mix together the tomatoes, green chiles,
   cilantro, olives and optional olive oil. Stir in the fish, then taste and season with

salt, usually about ¾ teaspoon, and the orange juice or sugar (the sweetness of the orange juice or sugar helps balance some of the typical tanginess of the *ceviche*). Cover and refrigerate if not serving immediately.

3. SERVING THE *CEVICHE*. Just before serving, stir in the diced avocado, being careful not to break up the pieces. For serving, you have several options: Set out your *ceviche* in a large bowl and let people spoon it onto individual plates to eat with chips or saltines; serve small bowls of *ceviche* (I like to lay a bed of frisée lettuce in each bowl before spooning in the *ceviche*) and serve tostadas, chips or saltines alongside; or pile the *ceviche* onto chips or tostadas and pass around for guests to consume on these edible little plates. Whichever direction you choose, garnish the *ceviche* with leaves of cilantro before setting it center stage.

WORKING AHEAD: The fish can be marinated a day in advance; after about 4 hours, when the fish is "cooked," drain it so that it won't become too limy. For the freshest flavor, add the flavorings to the fish no more than a couple of hours before serving.

Left: Ceviche
Below: Serving ceviche
at Neptuno Restaurant

Shrimp *Ceviche* "Cocktail"

CEVICHE DE CAMARÓN

Makes 3 cups, serving 6 as an appetizer

$^{1}/_{2}$ cup plus 2 tablespoons fresh lime juice

1 generous pound unpeeled smallish shrimp (I prefer the ones that
    are 41/50 count to a pound)

$^{1}/_{2}$ medium white onion, chopped into $^{1}/_{4}$-inch pieces

$^{1}/_{3}$ cup chopped fresh cilantro, plus several sprigs for garnish

$^{1}/_{2}$ cup ketchup

1 to 2 tablespoons vinegary Mexican bottled hot sauce
    (such as Tamazula, Valentina or Búfalo, the latter being
    on the sweet side)

About 2 tablespoons olive oil, preferably extra-virgin (optional,
    but recommended to smooth out sharpness)

1 cup diced peeled cucumber or jícama (or $^{1}/_{2}$ cup of each)

1 small ripe avocado, peeled, pitted and cubed

Salt

Several lime slices for garnish

Tostadas or tortilla chips, store-bought or homemade (page 136),
    or saltine crackers for serving

TRADITIONAL

1. COOKING AND MARINATING THE SHRIMP. Bring 1 quart salted water to a boil and add *2 tablespoons* of the lime juice. Scoop in the shrimp, cover and let the water return to the boil. Immediately remove from the heat, set the lid askew and pour off all the liquid. Replace the cover and let the shrimp steam off the heat for 10 minutes. Spread out the shrimp in a large glass or stainless steel bowl to cool completely.

    Peel and devein the shrimp if you wish: One by one, lay the shrimp on your work surface, make a shallow incision down the back and scrape out the (usually) dark intestinal tract. Toss the shrimp with the remaining $^{1}/_{2}$ *cup* lime juice, cover and refrigerate for about an hour.

2. THE FLAVORINGS. In a small strainer, rinse the onion under cold water, then

shake off the excess liquid. Add to the shrimp bowl along with the cilantro, ketchup, hot sauce, optional olive oil, cucumber and/or jícama and avocado. Taste and season with salt, usually about ½ teaspoon. Cover and refrigerate if not serving immediately.

3. SERVING THE CEVICHE. Spoon the *ceviche* into sundae glasses, martini glasses or small bowls; garnish with sprigs of cilantro and slices of lime. Serve with tostadas, tortilla chips or saltines to enjoy alongside.

WORKING AHEAD: The *ceviche* is best made the day it is served. The flavorings can be added to the shrimp a few hours in advance.

Peeking into a hidden courtyard

Salmon *Ceviche* with orange, capers and roasted green chile

CEVICHE DE SALMÓN A LA NARANJA

Makes 4 cups, serving 8 as an appetizer

1 pound very fresh skinless salmon fillets (you'll need about 1 ¼
*   pounds if the salmon has the skin—trim off the skin before*
*   proceeding), cut into ½-inch cubes or slightly smaller*
About ⅔ cup fresh lime juice
About ⅔ cup fresh orange juice
1 medium red onion, chopped into ¼-inch pieces
1 large fresh poblano chile
2 large seedless oranges
2 tablespoons drained capers
⅓ cup chopped fresh cilantro, plus some leaves for garnish
Salt
2 generous cups frisée lettuce (what you'll get from 1 small head)
Thin slices toasted French bread or special crackers for serving

CONTEMPORARY

1. MARINATING THE SALMON. Place the salmon in a 1½-quart glass or stainless steel bowl and stir in the lime and orange juices and onion. You'll need enough juice to cover the fish and allow it to float somewhat freely. Cover and refrigerate for 2 hours, until a piece of salmon looks "cooked" about halfway through—it'll still be translucent pink inside. Drain off all but a little of the juice.

2. THE FLAVORINGS. Roast the poblano over an open flame or on a baking sheet 4 inches below a very hot broiler, turning regularly until the skin is evenly blistered and blackened, about 5 minutes for an open flame, 10 minutes for the broiler. Cover with a kitchen towel and let stand for 5 minutes. Rub off the blackened skin, then pull or cut out the stem and the seed pod. Tear open and quickly rinse to remove any stray seeds and bits of skin. Cut into ¼-inch pieces and place in a large bowl.

    Cut the stem and blossom ends (tops and bottoms) off both oranges. Then, standing each orange on your cutting board and working close to the flesh, cut away the rind and all the white pith. Cut out the all-orange, no-white-pith segments: With a small sharp knife, cut between the segment-dividing white membranes, releasing perfect little segments (called *suprêmes*). Cut the segments in half and add to the bowl.

Stir in the capers, cilantro and marinated salmon (with the remaining juice). Taste and season with salt, usually about ¹/₂ teaspoon, then cover and refrigerate if not serving immediately.

3. SERVING THE *CEVICHE*. Divide the frisée among eight martini glasses or small decorative bowls. Spoon the *ceviche* into the center of the lettuce, lay on a leaf or two of cilantro and you're ready to share this wonderful dish with your guests. Serve with toasts or crackers.

WORKING AHEAD: This *ceviche* is best made the day it is served. After marinating the fish, the flavorings can be successfully added 4 or 5 hours ahead, but spoon the *ceviche* onto the lettuce when the guests are seated.

Preparing ceviche *at Neptuno*

QUESTIONS AND ANSWERS FROM OUR TESTING

WHICH FISH VARIETIES COMMONLY AVAILABLE IN AMERICAN MARKETS MAKE GOOD *CEVICHE*? While you can make *ceviche* from any fish, not all turn out a dish with pleasing texture or color. Firm fish with large flakes (sea bass, snapper, halibut, mahimahi) keep their shape and texture, but soft-fleshed fish with small flakes (trout and sole, for example) break up and seem mushy. Steaky fish like tuna and marlin also produce firm-textured pieces. Lighter-colored fish stay light-colored throughout the preparation, while dark flesh looks a little gray after marinating. In our restaurant, we typically make *ceviche* with marlin for firmness and light color, our second choice being tuna (which comes out darker but still firm). In Mexico, in Veracruz and Acapulco, two places famous for *ceviche*, cooks typically use fish from the stronger-tasting, darker-colored mackerel family, like sierra and kingfish. As long as those fish are the epitome of freshness, they'll be delicious, reasonably firm and lighter colored than tuna. Salmon, while becoming a beautiful orangy-pink color when marinated, is a moderately soft fish for *ceviche*. However, I've included a contemporary recipe that uses it because very fresh farm-raised salmon is fairly easy for landlocked folks to get and because salmon's richness is well balanced by citrus. In my recipe, I suggest marinating the salmon until only "half-done" to avoid problems with mushy or mealy texture. *Health considerations:* Avoid ocean fish like amberjack that are prone to parasites. (If you catch your own fish or shellfish from local waters, make sure the waters are approved for harvest.) The National Fisheries Institute recommends using frozen fish for *ceviche* (it must be frozen at 0°F, which usually means commercial freezing equipment) to completely wipe out chances of parasitic contamination. I have turned out nice-textured *ceviche* using frozen steaky fish like marlin and tuna.

WHICH OF THE REALLY TANGY CITRUS JUICES (LIME, LEMON OR KEY LIME) WORKS BEST IN THIS TYPE OF PREPARATION? In Mexico, cooks use either Tahitian/Persian hybrid limes (the ones most commonly available in our grocery stores) or the more highly prized little yellow-green key limes called *limón criollo*. Key limes have a distinctive flavor (more intensely citrusy-floral) and higher acid content, but in our tests both performed similarly in terms of length of time necessary to "cook" the fish. Lemon is the least acidic of the three citrus options and requires an extra half hour or so to "cook" the fish through. Taste, however, is substantially different for each of the three. Those who like bracingly tangy mouthfuls of complex flavor should seek out key limes. Those who like gentle, brisk sunniness will prefer lemons. The rest will remain in the more usual hybrid-lime camp.

(For my contemporary salmon *ceviche*, I mix lime juice with much-less-acidic orange, then use the combination to "half-cook" the salmon. Using a lime-orange mix in traditional *ceviche* would considerably lengthen the "cooking" time.)

WHAT QUANTITY OF JUICE IS NEEDED? Not wanting to use more juice than necessary, we tried making *ceviche* with only the amount of juice needed to coat, not cover, the fish—about 1 cup. Besides "cooking" the cubes of fish unevenly (some pieces were done an hour before others), the whole process took several hours longer. Our conclusion: The fish needs enough juice to more or less float freely.

WHAT AMOUNT OF TIME IS OPTIMAL FOR MARINATING THE FISH? For cubes about $1/2$ inch, 4 hours is the marinating time it takes for the fish to completely lose its raw-looking translucency. Two hours is about right for the "sashimi" center some prefer. Much longer than 4 hours will actually give the fish a slightly "overcooked" mealiness and a very strong lime flavor. Citrus juice penetrates firm-fleshed fish like tuna more slowly than it does softer fish like snapper.

WHAT IS KEY IN BALANCING FLAVORS AND TEXTURES IN GOOD *CEVICHE*? To some, it will seem obvious that adding a little sugar keeps the finished *ceviche* from tipping off the tangy scale—not enough sugar to make it taste sweet, just enough to offer a little perspective. For a gentler, more flavorful sweetness, I've suggested orange juice as an alternative to sugar. Salt plays a less obvious—but important—role; it is more difficult to use with a sure hand because our taste buds sometimes confuse salt and acid in these very tangy dishes. My recommendation is that if you're new to seasoning *ceviche*, taste your finished *ceviche* with no salt, then add salt a little at a time until you feel you've reached a perfect balance. For me, the best distribution of flavors and textures in classic *ceviche* comes from all the ingredients being chopped into pieces more or less the same size. And beautiful harmony is achieved with a little unctuous olive oil or avocado to smooth out the emphasis on tang.

REFINEMENTS: The marinating bowl is important: Plastic can easily pick up fishy, limy flavors, while aluminum can add tinniness to the mix. To tame the aggressiveness of raw onions, I've learned that adding them to the lime along with the fish pickles away any offensively strong taste. A sharp knife is essential for cutting fish fillets; dull blades tear at the rather delicate flesh. For safety's sake, after cutting fish, wash your cutting board and utensils with a mild bleach solution. If you have to keep fish for a day or so before marinating the *ceviche*, seal it in a plastic bag, pack it in ice and store it in the coldest part of the refrigerator.

Queso Fundido

 An earthy brick-colored casserole that holds a bubbling, sizzling blanket of melted cheese, strips of roasted peppers and crumbles of sharp, meaty sausage—who wouldn't dig into such food? If you're generous, you invite friends to join in, scooping up the flowing cheese. No food translates into more carefree fun than a singing dish of *queso fundido*.

In Mexico, *queso fundido* is largely proffered in restaurants in the northern part of the country. Imagine the scene: A huge trough of hot coals relentlessly radiating smoky heat toward split goats roasting on skewers. At the end of the open-fire assembly are several clay dishes atop an iron grill, making use of the edges of the coals. In them is spluttering cheese, crusting a bit on the bottom. Heady stuff.

Most cheese making in Mexico is a cottage industry, where simple, crumbly "garnishing" cheeses (the fresh *queso fresco*, the aged *queso añejo*) predominate. Melting cheeses, in fact, are relatively few, and they play a much less domineering role in Real Mexican Food than they do in America's "Mexican" food. *Queso fundido* is the exception. With America's penchant for melted cheese, you can understand why *queso fundido*—also called *queso flameado* in northern Mexico—has proliferated in Mexican restaurants in this country.

Though practically any melting cheese will work, in Mexico the dish is typically made from *asadero* or the mild cheddar-like Chihuahua (a type of cheese brought to the northern state of Chihuahua by German Mennonites in the 1920s). Stateside, the choices multiply. In my contemporary recipe, I suggest mozzarella, but that's only the first possibility.

With the right cheese as a base, *rajas* ("strips") of roasted poblano peppers create classic perfection. Raw poblanos start out with a medium-spicy, concentrated green-chile flavor that hints at green beans and parsley. When blistered over a flame, these qualities mellow into a sweet round harmony—to me, the quintessential complex Mexican flavor. Add some tangy chorizo sausage, and that melted cheese-and-poblano is all jazzed up.

My contemporary recipe shows you how to adapt the principles of *queso fundido*. I melt mozzarella and combine it with the earthbound flavors of mushrooms and a smoky chipotle chile that echoes the scent of a wood fire.

Have your guests seated at the table before you serve *queso fundido*—it's critical to catch the cheese at its most oozy. My instructions help you coordinate the warming of corn tortillas with the melting of the cheese. Yes, corn tortillas. Though decent ones aren't always as easy to find in the United States as their wheat flour counterparts, corn tortillas are number one in Mexico. And a better match, to my taste.

TRADITIONAL BENCHMARK: Strings of melted cheese, *hebras,* as they're called in Spanish, are the sine qua non of *queso fundido,* according to those Mexicans who claim it as their dish. For me, the cheese needs to have good flavor (but not be overbearing—a mild cheddar rather than a sharp one) so it welcomes other ingredients; it needs to have a *little* chewiness when it's melted (rather than be as runny as cream) to offer substance to scoop into the tortilla and transport to the mouth. And, in my opinion, *queso fundido* is like a one-note samba unless it's got a few good add-ins that contrast with the rich cheese, like tangy chorizo sausage and flame-roasted chiles.

WHEN TO THINK OF THESE RECIPES: Though northern Mexico, the homeland of the most famous *quesos fundidos,* doesn't exactly have a wintry clime, I think *queso fundido* is a perfect cold-weather dish. A casserole of *queso fundido* served before a cookout is a Mexican tradition, but serve only enough to tantalize, not satiate. For me, *queso fundido* is a casual main dish, a Sunday night supper, with some good tortillas and a tossed salad.

ADVICE FOR AMERICAN COOKS: A good corn tortilla to scoop the cheese into is the hardest ingredient for most Americans to obtain. Mexican chorizo sausage, while not available everywhere, can be replaced by another sausage or omitted. And a variety of large chiles and peppers is available everywhere nowadays, so make *queso fundido* with whichever ones you can get, even if they aren't poblanos.

Melted Cheese Casserole with Mexican sausage and roasted chiles

QUESO FUNDIDO CON CHORIZO Y RAJAS

Makes enough *queso fundido* for 12 soft tacos, serving
6 as an appetizer, 4 as a casual main dish

2 medium (about 6 ounces total) fresh poblano chiles
4 ounces (½ cup) Mexican chorizo sausage, store-bought (casing
    removed if there is one) or homemade (page 26)
1 medium white onion, sliced
Salt
12 corn tortillas, the fresher the better (store-bought are okay,
    but homemade [page 104] will really shine here)
8 ounces Chihuahua or other Mexican melting cheese, such as
    quesadilla or asadero (lacking Mexican cheese, queso
    fundido is delicious made with everything from Monterey
    Jack to mild cheddar), shredded (you'll have about 2 cups)
About 1 teaspoon or so of crumbled dried oregano, preferably Mexican

TRADITIONAL

1. ROASTING THE POBLANO CHILES. Roast the poblanos over an open flame or on a baking sheet 4 inches below a very hot broiler, turning regularly until the skin is evenly blistered and blackened, about 5 minutes for an open flame, about 10 minutes for the broiler. Be careful not to char the flesh, only the skin. Cover with a kitchen towel and let stand for 5 minutes. Rub off the blackened skin, then pull or cut out the stems and the seed pods. Tear the chiles open and quickly rinse to remove any stray seeds and bits of skin. Cut into ¼-inch-wide strips about 2 inches long.

2. THE CHORIZO-POBLANO MIXTURE. Heat the oven to 350°F. In a medium skillet (preferably nonstick), cook the chorizo over medium heat, stirring to break up any clumps, until half-cooked, about 5 minutes. (As the chorizo heats, it should render enough fat to cook the meat; if the mixture seems dry, add a little oil.) Add the onion and cook, stirring frequently, until the onion is richly golden and the chorizo cooked through, about 10 minutes. (If the mixture looks very oily, drain

it.) Stir in the poblano strips, taste and season with salt if you think the mixture needs some. Transfer the mixture to a 9- or 10-inch shallow baking dish, Mexican *cazuela* or pie plate.

3.   FINISHING THE *QUESO FUNDIDO.* Very lightly dampen a clean kitchen towel. Check the tortillas to make sure none are stuck together. Wrap them in the towel, then in foil, sealing the edges tightly. Place in the oven and set the timer for 7 minutes. (Alternatively, follow the directions on page 115 for heating tortillas in a microwave.)

When the timer goes off, stir the cheese into the warm chorizo mixture. Set in the oven alongside the tortillas and bake until the cheese is just melted but has not begun to separate or look greasy, about 5 minutes more. Sprinkle with the crumbled oregano and serve without a moment's hesitation, accompanied by the warm tortillas.

WORKING AHEAD: The chorizo-poblano mixture can be made a day ahead, covered and refrigerated; warm it in your baking vessel before stirring in the cheese and baking. *Queso fundido* doesn't hold well, so don't put it in the oven until everyone is ready to make tacos.

Right: Weighing Oaxacan string cheese
Left: Fresh cheese in wooden hoops

CHORIZO MEXICANO

● TANGY MEXICAN RED CHILE SAUSAGE

Mexican *chorizo,* unlike its namesake Spanish relative, is a fresh sausage, like American breakfast sausage or what most of us know as Italian sausage. Though it can be aged to improve the flavor and decrease the moisture, it's tasty used right away and requires very little equipment to make. Zesty from vinegar, dried chile, herbs and spices, *chorizo* gives a definitive flavor to the food of Mexico.

Makes about 2¹/₂ pounds fresh sausage

1¹/₂ pounds lean, boneless pork shoulder, cut into 1-inch pieces
*8 ounces pork fat (collect scraps trimmed from roasts or chops if you
    like, or even buy fatty bacon or salt pork—though the flavor will be
    different), cut into ¹/₂-inch cubes*
*12 medium (about 6 ounces total) dried ancho chiles, stemmed and
    seeded*
2 bay leaves
1¹/₂ teaspoons cinnamon, preferably freshly ground Mexican canela
¹/₈ teaspoon cloves, preferably freshly ground
1 teaspoon dried oregano, preferably Mexican
*1 tablespoon EACH fresh thyme leaves and marjoram leaves
    OR 1 teaspoon EACH dried thyme and marjoram*
Salt
¹/₄ cup cider vinegar

1. PORK AND PORK FAT. Place the cubed pork and pork fat (or one of the substitutes) into the freezer (to firm for uniform chopping) while you prepare the seasonings.

2. THE CHILES AND OTHER SEASONINGS. Tear the chiles into flat pieces and toast them in a dry heavy skillet or on a griddle heated over medium, pressing them flat with a metal spatula until they are aromatic, about 10 seconds per side. In a bowl, rehydrate the chiles for 20 minutes in hot water to cover;

place a small plate on top to keep the chiles submerged. Drain and transfer to a food processor or blender.

Pulverize the bay leaves in a mortar or spice grinder, then add to the food processor along with the cinnamon, cloves, oregano, thyme and marjoram and 1½ teaspoons salt (less if using bacon or salt pork). Measure in the vinegar and 2 tablespoons water and process until smooth, adding a little more water if necessary to keep everything moving through the blades. Press the mixture through a medium-mesh sieve into a large bowl.

3. GRINDING AND FLAVORING THE MEAT. Coarsely grind the meat either through the coarsest disk of a meat grinder or by pulsing it in a food processor (the blade needs to be sharp to avoid mashing the meat). Add the meat to the bowl with the seasonings and mix thoroughly. (It's best to cover and refrigerate the *chorizo* overnight for the flavors to meld.) Fry a little portion of the chorizo and taste for salt, adjusting as necessary.

WORKING AHEAD: Refrigerated, the *chorizo* keeps for about a week. It freezes well.

Market stall selling Oaxacan regional specialties: cheese, mole and chocolate

Melted Mozzarella Casserole with mushrooms and smoky chipotle chile

QUESO FUNDIDO CON HONGOS Y CHILE CHIPOTLE

Makes enough *queso fundido* for 12 soft tacos, serving 6 as an appetizer, 4 as a casual main dish

1½ tablespoons olive oil, preferably extra-virgin

1 medium red onion, sliced

6 to 8 ounces full-flavored mushrooms, such as shiitakes, oysters or practically any wild variety, stemmed (discard woody stems or finely chop them) and sliced (you'll have about 2 generous cups)

2 to 3 canned chipotle chiles en adobo, *seeded and thinly sliced*

Salt

12 corn tortillas, the fresher the better (store-bought are okay, but homemade [page 104] will really shine here)

8 ounces mozzarella, preferably whole-milk (but not "fresh" mozzarella, which will not melt) or Mexican quesillo, shredded (you'll have about 2 cups)

A generous ½ teaspoon chopped fresh thyme or generous 1 teaspoon chopped fresh epazote

A little black pepper, preferably freshly ground

CONTEMPORARY

1. **THE MUSHROOM MIXTURE.** Heat the oven to 350°F. In a large skillet (preferably nonstick), heat the oil over medium-high. Add the sliced onion and cook, stirring frequently, until softening and beginning to brown, about 5 minutes. Add the mushrooms and stir nearly constantly until they have softened and any juice they release has evaporated, about 5 minutes longer. Stir in the sliced chiles, then taste and season with salt, usually about ¼ teaspoon. Transfer the mixture to a 9- or 10-inch shallow baking dish, Mexican *cazuela* or pie plate.

2. **FINISHING THE *QUESO FUNDIDO*.** Very lightly dampen a clean kitchen towel. Check the tortillas to make sure none are stuck together. Wrap them in the towel, then in foil, sealing the edges tightly. Place in the oven and set the timer for 7 minutes. (Alternatively, follow the directions on page 115 for heating tortillas in a microwave.)

When the timer goes off, stir the shredded cheese into the warm mushroom mixture. Set in the oven alongside the tortillas and bake until the cheese is just melted, about 5 minutes more. Sprinkle with the thyme or *epazote* and black pepper and serve without a moment's hesitation, accompanied by the warm tortillas.

WORKING AHEAD: The mushroom mixture can be made a day or two in advance; refrigerate, well covered. Reheat the mixture before finishing the dish.

Left: Rustic red chile salsa Right: Taco and tostada vendor

Questions and Answers from Our Testing

Which cheeses available in the United States best replicate the prized cheese used in Mexico? Though in Mexico, this dish is frequently made from *asadero* cheese—it's stringy like a melted rich whole-milk mozzarella—other cheeses are often used there. Mild cheddar-like Chihuahua cheese will melt appropriately, as will Mexican-made Manchego and the rich cheese from the far northwest called *quesadilla*. On the north side of the border, look for flavorful but mild cheeses that are stringy when melted but not rubbery, not too fluid and not the kind that release their oil quickly when heated. These include most of the domestically made Chihuahua cheeses (the brand we use at our restaurant, Supremo, is a type of brick cheese made in Wisconsin) and the cheese sold in Mexican groceries as "quesadilla cheese." Other contenders are Monterey Jack (except the very rich Sonoma Jack, which melts like butter), most mild Muensters, whole-milk mozzarella (not fresh mozzarella, which doesn't really melt) and, to a lesser degree, cheddars and Colbys.

Is the stove top or oven best for thoroughly melting the cheese? While in Mexico the cheese for *queso fundido* is typically melted in a small earthenware dish over direct heat, we found replicating that technique a challenge. First, you have to find a slow-heating, flameproof vessel that you can serve in. Second, you have to have just the right cheese and the right temperature, or you'll end up with an oily, unpleasantly tough and stringy mess on your hands. Third, you have to stir the whole assembly very frequently, or it will melt unevenly. So, after several tests, we opted for warm add-ins mixed with shredded cheese, scooped into a wide shallow baking dish and melted quickly in the oven. The warm add-ins got the melting started, the long shreds controlled the melting rate and the wide baking dish encouraged quick melting. We finished the melting process in the all-around heat of the oven without stirring.

Why does fat separate from cheese, and what can you do to avoid it? If you leave *queso fundido* in the oven too long, the cheese will begin to overcook, causing the "casein to coagulate and separate from the fat and water into tough, stringy masses," to quote Harold McGee in his authoritative tome *On Food and Cooking*. Hard well-ripened cheeses can tolerate higher temperatures than soft cheese, he reports. So, with the semisoft cheeses that are appropriate here, go easy on the heat. And for the nicest look, make sure your add-ins aren't oily.

What is the best ratio of cheese to add-ins? While I love melted cheese as much as the next guy, I reach my limit pretty fast. To best enjoy *queso fundido*, I balance cheese and add-ins about fifty-fifty. That not only throttles the richness, but creates variety and interest with every bite.

Sopes *(Corn Masa Boats)*

You know how some of us love the mashed potatoes and gravy more than the roast? Or the sticky crust of the pie more than the filling? Well, then you understand some of the allure of *sopes*. My favorite ones are not about the meat or the filling. They're about crusty corn *masa*—and a little spicy salsa. So they're simplicity itself, the workaday, spicy, thick *masa* snacks into which you can sink your teeth.

Every day in most places in Mexico, you'll find cooks filling their griddles with thick *masa* cakes, edges pinched up to make boat shapes. There's a familiar earthiness to the flavor of these *sopes*, especially as they brown underneath, releasing a toasted-corn aroma. Topped with a spoonful of sharp salsa, a few pieces of sharp raw white onion and a scattering of sharp fresh cheese, they're the ultimate. And the perfectly timed dance of hands patting, pinching, crisping and topping these nibbles becomes the perfect prelude to the perfect bite.

When we lived in Guerrero, where the mountain air was as clear as the crystalline sunlight, Deann and I went to the closest market town, Tixtla, once a week for provisions. There, in the market plaza, a deft *señora* made *memelas*, the heartier, larger Guerrerense version of *sopes*. She stood over a wood-fired clay griddle rhythmically patting the pliant dough into five- or six-inch rounds, baking them on both sides, and then—this takes well-seasoned hands—pinching up a little wall of hot, still-soft dough around the edges. She left the *memelas* on the griddle for the bottom crust to develop a chewy crunch while she brushed the region's special roasty-flavored pork lard (*asiento*) across the top to soften and enrich it. Topped with salsa and the rest, these were a full, satisfying lunch.

For American cooks, however, *sopes* most often translate as an appetizer to pass around or even to serve as a dressed-up first course at the table, the way modern Mexican restaurants on both sides of the border are doing. If this is your first try at *sopes*, you may want to start with my contemporary potato *sopes*, simply because they're easy and the addition of the potato gives them an invitingly soft texture. In this version, toppings echo traditional ones, with the cilantro replaced by other herbs (watercress, arugula, basil) and Mexican *queso fresco* replaced by fresh goat cheese. The biggest difference between the two recipes, though, is that the griddle-crisping is replaced with a quick crisping tour through hot oil in the contemporary recipe. Traditional griddle-crisping, you see, is really the only part that takes practice to get right. Once you've mastered it, though, there's nothing quite like the combination of textures it gives.

TRADITIONAL BENCHMARK: The best *sopes*, like the best *gorditas*, combine the textures of crusty and soft—chewy/crusty underneath, meaty/soft on top—with bright-and-spicy toppings. It's all about proportion, thickness, griddle-heat and dexterity—but it's not difficult.

WHEN TO THINK OF THESE RECIPES: Traditional *sopes* are the purview of street cooks, and so they typically go straight from the griddle to the waiting mouth. In fact, that's the way the traditional ones *should* be served, since they can get tough and uninteresting as they cool. So make griddle-crisped *sopes* when you can be at the stove just before serving them—a casual gathering, for instance, where everyone's in the kitchen and you can feed your guests hot-off-the-griddle *sopes* one after another. The contemporary *sopes* work well as typical pass-around party appetizers because they're fried—though you do need to fry them shortly before serving.

ADVICE FOR AMERICAN COOKS: Make these soon and often, since *sopes* are made from traditional ingredients that are easily available.

Perfectly Simple *Sopes* (Masa Boats)

Makes 16 *sopes*, serving 8 as an appetizer

1 pound (2 cups) fresh smooth-ground corn masa *for tortillas*
OR 1³/₄ cups powdered masa harina *mixed with 1 cup plus*
2 tablespoons warm water
Salt
About ¹/₂ cup chopped white onion
Vegetable oil for the griddle
3 tablespoons asiento *(the dark, very roasty-tasting,*
crackling-filled lard from the bottom of the barrel)
OR 1¹/₂ tablespoons EACH vegetable oil and bacon
drippings
About ³/₄ cup salsa *(I recommend the Roasted Tomato–*
Green Chile Salsa on page 100)
About ¹/₃ cup grated Mexican queso añejo *or*
other dry grating cheese, such as Romano or Parmesan
About ¹/₄ cup chopped fresh cilantro

TRADITIONAL

I.   FORMING AND GRIDDLE-BAKING THE *SOPES*. Heat a well-seasoned or nonstick griddle or heavy skillet over medium. Put the *masa* (fresh or reconstituted) into a bowl and knead in ³/₄ teaspoon salt. If necessary, knead in a few drops of water to give the *masa* the consistency of soft cookie dough. Divide into 16 pieces, roll into balls and cover with plastic to keep them from drying out.

One by one, form the fat little tortillas that will become the *sopes*: Line a tortilla press with two pieces of plastic cut to fit the plates (to be on the safe side, cut them from a food storage bag; the thicker plastic usually works better for beginners). Gently press out a flattened ball of dough between the sheets of plastic to about 3¹/₂ inches in diameter (it should be a little less than ¹/₄ inch thick). Peel off the top sheet of plastic, flip the fat little tortilla—uncovered side down—onto the fingers of one hand and then gently peel off the second piece of plastic. In one flowing movement, roll the tortilla off your hand and onto the heated griddle or skillet. After about 1¹/₂ minutes, when the tortilla has loosened itself from the cooking surface and is lightly browned, flip it and cook for another minute or so—this cooking is just to set and brown the surface of the tortilla but not to cook the *masa* all the way through. While the first tortilla is cooking, continue pressing out others and adding them to the griddle or skillet; just be careful not to leave them on so long that they cook through.

Remove each lightly browned tortilla to a plate. Cool *just until handleable*, then use your thumb and index finger to pinch up a *masa* border about 1/2 inch high around the edge of the tortilla—in doing this you are transforming the fat little tortilla into a *sope*, a little *masa* boat. Press out the center to uniformly flatten it (see illustration, page 32.) Cool the *sopes*, then cover with plastic to keep them from drying out.

2. FINISHING THE SOPES. In a strainer, rinse the onion under cold water, then shake off the excess moisture. Set out the remaining ingredients near the griddle. Heavily oil the skillet or griddle (my 12-inch griddle takes about 1/4 cup to oil it properly) and heat over medium. Fill the griddle with a single uncrowded layer of *sopes*, flat side down, then brush each one with the *asiento* or oil-and-drippings combination. Spoon about 1/2 tablespoon of salsa into each *sope*, then sprinkle on a little chopped onion, grated cheese and chopped cilantro. Leave on the heat until the bottoms of the *sopes* begin to crisp and the salsa is warm, 1 to 1 1/2 minutes. (You may see the salsa boiling around the edges.) Serve on a warm platter or wooden board without a moment's hesitation—your guests will love biting into this simple perfection.

WORKING AHEAD: The *masa* base can be baked and pinched several hours ahead; cover the *sopes* and leave at room temperature. Once filled and heated through, they should go directly into a waiting mouth, although even after they've cooled to room temperature, they're still delicious.

SALSA ROJA • RED CHILE–TOMATILLO SALSA

This is one of the most versatile formulas to know, since you can go to practically any grocery store and find at least one variety of small hot dried chile. In a Mexican market (on either side of the border), the possibilities multiply quickly—from the nuttiness of cascabel to the punch of árbol chiles, the peanutiness of piquín, and the smoky sweetness of red chipotle (morita). As a rough guide, $1/2$ ounce dried chiles corresponds to 6 red chipotles (moritas), 4 tan chipotles, 16 árbols, 3 cascabels or $1/4$ cup piquín.

Makes about 1 $3/4$ cups

$1/2$ ounce small hot dried chiles, stemmed
6 large garlic cloves, unpeeled
1 pound (10 to 12 medium) tomatillos, husked and rinsed
Salt
Sugar, about $1/2$ teaspoon (optional)

1. TOASTING AND ROASTING. In an ungreased skillet over medium heat, toast the chiles, stirring for a minute until they are very aromatic (some will have slightly darkened spots on them). Transfer to a bowl, cover with hot water and rehydrate for 30 minutes.

    In the same skillet, roast the garlic, turning regularly, until soft and blotchy-dark in places, about 15 minutes. Cool and slip off the papery skin.

    Roast the tomatillos on a baking sheet 4 inches below a very hot broiler until soft, even blackened in spots, about 5 minutes on each side. Cool, then transfer the contents of the baking sheet (including any juices) to a blender or food processor.

2. FINISHING THE SALSA. Drain the chiles and add to the tomatillos along with the garlic. Puree, then scrape into a serving dish. Stir in enough water to give a spoonable consistency, usually about $1/4$ cup. Season with salt, usually 1 teaspoon, and the optional sugar. Refrigerated, the salsa keeps for several days.

Crispy Potato *Sopes* (*Masa* Boats) with salsa, goat cheese and herb salad

SOPES DE PAPA CON SALSA, QUESO DE CABRA
Y ENSALADA DE HIERBAS

Makes 18 sopes, serving 8 to 9 as a pass-around nibble

2 medium (about 8 ounces total) baking (a.k.a. Idaho or russet)
    potatoes, peeled and cut into large pieces
8 ounces (1 cup) fresh smooth-ground corn masa for tortillas
    OR 1 cup powdered masa harina mixed with ¹/₂ cup plus
    2 tablespoons warm water
Salt
Vegetable oil to a depth of ¹/₂ inch for frying
About 1¹/₂ teaspoons balsamic vinegar (optional)
³/₄ cup salsa (the Red Chile–Tomatillo Salsa on page 35 is
    delicious with the herbs)
2 generous cups loosely packed torn herb leaves (try watercress,
    arugula, mizuna, basil and the like)
About ¹/₂ cup crumbled goat cheese (choose a dryish one
    or ricotta salata or Mexican queso añejo)

CONTEMPORARY

1. THE DOUGH FOR THE *SOPES*. In a medium pan, boil the potatoes in salted water to cover until thoroughly tender, about 25 minutes. Drain and cool. Push the potatoes through a ricer or medium-mesh strainer into a bowl. Scrape the potatoes into a measuring cup. Discard all but 1 cup of the potatoes, return the 1 cup to the bowl and knead in the *masa* (fresh or reconstituted) and ³/₄ teaspoon salt. The dough should be the consistency of soft cookie dough.

2. FORMING AND BAKING THE *SOPES*. Heat a well-seasoned or nonstick griddle or heavy skillet over medium. Divide the dough into 18 portions, roll into balls and cover with plastic to keep them from drying out.

   One by one, form the fat little tortillas that will become the *sopes*: Cut two squares of plastic (to be on the safe side, cut them from a food storage bag; the thicker plastic works better for beginners). With your hands, gently flatten a ball of dough between the sheets of plastic to about 2 1/2 inches in diameter (it should be about 1/4 inch thick). Peel off the top sheet of plastic. Use your thumb and index finger to pinch up the dough into a border about 1/2 inch high around the edge to form the *sope*, the little boat. Flip the *sope*—uncovered side down—onto the fingers of one hand, then gently peel off the second piece of plastic. Now, flip the *sope* over onto the griddle or skillet, flat side down. After about a minute, when the *sope* has loosened itself from the cooking surface, remove it from the griddle. This cooking is just to set the bottom surface, not to cook the *masa* all the way through. While the first *sope* is cooking, continue shaping and adding others to the griddle or skillet. After cooking, to keep them from puffing oddly during frying, prick the bottoms of each one with a fork, being careful not to go all the way through. Cool, then cover the *sopes* with plastic to keep them from drying out.

3. FINISHING THE SOPES. In a deep heavy medium skillet or saucepan, heat 1/2 inch of oil to 350°F (it's best to use a thermometer; lacking one, you can judge the temperature by dipping the side of a *sope* in the oil—if it sizzles vigorously, it's ready). Meanwhile, turn on the oven to its lowest setting and set out a tray lined with paper towels to drain the *sopes*. Stir the balsamic vinegar (if you're using it) into the salsa and set out the herbs and crumbled cheese. A few at a time, fry the sopes until they are a rich golden brown, about a minute. Drain them upside down on the paper towels, then keep them warm in the oven.

When all the *sopes* are done, arrange them on a serving platter. Spoon about 1/2 tablespoon of salsa into each one, top with a tuft of the herbs and sprinkle generously with the cheese. Serve without hesitation.

WORKING AHEAD: The *sope* bases can be baked several hours ahead; cover them and leave at room temperature. Finish the frying just before you want to fill and serve these crisped delicacies.

Questions and Answers from Our Testing

Would making *sopes* with *masa harina* make them taste inferior to our favorite street stall version? As with other *antojitos* (corn *masa* snacks) that see hot oil, we found that traditional *sopes* made from readily available *masa harina* (dehydrated, powdered corn *masa*) tasted just about as good as those made from the harder-to-procure dough-like fresh-ground *masa*. It's important, however, for a wonderfully yielding—not dry—interior texture that the dough (especially the reconstituted *masa harina*) be as soft as is workable without being sticky. It's also good to know that when forming *sopes*, the dough cannot be overworked, toughening as, say, a pie dough would. There's no tightening gluten in *masa*, so if you're unhappy with the thick disk you've pressed out, just gather it back into a ball and start again.

How can we replicate the great combination of textures the street cooks achieve? *Stage one: the fat little tortillas.* Very practiced hands can clap a nugget of dough back and forth between the palms into a perfectly even round disk. It's like speaking a second language, I think: Unless you internalize the feel for it before puberty, it may never seem completely natural. Most of us use the dual plates of a tortilla press to flatten the dough—easy, efficient and nearly as good as the hand-patted ones. But these small disks can also be successfully formed by patting a ball of dough flat on a piece of plastic. Thickness (¼ inch) is important in achieving the best texture. *Stage two: griddle-baking the little tortillas.* This is like baking a tortilla—use a medium-hot griddle—though these cakes are thicker. The goal is simply to lightly brown the fat little tortilla, setting the exterior and bringing out the toasty corn flavor, without completely firming the *masa* inside. Do a test *sope* to learn just how long that takes. *Stage three: pinching the border.* Do this as soon as you can handle the heat, since nearly cooked warm *masa* molds more easily than cold *masa*. And for the best look and texture, pinch ¼-inch-thick edges up evenly—as straight up as possible. *Stage four: finishing traditional sopes.* This is the only step that's tricky. Once you've gotten the right temperature under your griddle and the right amount of oil on top (it's more than a film, but not quite enough to qualify as shallow-frying), you're home free. The dough in these little *sopes* is really already cooked, though if you tried to eat one without frying, it would seem heavy, mealy and uninteresting. Crisping the bottom on the greased griddle or skillet while letting the oil-brushed top soften with the salsa and other toppings transforms the *sope* from food for the birds to food fit for a king.

What is the right proportion of toppings? There are some places in Mexico where it has become tradition to pile on all manner of toppings. The hungry in those areas say they're going to have sausage *sopes* or shredded chicken *sopes*. This recipe for traditional *sopes* is different, more rustic and perfectly simple. As with all simple dishes, the ingredients have to be great and handled deftly. So if you've made a properly thick *sope* that's crusty underneath and soft on top, all you need in my opinion is a thin blanket of toppings—mostly salsa. A good dusting of *queso añejo*, the milky, tangy, dry grating cheese from Mexico, is integral in bringing together the flavors of *masa* and salsa.

Market meat stalls

Gorditas *(Corn Masa Pockets)*

You can probably imagine a not-so-long-ago era in which a favorite puffy, flaky, golden snack might have been called "Plumpies." Sounds sinister, I know, at the lean turn of the millennium. But "plumpies" still exist in the lingo of our southern neighbor. And they *are* plump. So plump that your hand cups them, so round that they sit agape welcoming savory, meaty, saucy fillings. Mexicans refer rather intimately to these beloved snacks as *gorditas,* "little fat ones."

A *gordita* begins as a thick raw-*masa* tortilla that's first cooked on the griddle, then slipped into hot oil to finish. In those transformative moments that follow, the disk of *masa,* in that magical interaction with just-right hot oil, puffs and crisps to a golden flaky shell while the moist interior finishes its cooking.

Most Mexicans I know love the soft texture of just-cooked *masa* as much as they love a crispy fried tostada. The *gordita* has the distinction of being both—crispy and soft. And, when stuffed, it becomes a sort of crispy version of Mexico's definitive soft-tortilla taco.

Like the taco, the *gordita* lies at the heart—and guts—of everyday street and marketplace cooking. In an instant, I can transport myself back fifteen years (my prerestaurant days) when I had the luxury of hours to roam the aisles of the brightly lit, modern Aguascalientes market in west-central Mexico, where hundreds of thick griddle-formed *gorditas* ballooned into flaky round snacks. Like most of the other hungry amblers, I always had trouble choosing from the many fillings beautifully displayed in *cazuelas* rigged up over stainless steel steam tables. Most were definitively flavored stewy dishes, simple homey concoctions, always including the classic *carne deshebrada* (shredded beef) so beloved in west-central and northern Mexico. Irresistible fare.

Gorditas can move out from the market or street stall to become casual, pass-around food for American homes. They've even become appetizers now at upscale Mexican restaurants in the United States. There's another reason to gravitate toward making *gorditas* where fresh-ground corn *masa* is difficult to get: Reconstituted *masa harina* (dehydrated, powdered corn *masa*) works well. A *masa harina* dough also works well with the twist I've added to my contemporary recipe—bacon bits. The tantalizing addition intensifies flavor, perfect for a meatless filling of mellow roasted poblano guacamole and biting arugula greens. Flavors that shout "Mexican" as well as "fresh and contemporary."

Made small, *gorditas* are animating openers for parties. You can griddle-bake a batch of fat three-inch cakes in advance and hold them under plastic. When your guests arrive, puff the *gorditas* in hot oil, then stuff them with something irresistible.

Be adventurous. Although shredded beef stands as a classic—I've included that recipe here—try chicken, mushrooms or shredded pork, or venture into lighter meatless fillings, as I have in the contemporary recipe. The fillings for any of the *tacos de cazuela* (see page 108), as well as many other fillings, work beautifully here. Whichever you try, I think you'll love holding these plump little rounded pockets of delight as you dive into them.

TRADITIONAL BENCHMARK: My most memorable *gordita* had several things going for it: Crusty enough on the outside to have a nice chew. Softened to a beautiful near flakiness by the frying. Thick enough to be satisfying without being heavy or doughy. Puffed nicely. Filled with just a little meaty something. And spiked with chile, fresh onion and a good aged cheese.

WHEN TO THINK OF THESE RECIPES: *Gorditas* are a nice starter, especially if you make them small (2½ to 3 inches). But, made a little larger (4 inches or so), they're substantial enough to be a casual meal. Say it's Friday evening: You don't have to think about the kids' homework or tomorrow's meetings, you've got a bag of *masa harina* and there's some leftover roast or chicken you can shred. *Gorditas* don't take very long, and the kids can help form them.

ADVICE FOR AMERICAN COOKS: These are simple to master, so they are a good place to start your hands-on learning about *antojitos* (corn *masa* snacks). The ingredients are easy to find.

Gorditas (Corn *Masa* Pockets) with Classic Shredded Beef

GORDITAS CON CARNE DESHEBRADA

Makes 10 filled pockets, serving 10 as a hefty snack,
4 to 5 as a casual main dish

1¼ pounds boneless beef chuck steak, cut into 4 pieces

3 small white onions, diced

4 garlic cloves, peeled and finely chopped

1 tablespoon vegetable oil, plus oil to a depth of ½ inch for frying

One 28-ounce can good-quality whole tomatoes in juice,
    drained and chopped
    OR 2 cups chopped ripe tomatoes

Fresh hot green chiles to taste (roughly 2 to 3 serranos
    or 1 to 2 jalapeños), stemmed, seeded (if you want a
    more refined-looking dish) and finely chopped

Salt

1 pound (2 cups) fresh smooth-ground corn masa for
    tortillas
    OR 1¾ cups powdered masa harina mixed with 1 cup
    plus 2 tablespoons warm water

⅓ cup all-purpose flour

1 scant teaspoon baking powder

About ⅓ cup grated Mexican queso añejo or other
    dry grating cheese, such as Romano or Parmesan

About ⅓ cup chopped fresh cilantro for garnish

TRADITIONAL

I. THE SHREDDED BEEF FILLING. In a medium saucepan set over medium heat, combine the meat with 2 quarts salted water, about *one-third* of the onions and *half* of the garlic and simmer until the meat is very tender, about 1½ hours. Strain, reserving the broth for another use. When the meat is cool enough to handle, shred it into coarse strands with your fingers or two forks—don't worry that there are bits of onion and garlic mixed with the meat.

Wash and dry the saucepan, set it over medium heat and add the *1 tablespoon* oil. When hot, add *half* of the remaining onions and cook until golden, about 6 minutes, then stir in the remaining garlic and cook for another minute. Add the tomatoes and chiles and cook until *most* of the juice has evaporated, about 3 minutes. Stir in the shredded meat and simmer for a few more minutes, then taste and season with about ½ teaspoon salt. Remove from the heat and set aside.

2. FORMING, FILLING AND GRIDDLE-BAKING THE *GORDITAS*. Heat a well-seasoned or nonstick griddle or heavy skillet over medium. Knead the *masa* (fresh or reconstituted) to make it pliable, adding a *little* water if necessary to achieve a soft-cookie-dough consistency. Knead in the flour, baking powder and ¾ teaspoon salt. Divide the dough into 10 portions and roll into balls; cover with plastic to keep from drying out.

Line a tortilla press with two pieces of plastic cut to fit the plates (to be on the safe side, cut them from a food storage bag; the thicker plastic usually works better for beginners). Gently press out a ball of dough between the sheets of plastic to about 4 inches in diameter (it'll be about ¼ inch thick). You've now made a *gordita*, which is what you call a fat tortilla. Peel off the top sheet of plastic, flip the *gordita* —uncovered side down—onto the fingers of one hand and gently peel off the second piece of plastic. In one flowing movement, roll the *gordita* off your hand and onto the heated griddle or skillet. Bake for about 1½ minutes, then flip and bake for another 1½ minutes on the other side. The *gordita* will be lightly browned and crusty on top and bottom, but still a little uncooked on the sides. Remove to a plate. Continue pressing and griddle-baking the remaining *gorditas* in the same manner.

3. FINISHING THE *GORDITAS*. When you're ready to serve, warm the shredded beef. Rinse the remaining onions in a small strainer under cold water and shake to remove the excess moisture. Have the cheese and cilantro at the ready.

In a deep heavy medium skillet or saucepan, heat the ½ inch oil over medium to medium-high until the oil is hot enough to make the edge of a *gordita* sizzle sharply (about 350°F on a deep-fry thermometer). One by one, fry the *gorditas*, turning them after they've been in the oil for about 15 seconds, until they're nicely crisp but not hard, about 45 seconds total. When they're ready, most will have puffed up a little, like pita bread. Drain on paper towels.

Once they all are fried, use a small knife to cut a slit in the thin edge of each one about halfway around its circumference, opening a pocket. As you cut them, fill each *gordita* with about ¼ cup shredded meat and a sprinkling of the onion, grated cheese and cilantro.

Line up the filled *gorditas* on a serving platter and pass them around (with plenty of napkins) for your guests to enjoy.

WORKING AHEAD: The shredded beef can be made several days ahead (cover and refrigerate), but the *gorditas* themselves are best griddle-baked the day they are served. Most definitely, you'll want to fry them at the moment before they're to be served.

LEFT: GORDITA (CORN *MASA* POCKET) WITH CLASSIC
SHREDDED BEEF (PAGE 42). RIGHT: CRISPY POTATO *SOPE*
(CORN *MASA* BOAT) WITH SALSA, GOAT CHEESE
AND HERB SALAD (PAGE 36)

Bacon-Flavored *Gorditas* (Corn *Masa* Pockets) with Roasted Poblano Guacamole

GORDITAS DE TOCINO CON GUACAMOLE
DE CHILE POBLANO

Makes 8 filled pockets. serving 8 as a hefty snack.
4 as a casual main dish

6 thick slices (8 ounces) smoky bacon

1 pound (2 cups) fresh smooth-ground corn masa *for tortillas*
OR 1 3/4 cups powdered masa harina *mixed with 1 cup plus*
2 tablespoons warm water

1 large fresh poblano chile

3 garlic cloves, unpeeled

2 large ripe avocados

1 to 2 tablespoons fresh lime juice, plus a sprinkling for the
arugula

Salt

2 cups young arugula leaves, stems removed (or fresh basil,
mizuna or tender spinach leaves)

About 1/3 cup chopped white onion

About 1/3 cup grated Mexican queso añejo or
other dry grating cheese, such as Romano or Parmesan

Vegetable oil to a depth of 1/2 inch for frying

1. FORMING AND GRIDDLE-BAKING THE *GORDITAS*. In a medium skillet, cook the bacon in a single layer over medium to medium-low heat until thoroughly crispy. Drain on paper towels, then cool and finely chop.

    Heat a well-seasoned or nonstick griddle or heavy skillet over medium. Knead the *masa* (fresh or reconstituted) to make it pliable, adding a *little* water if necessary to achieve a soft-cookie-dough consistency. Knead in half of the bacon. Divide the dough into 8 portions and roll into balls; cover with plastic to keep from drying.

    Line a tortilla press with two pieces of plastic cut to fit the plates (to be on the safe side, cut them from a food storage bag; the thicker plastic usually works better for beginners). Gently press out a ball of dough between the sheets of plastic to about 4 inches in diameter (it'll be about $1/4$ inch thick). You've now made a *gordita,* which is what you call a fat tortilla. Peel off the top sheet of plastic, flip the *gordita*—uncovered side down—onto the fingers of one hand and then gently peel off the second piece of plastic. In one flowing movement, roll the *gordita* off your hand and onto the hot griddle or skillet. Bake for about $1 1/2$ minutes, then flip and bake for another $1 1/2$ minutes on the other side, until lightly browned on both sides. Remove to a plate. Continue pressing and griddle-baking the remaining *gorditas* in the same manner. Cover with plastic wrap.

2. PREPARING THE GUACAMOLE. Roast the poblano over an open flame or on a baking sheet 4 inches below a very hot broiler, turning until the skin is evenly blistered and blackened, about 5 minutes for an open flame, 10 minutes for the broiler. Cover with a kitchen towel and let stand for about 5 minutes. Rub off the blackened skin, then pull or cut out the stem and the seed pod that's right below. Tear the poblano open and quickly rinse to remove any stray seeds and bits of skin. Roughly chop.

Roast the garlic cloves in an ungreased griddle or skillet over medium heat, turning frequently, until softened (they'll have dark splotches in spots), about 15 minutes. Cool and slip off the papery skins.

Combine the garlic with the poblano in a food processor and pulse several times to coarsely puree. Scrape into a bowl.

Halve each avocado by cutting straight down into it, knife blade running the length of the avocado, until you hit the large pit. Continue cutting around the avocado—around the pit—until you wind up where you started. Remove the knife and twist the halves apart. Scoop out the pit. Scrape the flesh from the skin into the bowl with the pureed poblano.

Using an old-fashioned potato masher or the back of a spoon, coarsely mash the avocado and flavorings together. Taste and season with the lime juice and about $1/2$ teaspoon salt. Cover with plastic wrap, pressing it directly against the surface; refrigerate.

3. FINISHING THE *GORDITAS.* When you are ready to serve, toss the arugula or its substitute with a sprinkling of lime juice and salt. Rinse the onion in a strainer under cold water, then shake to remove excess moisture. Have the guacamole, grated cheese and the remaining bacon at the ready.

In a deep heavy medium skillet or saucepan, heat ½ inch of oil over medium to medium-high until the oil is hot enough to make the edge of a *gordita* sizzle sharply (about 350°F on a deep-fry thermometer). One by one, fry the *gorditas*, turning them after they've been in the oil for about 15 seconds, until they're nicely crisp but not hard, about 45 seconds total. When they're ready, most will have puffed up a little, like pita bread. Drain on paper towels.

Once they all are fried, use a small knife to cut a slit in the thin edge of each one about halfway around its circumference, opening a pocket. As you cut them, fill each one with about 2 heaping tablespoons of guacamole, then stuff in a little of the dressed arugula and sprinkle with cheese, onion and bacon.

Line up the filled *gorditas* on a serving platter and pass them around (with plenty of napkins) for your guests to enjoy.

WORKING AHEAD: It's best to griddle-bake the *gorditas* shortly before they're served, then make the guacamole, fry the *gorditas*, fill them and serve. Not much working ahead here.

Grinding cooked corn into masa at tortilla factory

QUESTIONS AND ANSWERS FROM OUR TESTING

IS THERE A CRITICAL DIFFERENCE BETWEEN *GORDITAS* MADE FROM FRESH *MASA* AND THOSE MADE FROM RECONSTITUTED DRIED *MASA HARINA*? Fresh *masa* has the nicest texture and most compelling flavor, but once the *gordita* is griddle-baked, fried and filled, the differences between the harder-to-procure fresh stuff and the easy-to-get reconstituted dried version seem rather secondary.

DO ADD-INS LIKE BAKING POWDER, SALT AND FLOUR REALLY MAKE A DIFFERENCE? Adding flour and baking powder to the *masa* gives the *gorditas* a lighter, flakier texture and makes the dough a little easier to work with. Some cooks prefer to use plain *masa*—no add-ins. What they turn out is crustier and chewier, though with wonderful corn flavor. Both approaches have merit. Finally, some cooks may not even salt the *masa* (remember that the *masa*'s never salted when making plain corn tortillas). For me, saltless *gorditas* taste as if something's missing.

DO YOU HAVE TO HAVE A TORTILLA PRESS TO FORM *GORDITAS*? Though an inexpensive metal tortilla press turns out the most even disks, you can use a flat-bottomed plate or your fingers to flatten the balls of dough without substantially affecting the quality of your *gorditas*. Unevenness may, however, cause the *gorditas* to puff irregularly.

WHAT IS THE RIGHT AMOUNT OF TIME FOR GRIDDLE-BAKING *GORDITAS*? Cooking *gorditas* too long affects their final texture (too dry) and interferes with their ability to puff. Bake them just long enough to set and lightly brown the two sides, but not long enough to cook them through.

WHAT'S THE IDEAL TEMPERATURE FOR FRYING *GORDITAS*? Oil that is too cool results in greasy *gorditas*. Oil that is too hot will cause them to turn out hard. At 350°F the oil is just right. A heavy pan or pot will maintain the steadiest temperature. Exact oil temperature, however, is hard to judge when there's only a depth of 1/2 inch, given that most thermometers need more than that. So judge by the edge-sizzling test (the *gordita* should sizzle vigorously, not calmly or explosively). Oil that's about 350°F will have released that characteristic hot oil aroma into the kitchen and will present a slightly shimmery, ripply surface. Oil that starts to smoke is way too hot—dangerously hot—and, even if allowed to cool down, will give the *gorditas* a bad flavor.

DOES THE CUT OF BEEF FOR THE FILLING REALLY MAKE A DIFFERENCE? Chuck steak gives the nicest texture and flavor of all the beef cuts we tried. Round steak may be leaner, but it's less beefy tasting and dry to the point of mealiness.

DO FRESH TOMATOES ADD BETTER FLAVOR TO THE FILLING THAN CANNED? Despite their declassé reputation in gourmet circles, good-quality canned tomatoes offer a deep, rich flavor and beautiful moistness to this filling.

REFINEMENTS: *Dough consistency*: The softer the dough, the lighter and better-textured the end result. The dough should not crack around the edges when pressed out. If it does, knead in a little water before continuing. *Laying the* gordita *unrumpled on the griddle.* This technique requires a little practice, though it's one that's easier with a thick *gordita* than a thin tortilla. Most Mexican cooks unmold pressed-out *masa* onto one palm, positioned so that the bottom portion of the disk dangles off the hand. Slowly moving that hand over the griddle, they lay the tortilla on the hot surface, letting it "catch" first on the dangling side and then sweeping the hand out from under the tortilla in an underhand roll. One smooth, flowing motion ensures unrumpled tortillas. The overhand flip nearly always leads to unhappiness.

Quesadillas

There's something soulfully satisfying and elemental about coddling in your hands a piece of daily bread—from whatever tradition—wrapped around warm, giving cheese. Grilled cheese sandwiches are the perfect example for most of us, quesadillas for our neighbors to the south. But the quesadilla has learned to embrace more than the grilled cheese, welcoming a full imagination of fillings, sometimes even to the exclusion of cheese itself.

Quesadillas range from plain Jane to rustic adventurer to delicate sophisticate. Plain and everyday, a tortilla gets wrapped around a little cheese and crisped on a griddle with little thought, little planning. But in Oaxaca, quesadillas are a specialty, creations of epic proportions and memories. There they're generally called *empanadas*, and though the cooks everywhere make them wonderfully, there's an *empanada* alchemist, Señora Oliva Castro, in the Mercado de la Democracia. She thinly presses out a plate-sized disk—a huge tortilla—of fresh-ground corn *masa* and lays it on a clay griddle set over glowing coals. The *maestra* heaps the filling down the center of the tortilla (my favorite is torn squash blossoms, pulled local string cheese [*quesillo*] and a handful of *epazote* leaves), then folds the assembly in half, roughly sealing the edges together. When the meal-sized turnover is crusty and browned underneath, she tucks it underneath the coals, as we'd run something under a broiler. There it browns, emerging like a glorious calzone in rustic, rough-hewn splendor.

But crispy little quesadillas that rise from the oil with a golden patina have their own allure. These rich, tender little pockets almost give before the teeth touch them. What luxurious treats, whether you're street-side at a stall or in the relaxed atmosphere of a lovely restaurant! Think *croques-monsieurs* on the sidewalk in Paris or in an elegant brasserie.

It's easiest to start quesadilla making with the simplest crispy cheese-filled one, but do take the time to make the chile-spiked mushrooms to mingle with the cheese. When you're having a party, move on to the recipe for the crisp-fried beauties to pass around. Do not only *read* the recipe for the Oaxacan-style squash-blossom quesadillas. Sure it's fun to dream of the day when you'll have them on Oaxacan soil. But they're so wonderful that you simply have to make them. Besides, that'll give you the opportunity to dream up all kinds of add-ins when squash blossoms are nowhere to be found. That's how contemporary versions get started.

TRADITIONAL BENCHMARK: Each of the three different quesadilla styles has its benchmark. The one prepared from a ready-made tortilla (mostly a corn tortilla in Mexico, a flour one in the United States) that's folded around melting cheese and lightly crisped on a griddle is easy to make very good as long as the tortilla is fresh and the cheese is melting and tasty. When made from a corn tortilla (even if the tortilla is fresh and lightly brushed with oil), this type of quesadilla is a little chewier than one made from a flour tortilla. Our second recipe, the griddle-baked quesadilla made from *masa* that's pressed out, laid on the griddle, filled and folded, is best when the *masa* is pressed thin enough to be in proportion to the filling. It also needs to spend enough time on the griddle for the inner corn *masa* to cook (it should still be soft, but not raw tasting), the filling to heat through and the outside to toast to a chewy crustiness. The third recipe, the fried quesadilla, is perfect when the *masa* is pressed thin, there's an *epazote*-flavored nugget of melted cheese inside and the outside is crispy but tender and greaseless.

WHEN TO THINK OF THESE RECIPES: The simple ready-made-tortilla version is everyday eating. The rustic press-out-the-*masa* version is more of an adventure—an admittedly casual dish, but one that leaves a mighty impression. I often serve them when I've got a crowd coming and a hearty soup-stew like *pozole* (page 166) is on the menu; you will, however, have to dedicate the first part of the party to quesadilla making. The fried quesadilla is a rich pass-around mouthful; serve it with a little guacamole and a spicy, tangy salsa, then move on to dinner. Or pair these fried quesadillas with other *antojitos* for a casual all-passed feast.

ADVICE FOR AMERICAN COOKS: Be creative with quesadillas—they're so accommodating. We've spelled out suggestions in the ingredient lists.

GRIDDLE-BAKED SQUASH BLOSSOM QUESADILLAS
WITH *EPAZOTE* (PAGE 56)

Cheese-and-Mushroom Quesadillas

QUESADILLAS DE QUESO Y HONGOS

Makes 8 quesadillas, serving 8 as an appetizer,
4 as a light main course

2 tablespoons olive oil (preferably extra-virgin) or rich-tasting pork
lard, plus a little more for the tortillas

1 pound button mushrooms (or other flavorful mushrooms, such
as shiitake, oyster, cremini or chanterelles), cleaned and sliced
$^1/_4$ inch thick (you'll have about 4 cups)

Fresh hot green chiles to taste (roughly 2 to 3 serranos or 1 to 2
jalapeños), stemmed, seeded and thinly sliced

2 tablespoons chopped fresh epazote leaves
OR $^1/_4$ cup chopped fresh cilantro

Salt

8 fresh corn tortillas (or flour tortillas if good corn tortillas
are not available)

8 ounces Mexican melting cheese (Chihuahua, quesillo,
asadero or the like) or Monterey Jack, brick or mild
cheddar, shredded (you'll have about 2 cups)

About 1 cup salsa (I love the Roasted Tomato–Green Chile
Salsa on page 100)

TRADITIONAL

1. THE MUSHROOM FILLING. In a medium skillet, heat the 2 tablespoons oil or lard over medium. Add the mushrooms, chiles and *epazote* (if you're using cilantro, set it aside to add later), stir well and cover. Continue to stir every minute or so, replacing the cover each time, until the mushrooms have released a lot of juice, 4 to 5 minutes. Uncover and let briskly simmer until all the liquid has evaporated, about 3 minutes. Taste and season with salt, usually about $^1/_4$ teaspoon. Add the cilantro now, if that's what you're using.

2. FORMING AND GRIDDLE-BAKING THE QUESADILLAS. Heat a well-seasoned or nonstick griddle or heavy skillet over medium. Turn the oven on to its lowest setting. One by one, make the quesadillas: Lightly brush one side of each tortilla with

oil, then lay it oiled side down on the hot griddle. Spread with about ¼ cup of the cheese, leaving a ½-inch border all around. Spoon about 3 tablespoons of the mushroom mixture down the center of the cheese-covered tortilla. When the cheese begins to melt (but before the tortilla begins to crisp), fold the tortilla in half along the line of the filling. Cook, flipping the quesadilla every minute or so, until the cheese is completely melted and the tortilla crisps, about 5 minutes in all. As each quesadilla is done, transfer it to a baking sheet and keep warm in the oven.

3. SERVING THE QUESADILLAS. When all the quesadillas are done, set them out in a cloth-lined basket. Pass the salsa separately for each guest to spoon on.

WORKING AHEAD: The mushroom filling can be made several days in advance; cover and refrigerate. The quesadillas are best when prepared just moments before serving.

Señora Oliva scooping filling into quesadillas in Oaxaca market

Griddle-Baked Squash Blossom Quesadillas—with substitutes

QUESADILLAS ASADAS DE FLORES DE CALABAZA

Makes 8 quesadillas, serving 8 as an appetizer,
4 as a light main dish

2 dozen 4-inch-long squash blossoms (use less if they're larger, more
    if smaller)
    OR 2 cups small spinach and arugula leaves (if you have
    unsprayed nasturtium blossoms in the yard, use them in place
    of the arugula)
16 good-sized (2-inch-long) fresh epazote leaves, roughly chopped
    if large
    OR ¼ cup fresh cilantro leaves
8 ounces Mexican melting cheese (Chihuahua, quesillo,
    asadero or the like) or Monterey Jack, brick or mild
    cheddar, shredded (you'll have about 2 cups)
Salt
1 pound (2 cups) fresh smooth-ground corn masa for tortillas
    OR 1¾ cups powdered masa harina mixed with 1 cup plus
    2 tablespoons warm water
About 1 cup salsa (I love the Green Tomatillo Salsa on page 60)

TRADITIONAL

1. THE FILLING INGREDIENTS. Clean the squash blossoms by breaking off the
stems and the little thin green sepals at the base of each blossom. Pinch out or
break off the long pistils in the center of each flower. Tear or cut the blossoms,
including the bulbous base, into ½-inch-wide strips. If using spinach and arugula or nasturtium instead of the squash blossoms, set them at the ready, along
with the *epazote* or cilantro leaves and the shredded cheese.

2. FORMING AND GRIDDLE-BAKING THE QUESADILLAS. Heat a well-seasoned or
nonstick griddle or heavy skillet over medium. Turn the oven on to its lowest setting. Knead ½ teaspoon salt into the fresh or reconstituted *masa*. If necessary,
knead a few drops of water into the *masa* to give it the consistency of soft cookie

dough. Divide into 8 pieces, roll into balls and cover with plastic wrap to keep from drying out.

One by one, make the quesadillas: Line a tortilla press with two pieces of plastic cut to fit the plates (to be on the safe side, cut them from a food storage bag; the thicker plastic usually works better for beginners). Gently press out a flattened ball of dough between the sheets of plastic into a 7-inch circle. Peel off the top sheet of plastic, flip the tortilla—uncovered side down—onto the fingers of one hand and gently peel off the second piece of plastic. In one flowing movement, roll the tortilla off your hand and onto the preheated griddle or skillet.

Immediately spread on about ¼ cup of the cheese (leaving a ½-inch border all around), 2 leaves of *epazote* (or several of cilantro) and about 2 tablespoons of the sliced squash blossoms or their substitutes. After 30 to 45 seconds, when the tortilla has released itself from the cooking surface, fold it in half to enclose the filling. Press the edges together with your fingers (or the back of a spoon if you find the procedure a little too hot). Continue to cook, flipping the quesadilla every 30 seconds or so, until it is richly browned in places and crispy-crunchy, 6 to 7 minutes—a little longer than you might expect, but that's what it takes to get them done through. As you fold each quesadilla over, move on to the next. As they're done, keep them warm on a baking sheet in the oven.

3. SERVING THE QUESADILLAS. When all are done, set them out in a cozy cloth-lined basket. Pass the salsa separately for each guest to drizzle on *al gusto*.

WORKING AHEAD: The squash blossoms can be cleaned early in the day, the cheese shredded and the *masa* mixed and portioned. The quesadillas, however, aren't fabulous unless made just when you're ready to serve them.

Squash blossoms

Crispy-Fried Cheese Quesadillas

QUESADILLAS FRITAS

Makes 16 quesadillas, serving 8 or more as an
appetizer or pass-around nibble

1 pound (2 cups) fresh smooth-ground corn masa *for tortillas*
    OR 1³/₄ cups powdered masa harina *mixed with 1 cup plus*
    2 tablespoons warm water
2 tablespoons rich-tasting pork lard or vegetable shortening
¹/₄ cup all-purpose flour (use ¹/₃ cup if using masa harina)
Scant 1 teaspoon baking powder
Salt
12 ounces Mexican melting cheese (Chihuahua, quesillo,
    asadero *or the like*) or Monterey Jack, brick or mild
    cheddar, shredded (you'll have about 3 cups)
¹/₃ cup fresh epazote leaves, sliced if large
    OR ¹/₂ cup fresh cilantro leaves
Vegetable oil to a depth of ³/₄ inch for frying
About 1¹/₂ cups salsa (I love these with the tanginess of Red
    Chile–Tomatillo Salsa, page 35, or Classic Guacamole, page 4)

TRADITIONAL

1. THE DOUGH AND CHEESE. In a large bowl, knead together the *masa* (fresh or reconstituted), lard or vegetable shortening, flour, baking powder and ¹/₂ teaspoon salt. If necessary, work in a few drops of water to give the dough the consistency of a soft cookie dough. Divide into 16 pieces, roll into balls and cover with plastic to keep from drying out.

    Toss the cheese with the *epazote* or cilantro, then form it into 16 compact flattened football shapes about 3 inches long by 1¹/₄ inches wide; cover.

2. FORMING THE QUESADILLAS. One by one, make the quesadillas: Line a tortilla press with two pieces of plastic cut to fit the plates (to be on the safe side, cut them from a food storage bag; the thicker plastic usually works better for beginners). Gently press out a flattened ball of *masa* between the sheets of plastic into a 4-inch circle. Peel off the top sheet of plastic, lay a piece of the cheese mixture

on the right half of the tortilla and fold over the left half of the tortilla (plastic and all) to cover the cheese. Carefully press the edges of the turnover together (you'll be pressing through the plastic at this point), being careful not to trap air around the cheese. Now, peel off the plastic from the top side, flip the turnover onto your hand (uncovered side down) and peel off the rest of the plastic. Lay the turnover on a tray lined with plastic. Continue making the quesadillas, leaving at least ¹/₂ inch between them on the tray. Cover with plastic.

3. FRYING AND SERVING THE QUESADILLAS. In a deep heavy medium skillet or saucepan, heat ³/₄ inch oil to 375°F over medium to medium-high (it's best to use a thermometer here, but, lacking one, you can judge the temperature by testing the edge of a quesadilla in the hot oil: it should sizzle vigorously). Turn the oven on to its lowest setting and set out a baking sheet lined with paper towels. Two or three at a time, fry the quesadillas, turning them several times, until golden and crispy, about 2 ¹/₂ to 3 minutes. Drain on the paper towels and keep warm in the oven.

As soon as they are all fried, serve the quesadillas in a decorative basket lined with a cloth; don't forget to pass the salsa and/or guacamole for guests to spoon on to their liking.

WORKING AHEAD: You can form the quesadillas up to 3 days ahead. Refrigerate them on the tray, well covered. But fry these delectable morsels at the last moment—more than 5 or 10 minutes of holding in the oven will render them soggy.

Mounding squash blossoms to fill a quesadilla while tostadas crisp at edge of clay griddle

SALSA VERDE • Green Tomatillo Salsa

Whether you choose the verdant, slushy, herby freshness of the all-raw tomatillo salsa or the olive-colored, voluptuous, sweet-sour richness of the roasted version, tomatillos are about brightening tang. The buzz of fresh hot green chile adds thrill, all of which adds up to a condiment most of us simply don't want to live without.

Makes about 1 cup

8 ounces (5 to 6 medium) tomatillos, husked and rinsed
Fresh hot green chiles to taste (roughly 2 serranos or
    1 jalapeño), stemmed
5 or 6 sprigs fresh cilantro (thick stems removed),
    roughly chopped
Scant ¼ cup finely chopped white onion
Salt

FOR THE ALL-RAW VERSION: Roughly chop the tomatillos and the chiles. In a blender or food processor, combine the tomatillos, chiles, cilantro and ¼ cup water. Process to a coarse puree, then scrape into a serving dish. Rinse the onion under cold water, then shake to remove excess moisture. Stir into the salsa and season with salt, usually a generous ¼ teaspoon.

FOR THE ROASTED VERSION: Roast the tomatillos and chiles on a baking sheet 4 inches below a very hot broiler until darkly roasted, even blackened in spots, about 5 minutes. Flip them over and roast the other side—4 to 5 minutes more will give you splotchy-black and blistered tomatillos and chiles that are soft and cooked through. Cool, then transfer everything to a blender, including all the delicious juice that has run out onto the baking sheet. Add the cilantro and ¼ cup water, blend to a coarse puree and scrape into a serving dish. Rinse the onion under cold water, then shake to remove the excess moisture. Stir into the salsa and season with salt, usually a generous ¼ teaspoon.

Questions and Answers from Our Testing

What kind of store-bought tortillas make the best easy griddle-baked (cheese-and-mushroom) quesadillas? We made our very best quesadillas with just-made fresh-*masa* tortillas still hot from our griddle—not practical for most people looking for a quick dinner. Still passable, though a little chewier, were quesadillas made from fresh-that-day corn tortillas from a local tortilla factory, though we found the texture of even those to be improved by a light brushing of oil. No other corn tortillas were worth the effort. Flour tortillas, on the other hand, stay fresher longer because they contain fat . . . meaning that it's easier to find a good one for quesadillas. Conclusion: If you don't have fresh corn tortillas, make the easy griddle-baked quesadillas with good flour tortillas.

What cheeses are best for quesadillas? When you're looking for a Mexican taste and a texture that's not too molten or too rubbery, you're best off using one of the cheeses we describe for *queso fundido* on page 24. You'll have to experiment with other cheeses, though my recommendation for rustic griddle-baked and fried quesadillas is to look for a cheese that won't drown out the flavor of the *masa* and other fillings and flavorings.

Can *masa harina* produce as good a rustic griddle-baked or fried quesadilla as fresh *masa* can? Both the rustic griddle-baked and the fried quesadillas are best with fresh-ground corn *masa*—but they're also very good with reconstituted powdered *masa harina*. So use what you can get your hands on, but when using *masa harina*, make sure your dough is soft to ensure tenderness.

What traditional combinations make the best quesadilla fillings? When cheese is part of the mix in any of the quesadillas, the additional filling ingredients are usually small, rather sauceless pieces—from the smoked fish, poached shrimp and seared steak that I've eaten in northwestern Mexico to the potatoes and green chiles, squash blossoms and chorizo sausage farther south. Saucier, stewier fillings are often tucked into rustic griddle-baked and fried quesadillas made without cheese. Moist, flavorful shredded beef or pork, brains or stewed mushrooms are common choices. In making the easy griddle-baked quesadillas, cheese is a must, since something has to stick the two sides together. Raw *masa* seals to itself, so cheese is optional in the rustic griddle-baked and fried quesadillas. Just remember that when you're using moist fillings for fried quesadillas, they need to be fried the moment they're formed, or they'll soften and begin to fall apart.

What dough add-ins make the best gorditas? We tried the dough for fried quesadillas with plain *masa*, with salted *masa* and with *masa* containing salt, baking powder and fat. Kneading in all three produces the lightest, most tender quesadilla. For the rustic griddle-baked ones, salt was welcome, though a little oil or pork lard gives more tenderness.

Tostadas

Of all the personalities you find in the street-side snacks of Mexico, tostadas can be the raciest. They have a way of tingling the tongue, tangling the nostrils, even racing the pulse. I've most often found myself nibbling a tostada as I've ambled away from the jangling, glaring street stalls that stand cheek-by-jowl, each piled high with towers of wavy, not-quite-flat tortilla disks. These humble little spots entice shamelessly. They etch their presence in the impatient, pungent exhaust of traffic with their dangling naked bulbs and the biting, vinegary chile perfume they exude. You have to be pretty uptight not to succumb, knowing that any topping will take you on a ride with surprise twists and sharp-edged turns.

When I'm in the mood for a safer, modern ambiance, I head for the bright fluorescent-lit rooms of a *cafetería*, whose smooth-surfaced cleanness has a tendency to whitewash the sexy, racy tostadas' identity. Yet even here, the elemental balance of flavors and textures prevails.

Sadly, however, when we imported tostadas into the United States, we misunderstood something. Tostadas made a gradual transmutation, it seems to me, into the heavy over-laden taco salad—that giant, ultrarich deep-fried bowl of a flour tortilla filled with lettuce and rich dressing. So, if you feel you're awash in the American taco salad, reach for a life raft of original goodness: the Mexican tostada.

At their most basic, tostadas are simple, hand-held snacks with a playful insouciance that would rarely lead a cook or eater to carefully scrutinize their making. Take a look at my recipe for Black Bean–Chicken Tostadas. It's a flexible beauty—an appetizer, a light lunch, one of my favorite simple dinners. This version, a standard menu item straight out of the Mexican *cafeterías*, starts with a crisp-fried tortilla as a base—what's called in Mexico (confusingly for those who don't speak Spanish) a *tostada*. But the *tostada* base generously offers its name to the whole assemblage as well—crisp tortilla, toppings and all. And that assemblage stacks up nicely from a nutritional perspective: whole grains, legumes, chicken, cheese, fresh greens and salsa in healthy proportions. Notice also how the salsa and simply dressed romaine sharpen and define the dish.

I continue with those basic proportions in my contemporary tostada but move into the luxury corridor. Rich smoked salmon is laid up against black beans. Full-flavored salty smokiness is brought into perspective with earthy legumes. If you can get it, use the avocado leaf to add an anisey perfume to the beans. But don't skip the dressy dice of the fresh green avocado itself.

Now, you may wonder if either of these versions reveals raciness? Not really. That's the realm of the *manitas de puerco en vinagre,* pickled pigs' feet (see For the Adventurer, page 68). With a single wild bite of such varied, rich textures brought into focus with tanginess and spice, you're right there in the noisy, glary, giggle-infested ghetto of tostada stalls.

TRADITIONAL BENCHMARK: When I think of a really good tostada, a fiesta of textures and tastes comes to mind: a crispy tortilla that's tender enough to bite easily, but not so brittle that it falls apart in your hands, and toppings that offer softness (beans, avocado, cream, pigs' feet, boiled vegetables and so on), meatiness (chicken or sausage or even the smoked salmon of our contemporary recipe), freshness and crunchiness (raw onion, cilantro, radishes and lettuce) and spiciness (salsa or strips of pickled jalapeño).

WHEN TO THINK OF THESE RECIPES: Simple chicken tostadas are everyday lunch or dinner fare (for a meatless alternative, leave out the chicken), and they're so well balanced that you need little else but something to drink. The contemporary little salmon tostaditas are dressy and rich—an earthy pass-around appetizer for a nice dinner party rather than a simple meal-on-a-crispy-tortilla.

ADVICE FOR AMERICAN COOKS: All of the ingredients for tostadas are easily available. Just be sure not to succumb to the temptation to overburden the crisp tortilla platforms.

Black Bean–Chicken Tostadas with salsa and tangy romaine

TOSTADAS DE POLLO CON FRIJOLES

*Makes 10 tostadas, serving 10 as an appetizer,
5 as a light main course*

10 thin corn tortillas, preferably store-bought ones made of
   coarse-ground masa

Vegetable oil to a depth of $\frac{1}{2}$ inch for frying, plus 2 tablespoons
   for the beans

1 medium white onion, chopped

3 garlic cloves, peeled and finely chopped

2 cups cooked black beans (or any other type that appeals, such as red
   or pinto), liquid drained and reserved

Salt

2 cups coarsely shredded cooked chicken (buy a rotisserie chicken
   or poach chicken breasts, legs and/or thighs)

$\frac{3}{4}$ cup homemade crema (page 133), crème frâiche or sour
   cream, thinned with a little milk

1 cup salsa (the Green Tomatillo Salsa on page 60 is a
   good choice)

About $\frac{1}{2}$ cup grated Mexican queso añejo or other
   dry grating cheese, such as Romano or Parmesan

2 tablespoons cider vinegar

1 tablespoon olive oil, preferably extra-virgin

3 cups loosely packed sliced romaine ($\frac{1}{4}$-inch-wide slices are ideal),
   plus a little more for decorating the platter if you like

Sliced tomatoes (optional)

TRADITIONAL

1. THE TOSTADAS. If the tortillas are moist, lay them out in a single layer for a few minutes to dry to a leathery feel; rewrap them until you're ready to fry.

In a medium skillet, heat the $\frac{1}{2}$ *inch* vegetable oil over medium to medium-high. When the oil is hot enough to make the edge of a tortilla sizzle energetically, fry the tortillas one at a time: Lay a tortilla in the oil and, after about 15 seconds, use tongs to flip it over (this ensures that the tortilla will stay relatively flat). Continue to fry, pushing it down into the oil every few seconds. When the bubbling begins to subside and the tortilla has darkened just a bit (usually less than a minute total frying time), remove it from the oil and drain on paper towels. If they have been fried long enough, the tortillas should be completely crisp when cooled.

2. THE BEANS. Set a medium skillet (preferably nonstick) over medium heat and add the remaining *2 tablespoons* vegetable oil. When hot, add the onion and cook, stirring, until golden brown, about 7 minutes. Add the garlic, stir it around for a minute or so, and then add the beans. Using an old-fashioned potato masher, Mexican bean masher or the back of a large spoon, coarsely mash the beans, mixing in the onion and garlic as you go. Add enough of the reserved bean liquid (or water if you are using canned beans) to give the beans a soft consistency that barely holds its shape in a spoon. Taste and season with salt, usually about ¼ teaspoon if using already seasoned beans. Cover and set aside.

3. THE OTHER TOSTADA TOPPINGS. When you're ready to serve, set out the chicken, *crema* or sour cream, salsa and cheese. Set the beans over medium-low heat to warm them slightly. In a large bowl, mix together the vinegar and olive oil. Toss in the romaine. Season with about ¼ teaspoon salt.

4. LAYERING AND SERVING THE TOSTADAS. One by one, layer the tostadas: Spread a tostada with about 2 rounded tablespoons of warm beans (if they've thickened noticeably, stir in a little water or bean broth). Strew with 2 rounded tablespoons of chicken, then about ¼ cup of dressed lettuce. Drizzle on a scant tablespoon of cream, spoon about a tablespoon of salsa in the middle and dust generously with grated cheese.

Arrange the tostadas on a serving platter (you may want to first scatter extra sliced romaine and sliced tomatoes over the platter for a nice look), and you're ready to carry these treats to hungry eaters.

WORKING AHEAD: The tortillas are best when fried no more than a couple of hours before serving; don't refrigerate them, or they'll get soggy. The beans, however, can be made several days ahead (store them in the refrigerator, well covered); warm them when you're ready to serve. Layer the tostadas just before you're ready to eat them—even 15 minutes ahead will mean slightly soggy tostadas. Better yet, set everything out and let your guests build tostadas to their own liking.

Smoked Salmon–Black Bean Tostaditas

TOSTADITAS DE SALMON AHUMADO

Makes 24 tostaditas, serving 10 or more
as a substantial nibble

8 thin corn tortillas, preferably store-bought ones made of coarse-
ground masa

Vegetable oil to a depth of $^1/_2$ inch for frying, plus 2 tablespoons
for the beans

$^1/_2$ small white onion, chopped

2 garlic cloves, peeled and finely chopped

1 avocado leaf, crumbled (optional)

$1^1/_2$ cups cooked black beans, liquid drained and reserved

Salt

5 ounces smoked salmon (a less-expensive end piece or trimmings
are fine here), cut into $^1/_4$-inch cubes (you'll have 1 cup)

$^1/_4$ cup finely chopped ripe tomato

2 to 3 tablespoons thinly sliced green onions or garlic chives

2 tablespoons chopped fresh cilantro, plus 24 leaves for garnish

Fresh hot green chile to taste (roughly 1 serrano or $^1/_2$ jalapeño),
stemmed, seeded and finely chopped

$^1/_4$ teaspoon black pepper, preferably freshly ground

$^1/_4$ cup homemade crema (page 133), crème frâiche or sour
cream thinned with a little milk

Frisée lettuce or sliced romaine for lining the serving platter
(optional)

1. THE TOSTADITAS. If the tortillas are moist, lay them out in a single layer for a few minutes to dry to a leathery feel. Cut the tortillas into long triangles as illustrated on page 137; rewrap them until you're ready to fry.

   In a medium skillet, heat the $^1/_2$ inch oil over medium to medium-high. When the oil is hot enough to make the edge of a tortilla triangle sizzle energetically, fry them 3 at a time: Lay the tortilla triangles in the oil and after about

15 seconds, use tongs to flip them over. Continue to fry, pushing them down into the oil every few seconds. When the bubbling begins to subside and the triangles have darkened just a bit (usually less than a minute total frying time), remove from the oil and drain on paper towels.

2. THE BEANS. Set a medium skillet (preferably nonstick) over medium heat and add the remaining *2 tablespoons* oil. When hot, add the onion and cook, stirring, until golden, about 5 minutes. Add the garlic, stir for a minute or so, and then scrape into a food processor; add the optional avocado leaf and the beans. Process until smooth. Return to the skillet and stir in enough of the bean liquid (or water if you are using canned beans) to achieve a soft consistency—one that barely holds its shape in a spoon. Taste and season with salt, usually about 1/4 teaspoon if using already seasoned beans. Cover and set aside.

3. THE SALMON MIXTURE. In a small bowl, stir together the smoked salmon, tomato, green onions or chives, chopped cilantro, chile and black pepper. Taste and season with salt, usually about 1/4 teaspoon. Refrigerate covered for about 30 minutes.

4. ASSEMBLING AND SERVING THE TOSTADITAS. When you're ready to serve, warm the beans over medium-low heat; if they've thickened noticeably, stir in a little water or bean broth. Assemble the tostaditas: Spread the wide end of a tostadita with about a teaspoon of warm beans (you'll have some leftover beans for another use), then spoon on a generous teaspoon of the salmon mixture. Top with a little dollop of *crema* or sour cream and garnish with a leaf of cilantro.

Scatter frisée or sliced romaine (if using) over a platter. Arrange the tostaditas on it, and you're ready to pass your creations around.

WORKING AHEAD: The tortilla triangles taste freshest when fried no more than a couple of hours before serving; don't refrigerate them, or they'll get soggy. The beans can be made several days ahead (store them in the refrigerator, well covered) and rewarmed when you're ready to serve. Assemble the tostaditas just when you're ready for them, to avoid soft—rather than crisp—tostaditas.

Tostadas de Manitas de Puerco (Pigs' Feet Tostadas)

This classic Mexican dish, especially beloved in west central and central Mexico, can be made by replacing the chicken in the traditional recipe with pickled pigs' feet, either purchased or homemade; you can omit the beans, as most cooks do when building pigs' feet tostadas, and use a vinegary Mexican bottled hot sauce (like Tamazula) for the salsa.

To prepare 1½ pounds (2 medium) pigs' feet (ask the butcher to split them), simmer them slowly in water to cover in a large pot (add salt, bay leaves, garlic and chopped onion for flavor) until they're very tender, about 4 hours. Remove and cool, then cut out all the bones and knuckles. Chop what remains into rough ½-inch pieces. Make an *escabeche* of sliced onion, halved garlic cloves, sliced carrot and sliced jalapeños, first frying them in olive oil until crunchy-tender, then simmering briefly in half cider vinegar and half water—not even enough liquid to cover. Cool, season with salt, mix in the pigs' feet and let stand for at least several hours before assembling your pigs' feet tostadas.

Left: Cauldrons of hot chocolate and mole *at La Abuelita market stall*

Below: Rustic street taco

QUESTIONS AND ANSWERS FROM OUR TESTING

WHAT IS THE RIGHT TORTILLA FOR FRYING INTO A TOSTADA? *Corn v. flour tortillas:* Tostadas are always made from corn tortillas in Mexico, though in the States a flour tortilla version has become popular. I like richness as much as anyone, but a fried flour tortilla (already much richer than a corn tortilla) seems over the top. *Homemade v. store-bought:* Though homemade corn tortillas are the perfect accompaniment to a Mexican meal, they're usually too thick to produce a tender tostada. Store-bought corn tortillas are my first choice for frying into tostadas. *Tortillas made of smooth v. coarse-ground corn* masa: Many tortilla factories make a rather thin tortilla from coarsely ground corn *masa* especially for frying. Thinness makes it more tender, while the coarse-ground *masa* keeps it from puffing (and potentially trapping oil when fried). The coarser grind is obvious from the flecks in the finished tortilla. If special "frying" tortillas aren't available, choose any decent-looking corn tortilla and just watch out for the puffing. *Fresh v. stale tortillas:* Moist fresh tortillas typically absorb more oil during frying than dryish slightly stale ones. Special "frying" tortillas are generally made from drier *masa*, so they're drier to begin with. If your tortillas feel moist, let them dry in a single layer until leathery feeling to ensure that they don't come out greasy.

WHAT IS THE RIGHT WAY TO FRY A TORTILLA INTO A TOSTADA? Frying tostadas is easier than frying other corn *masa* creations. If you're careful to keep the tortilla submerged (no spots bubbling up above the level of the oil), there's little likelihood of its turning out hard or heavy. Oil that is too cool yields greasy tostadas; oil that is too hot inevitably creates a burnt flavor. At 350°F, the oil is just right. Exact oil temperature is hard to judge, however, when there's only a depth of ½ inch, given that most thermometers need more than that. So judge by the edge-sizzling test (the oil should sizzle vigorously, not calmly or explosively). Oil that's about 350°F will have released that characteristic hot oil aroma into the kitchen and will present a slightly shimmery, ripply surface. Oil that starts to smoke is way too hot—dangerously hot—and, even if allowed to cool down, will give the tostadas a bad flavor. A heavy pan or pot will maintain the steadiest temperature.

ARE THERE ALTERNATIVES TO FRYING THE TORTILLAS FOR TOSTADAS? In some places in Mexico, tender tortillas are crisped right on a dry griddle. The same crisping can be achieved in a 325°F oven, but the tortillas need to be thin and made from very-smooth-ground corn *masa*—otherwise they'll just be hard instead of tender and flaky. Even at their best, though, griddle- or oven-crisped tostadas will be harder than fried ones. Spraying both sides of the tortillas with vegetable oil before crisping them in the oven is an easy, decent alternative, but it still doesn't give the tenderness that frying does. Buying cellophane-wrapped packages of already-fried tostadas is an easy option for anyone living where there's a Mexican community; they can be passable, but they also can be pretty stale-tasting.

WHAT'S THE RIGHT BALANCE OF INGREDIENTS ON A TOSTADA? Simple food always shows off the quality of the ingredients, so choose well. Then think about the balance. In the traditional Black Bean–Chicken Tostadas, for instance, an inch of beans smeared over the tortilla would make the whole assembly go mushy. Too much chicken would be flexing muscles in an unexpected way. Too much salsa or cream would give a washed-out impression. And too much romaine would turn the whole thing into a salad—leaving guests wondering what the rest of those ingredients were there for. But each ingredient in the right balance makes the tostada experience one of symphonic proportions. In the contemporary Smoked Salmon–Black Bean Tostaditas, there is a slightly different balance. There, it's crispy (the tostada itself) against earthy (the black beans) against rich (the salmon and cream) against crunchy-fresh (green onions, tomato and cilantro). Texture is also the focus of the adventurous Pigs' Feet Tostadas. Crispy (the tostada) against chewy-tender-unctuousness (pickled pigs' feet—don't be tempted by the mushy canned varieties), all put into perspective with a shot of spicy, mouth-puckering hot sauce. Good cooking is like any art or craft. It's mostly about learning to achieve balance.

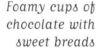

Foamy cups of chocolate with sweet breads

Tamales

If I can offer one piece of advice about making tamales, it's this: Don't make them by yourself.

I'm not saying that because tamales are particularly difficult—after all, the batter contains only a handful of ingredients. No, my advice springs more from my experience of the tamal-making ritual, which is a collective one, a special-occasion one. You gather with others to chatter, to anticipate, busying your fingers with mixing, folding, wrapping and tying. Finally, you inhale the unique aroma puffing out from the steamer, announcing the beginning of festivity. It's a fragrance that envelops your senses in air thick with the essence of earthy corn *masa,* woodsy corn husks, perhaps herbaceous banana leaves.

The whole sensory experience has become part of Mexico's collective consciousness, one that's carried into the middle of every fiesta, be it a baptism, birthday or Christmas. And the entire process leading up to the moment of biting into a steaming tamal is a kind of celebration of its own. It's a *tamalada,* the tamal-making party before the party.

Embrace the culture of the *tamalada* and you'll understand not just the "how" of tamales, but the "why." Perhaps the closest thing we have to this communal culinary rite is making cookies at Christmastime. But tamales offer a more complete experience, being served at the crescendo's end of a special day. They spark an explosion of merrymaking.

Though tamales come in innumerable shapes, sizes and flavors in Mexico and each is an expression of local pride, there are a few tamal generalities. Corn husks and banana leaves are common wrappers. Scalding steam is the typical heat used to cook them. And corn *masa*, the same elemental ingredient that's used to make corn tortillas, is as much a tamal's glory as the filling it contains.

Two of the most well known tamal fillings are chicken with green chile–tomatillo sauce and pork in red chile sauce, and here I've given directions for how to employ them both in making tamales with corn husks as well as banana leaves. Sweet tamales, like the pineapple-raisin version I offer here, are everyday fare in Mexico, frequently sold by street vendors to the hordes of hungry folks in markets, shops or offices who are in search of their midmorning *almuerzo*—that meal we'd consider a cross between breakfast and lunch. A cup of *atole*, the warm, comforting, thickish beverage with the gentle sweet allure of corn, cinnamon, even chocolate, is the classic accompaniment.

I end with a labor-light tamal casserole that was inspired by a Mexican friend's zucchini tamales. It's a recipe I developed to use easy-to-find dehydrated *masa harina* for tortillas and to sidestep the individual husk or leaf wrapping, combining the wonderful tamal essence with the lightness of zucchini and the smoky counterpoint of ham nuggets. Easy, functional, attractive and doable days in advance.

TRADITIONAL BENCHMARK: I'd be a fool to tell you that there is One Best Tamal, tamales being so varied and so imbued in Mexican culture with regional pride and the magic of mama's ministrations. But, not having a Mexican mama to offend, I can simply describe my favorites. I evaluate tamales on four criteria: tenderness, lightness, texture and taste. The ones I like best are moist and tender; they're light—almost fluffy—but not crumbly; they have an even texture that engages you with coarse flecks of corn; and their flavor is earthy-sweet from fresh-ground *masa*, rich from just the right amount of fat and aromatic from the husk or leaf wrapper. That isn't to say I wouldn't swoon over an everyday tamal bought from a street vendor at the edge of any Mexican town square (if they lack anything, it's usually the light texture). Or a slice of the ultracoarse *zacahuil* that's baked in a wood-fired oven. Or a wedge of the dense, earthy, pit-steamed *mucbipollo* that's made in Yucatan for Day of the Dead. Or a tremblingly light pudding-like tamal from the Gulf Coast area. Or a tender, flat-as-a-pancake, corn leaf–wrapped pre-Columbian-style tamal from Oaxaca. Or a compact, smooth-textured, four-sided *corunda* from Michoacan. When it comes to tamales, it's easy to go on and on.

WHEN TO THINK OF THESE RECIPES: In contemporary North America, the ritual of the *tamalada* (the tamal-making party) can fit right into the way many of us like to entertain—simply, casually. Cooking in a group can strengthen ties and be plain old fun. Make several varieties (plan on two or three tamales per person), and serve them at an informal party with a couple of salsas. Round out the menu (this is my American side talking) with a pot of beans and a big salad. Keep everything simple and focused on the tamales. Beer and limeade are my beverages of choice. Our contemporary tamal casserole is less work than individual-wrapped tamales, so it's great served at a small casual dinner or put out on a buffet.

ADVICE FOR AMERICAN COOKS: Look for fresh corn *masa* at a tortilla factory and some Mexican grocery stores, or dehydrated and powdered *masa* (called *masa harina*) in well-stocked chain groceries as well as Mexican groceries. Many Mexican groceries carry tubs or plastic pouches of *masa preparada*—typically fresh, coarse-ground corn *masa* that's been beaten with shortening or lard, salt, seasonings . . . and preservatives. *Masa preparada* is only as good as the ingredients that go into it. Fresh, roasty-tasting pork lard from a Mexican or German butcher, or lard you make yourself (see page 77), is by far the best. Corn husks are available in Mexican groceries. Banana leaves are often sold in Asian groceries, as well as Mexican ones, in the frozen food section. Keep in mind: Though the most perfect ingredients make tamales that are transcendent, second-choice ingredients still produce tamales that will deservedly garner compliments, so use what you can find, and get cooking.

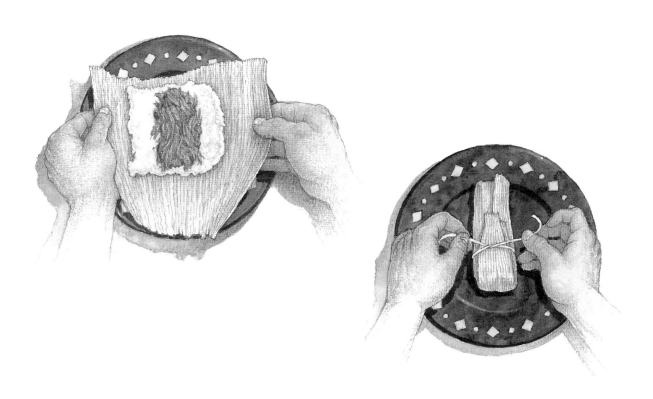

Green Chile Chicken Tamales

TAMALES DE POLLO CON CHILE VERDE

Makes about 24 tamales

One 8-ounce package dried corn husks

FOR THE FILLING:

1 pound (10 to 12 medium) tomatillos, husked and rinsed

Fresh hot green chiles to taste (roughly 4 to 6 serranos or 2 to 3 jalapeños), stemmed and roughly chopped

4 large garlic cloves, peeled and roughly chopped

1¹/₂ tablespoons vegetable or olive oil

3 to 3¹/₂ cups chicken broth

Salt

4 cups (about 1 pound) coarsely shredded cooked chicken, preferably grilled, roasted or rotisserie chicken

²/₃ cup roughly chopped fresh cilantro

FOR THE BATTER:

10 ounces (1¹/₄ cups) rich-tasting pork lard (or vegetable shortening if you wish), slightly softened but not at all runny

1¹/₂ teaspoons baking powder

2 pounds (4 cups) fresh coarse-ground corn masa *for tamales OR 3¹/₂ cups dried* masa harina *for tamales mixed with 2¹/₄ cups hot water*

TRADITIONAL

I.   PREPARING THE CORN HUSKS. Cover the husks with very hot water, weight with a plate to keep them submerged and let stand for a couple of hours, until they are pliable.

For forming the tamales, separate out 24 of the largest and most pliable husks—ones that are at least 6 inches across on the wider end and 6 or 7 inches long. If you can't find enough good ones, overlap some of the larger ones to give wide, sturdy surfaces to spread the batter on. Pat the chosen husks dry with a towel.

2. PREPARING THE FILLING. On a baking sheet, roast the tomatillos about 4 inches below a very hot broiler until soft (they'll blacken in spots), about 5 minutes; flip them over and roast the other side. Cool, then transfer to a food processor or blender along with all the delicious juice that has run onto the baking sheet. Add the chiles and garlic and process to a smooth puree.

   Heat the oil in a medium saucepan over medium-high. When it is quite hot, add the puree all at once and stir until noticeably thicker and darker, about 5 minutes. Add *2 cups* of the broth and simmer over medium heat until thick enough to coat a spoon quite heavily, about 10 minutes. Taste and season generously with salt, usually about 2 teaspoons. Stir in the chicken and cilantro; cool completely.

3. PREPARING THE BATTER. With an electric mixer on medium-high speed, beat the lard (or shortening) with 2 teaspoons salt and the baking powder until light in texture, about 1 minute. Continue beating as you add the *masa* (fresh or reconstituted) in three additions. Reduce the speed to medium-low and add *1 cup* of the remaining broth. Continue beating for another minute or so, until a half-teaspoon dollop of the batter floats in a cup of cold water (if it floats, you can be sure the tamales will be tender and light).

   Beat in enough of the remaining *¹/₂ cup* broth to give the mixture the consistency of soft (not runny) cake batter; it should hold its shape in a spoon. Taste the batter and season with additional salt if you think it needs some.

   For the lightest-textured tamales, refrigerate the batter for an hour or so, then rebeat, adding a little more broth or water to bring the mixture to the soft consistency it had before.

4. SETTING UP THE STEAMER. Steaming 24 husk-wrapped tamales can be done in batches in a collapsible vegetable steamer set into a large deep saucepan. To steam them all at once, you need something like the kettle-sized tamal steamers used in Mexico or Asian stack steamers, or you can improvise by setting a wire rack on four coffee or custard cups in a large kettle. Pour an inch or so of water into the bottom of the steamer and heat to a boil.

   It is best to line the rack or upper part of the steamer with some of the leftover corn husks to protect the tamales from direct contact with the steam and to add more flavor. Make sure to leave tiny spaces between the husks so condensing steam can drain off.

5. FORMING THE TAMALES. Cut twenty-four 8- to 10-inch pieces of string or thin strips of corn husks. One at a time, form the tamales (as shown in the illustration

on page 73): Lay out one of your chosen corn husks with the tapering end toward you. Spread about ¼ cup of the batter into about a 4-inch square, leaving at least a 1½-inch border at the end toward you and a ¾-inch border along the other sides (with large husks, the borders will be much bigger). Spoon about 1½ tablespoons of the filling down the center of the batter. Pick up the two long sides of the corn husk and bring them together (this will cause the batter to surround the filling). If the uncovered borders of the two long sides you're holding are narrow, tuck one side under the other; if wide, roll both sides over in the same direction around the tamal. (If the husk is small, you may feel more comfortable wrapping the tamal in a second husk.) Finally, fold up the empty 1½-inch section of the husk (to form a tightly closed "bottom," leaving the top open), and secure it in place by loosely tying one of the strings or strips of husk around the tamal. As they're made, stand the tamales on their folded bottoms in the prepared steamer. Don't tie the tamales too tightly or pack them too closely in the steamer—they need room to expand.

6. STEAMING AND SERVING THE TAMALES. When all the tamales are in the steamer, cover them with a layer of more leftover corn husks; if your husk-wrapped tamales don't take up the entire steamer, fill in the open spaces with loosely wadded aluminum foil to keep the tamales from falling over. Set the lid in place and steam over a constant medium heat for about 1¼ hours. Watch carefully to make sure that all the water doesn't boil away and, to keep the steam steady, pour *boiling* water into the pot when more is necessary.

Tamales are done when the husks peel away from the *masa* easily. Let the tamales stand in the steamer off the heat for a few minutes to firm up. For the best-textured tamales, let them cool completely, then steam again for about 15 minutes to heat them through.

WORKING AHEAD: Both filling and batter can be made several days ahead, as can the finished tamales; refrigerate, well covered. Resteam (or even microwave) the tamales before serving. For even more flexibility, batter, filling and finished tamales can all be frozen. Defrost finished tamales in the refrigerator overnight before resteaming.

MANTECA DE CERDO • Fresh Pork Lard

Okay, okay. I know I've said it before, but no one seems to remember: Lard has less than half the cholesterol and about one-third less saturated fat than butter! You won't drop dead if you eat a little of it every once in a while. And using it won't raise any questions about your moral fiber. In fact, it's delicious, digestible and the perfect flavor component in many Mexican dishes. When buying pork lard, I suggest you look for fresh-rendered lard from a Mexican or other ethnic butcher, rather than the hydrogenated pale blond bricks they sell in most groceries. Or, go through the easy steps of making it yourself.

Makes 1 ¾ cups

2 pounds pork fat (scraps trimmed off roasts and chops
are good here, but don't use salt pork or fatty bacon—
those flavors are very strong)

Cut the pork fat into 1-inch cubes. Spread it out in a deep baking dish and set it in an oven turned on to 275°F. Stir it every once in a while as the fat renders into a clear liquid. When the baking dish contains only clear liquid and browned bits, after about 2 hours, carefully remove the dish from the oven. (Letting the cracklings, as the browned bits are called, color richly gives the lard a fuller, roastier flavor.)

Let the lard cool to lukewarm, then strain. (The little browned bits are wonderful sprinkled over a salad.) Store the lard in a tightly sealed jar in the refrigerator—or freezer, if you're not going to use it all within a month.

Red Chile Pork Tamales

TAMALES DE PUERCO CON CHILE ROJO

Makes about 18 tamales

FOR THE FILLING:

16 medium (about 4 ounces total) dried guajillo chiles, stemmed,
    seeded and each torn into several pieces
4 garlic cloves, peeled and chopped
$^1/_2$ teaspoon black pepper, preferably freshly ground
$^1/_4$ teaspoon cumin, preferably freshly ground
$1^1/_2$ pounds lean boneless pork (preferably from
    the shoulder), cut into $^1/_2$-inch cubes
Salt

FOR THE BATTER:

10 ounces ($1^1/_4$ cups) rich-tasting pork lard (or vegetable
    shortening if you wish), slightly softened but not
    at all runny
$1^1/_2$ teaspoons baking powder
2 pounds (4 cups) fresh coarse-ground corn masa for tamales
    OR $3^1/_2$ cups dried masa harina for tamales mixed with
    $2^1/_4$ cups hot water
1 to $1^1/_2$ cups chicken broth

Two 1-pound packages banana leaves, defrosted if frozen

TRADITIONAL

1. PREPARING THE FILLING. In a blender or food processor, working in batches if necessary, combine the chiles, garlic, pepper and cumin. Add 3 cups water, cover and blend to a smooth puree. Strain the mixture through a medium-mesh strainer into a medium (3-quart) saucepan.

    Add the meat, 3 cups water and 1 teaspoon salt. Simmer, uncovered, over medium heat, stirring regularly, until the pork is fork-tender and the liquid is reduced to the consistency of a thick sauce, about 1 hour.

Use a fork to break the pork into small pieces. Taste and season with additional salt if necessary. Let cool to room temperature.

2. PREPARING THE BATTER. With an electric mixer on medium-high speed, beat the lard (or shortening) with 2 teaspoons salt and the baking powder until light in texture, about 1 minute. Continue beating as you add the *masa* (fresh or reconstituted) in three additions. Reduce the speed to medium-low and add *1 cup* of the broth. Continue beating for another minute or so, until a half-teaspoon dollop of the batter floats in a cup of cold water (if it floats, you can be sure the tamales will be tender and light).

Beat in enough additional broth to give the mixture the consistency of soft (not runny) cake batter; it should hold its shape in a spoon. Taste the batter and season with additional salt if you think necessary.

For the lightest-textured tamales, refrigerate the batter for an hour or so, then rebeat, adding enough additional broth or water to bring the mixture to the soft consistency it had before.

3. PREPARING THE BANANA LEAVES. Unfold the banana leaves and cut off the long hard sides of the leaves (where they were attached to the central vein). Check for holes or rips, then cut the leaves into unbroken 12-inch segments (you will need 18). Either steam the segments for 20 minutes to make them soft and pliable, or, one at a time, pass them briefly over an open flame or hot electric burner until soft and glossy.

4. SETTING UP THE STEAMER. Steaming 18 leaf-wrapped tamales can be done in batches in a collapsible vegetable steamer set into a large deep saucepan (if you stack the tamales more than two high, they will steam unevenly). To steam them all at once, you'll need something like the kettle-sized tamal steamers used in Mexico or Asian stack steamers, or you can improvise by setting a wire rack on four coffee or custard cups in a large kettle. Pour an inch or so of water into the bottom of the steamer and heat to a boil.

It is best to line the rack or upper part of the steamer with leftover scraps of banana leaves to protect the tamales from direct contact with the steam and to add more flavor. Make sure to leave tiny spaces between the leaves so condensing steam can drain off.

5. FORMING THE TAMALES. Cut eighteen 12-inch pieces of string or thin strips of banana leaves. One at a time, form the tamales: Lay out a square of banana leaf, shiny side up, and spread $^1/_3$ cup of the batter into an 8 x 4-inch rectangle over it

(as shown in the illustration below). Spoon 2 tablespoons of the filling over the left side of the rectangle of batter, then fold over the right third of the leaf so that the batter encloses the filling. Fold over the uncovered third of the leaf, then fold over the top and bottom. Loosely tie the tamales with string and set them in the steamer.

6. STEAMING AND SERVING THE TAMALES. When all the tamales are in the steamer, cover them with a layer of banana leaf scraps or leftover leaves. Set the lid in place and steam over a constant medium heat for about 1 1/4 hours. Watch carefully to make sure that all the water doesn't boil away and, to keep the steam steady, pour *boiling* water into the pot when more is necessary.

Tamales are done when the leaves peel away from the *masa* easily. Let the tamales stand in the steamer off the heat for a few minutes to firm up. For the best-textured tamales, let them cool completely, then steam them again for about 15 minutes to heat them through.

WORKING AHEAD: See Green Chile Chicken Tamales, page 74.

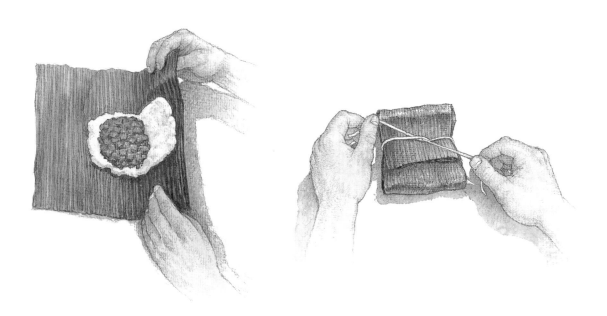

RED CHILE PORK TAMALES IN BANANA LEAVES (PAGE 78)

Sweet Tamales with pineapple and raisins

TAMALES DE DULCE CON PIÑA Y PASAS

Makes 24 tamales

One 8-ounce package dried corn husks

1 ripe medium pineapple, peeled, cored and cut into
rough cubes

10 ounces (1¼ cups) unsalted butter, rich-tasting pork lard
or vegetable shortening (or a combination), slightly
softened but not at all runny

1⅓ cups sugar

1½ teaspoons baking powder

Salt

2 pounds (about 4 cups) fresh coarse-ground corn masa
for tamales
OR 3½ cups dried masa harina for tamales mixed with
2¼ cups hot water

⅔ cup raisins

TRADITIONAL

1. PREPARING THE CORN HUSKS. Cover the husks with very hot water, weight with a plate to keep them submerged and let stand for a couple of hours, until they are pliable.

    For forming the tamales, separate out 24 of the largest and most pliable husks—ones that are at least 6 inches across on the wider end and 6 or 7 inches long. If you can't find enough good ones, overlap some of the larger ones to give wide, sturdy surfaces to spread the batter on. Pat the chosen husks dry with a towel.

2. PREPARING THE BATTER. In a food processor or blender, coarsely puree the pineapple. Measure out 2 cups puree (reserving the rest for another use). With an electric mixer on medium-high speed, beat the butter, lard and/or shortening with the sugar, baking powder and 1 teaspoon salt until light and fluffy in texture, about 3 minutes. Continue beating as you add the *masa* (fresh or reconstituted) in three additions. Reduce the speed to medium-low, then add the 2 cups pineapple puree. Continue beating for another minute or so, until a half-teaspoon dol-

lop of the batter floats in a cup of cold water (if it floats, you can be sure the tamales will be tender and light).

Beat in a little additional water if needed to give the mixture the consistency of soft (not runny) cake batter; it should hold its shape in a spoon.

For the lightest-textured tamales, refrigerate the batter for an hour or so, then reheat, adding enough additional water to bring the mixture to the soft consistency it had before.

3. SETTING UP THE STEAMER. Steaming 24 husk-wrapped tamales can be done in batches in a collapsible vegetable steamer set into a large deep saucepan. To steam them all at once, you need something like the kettle-sized tamal steamers used in Mexico or Asian stack steamers, or you can improvise by setting a wire rack on four coffee or custard cups in a large kettle. Pour an inch or so of water into the bottom of the steamer and heat to a boil.

It is best to line the rack or upper part of the steamer with some of the leftover corn husks to protect the tamales from direct contact with the steam and to add more flavor. Make sure to leave tiny spaces between the husks so condensing steam can drain off.

4. FORMING THE TAMALES. Cut twenty-four 8- to 10-inch pieces of string or thin strips of corn husks. One at a time, form the tamales: Lay out one of your chosen corn husks with the tapering end toward you. Spread about $1/4$ cup of the batter into a 4-inch square, leaving at least a $1\frac{1}{2}$-inch border at the end toward you and a $3/4$-inch border along the other sides (with large husks, the borders will be much bigger). Sprinkle a few raisins down the center of the batter. Pick up the two long sides of the corn husk and bring them together (this will cause the batter to surround the raisins). If the uncovered borders of the two long sides you're holding are narrow, tuck one side under the other; if wide, then roll both sides over in the same direction around the tamal. (If the husk is small, you may feel more comfortable wrapping the tamal in a second husk.) Finally, fold up the empty $1\frac{1}{2}$-inch section of the husk (to form a tightly closed "bottom," leaving the top open), and secure it in place by loosely tying one of the strings or strips of husk around the tamal (as shown in the illustration on page 73). As they're made, stand the tamales on their folded bottoms in the prepared steamer. Don't tie the tamales too tightly or pack them too closely in the steamer—they need room to expand.

5. STEAMING AND SERVING THE TAMALES. When all the tamales are in the steamer, cover them with a layer of more leftover corn husks; if your husk-

wrapped tamales don't take up the entire steamer, fill in the open spaces with loosely wadded aluminum foil to keep the tamales from falling down. Set the lid in place and steam over a constant medium heat for about 1 1/4 hours. Watch carefully to make sure that all the water doesn't boil away and, to keep the steam steady, pour *boiling* water into the pot when more is necessary.

Tamales are done when the husks peel away from the *masa* easily. Let the tamales stand in the steamer off the heat for a few minutes to firm up. For the best-textured tamales, let them cool completely, then steam again for about 15 minutes to heat them through.

WORKING AHEAD: The batter can be made several days ahead, as can the finished tamales; refrigerate, well covered. Resteam (or even microwave) the tamales before serving. For even more flexibility, batter, filling and finished tamales can all be frozen. Defrost finished tamales in the refrigerator overnight before resteaming.

Almuerzo
(mid-morning breakfast)

Casserole-Style Zucchini Tamal

TAMAL DE CALABACITAS EN CAZUELA

Serves 8 as a first course,
6 as a light main course

4 ounces (*1/2 cup*) unsalted butter, at room temperature
Salt
3/4 teaspoon baking powder
1 pound (*2 cups*) fresh coarse-ground corn masa *for tortillas*
     OR 1 3/4 cups dried masa harina *for tortillas mixed with*
     1 cup plus 2 tablespoons hot water
1/4 cup chicken broth
2 small (about 7 ounces total) zucchini, ends trimmed and
     coarsely shredded on the large holes of a grater
1/2 cup finely chopped ham
1/2 cup watercress leaves, roughly chopped, plus a
     few whole sprigs for garnish
1/2 cup finely sliced green onion, green part only
About 1*1/2 cups salsa (I prefer the Roasted Tomato–*
     Green Chile Salsa on page 100)

CONTEMPORARY

1. **PREPARING THE BATTER.** With an electric mixer on medium-high speed, beat the butter with 1 teaspoon salt and the baking powder until light in texture, about 1 minute. Continue beating as you add the *masa* (fresh or reconstituted) in three additions. Reduce the speed to medium-low, add the chicken broth, zucchini, ham, watercress and green onions and beat just long enough to mix the ingredients thoroughly.

2. **SETTING UP THE STEAMER.** Set up a steamer large enough to accommodate a 9-inch round cake pan or casserole dish, such as an Asian stack steamer, a Mexican tamal steamer or an improvised setup created by setting a wire rack on four coffee or custard cups in a large kettle. Pour an inch or so of water into the bottom of the steamer and heat to a boil.

3. **STEAMING THE TAMAL.** Scrape the batter into a 9-inch round cake pan or casserole dish. Cover the top lightly with parchment paper or buttered foil (this pre-

vents condensation from dripping onto the batter.) Place the tamal on the rack, cover the steamer tightly and steam over a constant medium heat for 1 1/2 hours. Watch carefully to make sure that all the water doesn't boil away and, to keep the steam steady, pour *boiling* water into the pot when more is necessary.

Let the tamal stand uncovered for 15 minutes after turning off the heat so it finishes firming up.

4. SERVING THE TAMAL. Cut the tamal into wedges and place on warm serving plates. Spoon about 3 tablespoons of salsa over and around each serving, garnish with watercress sprigs and serve.

WORKING AHEAD: The tamal batter (without the vegetables and ham) can be beaten up to 3 days ahead and refrigerated, tightly covered. Once the vegetables and ham have been added to the batter, you'll need to steam the tamal within hours. The finished tamal, however, can be made a day or two ahead, since it reheats beautifully in the steamer or microwave oven.

Corn nixtamal *(half-cooked hominy)*

QUESTIONS AND ANSWERS FROM OUR TESTING

Tamal batter could be called the "pie dough" of Mexican cuisine since it raises the same questions: Which kind of starch (flour for pie dough, *masa* for tamales) is best, which kind of fat is best and what's the best way to incorporate the ingredients? Answering these questions involved dozens and dozens of tests—most definitely the most involved testing we did for this book. Here are the results.

WHICH KIND OF CORN *MASA* IS BEST—FRESH OR DRIED, SMOOTH-GROUND OR COARSE-GROUND? Corn *masa* that is fresh and coarsely ground (the rough-looking paste—almost crumbly, but capable of being pressed together—called *masa quebrada* in some parts of Mexico and in California) makes tamales that have the fullest corn flavor and the moistest, most interesting texture. Dehydrated *masa* for tamales is my second choice (the only brand I've seen in the States is Maseca, and it's called *"masa instantánea de maiz para hacer tamales,"* or "instant corn masa mix for tamales"). It produces a beautiful light texture, though it lacks some of the earthy sweetness and toothsome textural irregularities of fresh coarse-ground *masa*. Tying for second place with the dehydrated *masa* for tamales is fresh *smooth*-ground *masa* for tortillas. It offers a lovely freshness of taste, but a denser, more uniform texture than fresh coarse-ground *masa*. My last choice when making tamales is dehydrated *masa* for tortillas (*masa harina* for tortillas). Tamales made from *masa harina*, eaten side by side with those made from fresh coarse-ground *masa*, are a little less flavorful, texturally uniform and a little denser, but still plenty acceptable, especially if the other ingredients are good.

IS LARD THE BEST FAT FOR TAMALES AND ARE THERE GOOD SUBSTITUTES? Lard is as central to tamales as butter is to puff pastry—replace the fat with something else, and the tamales or pastry isn't quite as appealing. That said, I will tell you that all these recipes will work with lard, vegetable shortening or butter. Here are my observations: Fresh, roasty pork lard (not the widely distributed grocery store brands of lard) offers the most complete and traditional flavor. Vegetable shortening (we used Crisco) produces the lightest texture, but to me not as satisfying a flavor; besides, nutritionists now confide that it's no better for us than lard. Butter's flavor overpowers the earthiness of the corn for some cooks, though I sometimes find it attractive.

WHAT IS THE BEST PROPORTION OF *MASA* TO FAT? Classic recipes for tamales in Mexico use *masa*-to-fat ratios that range from 4 : 1 to 2 : 1. To me, the leanest tamales seem dense and heavy, the richest seem greasy. I settled on 5 ounces of fat per pound of *masa*—closer to the lean end of the continuum, but enough fat to produce tender, flavorful tamales.

WHAT IS THE BEST WAY TO COMBINE THE INGREDIENTS? Rather than a pastry-making analogy here, I'll employ a cake-making one: For maximum lightness and tenderness, beat the fat well to incorporate air. Warm, runny fat won't incorporate air. Also, we found that batters made from hydrogenated vegetable shortening (Crisco) or hydrogenated lard (Armour) were lighter than those made with homemade lard. Flavor in both was lacking, however. For maximum moistness, the batter needs to be soft yet still able to hold its shape in a spoon. Though I've never seen cooks in Mexico do this, I discovered that *masa* absorbs liquid and thickens if allowed to stand for a couple of hours. So, for the moistest tamales, I recommend refrigerating the batter long enough for it to thicken, then beating in a little extra broth.

REFINEMENTS: *Leavening:* Cooks today usually rely on commercial baking powder to puff tamales to lightness. The old-fashioned way is to use *tequesquite*, the naturally occurring form of sodium bicarbonate (sold in many Mexican markets). Because tamales don't contain strongly acidic ingredients, *tequesquite*'s leavening is gentle, producing a lovely but less fluffy texture. To use *tequesquite* in these recipes, dissolve 1 teaspoon *tequesquite* (as best you can) in 1 cup boiling water with 6 tomatillo husks (for acidity), then use the water (but none of the undissolved grit or husks) as part of the liquid in the recipe.

Dried corn husks for tamales

Taquería Tacos with Grilled and Griddled Fillings

(Tacos al Carbón y Tacos a la Plancha)

Tacos al carbón, like the best hamburgers, entice all the senses: aromatic charcoal-seared meat, tongue-tingling poblano chiles and velvety soft corn tortillas, all served up with casual aplomb. And also like those hamburgers, *tacos al carbón* have long been considered a convenience food. So convenient, in fact, that most armchair historians put their origins with the roaming, utensil-free northern Mexican cowboy.

The spirit of that pull-up-and-eat culture lives on today in the *taquerías* of Mexico. Midmorning when hunger strikes or late at night when all restaurants and *cafeterías* close, you can find a neighborhood *taquería*—be it a makeshift stand in a doorway or a hundred-seater. Plainness is *de rigueur*, illuminated by unblinking naked bulbs. Perfectly woven into the fabric of Mexican life, these are the spots where the hungry from all groups—brick-layers, brash teenagers, bankers and politicians—gather for bitefuls of seared meat wrapped in soft tortillas sparked with hot chile.

Now, since not all *taquerías* have charcoal grills, the meat for the tacos may instead be seared on a *plancha*, a piece of rolled steel we'd call a griddle. My favorites are the griddles with a dome rising in the middle, under which a fire blares. That's the perfectly hot surface for searing a delicious sweet browned crust on chile-marinated pork or salty beef. The flat edges surrounding the dome are the perfect spot for browning onions and fresh green chiles to perk up the meat. Or for tender potatoes to crust to golden with bits of tangy chorizo sausage—a classic taco filling made even better with avocado salsa.

For grilled beef tacos, it's skirt steak that's popular—and certainly my choice. A simple squeeze of lime, gussied up with garlic and spices if you like, makes a bright-tasting marinade for that very beefy tasting cut of meat, which is enlivened with grilled poblano chile *rajas* (strips). My contemporary *tacos al carbón* recipe relies on the same simple, direct quality of the skirt steak taco except that it uses the fleshy, earthy juiciness of portobello mushrooms in place of the meat. And the ingredients for a salsa can be grilled right along with the mushrooms, creating a smoky, spicy echo.

My contemporary approach to griddling a taco filling is a twist on the thin-sliced pork *carne enchilada* sold all over Mexico. It's thin-pounded butterflied pork tenderloin slathered with spicy chipotle chile, seared and served with sun-dried tomato salsa dressed up with sunny Mediterranean olives.

With all these taco fillings to choose from, you can set yourself up for a casual, put-them-at-ease taco party, a *taquisa* in Mexican Spanish. Let your guests put together their own tacos as they like, maybe sitting down near the fire to lose themselves in the aromas that float from the grill.

TRADITIONAL BENCHMARK: When I think of great tacos with fillings off the griddle or grill, my mind wanders to a little hole-in-the-wall somewhere in northern Mexico (I can't even remember what city, it's been so long ago) where there was a glowing bed of hot coals over which perched a thick iron grate or griddle searing a smoky char into the edges of thin-sliced meat. The well-done meat (that may surprise you) was chopped into small pieces and rolled into a pair of hot thin corn tortillas. A tangy salsa shot through with the earthy fire of roasted chile completed my perfect taco. Well-seared crusty meat is essential, as are fresh corn tortillas.

WHEN TO THINK OF THESE RECIPES: Say some friends call up and ask if you want to do something fun for dinner. You know where to get good tortillas and the simple filling ingredients, and, if everyone pitches in making salsa and a salad (maybe a skillet of fried beans too), it won't take long at all to put together a treat the likes of which you probably can't get anywhere else.

ADVICE FOR AMERICAN COOKS: Filling and salsa ingredients are easy to come by (if chorizo is hard to find, choose another spicy sausage). So basically it's just the fresh corn tortillas that may stump you. Flour tortillas, since they stay fresh longer than corn, are an obvious substitute, but use them only after considering all your resources. Corn tortillas are the heart of the Mexican kitchen, so do your best to find them, or try making them when you can carve out the time.

GRILLED SKIRT STEAK TACO WITH ROASTED POBLANO *RAJAS*
(PAGE 92)

Grilled Skirt Steak Tacos with Roasted Poblano *Rajas*

TACOS DE ARRACHERA AL CARBÓN CON RAJAS

TRADITIONAL

Makes 12 tacos, serving 4 as a light meal

2 medium white onions, sliced into ¹/₂-inch rounds (keep the rounds
    intact for easy grilling)
3 garlic cloves, peeled and roughly chopped
3 tablespoons fresh lime juice
¹/₄ teaspoon cumin, preferably freshly ground
Salt
1 pound beef skirt steak, trimmed of surface fat as well as the
    thin white membrane called "silverskin"
3 medium (about 9 ounces total) fresh poblano chiles
Vegetable or olive oil for brushing or spritzing the onions
    and meat
A small bowlful of lime wedges for serving
12 warm, fresh corn tortillas (see page 115 to reheat store-bought
    ones or page 104 to make them from scratch)

1. **MARINATING THE MEAT.** In a food processor or blender, combine *one-quarter* of the onions, the garlic, lime juice, cumin and ¹/₂ teaspoon salt. Process to a smooth puree. Place the skirt steak in a nonaluminum baking dish. Using a spoon, smear the marinade over both sides of the skirt steak. Cover and refrigerate for at least 1 hour or up to 8 hours.

2. **MAKING THE GRILLED CHILE-AND-ONION *RAJAS*.** Turn on the oven to its lowest setting. Heat a gas grill to medium-high or light a charcoal fire and let it burn just until the coals are covered with gray ash and very hot. Either turn the burner(s) in the center of the grill to medium-low or bank the coals to the sides of the grill for indirect cooking. Set the cooking grate in place, cover the grill and let the grate heat up, 5 minutes or so.

    Lay the chiles on the hottest part of the grill, and cook, turning occasionally, until the skin is blistered and uniformly blackened all over, about 5 minutes. Be careful not to char the flesh, only the skin. Remove the chiles from the grill and cover with a kitchen towel.

While the chiles are roasting, brush or spray the remaining onion slices with oil and lay the whole rounds of onions on the grill in a cooler spot than you chose for the chiles. When they're starting to soften and are browned on the first side, about 10 minutes, use a spatula to flip them and brown the other side. Transfer to an ovenproof serving dish and separate the rings (if they haven't started separating during grilling).

Rub the blackened skin off the chiles, then pull out the stems and seed pods. Rinse briefly to remove any stray seeds and bits of skin. Slice into $1/4$-inch strips and stir into the onions. Taste the mixture and season it with salt, usually about $1/4$ teaspoon. Keep warm in the oven.

3. GRILLING THE MEAT. Remove the steak from the marinade and gently shake off the excess. Oil the steak well on both sides and lay it over the hottest part of the grill. Grill, turning once, until richly browned and done to your liking, about $1 1/2$ to 2 minutes per side for medium-rare (the way I like skirt steak).

4. SERVING THE TACOS. Cut the long piece of skirt steak into 3- to 4-inch lengths, then cut each section *across the grain* (that is, in line with the full length of the steak) into thin strips. Mix with the chiles and onions, season with a little salt and set on the table along with the lime wedges and hot tortillas, for your guests to make into soft tacos.

WORKING AHEAD: Thin steaks like skirt taste best with a relatively short tour in the marinade—1 to 8 hours. Leave them longer, and the marinade overpowers the flavor and saps the rosy color of the meat. The poblano-and-onion *rajas* can be made several hours ahead and left at room temperature; rewarm before serving. The steak, of course, must be grilled just before you're ready to eat.

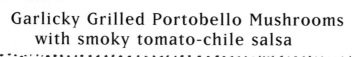

Garlicky Grilled Portobello Mushrooms
with smoky tomato-chile salsa

HONGOS ASADOS AL AJO CON SALSA POBLANA

Makes 12 tacos, serving 4 as a light meal

CONTEMPORARY

1 medium white onion, sliced into $^1/_2$-inch rounds (keep the rounds
    intact for easy grilling)
3 garlic cloves, peeled and roughly chopped
$^1/_4$ cup fresh lime juice
$^1/_4$ teaspoon cumin, preferably freshly ground
Salt
Six 4- to 5-inch (about $1^3/_4$ pounds total) portobello mushrooms,
    stems removed and caps wiped clean (you can use a spoon to
    scrape out the dark gills on the underside of the caps, though
    it's not really necessary)
A little vegetable or olive oil for the onion
12 ounces (2 medium-small round or 4 to 6 plum) ripe tomatoes
3 medium (about 9 ounces total) fresh poblano chiles
3 tablespoons chopped fresh cilantro
12 warm, fresh corn tortillas (see page 115 to reheat store-bought
    ones or page 104 to make them from scratch)

1.   MARINATING THE MUSHROOMS. In a food processor or blender, combine $^1/_3$ of
the onion, the garlic, *3 tablespoons* of the lime juice, the cumin and $^1/_2$ teaspoon
salt. Process to a smooth puree. Lay out the mushroom caps in a nonaluminum
baking dish. Using a spoon, smear the marinade over both sides of each mushroom cap. Cover and let stand for 1 hour.

2.   PREPARING THE SALSA. Heat a gas grill to medium-high or light a charcoal fire
and let it burn just until the coals are covered with gray ash and very hot. Either
turn the burner(s) in the center of the grill to medium-low or bank the coals to
the sides of the grill for indirect cooking. Set the cooking grate in place, cover the
grill and let the grate heat up, 5 minutes or so.

    Brush or spray the remaining onion slices with oil and lay in a single layer in the center (the least hot part) of the grill, along with the tomatoes. Set the chiles over the hottest part. Roast, turning everything occasionally, until the chiles' skin (but not the flesh) is blistered and uniformly blackened all over, about 5 minutes, and the onion and tomatoes are softened and browned in spots, 10 to 15 minutes, depending on their size and the heat. When the chiles are done, remove them and cover with a kitchen towel. Set the tomatoes aside on a plate. Finely chop the onion and scoop it into a bowl.

When the tomatoes are cool enough to handle, pull off their skins. Use a mortar to crush them, or place them in a food processor or blender and pulse until coarsely pureed. Add to the chopped onion.

Rub the blackened skin off the chiles, then pull out the stems and seed pods. Rinse briefly to remove any stray seeds and bits of skin. Chop into small bits and stir half into the tomato-onion mixture along with the remaining 1 *tablespoon* lime juice and the cilantro. Taste, season with salt, usually about ³/₄ teaspoon, and then scoop into a serving bowl.

3. GRILLING THE MUSHROOMS. Remove the mushrooms from the marinade, spray or brush them with oil and lay gill side up over the hot part of the grill. Cook until browned in spots, about 5 minutes, then flip and move to the center of the grill—the cooler part—and continue grilling until they feel a *little* limp but still have some body, about 10 minutes more.

4. SERVING THE TACOS. Cut the mushrooms into ¹/₄-inch strips. Scoop into a warm serving dish and mix with the remaining chopped poblanos. Season with salt, usually about ¹/₄ teaspoon. Set the mushrooms on the table along with the salsa and hot tortillas—everything you need for making wonderful soft tacos.

WORKING AHEAD: The mushroom caps can remain in their marinade for as long as 24 hours, covered in the refrigerator. The salsa will keep nicely (covered and refrigerated) for a day or so. The mushrooms are best cooked shortly before serving.

Potato-Chorizo Tacos with Simple Avocado Salsa

TACOS DE PAPAS CON CHORIZO Y SALSA DE AGUACATE

Makes 12 tacos, serving 4 as a light meal

3 (about 12 ounces total) medium red-skin or smallish
    Yukon Gold potatoes, peeled and cut into ½-inch cubes
    (about 2 cups)

Salt

12 ounces (about 1½ cups) Mexican chorizo sausage, store-bought
    (casing removed if there is one) or homemade (page 26)

1 small white onion, finely chopped

4 ounces (2 to 3 medium) tomatillos, husked, rinsed
    and roughly chopped

1 garlic clove, peeled

Fresh hot green chiles to taste (roughly 2 serranos or
    1 jalapeño), stemmed

1 large ripe avocado

12 warm, fresh corn tortillas (see page 115 to reheat store-bought
    ones or page 104 to make them from scratch)

TRADITIONAL

I. THE FILLING. In a medium (3- to 4-quart) saucepan, bring about 1 quart water to a boil. Add the cubed potatoes and heavily salt the water (about 2 teaspoons). Simmer until the potatoes are fully tender, about 10 minutes. Drain.

In a large (12-inch) heavy well-seasoned or nonstick skillet or griddle set over medium heat, combine the chorizo and onion; stir regularly, breaking up any clumps of sausage, until the onion is soft and the sausage cooked through, about 10 minutes. If the sausage has rendered more than a light coating of fat over the bottom of the skillet, pour out the excess.

Add the potatoes to the skillet and continue to cook over medium heat, stirring regularly, until the potatoes begin to brown, about 8 minutes. As the mixture cooks, mash everything together a little with the back of a spoon or a spatula, scraping up any crusty bits of potato, so that it roughly holds together (it'll look a little like hash). Cover and keep warm over the lowest heat.

2. **THE SALSA.** As the filling finishes cooking, make the salsa: In a food processor, combine the tomatillos, garlic and chiles. Pulse the machine until everything is finely chopped. Peel and pit the avocado, add the flesh to the processor and pulse until everything is well blended (the salsa will be the consistency of a light mayonnaise). Scrape the salsa into a serving bowl, taste and season with salt, usually about ¹/₂ teaspoon.

3. **SERVING.** Scrape the warm chorizo filling into a serving bowl and set on the table along with the avocado salsa and a basket of steaming tortillas. Supper is ready.

WORKING AHEAD: The chorizo-potato filling can be made a day or two ahead; cover and refrigerate. Reheat it in the microwave, in the oven covered with foil or in a skillet over medium to medium-low heat, adding a few drops of water if the mixture seems dry. The simple avocado salsa tastes fresh for only an hour or so after it's made.

Ancho chiles (foreground) and árbol chiles ready for sale

Seared Steak Tacos with Blistered Serranos and Browned Onions

TACOS DE BISTEC CON CHILES TORREADOS

TRADITIONAL

Makes 12 tacos, serving 4 as a light meal

12 to 24 fresh serrano chiles (depending on your penchant for
   hot food), stemmed
About 2 tablespoons rich-tasting pork lard, vegetable oil or bacon drippings
1 medium white onion, sliced ¼ inch thick
Salt
1½ tablespoons fresh lime juice
1 pound thin-cut beef (look for cecina, tasajo or butterflied
   skirt steak in a Mexican market or thin-cut round tip
   [⅛ to ¼ inch thick], also known as minute steak,
   sandwich steak or breakfast steak, in an American market)
About 1 cup salsa (such as the Roasted Tomato–Green Chile
   Salsa on page 100) or a bowlful of lime wedges for serving
   (optional)
12 warm, fresh corn tortillas (see page 115 to reheat store-bought
   ones or page 104 to make them from scratch)

1. THE CHILES. With a small sharp knife, cut straight down through each chile, starting just below the stem and continuing to the point, so that each chile is cut in half except for the spot at the stem end that holds it together. Rotate each chile a quarter turn and make a similar cut, giving you chiles cut into 4 long pieces held together at the stem end.

Measure *1 tablespoon* of the lard, oil or bacon drippings into a large (12-inch) heavy well-seasoned skillet (preferably cast-iron) or griddle and set over medium-high heat. When hot, add the chiles and onion slices (the chiles will begin to release their cough-provoking capsaicin, so your exhaust fan needs to be on) and stir almost continuously until the onion slices are richly golden, about 6 minutes. Sprinkle with salt, about ¼ teaspoon, and drizzle with the lime juice. Cook, tossing to thoroughly combine and to evaporate the liquid, then scoop into a serving bowl.

2. SEARING THE MEAT. Generously salt both sides of each piece of meat. Wipe out the skillet or griddle and return it to medium-high heat. Add the remaining *1 tablespoon* lard, oil or bacon drippings. When very hot (it'll just begin to smoke), lay in the meat in a single layer; if it doesn't all fit comfortably, you'll need to do this in two batches. Sear the meat on one side until browned, about 1½ minutes, flip it over and sear the other side. Meat for tacos *a la plancha* is generally cooked well-done. Transfer to your cutting board; tent with foil if you are searing the meat in batches.

3. SERVING. Chop the seared steak into ½-inch bits (most Mexican *taqueros* do this with a cleaver) and scoop into a serving bowl—a warm one makes a big difference in keeping the filling warm. Set on the table along with the chile mixture, salsa or lime wedges and warm tortillas, and your meal is ready.

WORKING AHEAD: This is last-minute fare. I have, however, made the seared chiles and onions a few hours ahead and found them quite agreeable, though they'll lose a little color and texture as they sit.

Early-morning marketing

SALSA DE MOLCAJETE

● ROASTED TOMATO–GREEN CHILE SALSA

You'll taste essence of Mexico in a bite of this salsa, though you may get more than you expect. Roasting focuses the tomatoes' sweetness and rounds out the typical green grassiness of fresh chiles, creating perfect harmony.

Makes about 2 cups

1 pound (2 medium-large round or 6 to 8 plum) ripe tomatoes
Fresh hot green chiles to taste (roughly 2 medium jalapeños or
    4 serranos)
3 garlic cloves, unpeeled
¼ cup finely chopped white onion
About ⅓ cup loosely packed chopped fresh cilantro
Salt
A dash of vinegar or squeeze of lime, if you think necessary

1. ROASTING. Roast the tomatoes on a baking sheet 4 inches below a very hot broiler until they're darkly roasted (they'll be blackened in spots), about 6 minutes. Flip them over and roast the other side—5 to 6 minutes more will give you splotchy-black and blistered tomatoes that are soft and cooked through. Cool. Working over the baking sheet, pull off and discard the blackened skins; for round tomatoes, cut out the hard cores where the stems were attached.

   Roast the chiles and garlic in a dry skillet or on a griddle over medium heat, turning them occasionally, until they are soft and darkened in places, about 5 minutes for the chiles, 15 minutes for the garlic. Cool, then slip the papery skins off the garlic.

2. FINISHING THE SALSA. Either crush the roasted garlic and chiles to a smooth paste in a mortar or chop them to near-paste in a food processor. If using a mortar, crush in the tomatoes one at a time, working them into a coarse puree. For a food processor, add the tomatoes and pulse to achieve a coarse puree.

   Scoop the chopped onion into a strainer and rinse under cold water. Shake to remove the excess moisture.

Transfer the salsa to a bowl, stir in the onion and cilantro and season with salt, usually a generous ½ teaspoon. Thin with a little water (usually about 2 tablespoons) to give it a spoonable consistency. Perk it all up with vinegar or lime if you wish.

WORKING AHEAD: Once the onion and cilantro have been added to the salsa, it should be eaten within a few hours. Without onion and cilantro, the refrigerated salsa base keeps for several days, though the flavors will dull.

Oaxacan clay mortar (chirmolera)

Spicy Chipotle Pork Tacos with Sun-Dried Tomato Salsa

TACOS DE PUERCO ENCHIPOTLADO CON SALSA DE JITOMATE PASADO

Makes 12 tacos, serving 4 as a light meal

2 (about 1 pound total) pork tenderloins

One 7-ounce can chipotle chiles en adobo

1 cup fresh orange juice, plus a little more if needed

1 cup (about 2 ounces) sun-dried tomatoes, halved

1 small red onion, finely chopped (generous ¹/₂ cup)

¹/₂ cup chopped pitted Kalamata olives

¹/₄ cup chopped fresh cilantro

About 1 tablespoon fresh lime juice

Salt

1 tablespoon vegetable oil, rich-tasting pork lard or bacon drippings

12 warm, fresh corn tortillas (see page 115 to reheat store-bought ones or page 104 to make them from scratch)

I. **BUTTERFLYING AND MARINATING THE PORK.** Lay 1 tenderloin on your cutting board and cut it in half. With a sharp knife, make a horizontal cut through one half (you'll be cutting parallel with the board) from one long side to within ¹/₄ inch of the other. This will allow you to fold open the meat like a book, using that ¹/₄-inch uncut side as a hinge. With a meat pounder or heavy mallet, pound the pork to between ¹/₄ and ¹/₈ inch thickness.

In a food processor or blender, thoroughly puree the chipotles with all their canning sauce. With a pastry or basting brush, liberally paint the butterflied meat on both sides with the pureed chipotles. Cover and refrigerate for at least an hour, or up to 24 hours. Repeat with the other tenderloin pieces. (There will be considerably more chipotle puree than you need; cover and refrigerate the leftover for up to 2 weeks and use it to marinate other meat, fish, poultry or vegetables.)

2. SOAKING THE SUN-DRIED TOMATOES. In a small saucepan, bring the orange juice just to a boil. Add the sun-dried tomatoes, stir well, cover and remove from the heat. Let stand, stirring once or twice, until softened, about 20 minutes.

3. PREPARING THE SALSA. Scrape the soaked tomatoes and the juice into a food processor or blender and measure in 1 tablespoon of the chipotle puree. Pulse the processor until the tomatoes are rather finely chopped (but not pureed). Scrape into a small serving bowl.

    Rinse the chopped onion under cold water, shake off the excess liquid and add it to the salsa along with the olives, cilantro and lime juice. Stir everything together, then taste and season with salt, usually about 1/4 teaspoon. Adjust the consistency to that of an easily spoonable salsa with additional orange juice or water if needed. Set aside at room temperature while you cook the meat.

4. SEARING THE MEAT. Set a large (12-inch) heavy well-seasoned or nonstick skillet or griddle over medium-high heat. Add the oil, lard or bacon drippings, brushing or spreading them around to evenly coat the surface (if using a nonstick surface, oil the meat instead of the pan). When the oil is very hot (it should just begin to smoke), lay one of the marinated meat pieces out flat in the pan. Sear on one side until beginning to brown, 2 to 3 minutes, flip it over and sear the other side, about 1 1/2 minutes. Transfer to a baking sheet and keep warm in a low oven. Sear the remaining meat and add to the baking sheet.

5. SERVING. Chop or slice the meat into smallish pieces and scoop into a warm serving bowl. Set on the table along with the salsa and warm tortillas, and your meal is ready.

WORKING AHEAD: The chile-coated meat (from Step 1) can be allowed to marinate for up to 24 hours. Longer than that, and the chipotles will overpower the pork flavor. The salsa is best made the day you are serving it.

TORTILLAS DE MAÍZ • CORN TORTILLAS

Mexican food without corn tortillas is like Chinese food without rice. Out of whack. Missing the very canvas on which to paint all those wonderful flavors. Now, the centrality of corn tortillas in Mexico may come as a surprise to you, since many of us north of the border don't choose corn tortillas with our Mexican food. The reason: We may never have eaten a good fresh one—a just-made one. Corn tortillas, you see, are at their peak for only a few hours after they're made. So, no matter what your circumstances, I encourage you to experience the aromatic moist tenderness of fresh homemade tortillas at least once.

Makes 15 tortillas

> *1 pound fresh-ground corn* masa *for tortillas*
> *OR 1 ³/₄ cups powdered* masa harina *for tortillas (such as Maseca brand) mixed with 1 cup plus 2 tablespoons hot tap water*

Heat a heavy rectangular griddle or (two skillets) to two different temperatures: one side (or one skillet) over medium to medium-low, the other over medium-high. Cut two squares of plastic to just cover the plates of a tortilla press (to be on the safe side, cut them from a food-storage bag; the thicker plastic is easier for beginners to work with).

Knead the *masa* (either fresh or reconstituted) with just enough water to make it soft (like cookie dough) but not sticky. The softer the dough, the more tender the tortillas—but don't make it so soft it sticks to your hands.

Open the press and lay one square of plastic on the bottom plate. Scoop out a walnut-sized piece of dough, roll it into a ball and center it in the middle of the plastic. Cover with the second sheet of plastic. Close the press and use the handle to flatten the ball into a 5- to 6-inch disk. Turn the plastic-covered disk of *masa* 180 degrees and press gently to even the thickness.

Open the press and peel off the top piece of plastic. Flip the uncovered side of the tortilla onto your palm, lining up the top of the tortilla with the top of your index finger. Starting at the top, peel off the remaining sheet of plastic. Part of the tortilla will be dangling off the side of your hand. Quickly lay the tortilla onto the cooler side of the griddle (or into the cooler skillet): Don't flip it off your hand, which always results in rumpled tortillas; instead, as you slowly sweep the tortilla away from you, let the dangling part catch on the hot surface, then roll your hand out from under the tortilla (the movement looks a little as if you are sweeping something off the griddle with the back of your hand).

Bake for 15 to 30 seconds—just until the tortilla releases itself from the griddle. It'll look just a tiny bit dry around the edges, but don't leave it too long, or it will turn out dry and heavy. Flip onto the hotter side of the griddle (or into the hotter skillet) and bake until splotchy brown underneath, 30 to 45 seconds. Turn once again, leaving it on the hot side, and bake for another 30 to 45 seconds to brown. During these last few seconds of baking, a perfectly made tortilla will puff up like pita bread. If yours doesn't, it may have been baked too long on the first side or may not have been baked on a hot-enough surface.

Transfer to a cloth-lined basket and continue making tortillas, stacking them one on top of another and keeping them covered. As the cloth traps the steam, the tortillas will complete their final little bit of "cooking."

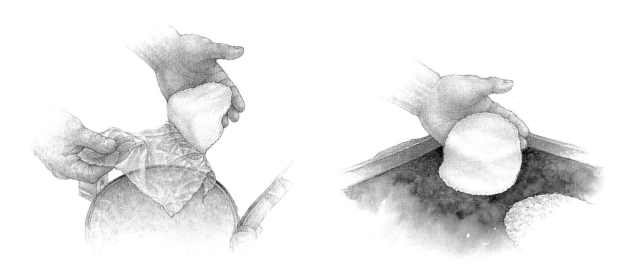

QUESTIONS AND ANSWERS FROM OUR TESTING

WHAT IS THE BEST MEAT FOR MAKING THESE GRILLED OR GRIDDLED TACOS? We've called for skirt steak to grill and thin-sliced sheets of *bistec* (beef of various cuts) to griddle-sear, but they are in fact interchangeable according to many Mexican cooks. I've focused on skirt steak for grilling, simply because it's thicker (unless you have gotten skirt steak that has been butterflied, as in many Mexican markets), giving you a more satisfying, steaky texture for the extra effort of firing up the grill. In most of our local Mexican markets in Chicago, we find thin-sliced *bistec* in all the butcher cases, labeled simply *bistec* or *bistec para asar* (an unspecified cut of beef—it usually seems to be from the round—for grilling or griddle-searing), *bistec de aguayon* (cut from the sirloin strip) or *bistec de bola* (cut from the round). Choose *bistec de aguayon* for the tenderest; flavorwise, they're all similar—and good. *Arrachera* (skirt steak), however, has a beefier taste than any of the above. In most of the Mexican groceries, the butchers sell the less tender inner skirt steak, butterflied to half the thickness of the already-thin original and then run through a tenderizing machine.

From groceries outside the Mexican community, we have tried thin-sliced minute, sandwich and breakfast steaks to stand in for Mexican *bistec*, all of which work well for griddle-searing—most are cut from the round. In our tests, thin-sliced sirloin tip and strip steak both yielded dry results.

When choosing skirt steaks to grill, you can go with the butterflied, tenderized Mexican-market variety or pieces of tender unbutterflied outer skirt steak (it's available in most chain groceries and is more expensive). The meat needs to be trimmed of most fat and any chewy silvery skin that may still cover some of the edges.

Chorizo is readily available in Mexican markets and in many well-stocked grocery stores. Quality varies greatly. I usually have better luck with the local butcher shop–made varieties than the commercially packaged ones, but the best one I can find in the United States is one I make myself. A good simple recipe is on page 26.

HOW SHOULD THE MEAT BE MARINATED? If meat is marinated in Mexico, the most common approach is a simple brush of lime juice and a sprinkling of salt. It's not intended to tenderize the meat (if you soak meat in lime juice long enough to tenderize a tough cut, the meat will lose all its color and be inedibly tart). It's for flavor. And to me it's just perfect . . . when you add a little garlic, perhaps a little cumin. That's the treatment we suggest for the grilled skirt steak. For the griddle-seared beef tacos, we recommend that the added flavor come primarily from salt and a hot griddle, since tanginess comes along with the quick-cooked onions and green chiles drizzled with lime.

DOES ONE GRILL WORK BETTER THAN ANOTHER? This dish involves fast, direct-heat cooking of the meat, so your heat source and cooking surface are both important. In my experience, fires that are not very hot and grill grates that simply won't hold heat produce disappointingly weak results. Cast-iron or heavy stainless steel grates produce the best results. A gas grill is easy, but it doesn't give quite the same enticing flavor to quickly seared meat.

ARE ALL GRIDDLES CREATED EQUAL? As with grill grates, heavier griddles (and skillets) hold heat better than lighter ones. I especially like cast iron because not only does it hold heat, but it holds and distributes the heat evenly. When working with other materials, you'll generally need a higher heat. And though they're a snap to clean up, nonstick surfaces don't seem to get as hot as the metal underneath. So what's underneath becomes even more important. Make sure your nonstick surface is covering a *heavy* griddle or skillet for best results.

*Youngster
anticipating
a just-baked
corn tortilla*

Home-Style Tacos with Casserole Fillings
(Tacos de Cazuela)

Thickish, earthy-smelling, steamy corn tortillas—the typical wrap for a soft taco in Mexico—have the strength to roll around any filling, even the juicy, slow-simmered dishes that are the everyday expression of Mexico's home cooking. These dishes are native stews that fuse a complexity of flavors, from chiles and sweet garlic to pungent herbs and ripe tomatoes, and they do so in *cazuelas*, vessels made of the earth itself.

Though it's easy to translate *cazuela* as "casserole," there's a lot more to it than that. Glazed shiny hard on the inside and left chalky unglazed earthenware outside, the *cazuela*, unlike our common casserole dish, can sit directly over a flame. There it absorbs heat evenly into its thick base and walls. Chile purees for *moles* are seared in *cazuelas*, cheese is melted in *cazuelas*, homey stews to fill tacos—*tacos de cazuela*—are simmered in *cazuelas*. And each preparation takes on an earthiness from the vessel.

Where muscley, meaty *tacos a la plancha* and *tacos al carbón* are strictly born of the hungry communal street life of Mexico, most fillings for *tacos de cazuela*—sometimes called *tacos de guisados*, stewed-filling tacos—simmer beguilingly back at home's hearth: Mom's Cooking stews in those pots, simple and satisfying and ready to be wrapped in fresh tortillas. And when (or if) you find the same sort of preparations in market stalls or spiffy *taquerías*, you can be sure it's hominess that's being offered.

The fact that the tortilla is a sturdy flatbread means it scoops well, preserving more delicious juices for the eater. And two of the *cazuela* taco fillings I've included here are full of juices. The Mexican-style zucchini filling simmers with ripe tomatoes, roasted poblanos and corn in a glossy coat of thick cream. It just begs to be spooned into tortillas for do-it-yourself soft tacos. The guajillo-spiked pork-and-potato filling has to do no pleading. Every spoon in close proximity goes for the rich sauce of self-assured, garlicky red chile tempered with a little tomato, cubes of potato and the rich juices of tender pork.

Mexicans aren't typically fussy about the temperature of most of the food set before them. In fact, there are even places in Mexico where cool or room-temperature taco fillings are celebrated. Hot tortillas, cool fillings—for me there's nothing better on a warm day. Which is why I put a spin on one of my favorite cool Yucatecan taco fillings, creating a contemporary chipotle chicken salad filling. It combines the crunch of shredded Napa cabbage with meaty chicken in a smoky, chipotle-infused vinaigrette, then tops everything with avocado and tangy cheese. Easy to make ahead and a nice addition to the other fillings if you're setting out all three for an informal *taquisa* (taco party).

TRADITIONAL BENCHMARK: *Tacos de cazuela* are going to be great if the tortillas are fresh and hot and the filling is thickish and beautifully seasoned—a little spicy, a little rich, a little complex, a little varied in its textures. Above all, good *tacos de cazuela* make you feel comfortable, always welcoming you back for another bite.

WHEN TO THINK OF THESE RECIPES: Okay, these recipes are more involved than opening a box of macaroni and cheese, but they're right when you want that same kind of easy feeling: say when friends come into town and you just want to relax together with a little good food (I'd include a big salad of young greens, balsamic vinegar, olive oil and sea salt), maybe a bottle of wine and some Buena Vista Social Club on the stereo. A creamy classic flan (page 308) would be the perfect end to the meal.

ADVICE FOR AMERICAN COOKS: Finding good fresh tortillas is the biggest challenge, and you may just want to make them yourself to ensure the best. Homemade ones are going to be thickish; factory-made ones are thin, so in Mexico, they often make tacos with a pair of tortillas to ensure that the filling stays inside. For the pork filling, dried guajillo chiles may not be as easily available to you as New Mexico or California chiles, but any of those will work. Just remember to substitute the same *weight* of chiles. For the zucchini dish, if you can locate (or even *grow*) some of the Mexican *calabacitas*, the dish will really sing. If zucchini isn't your favorite, try yellow crookneck or pattypan squash. And poblanos? Any large pepper from Anaheim (long green) to chilaca to red bell will make a tasty mixture. Again, substitute weight for weight.

Mexican-Style Zucchini Tacos

TACOS DE CALABACITAS A LA MEXICANA

Makes about 6 cups, filling about 24 tacos,
serving 6 as a casual meal

1 1/2 tablespoons vegetable oil

1 medium white onion, chopped

1 pound (2 medium-large round or 6 to 8 plum) ripe tomatoes,
    roughly chopped
        OR two-thirds of a 28-ounce can good-quality whole tomatoes in
        juice, drained

2 garlic cloves, peeled and finely chopped

2 large fresh poblano chiles

1 large ear corn, husked and kernels cut off (about 1 cup)

4 medium (about 1 1/2 pounds total) zucchini—or use the Mexican
    round or teardrop-shaped, light green calabacitas—trimmed
    and cut into 1/2-inch cubes (about 5 cups cubes)

Leaves from 1 sprig fresh epazote, roughly chopped
        OR 3 tablespoons chopped fresh cilantro

2/3 cup homemade crema (page 133), crème fraîche or
    heavy (whipping) cream

Salt

1/2 cup (about 2 ounces) crumbled Mexican queso fresco or
    other crumbly fresh cheese, such as salted pressed farmer's
    cheese or feta

24 warm, fresh corn tortillas (see page 115 to reheat store-bought
    ones or page 104 to make them from scratch)

TRADITIONAL

I. PREPARING THE FLAVORING BASE. Measure the oil into a large (12-inch) skillet
    set over medium-high heat. Add the onion and cook, stirring frequently, until richly
    browned, about 8 minutes. While the onion is cooking, coarsely puree the tomatoes
    in a food processor or blender. Add the garlic to the browned onion and cook for 1
    minute, stirring, then add the tomatoes. Reduce the heat to medium-low, cover the
    skillet and cook, stirring occasionally, for 5 minutes. Remove from the heat.

2. ROASTING THE CHILES. Roast the poblanos directly over a gas flame or on a baking sheet 4 inches below a very hot broiler, turning regularly, until the skin has blistered and blackened on all sides, about 5 minutes for an open flame, about 10 minutes for the broiler. Cover with a kitchen towel and let stand for 5 minutes. Rub off the blackened skin, then pull out the stems and seed pods. Rinse briefly to remove any stray seeds and bits of skin. Slice into ¼-inch strips.

3. FINISHING THE DISH. Uncover the skillet and set over medium-high heat. Stir in the poblanos, corn, zucchini, *epazote* or cilantro and the *crema* (or one of its stand-ins). Cook, stirring frequently, until the zucchini is crisp-tender and the liquid has thickened enough to coat the vegetables nicely, about 8 minutes. Taste and season with salt, usually about 1 teaspoon. Serve in a decorative bowl, sprinkled with the crumbled cheese, and pass the hot tortillas separately for do-it-yourself tacos.

WORKING AHEAD: If you find it helpful, the dish can be prepared a day ahead through Step 2; refrigerate the flavoring base and chiles separately, well covered. Return the mixture to the skillet and finish Step 3 just before serving.

Left:
First-quality
guajillo chiles
Right: The way
to the market

Guajillo-Spiked Pork-and-Potato Tacos

TACOS DE PUERCO Y PAPAS AL GUAJILLO

Makes about 4 cups filling for 12 to 16 tacos,
serving 4 as a casual meal

8 medium (2 ounces total) dried guajillo chiles, stemmed, seeded and
    torn into flat pieces
12 ounces (2 medium-small round or 4 to 6 plum) ripe tomatoes,
    roughly chopped
    OR one 15-ounce can good-quality whole tomatoes in juice,
    drained
3 large garlic cloves, peeled and roughly chopped
1 1/2 tablespoons vegetable oil or rich-tasting pork lard
1 pound lean boneless pork (preferably from the shoulder),
    cut into 1/2-inch cubes
Salt
4 medium (about 1 pound total) boiling potatoes, such as
    red-skins, cut into 1/2-inch cubes
3 tablespoons chopped fresh cilantro for garnish
12 to 16 warm, fresh corn tortillas (see page 115 to reheat store-
    bought ones or page 104 to make them from scratch)

TRADITIONAL

1.   THE CHILE SAUCE BASE. Toast the chile pieces a few at a time in a dry heavy skillet or on a griddle heated over medium, pressing them flat against the hot surface with a metal spatula until they are aromatic, about 10 seconds per side. (If the heat is right, you'll hear a slight crackle when you press them down, but you shouldn't see more than the slightest wisp of smoke; the inside surface of the chile should look noticeably lighter.) In a bowl, rehydrate the chiles for 20 minutes in hot tap water to cover; place a small plate on the top to keep the chiles submerged.

Use a pair of tongs to transfer the rehydrated chiles to a food processor or blender. Measure in 1 cup water, add the tomatoes and garlic and process to a smooth puree. Leave in the blender or food processor while you brown the meat.

2. MAKING THE FILLING. In a small (3- to 4-quart) pot, preferably a Dutch oven or Mexican *cazuela*, heat the oil or lard over medium-high. When quite hot, add the pork in a single layer (do this in batches if necessary; don't crowd the pan, or the meat will not brown nicely). Cook, turning the pieces, until richly browned all over, about 10 minutes. If working in batches, transfer the browned pork to a plate while you brown the rest; when all the meat is browned, return all the pork to the pot. Push the chile puree through a medium-mesh strainer directly into the pot. Cook, stirring frequently, until the saucy mixture is as thick as tomato paste, 6 to 8 minutes.

   Stir in 3 cups water and 1 teaspoon salt. Partially cover and simmer over medium-low heat, stirring often, for 20 minutes. Stir in the potatoes. Partially cover and cook, stirring often, until the potatoes and meat are both thoroughly tender but not falling apart, 20 to 30 minutes more. By that time, the sauce should have thickened to the consistency of canned tomato sauce—if it is too thick, add a little water; if too thin, cook uncovered to reduce. Taste and adjust the seasoning with salt if necessary.

3. FINISHING THE DISH. Scoop the hot pork-and-potato mixture into a serving bowl, sprinkle with the chopped cilantro and carry to the table, along with the warm tortillas.

WORKING AHEAD: This taco filling can be made a few days ahead (it actually improves after a day or two); store it covered in the refrigerator. Reheat the filling shortly before serving, adding a few drops of water if the mixture looks dry. It is also a sturdy enough preparation to hold in a low oven, covered with a lid or foil, for an hour or so.

Chipotle Chicken Salad Tacos

TACOS DE POLLO EN ENSALADA ENCHIPOTLADA

Makes about 4 cups, filling 12 to 16 tacos,
serving 4 as a casual meal

2 tablespoons balsamic vinegar (*no need to use your very best
balsamico here*)
$^1/_3$ cup olive oil, preferably extra-virgin
2 canned chipotle chiles en adobo, *finely chopped*
Salt
$^1/_2$ small head Napa cabbage, *thinly sliced* (about $2^1/_2$ cups)
1 large carrot, *peeled and chopped into* $^1/_4$-inch pieces
1 small red onion, *thinly sliced*
$^1/_4$ cup chopped fresh cilantro
$1^1/_2$ cups coarsely shredded cooked chicken, preferably grilled,
roasted or rotisserie chicken
1 large ripe avocado, *peeled, pitted and cut into* $^1/_2$-inch cubes
$^1/_3$ cup coarsely grated Mexican queso añejo or other dry
grating cheese, such as Romano or Parmesan
12 to 16 warm, fresh corn tortillas (*see page 115 to reheat store-
bought ones or page 104 to make them from scratch*)

CONTEMPORARY

1. **THE FILLING.** In a large bowl, whisk together the vinegar, olive oil and chipotles. Season generously with salt, usually about a generous $^1/_4$ teaspoon. Add the cabbage, carrot, onion, cilantro and chicken. Toss everything together and let stand for 15 minutes. Taste and season with additional salt if necessary.

2. **FINISHING THE DISH.** Scoop the filling into a wide shallow serving bowl, dot with the cubed avocado and dust generously with the cheese. Set on the table with the warm tortillas, and you're ready for some great roll-them-yourself tacos.

WORKING AHEAD: The chicken filling is best eaten the day it is made, though it will keep for several hours in the refrigerator.

REHEATING CORN TORTILLAS

There are several methods for reheating corn tortillas: dry heat (gas flame), moist heat (steamer and microwave) and oily heat (dry-frying).

Dry heat: This easy method works only if your tortillas have been made that day. Heat the tortillas directly over the flame (or on a griddle or skillet), flipping them until toasty and pliable.

Moist heat of a steamer: This is easier for larger quantities of corn tortillas, especially if you need to hold them hot for a little while. Pour $1/2$ inch water into the bottom of the steamer, then line the steaming basket with a clean heavy kitchen towel. Lay the tortillas in the basket in stacks of 12 (a small vegetable steamer will accommodate only one stack; a large Asian steamer will hold three or four stacks). Fold the edges of the towel over the tortillas to cover them, set the lid in place, bring the water to a boil and let boil only for 1 minute, then turn off the fire and let stand, covered, for 15 minutes. If you wish to keep the tortillas hot for up to an hour, slip the steamer into a low oven or reheat the water periodically.

Moist heat of a microwave: This easy method works best with no more than a dozen tortillas. Drizzle a clean kitchen towel with 3 tablespoons water and wring the towel to evenly distribute the moisture. Use the towel to line a microwave-safe casserole dish (8 or 9 inches in diameter is best). Lay in a dozen tortillas, cover with the towel and the lid, then microwave at 50 percent power for 4 minutes. Let stand for 2 to 3 minutes. The tortillas will stay warm for 20 minutes.

Oily heat: Though it's not much a part of home cooking, street vendors of seared-meat tacos reheat fresh tortillas with the heat of a slightly oily griddle—they're not so much frying the tortillas (which would mean completely submerging the tortillas in oil) as griddle-heating them with a tiny bit of oil.

When just-baked tortillas come off the griddle or when they've been reheated, they're traditionally kept warm in a tightly woven basket (*chiquihuite*) lined with a cloth; some have lids, others don't. In the Yucatan, they use hollowed-out gourds. And in modern households, they use Styrofoam containers—which are so efficient that they now come in many decorated styles. If you're having a party, hold hot tortillas in an insulated chest (like an ice chest) lined with a towel.

Questions and Answers from Our Testing

Is a traditional Mexican earthenware *cazuela* essential to get the right flavor? Though earthenware *cazuelas* are a beautiful, romantic and satisfying pleasure to use, in Mexico they're being replaced quite regularly by enameled steel, aluminum and stainless steel vessels. Which isn't to say *cazuelas* are not good. They cook more evenly than practically any alternative, holding and distributing heat perfectly for long, slow simmers, and they add an almost indescribable flavor that links stew to *terroir* through generations of tradition. The difficulty with *cazuelas* is that they are heavy and rather fragile. And some have suggested they're not too good for your health, because most *cazuelas* are finished with lead glazes. So, if you've brought back a treasured one from a Mexican sojourn, you need to know the facts: Lead leaches out with *time* and *acid*. To be on the safe side, don't cook long-simmered acidic dishes in a *cazuela*. And don't store anything acidic in a *cazuela*. And remember that you're probably picking up more lead in your everyday ramblings than you'd get from the use of a handsome *cazuela* a couple of times a year. My motto: Life's not very rich if you're not surrounded by simple beauty.

Are really *full* tacos better than ones with less filling? After eating tacos extensively on both sides of the border, I'm convinced that the amount of filling is critical. In Mexico, tacos are as much about good corn tortillas as they are about the filling, and lots of filling is not necessarily better. Think of it this way: We'd never make an overstuffed sandwich on wafer-thin sheets of bread, or a pasta dish that was all sauce and add-ins, hardly a penne or fettuccine in sight. If you have full-sized (6-inch) corn tortillas, ¼ cup of filling is the *most* you should use to give the right balance.

How saucy should the filling be? If you want satisfied guests and no cleaning bills, there's only one consistency that will work for a stewy taco filling—thick enough that the sauce clings with both hands to the chunks, but not so thick that it seems pasty.

Does the cut of pork make a difference in the pork filling? In our testing, pork loin, pork tenderloin and fresh ham (leg) all proved too lean or stringy for this treatment. Shoulder is juicy and tender.

What's the easiest way to get the roundest, most complete flavor from guajillo chiles? After years of tests with dried chiles, I've settled on the method that I've employed here. It's not as easy as spooning chile powder into the pot, but it's the only way I've found to get rich, round, full chile flavor. You toast and soak the cleaned dried chiles, then drain and puree them with fresh water, strain the puree and cook it until it's as thick as tomato paste. Toasting adds depth and richness, draining off the soaking liquid ensures little bitterness, straining gets rid of annoying skins and cooking the pureed chiles to a paste rounds out the rough edges.

WHAT ARE THE TASTE AND TEXTURAL DIFFERENCES BETWEEN ZUCCHINI AND MEXICAN *CALABACITAS*? Though all squash is originally native to Mexico, the soft-skinned summer squash that we eat most in the United States is the Italian cultivar called zucchini. The light-green round or pear-shaped cultivar that's most popular in Mexico is sweeter and has a more compact texture than the zucchini. But it blemishes more easily, so it isn't great for shipping and shelf life. To grow these beauties, choose *ronde de nice* (a similar French cultivar) or *tatume* or Mexican *calabacita*. Look for them in Latin American (mostly Mexican) or Middle Eastern markets.

REFINEMENTS: Mexican *crema* (homemade, page 133, or store-bought) or *crème fraîche* gives a wonderful tang to the squash filling; heavy cream is beautiful, if less tangy; and store-bought sour cream will curdle when heated.

Making soft tacos

Enchiladas

Meet the fraternal twins of the enchilada household: There's the one you know, with its spicy-sauced corn tortilla rolled around chicken, beef or what-have-you. And if you happen to be in the right regions of Mexico, you can experience the thrill of another enchilada, a racy street-style enchilada in which the tortilla is tightly clad with red chile sauce as it sears on a hot iron griddle. It's that seared version—the "dip the tortilla in chile sauce, then fry it" version—that illustrates the very essence of enchilada.

Language tells it all. Tortillas that become enchiladas are not en-cased or en-robed; they're en-*chilied* tortillas: *tortillas enchiladas,* as the full Spanish phrase goes; simply *enchiladas* for short. So, if tortillas are the "canvas" of Mexican cuisine, then these enchiladas are that canvas with a chile wash.

In Mexico, the fraternal enchilada twins inhabit different spheres. The first, more common type comes from the home kitchen or perhaps the home-away-from-home kitchen (*cafeterías,* market *fondas,* the simple mom-and-pop places called *cocinas económicas,* even some fancy restaurants). They are served at practically any time of day. And their sauces vary widely, from simple tomato or tomatillo to vibrant red chile or *mole,* some regions even giving each flavor of sauced tortilla a sauce-specific name—*enjitomatada* (tomato sauce), *entomatada* (tomatillo sauce), *enmolada* (*mole*). Some come with a dusting of dry grating cheese; others have sliced onion, cilantro or parsley, or a spoonful of cream; and still others are blanketed with the oozy melted cheese we typically associate with enchiladas north of the border.

But the seared street-style enchilada conjures up a specific place and time. It's eight in the evening and the shopkeepers are bringing down the metal grates over their store windows. As if by signal, the number of people on the streets begins to swell as folks pour out of doorways for the leisurely evening walk that is a ritual of old-fashioned Mexican life. Friends cluster spontaneously. And just as naturally, they eat an almost wickedly delicious supper (*cena*) from the street vendors—a smorgasbord of tacos, *sopes,* tamales, tostadas and, in many places, simple-and-savory red chile–seared tortillas they call enchiladas, *enchiladas rojas, enchiladas de la plaza* or any number of regional monikers.

Enchiladas suizas (literally, Swiss enchiladas) are based on the saucy variety—tortillas rolled around coarse shreds of chicken, their surface burnished with melted cheese. But *enchiladas suizas* pay homage to a distant land where cream rules. By most accounts, these enchiladas were brought into the collective Mexican consciousness by Sanborns, the coffeeshop and drugstore that is an international travelers' (and upwardly mobile Mexicans') refuge. The version created there in the '50s by Teresa Montaño has a tomatillo-based sauce, though a tomato-based one is common in some cooks' riff on the theme.

Though perhaps not as familiar feeling as *enchiladas suizas,* dip-and-fry red chile enchiladas are simple—after frying a couple of tortillas, you'll be comfortable with making them. These uncomplicated enchiladas are really a celebration of spicy tortillas, filling optional. The counterpoint of zesty grated cheese, crisp lettuce and raw onion makes them delicious perfection.

And for brunch, top these red chile enchiladas (not folded or rolled) with eggs sunnyside up. A spoonful of red-chile hash browns, a sprinkle of sharp cheese and a little stack of tangy lettuce completes this contemporary take on some of my favorite enchiladas.

TRADITIONAL BENCHMARK: No matter what the style, the tortillas in the best enchiladas are supple and toothsome, but never mushy. The proportion of sauce to filling (if there is any) and toppings should be balanced to give the tortilla first billing. All the other elements play a supporting role, offering textures and tastes from raw-and-crunchy to spicy to meaty.

WHEN TO THINK OF THESE RECIPES: I occasionally like to serve a single enchilada as the first course of a dressy meal, but enchiladas are usually considered casual main-course fare. They take a little time to make, but the reward is more than worth it.

ADVICE FOR AMERICAN COOKS: Start with the sauced enchiladas—they're the easiest and closest to what you may already know. Then procure dried chiles and master the dip-and-fry version.

Creamy Enchiladas with Chicken, Tomatoes and Green Chile

ENCHILADAS SUIZAS

Serves 4 to 6

3 pounds (6 medium-large round or about 20 plum) ripe tomatoes
  OR two 28-ounce cans good-quality whole tomatoes in juice, drained
Fresh hot green chiles to taste (roughly 3 serranos or 2 jalapeños), stemmed
1 1/2 tablespoons vegetable oil or rich-tasting pork lard, plus a
  little oil for brushing or spraying the tortillas
1 medium white onion, chopped
2 cups chicken broth, plus a little extra if needed
Salt
1/2 cup homemade crema (page 133), crème fraîche or
  heavy (whipping) cream
About 2 cups coarsely shredded cooked chicken, preferably
  grilled, roasted or rotisserie chicken
2/3 cup shredded Mexican melting cheese (Chihuahua,
  quesadilla, asadero or the like) or Monterey Jack, brick
  or mild cheddar
12 corn tortillas
A few sliced rounds of white onion, separated into rings, for garnish
Sprigs of fresh cilantro for garnish

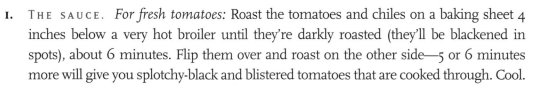

TRADITIONAL

I. THE SAUCE. *For fresh tomatoes:* Roast the tomatoes and chiles on a baking sheet 4 inches below a very hot broiler until they're darkly roasted (they'll be blackened in spots), about 6 minutes. Flip them over and roast on the other side—5 or 6 minutes more will give you splotchy-black and blistered tomatoes that are cooked through. Cool.

Working over your baking sheet, pull off and discard the blackened tomato skins and, for round tomatoes, cut out the hard cores. Transfer the tomatoes and chiles to a food processor or blender, along with all the juices on the baking sheet. Blend to a smooth puree.

For canned tomatoes: In a small dry skillet, roast the chiles over medium heat, turning regularly, until they're soft and splotchy-black, about 5 minutes. Place in a blender or food processor along with the drained canned tomatoes. Blend to a smooth puree.

In a medium (4- or 5-quart) pot (preferably a Dutch oven or Mexican *cazuela*), heat the oil or lard over medium heat. Add the onion and cook, stirring regularly, until golden, about 7 minutes. Raise the heat to medium-high, and, when the pot is noticeably hotter, stir in the tomato puree. Cook, stirring, until darker in color and thickened to the consistency of tomato paste, 10 to 15 minutes. Stir in the broth, partially cover and simmer for 15 minutes. Taste and season with salt, usually about ½ teaspoon. The sauce should have a slightly soupy consistency—not as thick as spaghetti sauce. If it is too thick, stir in a little additional broth. Keep warm over low heat.

2. OTHER PRELIMINARIES. Stir the *crema* (or one of its stand-ins) into the sauce. Put the chicken in a bowl and stir ½ cup of the sauce mixture into it. Taste and season with additional salt if you think it needs it. Have the cheese at the ready.

3. FINISHING THE ENCHILADAS. Heat the oven to 350°F. Smear about ¼ cup of the sauce over the bottom of each of four to six 9-inch individual ovenproof baking/serving dishes or smear about 1 cup of the sauce over the bottom of a 13 x 9-inch baking dish. Lay the tortillas out on a baking sheet (two sheets if you have them, for more even heating), and lightly brush or spray both sides of the tortillas with oil. Bake just to warm through and soften, about 3 minutes. Stack the tortillas and cover with a towel to keep warm.

Working quickly so the tortillas stay hot and pliable, roll a portion of the chicken up in each tortilla, then line them all up in the baking dish(es). Douse evenly with the remaining sauce, then sprinkle with the cheese. Bake until the enchiladas are hot through (the cheese will have begun to brown), about 15 minutes. Garnish with the onion rings and cilantro sprigs. These are best served piping hot from the oven.

WORKING AHEAD: The sauce can be made a day or two ahead; refrigerate covered. Once the tortillas have been heated in the oven, you need to work quickly and steadily toward serving in order to preserve their beautiful texture. Once out of the oven, the finished dish softens to near mush over a period of 15 to 20 minutes.

Red Chile Enchiladas, Street-Style

ENCHILADAS ROJAS

Serves 4

5 medium (2 $^1/_2$ ounces total) dried ancho chiles,
    stemmed and seeded
2 garlic cloves, peeled and roughly chopped
Salt
$^1/_2$ cup grated Mexican queso añejo or other dry grating
    cheese such as Romano or Parmesan
1 small white onion, thinly sliced
2 cups coarsely shredded cooked chicken, preferably grilled,
    roasted or rotisserie chicken (optional)
12 corn tortillas
About $^1/_3$ cup vegetable oil or rich-tasting pork lard
4 loosely packed cups sliced ($^1/_4$-inch) romaine lettuce
1$^1/_2$ tablespoons vinegar (cider vinegar works nicely here)

TRADITIONAL

1. THE SAUCE. Heat a dry heavy skillet or griddle over medium. Tear the chiles into flat pieces, then toast them a few at a time: Use a metal spatula to press the chile pieces flat against the hot surface, skin side up, until they are aromatic and have lightened in color underneath, about 10 seconds. (If the heat is right, you'll hear a slight crackle when you press them down, but you shouldn't see more than the slightest wisp of smoke.) Place in a bowl, cover with about 3 cups very hot tap water, lay a small plate on the chiles to keep them submerged and soak for 20 minutes to rehydrate.

    Use a pair of tongs to transfer the rehydrated chiles to a food processor or blender. Measure 1$^1/_2$ cups of the soaking liquid and add it to the chiles along with the garlic. Blend to a smooth puree, then push through a medium-mesh strainer into a pie plate. The consistency should be like that of canned tomato sauce. Taste (the sauce will be a little rough on the tongue at this point) and season highly with salt, usually about $^1/_2$ teaspoon.

2. OTHER PRELIMINARIES. Set out the grated cheese and sliced onion. If using the

optional chicken, warm it in a microwave or in a small skillet over medium-low heat (for stove-top heating, you'll want to dribble in a little water to keep it from sticking).

3. FINISHING THE ENCHILADAS. Heat the oven to 350°F. Place the sauce and tortillas near the stove, with a baking sheet beside them. Set a small (8-inch) skillet (preferably nonstick) over medium heat and add *1 tablespoon* of the oil or lard. When the oil is hot, dip both sides of a tortilla into the sauce, then lay it in the oil. Let it sear and sizzle for about 20 seconds, then use a small spatula to flip it over. Sear the other side for about 20 seconds. Transfer to the baking sheet, folding it in half. Continue dipping and frying the remaining tortillas, wiping out the pan occasionally and then heating another tablespoon of oil or lard to fry a new batch. Arrange the fried, folded tortillas in groups of three, overlapping them. Pop them into the oven to heat through, about 5 minutes.

    While the enchiladas are heating, in a small bowl, toss the lettuce with the vinegar and a good sprinkling of salt.

    Divide the warm enchiladas among four dinner plates and sprinkle liberally with the grated cheese. Top with the sliced onion, chicken (if you are using it) and a generous portion of the dressed romaine. These wait for no one.

WORKING AHEAD: The sauce will keep for several days in the refrigerator, well covered, though you may notice the garlic flavor becoming a little stronger. If the sauce has thickened to more than the consistency of canned tomato sauce, thin it with a little water before using. Once you start frying the enchiladas, though, the short fuse to dinnertime has been lit—these can survive for only 30 minutes before the final 5-minute warming.

Red Chile Brunch Enchiladas with Spicy Potatoes and Fried Eggs

ALMUERZO ENCHILADO

Serves 4

4 medium (2 ounces total) dried ancho chiles, stemmed and seeded

4 medium (1 ounce total) dried guajillo chiles, stemmed and seeded

3 garlic cloves, peeled and roughly chopped

Salt

4 medium (1 pound total) boiling potatoes, scrubbed and cut into
    rough $^1/_2$-inch cubes

About 6 tablespoons vegetable oil or rich-tasting pork lard

1 small white onion, chopped

8 corn tortillas

4 large eggs

2 loosely packed cups sliced ($^1/_4$-inch) frisée (a.k.a. curly endive)
    lettuce—or use romaine if you like it better

$1^1/_2$ tablespoons vinegar (cider vinegar works nicely here)

$^1/_3$ cup grated Mexican queso añejo or other dry
    grating cheese, such as Romano or Parmesan

CONTEMPORARY

I. THE SAUCE. Heat a dry heavy skillet or griddle over medium. Tear the chiles into flat pieces, then toast them a few at a time: Use a metal spatula to press the chile pieces flat against the hot surface, skin side up, until they are aromatic and have lightened in color underneath, about 10 seconds. (If the heat is right, you'll hear a slight crackle when you press them down, but you shouldn't see more than the slightest wisp of smoke.) Place in a bowl, cover with 3 cups very hot tap water, lay a small plate on the chiles to keep them submerged and soak 20 minutes to rehydrate.

Use a pair of tongs to transfer the rehydrated chiles to a food processor or blender. Measure $1^1/_2$ cups of the soaking liquid and add it to the chiles along with the garlic. Blend to a smooth puree, then push through a medium-mesh strainer into a pie plate. The consistency should be like that of canned tomato sauce. Taste (the sauce will be a little rough on the tongue at this point) and season highly with salt, usually about $^1/_2$ teaspoon.

2. THE POTATOES. Simmer the potatoes in salted water to cover until just barely tender, about 10 minutes. Drain.

    In a large (12-inch) skillet (preferably nonstick), heat *2 tablespoons* of the oil or lard over medium heat. Add the onion and cook, stirring regularly, until translucent, about 5 minutes. Add the potatoes and continue cooking, turning and scraping up any browned bits, until richly browned and crusty, 15 to 20 minutes. Stir in $^1/_4$ cup of the sauce and cook for another 5 minutes, then remove from the heat.

3. THE ENCHILADAS. While the potatoes are cooking, make the enchiladas. Heat the oven to 350°F. Place the sauce and tortillas near the stove with a baking sheet beside them. Set a small (8-inch) skillet, preferably nonstick, over medium heat and add *1 tablespoon* of the oil or lard. When the oil is very hot (just beginning to smoke), dip both sides of a tortilla into the sauce, then lay it in the oil. Let it sear and sizzle for about 20 seconds, then use a small spatula to flip it over. Sear the other side for another 20 seconds. Transfer to the baking sheet, laying it out flat. Adding additional oil to the skillet as needed, continue dipping and frying the remaining tortillas, wiping out the skillet occasionally. Lay the tortillas on the baking sheet in groups of two, about half overlapping each other.

    Divide the potatoes among the chile-seared tortillas and place in the oven to warm, 5 to 10 minutes. Meanwhile, wash and dry the large skillet and set over medium to medium-low heat. Add *1 tablespoon* of the oil or lard. When warm (not too hot), crack in the eggs, cover the pan and cook until as done as you like, about 3 to 4 minutes for set whites and slightly runny yolks.

    While the eggs are cooking, in a small bowl, toss the lettuce with the vinegar and a good sprinkling of salt. Put an enchilada-potato stack on each of four dinner plates and top with a fried egg, then a portion of the dressed lettuce and a generous sprinkling of the grated cheese. You've made your guests a brunch they'll never forget.

WORKING AHEAD: The sauce can be made ahead (thin it with a little water if it has thickened to more than the consistency of canned tomato sauce), as can the fried-and-chilied potatoes. At serving time, then, there's not much left besides rewarming the potatoes, searing the tortillas and frying the eggs. Who wants to do more than that on a weekend morning?

CREAMY ENCHILADAS WITH CHICKEN, TOMATOES
AND GREEN CHILE (PAGE 120)

Questions and Answers from Our Testing

Which are the right tortillas for enchiladas? Tortillas for the best enchiladas should be fairly fresh. And thickish, sturdy (some would say dense) ones are generally better than most thin ones. On the other hand, we tested this recipe with the widely distributed Azteca brand tortillas (thin and not very fresh) bought from the refrigerated food case of a local chain grocery store, and they were quite good—I'd say the best use I've found for those tortillas. If you make your own tortillas, make sure that the *masa* is as soft as is workable or your tortillas will crack when they're folded or rolled. For the best results, let homemade tortillas cool before using in these recipes.

Is there an alternative to frying tortillas for saucy enchiladas? In other books, I've encouraged steam-heating cold tortillas to make them pliable for enchiladas, but that method can yield mushy enchiladas unless you are working with rather thick tortillas. Otherwise, you should do what most Mexican cooks do: soften cold, stiff tortillas by quickly frying them one by one (this also gives them a stabilizing firmness that keeps them from falling apart), then pat them dry on paper towels. Another successful method for softening tortillas, we discovered, is brushing or spritzing the tortillas with oil and heating them in the oven. This method has several advantages: It involves less fat, it's easy and it doesn't leave behind any "hot oil" smell in the kitchen. That method doesn't, however, work very well with very thin, tender tortillas; they require one-by-one frying.

What is the best equipment for dip-and-fry enchiladas? In Mexico, the street vendors use a large (2 x 3-foot) griddle with a shallow well in the center for frying. The fire is directly under that well, so a chile-dipped tortilla can be slid in to sear, happily spattering onto the edges of the griddle, before it's retrieved to a warm spot on the sides, waiting to be served. A well-seasoned wok is a good substitute (giving room to catch spatters), as is a small (8-inch) nonstick skillet (easier to manage, but messier on the stove).

Do dip-and-fry enchiladas need to be made at the last minute? I had always thought these enchiladas needed to be eaten the second they're ready. But, happily, after several tests, we learned that the chile-coated, fried tortillas can be held at room temperature for 30 minutes before being popped in the oven for a quick reheat. They come out just great—and it gives you time to clean up the kitchen before serving.

Refinements (*Enchiladas Suizas*): *Tomatoes v. tomatillos:* The acidity tomatillos add is wonderful against the richness of the cream. To make that choice, replace tomatoes with an equivalent weight of tomatillos. *Individual v. large casserole:* It's tricky to lift nice-looking portions of saucy enchiladas from a large baking dish, so I recommend investing in some individual casserole dishes (inexpensive stoneware ones are wonderful) so that you can bake individual portions. *Covering the tortillas completely:* A common oversight for most American cooks is not covering the tortillas completely with sauce, leaving exposed edges of the tortillas to dry out.

REFINEMENTS (*ENCHILADAS ROJAS*): *Ancho v. other dried chiles:* Ancho chiles make a velvety, full-flavored sauce and using their soaking liquid here gives an appropriately rustic oomph that I like. Other chiles can be woven in for varied flavors. Guajillo adds brightness and can easily be used for up to half of the weight of the dried chiles. A little smoky chipotle jazzes up the sauce. *Consistency of sauce:* For the sauce to coat appropriately, it needs to be the consistency of canned tomato sauce. Too thin means bland tortillas; too thick means overly intense mouthfuls. *Lard v. vegetable oil:* In Mexico, some street vendors use a roasty fresh pork lard for frying the enchiladas. In my opinion, lard (or a combination of lard and oil) is the way to go if you can get good fresh lard. It's like the difference between potato pancakes fried in butter and those fried in oil. Richer, yes, but with a complete flavor.

A few of the varieties of beans in the Oaxaca Market

Chilaquiles (Tortilla Casserole)

Chilaquiles—they're so ingrained in the cultural consciousness that most Mexicans don't even know the word means "chiles and greens" in Nahuatl, the ancient tongue of the ancestors. They only know the soulful texture of crisp tortillas softening in brothy sauce, which resist just a little as you sink your teeth in deeply. They appreciate the spiciness of chile against the earthiness of corn. And their mouths water, loving how smoothly the *chilaquiles* go down, how agreeably they stick to the ribs.

One of my nineteenth-century Mexican cookbooks defines *chilaquiles* as a soup with unfried day-old tortillas in it. (Think of "soup" here in the same way Mexicans consider rice a soup, a *sopa seca*, a dry soup, that moves from brothy to not-so-brothy as it cooks.) I've tried that old-fashioned recipe, and the result is . . . well, akin to coarse-textured mush. In modern-day Mexico's version, the tortillas are fried first, like chips, giving them a more toothsome texture in the brothy sauce. That is, if you eat the *chilaquiles* right away and if you've used crisp-fried tortillas with some heft to them—not the thin melt-in-your-mouth kind we Americans prefer for noshing.

In a Mexican home kitchen, *chilaquiles* are easy-to-fix, substantial everyday fare—like the eggless hard-wheat pastas of the Italian *cucina povera* or the chewy northern Chinese noodles. Sure, *chilaquiles* are modest by nature—a handful of old tortillas and a little something to flavor them—but that doesn't diminish how soul-satisfying they are.

The improvisations that have flourished around *chilaquiles* are also direct and sturdy. My traditional Chipotle *Chilaquiles* begin with a simmering pot of tomato broth flecked with the smoky sizzle of chipotle chiles. In go those thickish chips, then I set a lid in place and turn off the heat. Over the next few minutes, the chips soften perfectly to that almost indescribable chew, infusing themselves with quintessential Mexican flavor.

Spoon the chilaquiles into a deep plate as you would saucy pasta. A sprinkling of full-flavored dry grating cheese, like Mexican *queso añejo,* is a must to focus the flavors; a drizzling of cream is heaven, and sliced raw onion provides the perfect fresh crunchy counterpoint.

If you get the *chilaquiles* to the table right away, you'll create memories. But that's not always possible. So I've supplied a recipe for baked *chilaquiles*—a rustic "lasagne" of sorts. It holds better than the stove-top version (the richness of melted cheese keeps the tortillas intact longer). Though you can add cream to the tomato-chipotle sauce in the first recipe and use it for the baked version, I love baked *chilaquiles* made with tomatillos and fresh green chile.

TRADITIONAL BENCHMARK: Though I'd doubtless eaten *chilaquiles* before I was twenty-four, the first plate I remember—*really* remember—was in a small restaurant in Oaxaca. To this day, it's my benchmark: an oval plateful of thickish tortillas with a texture halfway between crisp and tender (definitely not mushy), all coated and infused with a brothy, *epazote*-flecked tomato sauce containing a gentle wake-up call of smoky chile. Several years later, I was living above a *cafetería* in Mexico City and regularly ate similar platefuls of equally great-textured *chilaquiles*, though these were always made with tomatillo sauce. To me, the sauce isn't as important as the proportions, garnishes and length of time the tortillas spend in the sauce.

WHEN TO THINK OF THESE RECIPES: *Chilaquiles* are home-style fare, for Wednesday night dinner, say, when you want something with a little thrill. A salad completes the picture. They work for brunch (top with ham) or, when made meatless, as an accompaniment to roast chicken or grilled steaks.

ADVICE FOR AMERICAN COOKS: Chips (either store-bought or homemade) are the only challenge to perfect *chilaquiles*, since they need to be thick enough to absorb just the right amount of sauce without falling apart. Otherwise, the basic approach to making *chilaquiles*, like making most simple pasta dishes, welcomes flights of imagination, traditional or not.

Chipotle *Chilaquiles* (Tortilla "Casserole")

CHILAQUILES AL CHIPOTLE

Serves 4 as a casual main dish

12 (10 ounces total) corn tortillas, cut into sixths and fried or baked
    to make chips (see page 136)
    OR 8 ounces (8 to 12 loosely packed cups, depending on thick-
    ness) thick, homemade-style tortilla chips (such as ones you buy
    at a Mexican grocery)
One 28-ounce can good-quality whole tomatoes in juice, drained
    OR 1$^1/_2$ pounds (3 medium-large round or 9 to 12 plum)
    ripe tomatoes
2 to 3 canned chipotle chiles en adobo
    OR 2 to 3 dried chipotle chiles, stemmed
1$^1/_2$ tablespoons vegetable or olive oil
1 large white onion, sliced $^1/_4$ inch thick
3 garlic cloves, peeled and finely chopped
2$^1/_2$ cups chicken broth, vegetable broth or water,
    plus a little extra if needed
Salt
About $^1/_3$ cup homemade crema (page 133), crème fraîche or
    store-bought sour cream thinned with a little milk
1$^1/_2$ cups coarsely shredded cooked chicken, preferably grilled,
    roasted or rotisserie chicken (optional)
$^1/_4$ cup grated Mexican queso añejo or other dry
    grating cheese, such as Romano or Parmesan
2 cups sliced red Swiss chard leaves or lamb's-quarters (quelites)
    (optional)
3 tablespoons roughly chopped fresh epazote
    OR $^1/_2$ cup chopped fresh cilantro

TRADITIONAL

1. THE CHIPS. Make the chips or measure out the store-bought chips.
2. THE BROTHY SAUCE. If using canned tomatoes, place them in a blender jar. If using fresh tomatoes, spread them onto a baking sheet and place 4 inches below

a very hot broiler. Roast until splotchy-black and thoroughly soft, about 6 minutes per side. Cool. Peel (collecting the juices) and, for round tomatoes, cut out the hard cores. Transfer to a blender, juices and all.

If using canned chipotles, add them to the blender, seeds and all. If using dried chipotles, toast them in a dry skillet over medium heat for about a minute, turning frequently, until very aromatic. Place in a small bowl, cover with hot tap water and let rehydrate for 30 minutes. Drain and add to the blender.

Blend the tomatoes and chiles to a slightly coarse puree, one that still retains a little texture. You should have about 2 1/4 cups puree.

Set a medium (4- to 5-quart) pot or Dutch oven or a large (12-inch) deep skillet over medium heat—you'll need a lid for whichever vessel you choose. Measure in the oil, add *half* of the onion and cook, stirring regularly, until golden, about 7 minutes. Add the garlic and stir for another minute, then raise the heat to medium-high. Add the tomato puree and stir nearly constantly for 4 to 5 minutes, until the mixture thickens somewhat. Stir in the broth or water and season with salt, usually about 1/2 teaspoon if you are using salted chips. (Cover the pot and turn off the heat if not continuing with Step 3 right away.)

3. COOKING AND SERVING THE *CHILAQUILES*. Set out the remaining onion, the *crema* (or its stand-in), chicken (if using) and cheese. Put the pot over medium-high heat until the brothy sauce boils. Stir in the chard or lamb's-quarters (if using), the *epazote* (if using cilantro, set it aside to add later) and the tortilla chips, coating all the chips well. Let return to a rolling boil, cover and turn off the heat. Let stand for 5 minutes (no longer).

Uncover the pot and check that the chips have softened nicely—they should be a *little* chewy, definitely not mushy. (If they're too chewy, stir in a few tablespoons more broth, cover and set over medium heat for a couple minutes more.) Sprinkle with the cilantro, if that's the herb you're using.

Spoon onto warm plates. Drizzle with the *crema* (or its stand-in), strew with the sliced onion and optional chicken and dust generously with the cheese.

WORKING AHEAD: The brothy sauce (Step 2) can be completed up to 3 or 4 days ahead; store in the refrigerator, covered. *Chilaquiles* lose texture once they're made, so complete the simple tasks of cooking and serving them when everyone's ready to eat. Homemade chips for *chilaquiles* are fine made a day or two in advance.

CREMA MEXICANA • MEXICAN-STYLE THICK CREAM

This is the luscious stuff that burns a simple dish into your memory. A little edgy, a little nutty and really voluptuous. Did they ever call Marilyn Monroe *crema*?

Makes about 1 cup

1 cup heavy whipping cream
¹/₄ cup good-quality commercial sour cream with
    active cultures
    OR 2 tablespoons buttermilk with active cultures

In a small saucepan, heat the cream just long enough to take the chill off—to bring it to body temperature. If you have ready access to a low-range instant-read thermometer, it should be about 100 degrees. Off the heat, whisk in the sour cream (or buttermilk) and pour into a glass jar. Set the lid on the jar (but don't tighten it), then place the jar in a warmish place (it shouldn't be over 90 degrees). After 12 hours, the cream should be noticeably thicker. Refrigerate (you can tighten the lid now) for at least 4 hours or, better yet, overnight to complete the thickening. *Crema* will last for at least a week in the refrigerator.

Baked Tomatillo–Green *Chilaquiles* (Tortilla "Casserole")

CHILAQUILES VERDES HORNEADOS

Serves 6 as a casual main dish,
10 as an accompaniment

18 (15 ounces total) corn tortillas, cut into sixths and fried or baked to
    make chips (see page 136)
    OR 12 ounces (12 to 18 loosely packed cups, depending on
    thickness) thick, homemade-style tortilla chips (such as ones
    you buy at a Mexican grocery)
2 pounds (20 to 24 medium) tomatillos, husked and rinsed
Fresh hot green chiles to taste (roughly 4 serranos or 2 jalapeños),
    stemmed
2 tablespoons vegetable oil or olive oil
1 medium white onion, sliced $^1/_4$ inch thick
4 garlic cloves, peeled and finely chopped
$^2/_3$ cup homemade crema (page 133), crème fraîche or
    heavy (whipping) cream
3 cups chicken broth, vegetable broth or water
Salt
4 ounces cooked ham, cut into $^1/_2$-inch dice (optional)
3 tablespoons roughly chopped fresh epazote
    OR $^1/_2$ cup chopped fresh cilantro
4 ounces Mexican melting cheese (Chihuahua,
    quesadilla, asadero or the like) or Monterey Jack, brick or
    mild cheddar, shredded (you'll have about 1 cup)

TRADITIONAL

1. THE CHIPS. Make the chips or measure out the store-bought chips.
2. THE BROTHY SAUCE. Roast the tomatillos and green chiles on a baking sheet 4 inches below a very hot broiler until darkly roasted, even blackened in spots, about 5 minutes. Flip them over and roast on the other side—4 or 5 minutes more will give you splotchy-black and blistered tomatillos and chiles that are soft

and cooked through. Cool, then transfer everything to a blender, being careful to scrape up all the delicious juice that has run out onto the baking sheet. Blend to an almost smooth puree. There should be about 2 1/2 cups puree.

In a medium (4- to 5-quart) pot or Dutch oven, heat the oil over medium. Add the onion and cook, stirring regularly, until golden, about 7 minutes. Stir in the garlic and cook another minute, then raise the heat to medium-high. Add the tomatillo puree and stir constantly for 5 minutes or so, until the mixture has reached a full boil. Stir in the *crema* (or one of its substitutes) and broth or water. Season with salt, usually about 3/4 teaspoon if you are using salted chips.

3. COOKING AND SERVING THE *CHILAQUILES*. Heat the oven to 400°F. Scoop the chips into a 13 x 9-inch baking dish. You may have to press down on them, crushing them just a little, to get them to fit. Sprinkle with the optional ham.

Bring the sauce to a boil and stir in the *epazote* or cilantro, then ladle the sauce over the chips. Gently press the chips into the sauce to ensure they're evenly coated (though a few may be sticking out). Evenly spread the shredded cheese over the top and set in the oven. Bake until lightly browned on top and bubbling around the edges, about 15 minutes. Carry your *chilaquiles* to the table or buffet.

WORKING AHEAD: Though the sauce (Step 2) can be prepared as much as 4 days ahead and kept covered in the refrigerator, the *chilaquiles* will have the most delectable texture when served shortly after baking.

Shelling freshly
harvested beans

TOTOPOS FRITOS O HORNEADOS

● FRIED OR BAKED TORTILLA CHIPS

If you're going to use these chips for *chilaquiles*, you should buy medium-thick tortillas, ones that weigh 10 ounces per dozen. Choosing these will yield the right weight/volume for making Chipotle *Chilaquiles* (for the Baked Tomatillo Green *Chilaquiles*, you'll need 1½ times the recipe—18 tortillas). For snacking chips, choose the thinner, drier tortillas that are made from more coarsely ground corn—especially for frying light, crisp and greaseless. Baked chips can be nearly as good as fried ones (especially right out of the oven), and they are leaner. We counted: Baked chips take about 80 spritzes of oil (a total of 1 tablespoon oil spritzed over 12 tortillas).

Makes enough for 6 to 8 as a snack, or the right amount to use in making Chipotle Chilaquiles

12 corn tortillas
Vegetable oil to a depth of at least 1 inch (1½ inches is
     even better) for frying
          OR vegetable oil in a spray bottle
Salt

1. THE TORTILLAS. For the crispest, most greaseless chips, the tortillas you start with should not be at all warm or moist—in fact cold, dryish, slightly stale tortillas are best. Separate the tortillas (make sure none are stuck together) and cut each into 6 wedges (it's most efficient to cut stacks of 4 or 5 tortillas). For dramatic-looking chips that are perfect for serving *ceviche* or other pass-around appetizers, cut the tortillas as illustrated on page 137. Spread out the wedges on your cutting board to air-dry for a few minutes.

2. OPTION 1: FRYING THE TORTILLAS. In a heavy pot, preferably at least 8 inches across and 3 to 5 inches deep, heat 1 to 1½ inches of oil over medium to medium-high. For greatest consistency, attach a deep-fry thermometer and adjust the heat to keep the oil at 375°F. Lacking a thermometer, the most accurate way to judge temperature is with your nose—at about 325°F, the oil will begin to give off that characteristic hot oil smell—and with your eyes—you'll

notice a shimmering surface on the oil (but no smoking) when it's about 375°F. You should also use good old trial-and-error: Lay a tortilla triangle in the oil, and if it sizzles happily, the temperature's about right; if it languishes with a only a trickle of bubbles, the oil's too cool; or, if it gets zapped unmercifully, you've got smoking-hot oil that is dangerous and will give the chips a bad taste.

Working with a small handful (about 12 pieces) at a time, fry the chips, stirring them around nearly constantly, until they've darkened just a shade and the bubbling has slowed way down, 45 seconds to a minute. Use tongs or a skimmer to remove them from the oil and drain on paper towels. Sprinkle with salt.

OPTION 2: BAKING THE TORTILLAS. Heat the oven to 375°F. Spread the triangles into a more-or-less single layer on two baking sheets. Using a spray bottle of oil, evenly mist them on both sides. Bake, stirring them around once or twice, until they're crisp and slightly golden, 10 to 15 minutes. Sprinkle with salt.

WORKING AHEAD: Allowed to cool completely and stored in an air-tight container, chips for snacking are okay for several days after they're made. But just-made chips are heads-and-shoulders above chips made even, say, 2 hours before. For *chilaquiles,* they can be made a week or so ahead.

VARIATION: *Tostadas:* To make these flat crispy disks, fry or bake whole tortillas as directed above.

Questions and Answers from Our Testing

What tortillas make the best chips for *chilaquiles*? After making chips from a wide variety of corn tortillas, we discovered that there are two qualities to consider: the thickness and the density of the tortillas. The good news is that most corn tortillas you can buy (or any that you make) will work. However, thicker ones and denser ones (those made from coarser-ground corn) are best. To learn if your tortillas are as thick as my favorites, weigh them: A dozen 6-inch corn tortillas that are thick enough for this preparation should weigh 10 ounces. Though I'm not wild about the widely distributed Azteca brand corn tortillas, they make good-textured *chilaquiles*. If your tortillas are moist, let them dry out in a single layer before frying, to prevent oil absorption. Flour tortillas aren't an option here, since they produce a glutinous mass if made into *chilaquiles*.

Do store-bought chips make good *chilaquiles*? Yes, if they are thick ones (thicker than any of the nationally distributed brands). Typical thin tortilla chips turn into mushy *chilaquiles*. The only chips that I really like from my local groceries look homemade—like home-fried tortilla chips—and are made by a local Mexican-owned tortilla factory. Volume measurements of chips are difficult; it's best to weigh them.

Are *chilaquiles* made from baked chips as good as those made from fried chips? *Chilaquiles* can be made with either baked or fried chips. The denser and thicker the tortillas, the better luck you'll have when you choose to bake the tortillas.

What is the best proportion of sauce to tortillas? The trick to perfect *chilaquiles* is having the right amount of brothy sauce for your tortillas to absorb, leaving enough to pool a little when the *chilaquiles* are spooned onto the plate. If you follow our recipes carefully, you'll reap the benefit of our many tests. Baked *chilaquiles* that are not served right away will have a more compact texture. But they're still excellent.

What is the best way to cook *chilaquiles*? After making thousands of orders of simmered *chilaquiles* in our restaurant, I made a discovery: If you don't simmer the *chilaquiles* after adding the chips, they'll have a beautiful, even texture. Here is my foolproof method: Bring the sauce to a boil once you've added the chips, *turn off the heat* and let the mixture stand, covered, for a few minutes. There's no bubbling to break up the chips.

Refinements: *Tomatoes*: Though I like to cook with fresh ingredients as much as possible, *chilaquiles* made with canned tomatoes are almost indistinguishable from those made from fresh ripe ones. Canned whole round tomatoes yield *chilaquiles* with a more Mexican texture than canned plum tomatoes do. *Doubling the stove-top* chilaquiles *recipe*: If you want to double the recipe for stove-top *chilaquiles*, you'll need to use a larger (7- to 8-quart) pot, to ensure even cooking.

Soups, Stews and Sides

Mexican Chicken Soup

The singsong, clamoring chant of *fonda* cooks in Mexico suffuses the pungent market air like the sound of crickets and cicadas on a warm summer evening. "*Hay caldo de pollo, caldo de res, albóndigas, mole.*" There's chicken soup and beef soup, meatballs and *mole*. And with their determined tones, these menu cantors are inviting — exhorting— you to pull up a stool or chair and let them set before you a big, steaming bowl of their best fare.

Chicken soup fills a great many of those bowls, because, as in almost every culture, chicken soup brings you back home—even if just in spirit—for reviving sustenance that simply tastes wonderful. It brings to mind the fact that in most Mexican homes a pot of simmering golden liquid, chicken bobbing about in it, anchors one part of the kitchen. The mint-perfumed broth, with a few cubes of vegetables added, can open the traditional multicourse midday repast (*comida*), the chicken itself following as part of the main dish. Or, late in the day, an assemblage of broth, chicken and rustic slabs or slices of vegetables can be a one-dish supper (*cena*). Wherever the simple broth finds its presentation, there are four traditional last-minute brighteners that make it Mexican: fresh-squeezed lime, fiery green chile, juicy white onion and aromatic cilantro.

Soup bowls run big in Mexico, and meal-in-a-bowl soups explain why. A simple meal of soup is as typical there as a sandwich is here. And, as with basic sandwiches, everyday soups like *caldo de pollo* rarely find their way into classic cookbooks in Mexico. It seems everyone knows how to make them.

Nowadays a pot of homemade chicken soup has become an occasion in many of our busy homes. So we may need to be reminded how to make this most elemental dish—this dish that dates back to the beginning of time, certainly to pre-Columbian times, when long-simmering fowl in hand-formed earthenware pots defined True Flavor.

We start with a good meaty chicken. And if we want authentic Mexican flavor, it should be free-range (which develops the right chew and richness) and have been fed marigold petals to turn its skin (and, consequently, the broth) the color of the setting sun. Then the herbs, the *hierbas de olor*—bundled bunches of thyme, marjoram and bay—infuse their aroma. A little white onion, garlic and carrots complete the simple, uncomplicated flavors that never fail to satisfy. Potatoes and corn add substance. And other vegetables add character, whether the sweetness of tomato or the fresh greenness of chayote and green beans.

A dish I find as compellingly imperative as traditional chicken soup is our contemporary Spicy Grilled Chicken Soup. The chicken is first marinated in spicy green chiles, then grilled to a smoky crispy-crustiness and finally nestled in that chicken broth studded with beautiful fresh vegetables. Just the dish for warm weather, after working in the garden or shopping at a farmers' market.

If you're cooking in Mexico or live near a great produce market or have access to a garden of squash plants, think of Mexican chicken soup with golden shreds of fresh squash blossoms. They're beautiful and, yes, a touch exotic. Delicately flavored as they are, squash blossoms are easy to love.

TRADITIONAL BENCHMARK: I don't like chicken soup that's too rich, too demanding. As with good bread or good salad, the best chicken soup only comes into full consciousness when you're about halfway through the bowl. That's when the, "Oh yeah. This is really good soup!" should hit. The broth should be flavorful, but in true Mexican style, it shouldn't be concentrated, too vegetal (celery isn't a part of most Mexican broths) or bitter with too many herbs. In my favorite chicken soups, there are beautifully cooked vegetables (not mushy overdone ones), contrasting with the raw freshness of chile, lime, raw onion and cilantro.

WHEN TO THINK OF THESE RECIPES: Soup knows no season at Mexican tables. But since many Americans ascribe to the limiting winter-only soup habit, I felt a challenge to create the perfect summer soup, a contemporary Spicy Grilled Chicken Soup. Of course, traditional Meal-in-a-Bowl Ranch-Style Chicken Soup is good year round too, perfect for small, very casual gatherings. You just have to be in the mood for offering homey comfort, since there's a *"te quiero"* message in every bowl.

ADVICE FOR AMERICAN COOKS: None, really. After all, it's just chicken soup.

Meal-in-a-Bowl Ranch-Style Chicken Soup

CALDO DE POLLO RANCHERO

Serves 6 as a light main course

One 5-pound roasting chicken, cut up (see page 144 for details;
    see Questions and Answers, page 149, for other chicken choices),
    neck, back and wings reserved
Salt
4 garlic cloves, peeled and finely chopped
1 medium white onion, finely chopped
3 bay leaves
$^1/_2$ teaspoon EACH dried marjoram and thyme (or a rounded
    teaspoon EACH if you have fresh herbs)
1 pound (2 medium-large round or 6 to 8 plum) ripe but firm
    tomatoes, cut into $^1/_2$-inch cubes
    OR 1 pound (2 medium) chayote, peeled (if you wish),
    pitted and cut into $^1/_2$-inch cubes
2 sprigs fresh mint
2 to 3 medium carrots, peeled and cut into $^1/_2$-inch
    cubes
8 small (about 1 pound) boiling potatoes (such as
    red-skins), scrubbed and halved
2 large ears corn, husked and cut across the cob into
    1-inch sections
1 cup trimmed green beans, cut into $^1/_2$-inch pieces and
    steamed until barely tender (optional)
3 to 4 fresh jalapeño chiles, stemmed, seeded and finely chopped
$^1/_2$ cup chopped fresh cilantro
2 limes, cut into wedges

TRADITIONAL

1. THE CHICKEN AND BASIC BROTH. Measure 4 quarts of water into a soup pot (an 8-quart pot works best here). Add the chicken back, neck and wings along with 2 teaspoons salt. Bring to a boil, then reduce the heat to maintain a gentle

simmer. Skim off the grayish foam that rises during the next couple of minutes. Add the garlic, *half* of the onion, the bay leaves, marjoram and thyme and simmer gently, uncovered, for about 1 hour. Add the legs and thighs and simmer for 10 minutes, then add the breast pieces. When the broth returns to a simmer, cover the pot and turn off the heat. Let stand for 30 minutes.

Transfer the legs and thighs to a plate. Cut the two breast pieces crosswise in half and add to the plate. Remove and discard the back, neck and wings. Spoon off all the fat that has risen to the top of the broth.

2. COOKING THE VEGETABLES. Add the tomatoes or chayote to the pot along with the mint, carrots and potatoes. Partially cover and simmer for 20 to 25 minutes, until the potatoes are tender but firm. Taste the soup and season it with salt, usually about a generous teaspoon.

3. FINISHING AND SERVING THE SOUP. Just before you're ready to serve, add the corn, optional green beans and cooked chicken to the pot. Simmer gently for 5 to 10 minutes to warm everything through, and you're ready to serve.

Ladle a portion of the soup into each of six warm large wide soup bowls, making sure each has 1 or 2 pieces of chicken and a little of each vegetable. Scoop the remaining onion into a small bowl and set on the table along with bowls of the chopped chiles, chopped cilantro and lime wedges, for guests to sprinkle on or squeeze in to their liking. Guests will need a knife and fork for the chicken.

WORKING AHEAD: Preparing the broth and cooking the chicken can be completed a day or so ahead. Refrigerate the broth and chicken pieces separately. (It'll be easier to degrease the broth if you chill it.) Flavoring the broth and finishing the soup should be done shortly before serving.

Caldo de Pollo con Flores de Calabaza (Squash Blossom Chicken Soup)

This is easy to make if squash blossoms are available. Simply gather 18 to 24 blossoms. Clean off the spiky little green sepals on the exterior of the base of the flowers, then cut off the stems (leave the bulbous base intact). Dislodge the fuzzy golden stamen that sticks up inside each flower; discard. You can cut the flowers into $1/2$-inch slices either crosswise or lengthwise (lengthwise shows off the petals better) or leave them whole. Add to the hot soup 1 minute before ladling it into the bowls. To accentuate the lovely blossoms, you may want to cut the kernels from the corncobs (rather than cooking the corn, cob and all) and chop the potatoes into smaller pieces.

HOW TO CUT A CHICKEN INTO SERVING PIECES

With a large knife or cleaver, cut through the skin between one leg and the body, then pry the leg away from the body, exposing the white hip joint where leg and body join. Cut through the joint, freeing the leg-thigh section, then cut through the joint where leg meets the thigh. Repeat on the other side.

With kitchen shears (or your knife or cleaver), cut down through the small rib bones on each side of the backbone. Set the back aside to use in making broth.

Pry each of the wings away from the breast and cut through the joints where they attach to the body; set them aside with the back. With the breast section skin side up, open out the sides so that you can press the center firmly down, nearly flattening it and loosening the breastbone. Use your knife or cleaver to cut straight down through the breast following the line of the breastbone, splitting the breast in two (this takes a sharp knife and a little strength).

SPICY GRILLED CHICKEN SOUP WITH SUMMER VEGETABLES
(PAGE 146)

Spicy Grilled Chicken Soup with summer vegetables

CALDO DE POLLO ASADO CON VERDURAS
DE LA HUERTA

Serves 4 as a light main course

Fresh hot green chiles to taste (roughly 4 serranos or 2 jalapeños),
    stemmed
2 tablespoons olive oil, preferably extra-virgin, plus a little
    to brush on the corn
Juice of 1 lime
Salt
$^1/_2$ teaspoon black pepper, preferably freshly ground
8 medium (2 pounds total) bone-in chicken thighs
3 quarts good chicken broth, store-bought or homemade (page 148)
3 garlic cloves, peeled and roughly chopped
1 small white onion, chopped
1 pound (2 medium-large round or 6 to 8 plum) ripe tomatoes,
    cut into small cubes
4 sprigs fresh mint
2 large ears corn, husked
6 young carrots, peeled and cut into small cubes
    OR 12 baby carrots, peeled
12 very small (about 12 ounces total) new potatoes, scrubbed
    and quartered
2 limes, cut into wedges, for garnish

CONTEMPORARY

1. SEASONING THE CHICKEN. Very finely chop the chiles, seeds and all, with a knife or a food processor (a small one works best). In a small bowl, combine the chiles with the olive oil, lime juice, $^1/_2$ teaspoon salt and the pepper. Lay out the chicken thighs in a baking dish and smear the chile mixture over both sides; cover and refrigerate. (The chicken can marinate overnight—it'll just get spicier.)

2. THE BROTH. In a medium-large (6-quart) pot, combine the broth, garlic, onion,

half of the tomatoes and *1 mint sprig*. Bring to a boil, then reduce the heat so that the liquid simmers briskly and let cook, reducing and reducing, until it reaches two-thirds of its original volume (2 quarts), about 30 minutes. Strain, discard the solids and return the broth to the pan.

3. PREPARING THE GRILL. Heat a gas grill to medium-high or light a charcoal fire and let it burn just until the coals are covered with gray ash and very hot. Either turn the burner(s) in the center of the grill off or bank the coals to the sides of the grill for indirect cooking. Set the cooking grate in place, cover the grill and let the grate heat up, 5 minutes or so.

4. GRILLING THE CHICKEN AND FINISHING THE SOUP. When the grill is ready, lay the chicken skin side up in the center of the grill (not over direct heat). Cover and cook for about 25 minutes, until the chicken is richly browned, the juices run clear and the meat easily separates from the bone. After the chicken has cooked for 20 minutes, lightly brush the corn with oil, sprinkle it with salt and lay it directly over the heat. Grill, turning it regularly, until richly golden and tender, about 5 minutes or so.

   While the chicken is cooking, bring the broth to a boil over high heat and add the carrots, potatoes and remaining tomatoes. Regulate the heat so that the broth simmers gently until the carrots and potatoes are tender, about 15 minutes. Taste and season with salt if necessary.

   When the chicken is ready, ladle a portion of the broth and vegetables into each each of four warm soup bowls. Set 2 thighs in each bowl. Standing the corn on end and holding it with a pair of tongs (it's hot!), use a sharp knife to cut the kernels from the cobs. Sprinkle the corn over each bowl, garnish with a few leaves of mint and you're ready for a good dinner. Pass the lime wedges for each guest to squeeze on to his or her liking.

WORKING AHEAD: The broth can be made several days ahead and stored in the refrigerator well covered. If you like really spicy food, you can marinate the chicken a day ahead, but grill it and the corn shortly before serving. Both chicken and corn will hold fine for an hour in a low oven, covered with foil.

CALDO DE POLLO BÁSICO • BASIC CHICKEN BROTH

Chicken broth in Mexico is typically gentle in flavor and used to weave in a light richness. You can add carrots if you wish—some Mexican cooks even add celery—though a simple, chickeny broth is favored by most. Which explains the quantity of chicken in the following recipe.

Makes about 2 quarts

1 medium 3¹/₂-pound chicken, preferably a good-tasting free-range one,
    cut into pieces
    OR 3 pounds chicken wings or bones (such as necks or carcasses)
1 medium white onion, sliced
3 to 4 garlic cloves, peeled and halved
3 to 4 bay leaves (use the skinny Mexican bay laurel leaves for
    authentic flavor)
2 to 3 sprigs EACH fresh marjoram and thyme
    OR a generous ¹/₂ teaspoon EACH dried marjoram and thyme

In a medium (6-quart) soup pot, combine the chicken, onion, garlic, bay, marjoram and thyme. Add 4 quarts of water, set over medium-high heat and let come to a simmer. Skim off the grayish foam that rises during the first few minutes of simmering, then partially cover and reduce the heat to keep the liquid at a very gentle simmer. If using a cut-up whole chicken, cook for 45 minutes. Remove the chicken pieces, let cool until handleable and pull the meat from the bone (reserve it for enchiladas or the like); return the bones to the simmering broth for another hour. If using chicken wings or bones, let simmer for 2 hours.

Strain through a fine-mesh strainer and discard the solids. Let the broth rest long enough for the fat to rise to the top, then spoon it off. Covered and refrigerated, the broth will keep for several days in the refrigerator. It freezes beautifully.

QUESTIONS AND ANSWERS FROM OUR TESTING

WHAT IS THE BEST, MOST EASILY AVAILABLE CHICKEN FOR SOUP? As a general rule, larger chickens have more flavor than smaller ones, and they're less tender—perfect for simmering. Since the old stewing chickens (a.k.a. stewing hens or boiling fowl) seem to be less and less available these days, we chose to make our *caldo de pollo* from the other large chicken in the market—the roasting chicken. Roasters are younger (8 to 10 months old), more tender and a little fattier than stewing chickens, so they cook in less time. For the roaster, we've specified a longer cooking time for legs and thighs than for breasts to ensure juicy meat. In Mexico, market stewing chickens have a more developed (read: gamy) taste than our stewing chickens, and their muscles are so well exercised that they need to bubble around in the pot for a long time.

HOW CAN YOU GET THE BEST BALANCE OF TEXTURE AND FLAVOR FROM THE VEGETABLES FOR TRADITIONAL CHICKEN SOUP? There's always a trade-off in soup making: If you simmer vegetables long enough for them to give up their flavor into the broth, they become mushy. After several tests, we decided that we liked adding half the onions (the other half is used raw as a garnish) to the garlicky, herby broth and simmering them until they were spent. Then in go the rest of the vegetables at the right time to ensure they're cooked perfectly in the now-richly flavored broth. The tomatoes for this soup should be red-ripe but firm enough to dice.

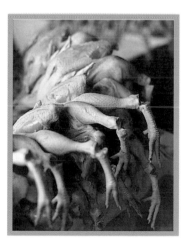

In Mexico they do it a little differently

Tortilla Soup

 Yesterday's bread, first crisped to give new life, then set adrift in nourishing broth, softening as it soaks in the goodness—that's a recipe for soup of lasting memory. And tortilla soup is all of that. Like French onion soup, the world's most famous bread-topped potage, the Mexican "bread" soup is classic and timeless.

The daily bread of Mexico, the corn tortilla, is a bread so immediate and fresh that (just like real French bread) it goes stale quickly. And that reality has given rise to myriad creative uses for "leftovers," from enchiladas to casseroles to dumplings. In soup, the stale tortillas find a perfect Mexican expression: toasty, corny, crisp-but-softening tortilla strips afloat in comforting tomato-laced broth, jazzed, as you might expect, with flavor bursts and textural contrasts.

Elemental though it is (I suspect that tortillas in broth have been eaten since time immemorial), Tortilla Soup has become a Dish, worthy of animated argument—the proper choice and handling of the dried chile, the quantity of tomato, the indispensability of *epazote*. It's at once restaurant fare and home fare—the kind of dish that can be dolled up while staying true to its down-to-earth roots.

So it appeals to all kinds of cooks, from those looking for a simple repast to those with a flair for the dramatic. In the classic recipe below, you can place the add-ins—the cheese, avocado and chile—in the bottom of warm wide soup bowls, ladle the fragrant soup over them and christen with a climactic tangle of crispy tortilla strips and crumbled toasted chile. Or simply set out a platter of all that delicious goodness and invite your guests to festoon their own steaming bowls.

But tradition guides my contemporary tortilla soup, too. The toasted pasilla chile flavor gives way to the smokiness of chipotle and the fresh, tangy *queso fresco* becomes goat cheese. Watercress and avocado deliver the fresh herbal vitality, while earthy mushrooms anchor all the flavors to culinary bedrock.

TRADITIONAL BENCHMARK: My favorite tortilla soup dances salsa in the bowl. While swaying with deep, sweet tones, it surprises with colorful flourishes. It gently slides its hand around your waist, then does an unexpected turn with the muscle of herby *epazote*.

It tickles you with tangy fresh lime, then nudges you gently with fresh cheese and creamy avocado. And then comes the whirlwind of turns—crumbled bits of toasted black-red pasilla chile exploding with delectable energy, revealing just how thrilling life can be.

WHEN TO THINK OF THESE RECIPES: A small bowl of tortilla soup is a dramatic way to begin a meal, but the soup is also satisfying enough to be the main attraction.

ADVICE FOR AMERICAN COOKS: This is one of the easiest classic Mexican dishes for American cooks—if you factor out the dried pasilla chile and *epazote*. Though both could be left out, the soup would lack that inimitable Mexican stamp. Some toasted dried chile is a must in my opinion—in western Mexico, a good number of cooks use dried ancho chile, which is more readily available in the United States than pasilla. *Epazote* adds a rustic, Mexican flavor, but you'll still like the soup made without it.

Fresh-baked
corn tortillas,
sold by the kilo

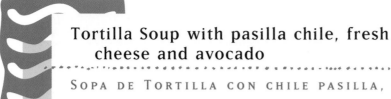

Tortilla Soup with pasilla chile, fresh cheese and avocado

SOPA DE TORTILLA CON CHILE PASILLA,
QUESO FRESCO Y AGUACATE

Serves 6 as a first course, 4 as a light main dish

6 corn tortillas
Vegetable oil to a depth of $^1/_2$ inch for frying
4 garlic cloves, peeled and left whole
1 small white onion, sliced
2 dried pasilla chiles (or 1 dried ancho), stemmed, seeded and
    torn into several flat pieces
One 15-ounce can good-quality whole tomatoes in juice, drained
    OR 12 ounces (2 medium-small round or 4 to 6 plum)
    ripe tomatoes, cored and roughly chopped
6 cups good chicken broth, store-bought or homemade (page 148)
1 large sprig fresh epazote, if you have it
Salt
6 ounces Mexican queso fresco or other crumbly
    fresh cheese, such as salted, pressed farmer's cheese or
    feta, cut into $^1/_2$-inch cubes
    OR 6 ounces Mexican melting cheese (Chihuahua,
    quesillo, asadero, or the like) or Monterey Jack, brick or
    mild cheddar, shredded (you'll have about $1^1/_2$ cups)
1 large ripe avocado, peeled, pitted and cut into $^1/_2$-inch cubes
1 large lime, cut into wedges

1. FRYING THE TORTILLAS. Cut the tortillas in half, then cut crosswise into $^1/_4$-inch strips. In a medium-large (4-quart) saucepan, heat $^1/_2$ inch of oil over medium to 350°F. (Using a thermometer is most accurate, but there are other reliable clues: The oil releases that "hot oil" aroma and its surface begins shimmering. Without a thermometer, test the edge of a tortilla strip to ensure that it sizzles vigorously. Remember, smoking oil is dangerously overheated and will give the tortilla strips

a bad taste.) Add half the tortilla strips. Stir around in the oil nearly constantly until they are golden brown and crispy. With a slotted spoon, scoop them out and drain on paper towels. Repeat with the remaining tortillas.

2. OTHER PRELIMINARIES. Pour off all but a thin coating of hot oil from the saucepan and return to the heat. Add the garlic and onion to the pan and cook, stirring regularly, until golden, about 7 minutes. Use the slotted spoon to scoop out the garlic and onion, pressing them against the side of the pan to leave behind as much oil as possible, and transfer the garlic and onion to a blender or food processor.

   Add the chile pieces to the hot pan. Turn quickly as they fry, toast and release a delicious aroma—about 30 seconds in all. Too much frying/toasting will make them bitter. Remove and drain on paper towels. Set the pan aside.

3. THE BROTH. Add the tomatoes to the blender containing the garlic and onion and process to a smooth puree. (If using fresh tomatoes, strain the puree to get rid of the pieces of tomato skin.) Set the saucepan over medium-high heat. When hot, add the puree and stir nearly constantly until it has thickened to the consistency of tomato paste, about 10 minutes. Add the broth and *epazote* and bring to a boil, then partially cover and gently simmer over medium to medium-low heat for 30 minutes. Taste and season with salt, usually $\frac{1}{2}$ teaspoon, depending on the saltiness of your broth.

4. SERVING THE SOUP. Divide the cheese and avocado among the soup bowls. Ladle a portion of the broth into each bowl, top with a portion of the tortilla strips and crumble on a little toasted chile. Carry these satisfying bowls of soup to the table and offer your guests wedges of lime to squeeze in to their liking.

WORKING AHEAD: Steps 2 and 3 can be completed several days ahead (which means you'll have the soup virtually ready to serve). Store the soup in the refrigerator, covered. The tortilla strips (Step 1) will begin to taste stale if they're not served the day fried.

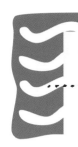

Mushroom-Studded Tortilla Soup with chipotle chiles and goat cheese

SOPA DE TORTILLA Y HONGOS CON CHILE CHIPOTLE
Y QUESO DE CABRA

Serves 6 as a first course, 4 as a casual main dish

1 ½ tablespoons vegetable oil or rich-tasting pork lard, plus
    a little oil to spray or brush on the tortillas
4 garlic cloves, peeled and left whole
1 small white onion, sliced
One 15-ounce can good-quality whole tomatoes in juice, drained
    OR 12 ounces (2 medium-small round or 4 to 6 plum) ripe
    tomatoes, cored and roughly chopped
6 cups good chicken broth, store-bought or homemade (page 148)
8 ounces full-flavored mushrooms (I love shiitakes here), stemmed
    (discard woody stems or finely chop them) and sliced ¼ inch
    thick (you'll have about 2 generous cups slices)
    OR 1 ½ ounces dried shiitake, chanterelle or porcini
    mushrooms, soaked in hot water for 30 minutes, then
    drained and sliced ¼ inch thick
Salt
6 corn tortillas
2 to 3 canned chipotle chiles en adobo, *removed from the
    canning sauce*
4 ounces goat cheese, cut or broken apart into roughly
    ½-inch cubes
1 large ripe avocado, peeled, pitted and cut into ½-inch cubes
1 large bunch watercress, leaves only

CONTEMPORARY

I. THE SOUP. In a medium-large (4-quart) saucepan, heat the oil or lard over
    medium. Add the garlic and onion and cook, stirring regularly, until golden,
    about 7 minutes. Use a slotted spoon to scoop up the garlic and onion, pressing
    them against the side of the pan to leave behind as much oil as possible and

transfer to a food processor or blender; set the pan aside. Add the tomatoes to the garlic and onion and process to a smooth puree.

Set the saucepan over medium-high heat. When hot, add the puree and stir nearly constantly until it has thickened to the consistency of tomato paste, about 10 minutes. Add the broth and sliced mushrooms and bring to a boil, then partially cover and gently simmer over medium to medium-low heat for 30 minutes. Taste and season with salt, usually ½ teaspoon, depending on the saltiness of your broth.

2. TOASTING THE TORTILLAS. Heat the oven to 375°F. Cut the tortillas in half, then cut crosswise into ¼-inch strips. Spread out the tortilla strips in a single layer on a baking sheet and spray or lightly brush with oil and toss to coat evenly. Set in the oven and bake, stirring around every couple of minutes or so, until lightly browned and crispy, about 8 minutes.

3. SERVING THE SOUP. Cut open the chipotle chiles and scrape out their seeds. Cut the chiles into thin strips. In each soup bowl, place a portion of the cheese and cubed avocado, a generous sprinkling of the watercress leaves and a few strips of chipotle. Ladle the broth into the bowls, top each with a little handful of crispy tortilla strips and you're ready to eat.

WORKING AHEAD: Step 1 can be done several days in advance—in fact, the soup gets better with a day or two for the flavors to mingle. Store made-ahead soup in the refrigerator, covered. Complete Steps 2 and 3 shortly before serving.

Questions and Answers from Our Testing

What kind of tortilla is best for frying into the strips for the soup?
Though I wouldn't hesitate to make tortilla soup with practically any corn tortilla, my first choice for taste and texture is a tortilla that's thickish and slightly dry. Crispy strips made from that kind of tortilla soften slowly in the soup. Flour tortillas are not an option here, since they would turn into a mushy mass.

Is there an alternative to frying the tortillas? Frying tortilla strips in too little oil is always disappointing; they never crisp evenly and always seem grease-soaked. So I've called for 1/2 inch of oil to do the task right. There are times, however, when classic tortilla soup beckons but the smell of hot oil discourages. So we tried using lightly oiled, oven-baked tortilla strips and were very pleased with the outcome. (Step 2 of the contemporary tortilla soup recipe describes the process.) Another alternative is to use store-bought thick tortilla chips, slightly broken up.

What is the best way to prepare the dried chile? For this traditional soup garnish, you can dry-toast the chile on a dry griddle or in a skillet, but I prefer the richer, darker taste and more crumbly texture that come from oil-toasting.

What strength of broth makes a soup with the most balanced flavor?
The flavor of homemade chicken broth really soars here. In testing, we used a typical Mexican-style broth (page 148), because it is lighter than its European counterpart. Most European-style stock tips the flavor scale toward meat rather than keeping it in the vegetable/chile realm, and that misses the point of this soup. We also tested the recipes with canned chicken broth and found its flavor in the soup easily acceptable. We prefer the low-sodium variety because it gives us control over the final flavor.

Mexican Seafood Stew

The weather is hot as I write this, the air thick and moist, almost suffocating. My only relief comes from a gentle ameliorating coolness radiating from the tile-topped table here in this open-air restaurant on the Veracruz shore. Odd as it may seem given my circumstances, the only dish that appeals is a brothy bowl of *caldo de mariscos* (Mexican seafood stew), the primary seasoning of which seems to be the tangy sea air. Whether I'm in a waterfront restaurant in Veracruz or in landlocked Mexico City or Chicago, I invariably have the same experience with seafood stew. It's a dish that always speaks the same language, the language of life's other dimension, the language of the sea.

Classic Mexican seafood stew is a medley of fresh seafood floating in tomato-flavored broth. Plain as that may sound, there is nothing pedestrian about it. I revel in the transparent energy that jumps out of the bowl. At Chicago's Maxwell Street Market on Sundays, or at one of the many *coctelerías* (seafood cocktail shops) that dot Mexican city streets or at mountainous Oaxaca City's Neptuno restaurant (where you're served a cup of this stew as you're seated), *caldo de mariscos* welcomes with an ingenuous, lively grace.

Since Mexican soups and stews generally do not showcase complex stocks (they let chiles and other vegetables sing with clear purity), for this traditional seafood stew, the cook's work is quite simple. Simple until you taste what's ladled into the bowl: The flavors of long-simmered squid, finfish and shellfish knit together in the punchy, brothy, herb-infused liquid to create a memorable mouthful. My contemporary recipe here doesn't have the benefit of simmered squid or the full variety of seafood, so I started that recipe with a light chicken broth for body. Given dimension with tomato and *epazote*, the chicken broth creates a harmonious and richly flavored soup base to welcome grilled shrimp. Both recipes speak of an elegant economy of time and ingredients.

TRADITIONAL BENCHMARK: Though most of the seafood stews I remember fondly are ones I've eaten seaside, I have no intention of baiting you in these recipes with fabulous dishes you can't possibly reproduce yourself. The truth of the matter is, you *can* make great seafood stew practically anywhere. My benchmark is a stew with a simple broth that echoes piscine flavors—while taking them to another level. It is rich, but not thick or domineering. And it is filled with a variety of tastes and textures, from flaky fish to meaty shrimp and tender squid or octopus. I always like to include, too, cubes of earthy potato for contrast. And since it's Mexican, the stew needs a little spiciness, the sweet-tart balance of good tomatoes and the self-confidence of herbs like *epazote* (not the mellowness of the more European marjoram, thyme and bay).

WHEN TO THINK OF THESE RECIPES: Of all the truly special-occasion dishes I know, seafood stew is one of the easiest, most impressive ways to celebrate. It can be economical too: In testing, we bought all the ingredients from a well-stocked grocery store for under $20. To flesh out the meal, make some *sopes* (page 33) to get the party started, then serve big steaming bowls of the stew with warm tortillas or crusty French bread (bread is customary in Mexico with this dish). Toss a big salad of beautiful young lettuces with a good vinaigrette to accompany or follow the stew, then end with a big cake, if that's what's called for.

ADVICE FOR AMERICAN COOKS: Since procuring decent seafood has long been a challenge for most American cooks, I'm happy to report that more and more cities now have good fish markets, and dependable seafood in good grocery stores is becoming more common. Here is another hint: Look in Asian markets. Their clientele is very demanding when it comes to the fruits of the sea.

Dishing up soup

Mexican Seafood Stew

CALDO DE MARISCOS

Serves 6 generously as a main course

1 pound cleaned squid or 1¹/₂ pounds uncleaned

1 large white onion, sliced

6 garlic cloves, peeled and roughly chopped

3 bay leaves

1¹/₂ pounds (3 medium-large round or 9 to 12 plum) ripe tomatoes,
   roughly chopped
   OR one 28-ounce can good-quality whole tomatoes in juice, drained

2 tablespoons olive oil, preferably extra-virgin

1 to 2 large sprigs fresh epazote (or a small handful of
   fresh cilantro or parsley sprigs, if no epazote is at hand)

2 to 3 dried árbol chiles, stemmed, seeded and broken into small pieces

Salt

6 medium (about 1¹/₂ pounds) boiling potatoes (such as
   red-skins), scrubbed and quartered

1 pound (about 24) medium-large shrimp

1 pound boneless, skinless fish fillets (for best flavor and nice
   large flakes of fish in the stew, choose meaty or large-flake
   fish such as grouper, snapper, halibut, catfish, sea bass
   or the like), cut into 1-inch cubes

2 to 3 limes, cut into wedges

TRADITIONAL

1. THE SQUID AND BROTH. If the squid is frozen, defrost it in the refrigerator (allow 24 hours) or under dribbling cold water (it'll take about 45 minutes). If the squid has not been cleaned, clean each one as follows: Grasp the head/tentacles firmly in one hand, the body in the other, and gently but firmly pull the two sections apart. The innards, including the ink sac, will come out connected to the head. Cut the head away and discard everything above the point where the tentacles come together. In the body cavity, feel for the hard quill. Grasp the body firmly as you pull it out. Rinse the body cavity and tentacles well. Cut the bodies into 1-inch sections and cut the tentacles in half if they are large.

Place the squid in a medium (4- to 5-quart) pot (preferably a Dutch oven or Mexican *cazuela*), measure in 2 quarts of water and add *half* of the onion and *half* of the garlic. Add the bay leaves and bring to a simmer, then partially cover the pot and reduce the heat to keep the liquid at a very gentle roll. Cook until the squid is thoroughly tender, about 25 minutes. Strain, reserving the solids (discard the bay leaves). Measure the liquid: You should have about 6 cups (if you have too little, add water; if too much, either pour off the excess or quickly boil the whole thing down to 6 cups). Wipe out the pot and set aside.

2. THE FLAVORED STEW BASE. In a blender or food processor, combine the remaining onion and garlic with the tomatoes and process to a smooth puree. Add the oil to the pot and heat over medium-high. When hot enough to make a drop of the puree sizzle sharply, add it all at once and stir continually until darker in color and cooked down to the consistency of tomato paste, 10 to 12 minutes. Stir in the squid broth, *epazote* (or its stand-in) and chiles. Taste and season generously with salt, usually about 1½ teaspoons.

Add the potatoes, partially cover the pot and simmer over medium to medium-low heat until the potatoes are tender, about 15 minutes.

3. FINISHING THE STEW. While the potatoes are cooking, peel the shrimp, leaving their final joint and tails intact. Devein each shrimp by making a shallow incision down the back and scraping out the dark (usually) vein-like intestinal tract.

When the potatoes are tender, raise the heat a little under the pot and add the fish cubes. Partially cover the pot, and when the broth returns to a gentle boil, set the timer for 3 minutes. When the timer rings, uncover the pot and add the squid (and any onions and garlic clinging to them) and shrimp. Set the lid in place, turn off the heat and let stand for 3 to 4 minutes to gently finish the cooking. (If the shrimp are large and refrigerator-cold, let cook for 1 minute before turning off the heat.) I like the rustic nature of the *epazote* floating in the soup; if you don't, fish it out.

Ladle the soup into deep bowls, and you're ready to present your guests with an aromatic treat, accompanied by lime wedges for each to squeeze in to his or her liking.

WORKING AHEAD: The squid and broth can be made several days in advance; refrigerate separately, covered tightly. The stew base—minus the potatoes—actually improves in flavor if made several hours (or up to a day) in advance.

Spicy Grilled Shrimp Stew

CALDO DE CAMARÓN ASADO

Serves 6 generously as a main course

1 small white onion, sliced ¼ inch thick

3 garlic cloves, peeled and roughly chopped

1½ pounds (3 medium-large round or 9 to 12 plum)
　　ripe tomatoes, roughly chopped
　　OR one 28-ounce can good-quality whole tomatoes in juice, drained

2 tablespoons olive oil, preferably extra-virgin, plus additional
　　for brushing or spraying the shrimp and vegetables

6 cups good chicken broth, store-bought or homemade (page 148)

1 to 2 large sprigs fresh epazote (or a small handful of fresh cilantro or
　　parsley sprigs, if no epazote is at hand), plus 6 sprigs for garnish

2 pounds (about 48) medium-large shrimp

12 bamboo skewers, about 7 inches long, soaked in water for
　　at least 20 minutes

Salt

About 2 tablespoons pure ground chile (buy ancho,
　　guajillo or New Mexico chile, or substitute a
　　little cayenne

3 medium (about 1½ pounds) sweet potatoes (I especially
　　like the purple-skinned Mexican sweet potatoes called
　　camotes morados), peeled and sliced ½ inch thick
　　OR 3 medium chayotes (about 2 pounds), halved, pits removed
　　and sliced ½ inch thick
　　OR 3 large (about 1½ pounds) Yukon Gold potatoes, scrubbed
　　and sliced ½ inch thick

CONTEMPORARY

1. THE FLAVORED STEW BASE. In a blender or food processor, combine the onion and garlic with the tomatoes and process to a smooth puree.

　　In a medium (4- to 5-quart) pot (preferably a Dutch oven or Mexican *cazuela*), heat the oil over medium-high. When hot enough to make a drop of the puree sizzle sharply, add it all at once and stir continually until darker in color and cooked down to the consistency of tomato paste, 10 to 12 minutes. Stir in the broth and *epazote* (or its stand-in), partially cover and simmer over medium-low heat for about 30 minutes.

2. PREPARING THE SHRIMP. While the broth is simmering, peel the shrimp, leaving their final joint and tails intact. Devein each shrimp by making a shallow incision down the back and scraping out the dark (usually) vein-like intestinal tract. Impale the shrimp on the skewers (about 4 on each), being careful not to bunch them too tightly. Lay them out flat on a tray and sprinkle them generously on both sides with salt and ground chile.

3. FINISHING THE DISH. Heat a gas grill to medium or light a charcoal fire and let it burn until the coals are covered with gray ash and medium-hot. Set the cooking grate in place, cover the grill and let the grate heat up, 5 minutes or so. Taste the broth and season it with salt, usually about ¾ teaspoon; keep warm, covered, over low heat.

Generously brush or spray the sliced sweet potato, chayote or potato with olive oil, sprinkle both sides of each piece with salt and grill, turning occasionally, until soft through, 10 to 15 minutes. Divide among six large soup bowls.

Lightly brush or spray the shrimp with olive oil and lay on the grill. Cook until just done through, 2 to 3 minutes per side.

Ladle the steaming broth over the vegetables in each soup bowl. Lay 2 skewers of shrimp in each bowl (they'll rise dramatically from the broth, toward the edge of the bowls). Garnish each with an herb sprig and you're ready to present this dramatic, lusty soup to your guests.

WORKING AHEAD: The flavored stew base is excellent when made hours—even a day or two—in advance; just before serving, reheat it and adjust the seasonings and the consistency by thinning it with broth if necessary. The vegetables and shrimp should be grilled just before serving.

Very fresh Gulf shrimp, heads still on

QUESTIONS AND ANSWERS FROM OUR TESTING

WHAT IS THE SIMPLEST BROTH YOU CAN MAKE TO BOTH WEAVE TOGETHER ALL THE FLAVORS AND PROVIDE RICH COMPLETENESS TO THE SOUP? Many cooks start a great seafood soup or stew with fish stock made from fish bones or heads, vegetables or herbs. That's wonderful, but not easily feasible for many American cooks, since fish bones and heads are less and less available these days at fish counters and markets. So we tested our classic recipe using chicken broth, an ingredient I've relied on for years to enrich other fish dishes. The flavor was very good, but, to my taste, the chicken broth muddied an otherwise clear flavor. However, if you simmer squid Mexican-style (that is, long enough to become thoroughly tender), it produces a sweet, slightly exotic-tasting, moderately rich broth. The color is a little odd (purplish), but that gets painted over by the addition of tomatoes. For the contemporary grilled-shrimp version, we did use chicken broth, which gave the right richness and body for the bolder flavor of the grill.

WHAT IS THE BEST, MOST EASILY AVAILABLE VARIETY OF SEAFOOD FOR THE STEW? My goal here is a recipe that's useful for folks all across the United States. So I chose to rely primarily on readily available seafood that freezes well (squid and shrimp), leaving only good-quality fresh finfish to sniff out. Truth be told, occasionally I've relied on good frozen finfish when the fresh finfish options were slim.

Some guidelines for buying seafood that has been frozen: Buy it frozen rather than defrosted, so that you can judge its integrity. There should be no signs of defrosting and refreezing (irregular ice crystals around the outside) or freezer burn (dried-out edges). Once defrosted, there should be no off or iodine odors.

Fresh finfish that glistens and has a translucency is the freshest; it should have no odor other than that of the sea. Fish with small flakes (like sole or flounder) will fall apart in the stew, so I suggest large-flake fish. Strong-flavored fish like kingfish, mackerel, bluefish and salmon would dominate the otherwise delicious balance here, so I veer away from them.

WHAT IS THE RIGHT BALANCE OF INGREDIENTS? The richest seafood soups and stews are created with a variety of seafood. We chose the squid for its soft, toothsome texture and slightly sweet, earthy flavor; the shrimp for its crispness and sweet burst of flavor; and the finfish for its lovely soft flakiness and definitive saltwater taste. To me, seafood stew is too much of one thing without the grounding influence of potatoes (or other starchy vegetable) to add contrast. Tomato adds bright acidity—and sweet depth if you cook it the way we've suggested. Herbs, especially *epazote*, add a sophisticated greenish note. And chile accelerates your enjoyment—as long as you don't put too much in. Remember, the chile will taste hotter and hotter the longer it's in the soup.

Pozole (Pork and Hominy Stew)

 In its most authentic form, certainly its most rural, *pozole* is an earthy and aromatic stew, simmering in a huge cauldron over red-hot embers. Its perfume permeates homes and neighborhoods, drawing people to it, creating community.

Anyone who is acquainted with *pozole* knows that it's the intertwining aromas and textures that attract—the succulent pork and the meaty kernels of hominy cooked from dried corn, prodded awake by pungent Mexican oregano, crunchy raw radish and cabbage and piercing lime and red chile. Enjoy a big bowl of *pozole* and you ride the crest of a day-long buildup toward rib-sticking fiesta food.

Pozole, however, announces "fiesta" more casually, than, say, *mole* or tamales. Its announcement often starts with subtle signals a day ahead, at least in rural areas—the ritual dance of fire building, filling the pot, adding each ingredient and, above all, patiently pinching off the pointy nub (the germ end) of each half-cooked corn kernel ("deheading" the *nixtamal*). That takes time, but it also marks time, the movement toward a special, soulful moment. So, if you choose the kernel-by-kernel process, think of it as the Mexican cultural equivalent of hand-cranking the spit at an old-fashioned American pig roast. Few things progress more slowly than either of these, but it's that tending, that loving loitering, that builds communal anticipation.

Deheading the corn aside, *pozole* can be practical in modern America—in the hubbub of our time-starved, complex lives. It is a magnificent stew, the perfect one-dish party fare. It simmers almost unattended, nothing's very complicated and the end result just can't help but please a crowd. *Pozole* just may help us relearn the lessons of community and celebration.

TRADITIONAL BENCHMARK: The best *pozole*, like perfect Japanese noodle broth or bouillabaise, is a work of art—one that is achieved with dedication. It's simple, so the stew must start with just the right ingredients. First, there's hominy corn to give a toothsome, tender grain. Then broth that has a voluptuous texture and complex flavor that's only achieved by using meat and bones from different (some might say "less respectable") cuts. And whether your favorite is *pozole blanco* (without the chile in the broth) or *pozole rojo* (dried red chile well integrated), the best bowlfuls taste of long-simmered tradition with a healthy dose of garlic. Plus a dash of dried Mexican oregano and chopped radish, cabbage and lime added by each guest *al gusto*, with freshly fried tostadas offered for nibbling.

WHEN TO THINK OF THIS RECIPE: We *norteamericanos* typically think of warming soups and stews only in cold weather. In Mexico, the *pozole* pot goes onto the stove any time the cook needs to feed a crowd and, at the same time, let them know there's something special in the air. *Pozole* is so thoroughly woven into Mexican life that even the celebration of the week's end (or the arrival of Thursday in Guerrero) is occasion for a steaming bowl— though more and more frequently brought home from a neighborhood vendor or enjoyed at a local eatery.

ADVICE FOR AMERICAN COOKS: The right corn for *pozole* is the only significant hurdle here. My preference is to buy *nixtamal* (half-cooked hominy) from a tortilla factory, but that's not practical for most cooks. Rather than open a can of hominy, I'd look for dried American Southwestern *pozole* corn (available from specialty markets or by mail-order) as a second choice. Pork is available everywhere (though the shanks and trotters may require a special order); ancho chiles are available in well-stocked groceries, all Mexican groceries and by mail (guajillo or New Mexico chiles can be substituted); and Mexican oregano is bottled by major spice companies (read the fine print).

Left: Santo Domingo church, Oaxaca Right: Rock cal (calcium oxide) for cooking corn

Red Pork and Hominy Stew

POZOLE ROJO

Makes about 8 1/2 quarts, serving 12 generously
as a main course

2 pounds (about 5 cups) fresh or frozen nixtamal corn, well rinsed
   OR 1 1/2 pounds (4 cups) American Southwestern dried pozole
   corn (see Sources, page 361)
1 head garlic, cloves broken apart, peeled and halved
3 1/2 pounds (1 1/2 medium) pork shanks, cut into 1 1/2-inch-thick
   pieces (you'll have to ask the butcher to cut this for you)
1 1/2 pounds (2 medium) pork trotters (a.k.a. fresh pigs' feet),
   cut lengthwise in half (you'll have to ask the butcher
   to do this for you too)
1 1/2 pounds bone-in pork shoulder, cut into 3 or 4 large pieces
   (again, ask the butcher)
Salt
2 large white onions, rather finely chopped
8 medium (4 ounces total) dried ancho chiles, stemmed and seeded
3 limes, cut into wedges
6 cups thinly sliced cabbage or head lettuce (though not
   traditional, I love Napa cabbage for pozole)
15 radishes, thinly sliced
3 to 4 tablespoons dried Mexican oregano
2 tablespoons coarsely ground dried hot red chile (optional)
24 tostadas (crisp-fried corn tortillas), store-bought or
   homemade (see variation on page 137)

TRADITIONAL

I.   COOKING THE CORN. The most careful cooks like to remove the hard, pointy
     end—the germ—of each lime-treated corn kernel (*nixtamal*) so that the kernels
     will splay into a rough flower shape as they cook. A fingernail or small knife
     works well for this job, along with a lot of patience. (This step is impractical when
     using American Southwestern dried *pozole* corn.)

Measure 6 quarts of water into a large (10-quart or so) pot and add the corn (either the rinsed *nixtamal* or the dried corn) and garlic. Bring to a boil, partially cover the pot and simmer gently over medium-low heat until the corn is *thoroughly* tender—at a minimum allow 2 to 3 hours for *nixtamal*, about 5 hours for dried corn. Add water as necessary to keep the water level more or less constant. Slower, longer cooking only means better *pozole*, as evidenced by the fact that in many places in Mexico huge pots of the fragrant mixture simmer over wood fires overnight before a fiesta.

2. THE MEAT. While the corn is simmering, cook the meat. Place all the meats in another large pot, cover with 4 quarts of water, add 2 tablespoons salt and bring to a boil, skim off the grayish foam that rises during the next few minutes, then add *half* the chopped onions. Partially cover the pot and simmer over medium-low heat until all the meat is thoroughly tender, about 2 hours. Remove the meat from the broth and let cool. Or, if time allows, cool the meat in the broth for the best flavor and texture, then remove it.

    Skim the fat from the broth; you'll have 2 generous quarts broth. Pull off the meat from the pork shanks and pull the shoulder meat into large shreds. Cut the bones and knuckles out of the trotters. Discard the bones and knuckles, then chop what remains into ½-inch pieces. Add to the shredded meat (there will be about 6 cups meat in all). Cover and refrigerate if not serving within an hour.

3. SEASONING THE POZOLE. While the corn and meat are cooking, rehydrate the ancho chiles in enough hot water to cover (lay a small plate on top to keep them submerged) for about 20 minutes. Puree the chiles, liquid and all, in batches if necessary in a blender or food processor.

    When the corn is tender, press the chile mixture through a medium-mesh strainer (this removes tough chile skins) directly into the simmering liquid. Add the pork broth and 1 tablespoon salt, partially cover and simmer for 1 hour.

4. SERVING. When you're ready to serve, set out bowls of the condiments for your guests to add to their steaming, fragrant bowlfuls *al gusto*: the lime wedges, sliced cabbage or lettuce, sliced radishes, oregano and optional ground chile. Scoop the remaining chopped onion into a strainer, rinse under cold water and shake off the excess, then place in a bowl and set out with the other condiments.

    Add the meat to the simmering *pozole* and check the consistency: It should look hearty—chock-full of hominy with bits of meat—but brothy enough to be thought of as a soup or brothy stew. If necessary, add water. Taste the *pozole* and season with additional salt if you think it's necessary; since hominy soaks up a surprising amount of salt, you may need as much as another tablespoon.

Either serve your *pozole* extravaganza (brothy stew plus garnishes and go-withs) buffet-style or ladle portions of the *pozole* into large soup bowls and deliver them to your guests, then pass around the condiments. Before sprinkling it over the bowl, each guest should powder the whole-leaf oregano by rubbing it between his or her palms. The crushed red chile is for those who really like spice. The tostadas are eaten as an accompaniment on the side.

WORKING AHEAD: *Pozole* prepared through Step 3 keeps very well—even improves—for several days, refrigerated. The biggest hurdle for most cooks is cooling it down quickly enough (I highly recommend immediately dividing finished *pozole* among at least four 2- to 3-quart containers for quick cooling) and finding enough space in the refrigerator.

RED PORK AND HOMINY STEW (PAGE 166)

QUESTIONS AND ANSWERS FROM OUR TESTING

WHAT'S THE BEST CORN FOR *POZOLE*? *Homemade* nixtamal: Traditional cooks start with dried field (grain) corn and cook it with *cal* (slaked lime) or wood ashes until the kernels' hulls have turned vivid yellow and softened to a sticky consistency, then they wash it thoroughly so it is free of any traces of hull. Corn prepared in this manner is called *nixtamal* (see photograph, page 86). If you want to go to that effort, search in Mexican groceries for the dried, big-kernel *maíz cacahuacintle* that is so prized in Mexico for *pozole*. If that corn isn't available, look in those same stores for dried corn labeled "corn for *pozole*" or "*maíz para pozole*." *Cal* is generally sold there too. On the other hand, you may want to save this procedure for the time you rent a house in San Miguel and have Mexican neighbors to help you. *Purchased* nixtamal: You can skip the step of boiling dried corn with the *cal* by simply buying freshly cooked, damp *nixtamal* at a tortilla factory. Some Mexican groceries also sell *nixtamal* in bags in the refrigerated or frozen case. It freezes beautifully. *Southwestern dried pozole corn*: Making your own *pozole* with what's typically called in the American Southwest "dried *pozole* corn" (*nixtamal* that has been washed and re-dried) produces nearly indistinguishable results from *pozole* made of fresh *nixtamal*. It's available in specialty markets and by mail-order, keeps on the shelf for a year and is not expensive. Most package directions tell you to soak it overnight before simmering. We found that unnecessary, though the cooking time for unsoaked corn was considerably longer than for soaked.

IS IT NECESSARY TO REMOVE THE POINTY END (TO DEHEAD) OF THE CORN? The name *pozole* comes from the Aztec word for "foam." And what gives the preparation a foamy appearance was the multitude of kernels that had blossomed like little stubby flowers, having had their pointy germ ends picked off kernel by kernel. Deheading corn kernels is not a procedure I'm inclined to do frequently. Make *pozole* a few times and, if it becomes one of your specialties, you may want to start plucking to make it even more special—preferably with the help of a few friends.

WHAT ACCESSIBLE CUTS OF PORK WILL GIVE TRADITIONAL FLAVOR AND TEXTURE? The best *pozole* I've ever tasted was made with the whole animal—including, specifically, the head. The head adds inimitably delicious flavor and rich texture to the pot, though that may not be enough to convince most American cooks to get one. Besides the fact that it would have to be ordered from an ethnic butcher (my grocery store butcher wants nothing to do with special-order heads), this recipe would require only half a head, creating an even more uncomfortable situation for many cooks. So shanks and pigs' feet stand in for the head, and I think they do so admirably. If you can't manage pigs' feet, you'll be settling for a broth without that beautiful silkiness. Shanks add rich and complex flavor.

WHAT IS THE MOST EFFICIENT WAY TO COOK THE CORN AND THE PORK? While it's common to add the pork to the corn-cooking pot when the corn is half-done, I've always struggled with that. Sure it works, but I find myself endlessly fishing out pieces of pork and bone that have broken away. When I tried simmering the two separately, in order to easily strain out the meat, struggles ceased. The pork broth goes into the pot to enrich the corn during the final simmering.

IS IT NECESSARY TO TOAST THE DRIED ANCHO CHILES TO GET GOOD FLAVOR? While for salsas and sauces, toasting dried chiles heightens flavor while leveling out any bitterness, we found that the procedure contributed little in this dish. There's not much chile to begin with, and it gets a long, mellowing simmer.

WHICH OF THE GARNISHES AND GO-WITHS ARE BEST? *Cabbage v. lettuce:* Probably more lettuce—thinly sliced head lettuce—is eaten in *pozole* in Mexico than cabbage. It's got a light sweet crunch, but to my taste it's not that flavorful. Regular cabbage has been my preference for years, but lately I like Napa cabbage. Its tenderness approaches that of head lettuce (a little more substantial), but it has more flavor. *Tostadas:* Crispy, golden disks of corn tortilla are great—and traditional—to munch along with the *pozole*. If you don't feel like making them and no good commercial ones are within your reach, replace them with the best corn tortilla chips you can procure. You'll need about a pound.

Fresh field corn

Rice

In 1888, Mexican cook Guadalupe Rivera wrote, "We make general use of [rice], since there isn't a stew or sweet into which it can't be incorporated." And that's pretty remarkable, given that rice wasn't known in Mexico until the Spaniards arrived, and, more important, that folks in Mexico have relied almost exclusively on beans and corn for daily nourishment since time immemorial. Rice hasn't supplanted those New World native staples, though it has found an honored role in Mexico's daily nutrition.

But it didn't happen overnight. In fact, for centuries after the first rice arrived in Mexico (most researchers believe that happened shortly after the sixteenth-century Spanish conquest), it seems only to have been woven in here and there, without taking the leap to near-staple status. You'd find it in Spanish-inspired desserts and savory dishes like *arroz a la valenciana* (Valencia-style rice with tomatoes and garlic), in soups, in patties and fritters, even in a cold drink (*horchata de arroz*, page 316). It was not served by the spoonful to accompany other dishes. That didn't happen until those eating the Spanish-rooted rice dishes began to welcome inventions like rice tamales. When rice found a home in native dishes, the grain was on its way to becoming a naturalized citizen.

I haven't uncovered exactly when, in Mexico, "Valencia-style rice" changed its name to "Mexican rice." But for at least a century now, a tomato-red rice in that Valencia style (with a few chiles added) has held a revered place as the second course in Mexico's midday meal or as the perfect accompaniment to *mole*, Mexico's national dish. Today, rice has joined corn and beans as daily must-haves.

From a nutritional point of view, of course, we've all heard that in diets light in animal proteins, beans and rice eaten together can satisfy all your protein needs. Mexico, however, already had the "vegetable protein" bases covered with the combination of beans and corn. Still, Mexican cooking and eating found a welcome place for rice, revealing, I think, the cuisine's vegetarian underpinnings—beans, corn tortillas, rice and salsa continue as everyday mainstays.

Mexican rice cooking begins with frying the raw rice. I've never come across a definitive historical reason for it, but I have my hunch: The Mexicans learned the technique from the Spaniards, who had learned it from the Arabs (who dominated Spain for nearly eight centuries), and the Arabs had convinced the Spaniards that rice should cook into separate grains like their beloved couscous (or like the long-grain rice pilafs they knew from India). But the rice they had to work with was a relatively short-grain, somewhat sticky rice, so separate grains were a challenge. Frying the raw rice, they discovered, changed the starch on the outside of the grains, making the grains less sticky. Many people today call this raw-rice-frying method pilaf-style, since it produces separate grains like you'll find in the famous pilafs of India and the Middle East.

A lot of Mexican rice (especially in chain eateries) is pretty uninspiring, though, so you may wonder why I have devoted so much attention to it. I've done so because good rice, well prepared in the Mexican pilaf-style, is unbelievably delicious and satisfying. Mexico grows a lot of rice, much of it a plump *medium*-size grain that I think has a wonderful texture and flavor. Prepared either with tomatoes and vegetables in the most well known version, or with garlic and, occasionally, the cooking bananas they call plantains (a Gulf Coast tradition), Mexican rice can be almost a meal in itself. For sure, our contemporary recipe, with spinach, cheese and chiles added to the rice offers complete satisfaction on many levels.

TRADITIONAL BENCHMARK: Most types of rice have a light flavor—slightly sweet, comforting, never challenging. So, what makes one rice better than another? For me, it's texture. And the texture of perfectly cooked Mexican rice is substantial, almost meaty in its chew, not dry, broken or mushy. Perfect Mexican rice is also infused with the gentle flavor of salted broth and flecked with aromatic bits of onion and garlic. If it has a reddish hue, there'll be a lingering rich sweetness of cooked tomato.

WHEN TO THINK OF THESE RECIPES: Rice is welcome at practically any meal, from brunch to a quick supper to a fancy dinner party. Simple grilled meats or tomato-sauced main dishes go particularly well with red tomato rice. I find garlicky Mexican-style white rice to be the perfect accompaniment to complex *moles* and stew-like preparations. To tell the truth, the simple rustic combination of any well-made Mexican rice, fried beans and a salad is one of my favorite, simple, everyday light meals. Our contemporary rice with chiles, spinach and cheese also makes a great main dish or buffet offering.

ADVICE FOR AMERICAN COOKS: I know from experience that rice cooking can be tricky, so I've carefully specified the correct proportions, equipment and cooking temperature. Finding the ingredients is easy.

Red Tomato Rice

ARROZ ROJO

Makes 6 cups, serving 6 to 8

12 ounces (2 medium-small round or 4 to 6 plum) very ripe tomatoes,
    cored and roughly chopped
      OR one 15-ounce can good-quality whole tomatoes in juice,
    drained
$1/2$ small white onion, roughly chopped
2 garlic cloves, peeled and halved
$1^3/4$ cups chicken broth or water
Salt
$1^1/2$ tablespoons vegetable oil
$1^1/2$ cups white rice, preferably medium-grain
2 medium carrots, peeled and chopped into $1/4$-inch cubes
Fresh hot green chiles to taste (roughly 3 serranos or 2 jalapeños),
    a slit cut down the length of each one
$1/4$ cup coarsely chopped fresh flat-leaf parsley
$1^1/2$ cups defrosted frozen peas or cooked fresh peas (tender, tiny ones will
    need to simmer as little as 4 minutes, larger ones as much as 15)

TRADITIONAL

1. THE TOMATO FLAVORING AND BROTH. In a blender or food processor, combine the tomatoes (raw or drained canned) with the onion and garlic. Blend to a smooth puree; you should have 1 generous cup.

   In a small saucepan or in a microwave oven, heat the broth or water until steaming; stir in about $3/4$ teaspoon salt if using lightly salted broth, $1^1/2$ teaspoons if using unsalted broth or water. Cover and keep warm.

2. FRYING THE RAW RICE. In a medium (3-quart) saucepan (one that's about 8 inches in diameter is perfect for even cooking) with a tight-fitting lid, heat the oil over medium. When hot, add the raw rice and stir regularly until the grains have turned from translucent to milky-white, 5 to 6 minutes—it is fine if some of the grains begin to brown. Add the tomato mixture and carrots and stir around

a couple of times, then let cook until any liquid is reduced and the mixture is somewhat dry-looking, 2 to 3 minutes.

3. SIMMERING THE RICE. Add the warm broth or water, chiles and parsley, stir thoroughly and scrape down any rice grains clinging to the side of the pan. Cover and cook over the lowest heat for 15 minutes—the temperature should be low enough that only the slightest hint of steam escapes from the lid.

Remove the pan from the heat, uncover it and quickly distribute the peas over the rice. Re-cover and let stand for 5 minutes. Uncover and test a grain of rice: if it's still a little hard, re-cover the pan and set over low heat for about 5 minutes; if the rice has absorbed all the liquid (and is completely dry), sprinkle on 2 table-spoons of water before returning it to the heat.

As soon as it is done, gently fluff the rice to release the steam and stop the cooking, then turn it into a warm bowl—and it's ready to serve. You can remove and discard the chiles if you wish, or pull them out to use as decoration on top of the rice.

WORKING AHEAD: This preparation actually works very well when cooked ahead and reheated. Make the recipe as directed, but don't add the peas. When the rice is cooked, turn it out onto a baking sheet in a shallow layer to cool; refrigerate, covered, for up to 3 days. When ready to serve, mix in the cooked or defrosted frozen peas and reheat in a microwave oven or a steamer. Or reheat on a baking sheet, covered with foil, in a 325°F oven until heated through, about 15 minutes.

Market vendor with basket of native "pleated" tomatoes

Classic Mexican White Rice

ARROZ BLANCO

Makes 5 cups, serving 5 or 6

2 ¹/₂ cups chicken broth or water
Salt
2 tablespoons vegetable oil or olive oil
1 ¹/₂ cups white rice, preferably medium-grain
1 small white onion, chopped
2 garlic cloves, peeled and finely chopped
1 tablespoon fresh lime juice
3 tablespoons roughly chopped fresh flat-leaf parsley,
    for garnish
Fried Plantains (page 322) (optional)

TRADITIONAL

1. HEATING THE LIQUID. In a small saucepan or microwave oven, heat the broth or water until steaming; stir in about ³/₄ teaspoon salt if using salted broth, 1 ¹/₂ teaspoons if using unsalted broth or water. Cover and keep warm.

2. FRYING THE RICE. In a medium (3-quart) saucepan (one that's about 8 inches in diameter is perfect for even cooking) with a tight-fitting lid, heat the oil over medium. When hot, add the raw rice and onion and stir regularly until the grains have turned from translucent to milky-white, 4 to 5 minutes. Add the garlic and stir for a few seconds, until fragrant. For beautiful white rice, the grains should not brown.

3. SIMMERING THE RICE. Add the warm liquid and lime juice, stir thoroughly and scrape down any grains that are clinging to the side of the pan. Cover and cook over the lowest heat for 15 minutes—the temperature should be low enough that only the slightest hint of steam escapes from the lid.

    Remove the pan from the heat and let stand covered for 5 minutes. Uncover and test a grain of rice: If it's still a little hard, re-cover the pan and set over low heat for about 5 minutes; if the rice has absorbed all the liquid (and is completely dry), sprinkle on 2 tablespoons of water before returning it to the heat.

    As soon as the rice is done, sprinkle on the parsley and gently fluff the rice to release the steam and stop the cooking, then turn it into a warm bowl. It's ready to serve, garnished with the fried plantains if you wish.

WORKING AHEAD: The rice can be successfully made ahead: Turn it out onto a baking sheet in a shallow layer to cool, then cover and refrigerate for up to 3 days. When ready to serve, reheat in a microwave oven or a steamer. Or reheat on a baking sheet, covered with foil, in a 325°F oven until heated through, about 15 minutes. Toss in the parsley and serve.

Fresh native garlic brought to the market in bundles

ARROZ MEXICANO A LA MEXICANA
● MEXICAN RICE COOKED THE MEXICAN WAY

Our rice—and the way we feel comfortable cooking it—is a little different from its Mexican counterpart. Here's the classic Mexican version, should you find yourself in Mexico or at a Mexican grocery with imported Mexican rice.

Makes 5 cups, serving 5 or 6

1 1/2 *cups Mexican-milled white rice (it will be imported*
    if you're doing this in the United States)
3 1/2 *cups chicken broth or water*
Salt
1 cup vegetable oil
1 small white onion, chopped
2 garlic cloves, peeled and finely chopped
3 tablespoons roughly chopped fresh flat-leaf parsley, for garnish

1. SOAKING THE RICE AND HEATING THE LIQUID. Place the rice in a medium-mesh strainer and wash under cold running water until the water runs clear. Scoop it into a bowl, cover with cold water and let stand for 20 minutes, then pour into the strainer and drain for 15 minutes.

    Heat the broth or water in a small saucepan or in a microwave oven until steaming; stir in 3/4 teaspoon salt if using salted broth, 1 1/2 teaspoons if using unsalted broth or water. Cover and keep warm.

2. FRYING THE RICE. In a medium (3-quart) saucepan, heat the vegetable oil over medium. When hot, add the rice (it will sputter) and stir almost constantly for a minute or so, until the rice floats freely, no longer clumping. Continue to fry the rice, stirring occasionally, until it has turned milky-white, 7 to 8 minutes. Pour into a strainer set over a bowl; do not wash the pan. Let the rice drain for 5 minutes (the oil can be refrigerated for use later).

In the still-oily pan, fry the onion over medium heat until translucent, 3 to 4 minutes. Add the garlic and stir for a few seconds until aromatic, then add the rice and broth.

3. SIMMERING THE RICE. Simmer briskly, uncovered, stirring every once in a while, for 7 to 10 minutes, until the liquid drops below the surface of the rice—you'll see small steam holes appear. Turn the heat to low and cook, without stirring, until you no longer hear gurgling liquid, about 8 minutes. Remove from the heat and cover the pan with a folded kitchen towel to trap the steam. Let rest for 20 minutes.

Fluff the rice with a fork to release trapped steam and stop the cooking. Stir in the chopped parsley, and it's ready.

This *is Mexico*

Rice with Roasted Poblano, Spinach and Fresh Cheese

ARROZ AL POBLANO CON ESPINACAS
Y QUESO FRESCO

Makes 6 cups, serving 6 to 8

3 medium (about 9 ounces total) fresh poblano chiles
2 cups chicken broth or water
Salt
2 tablespoons vegetable oil or olive oil
1 1/2 cups white rice, preferably medium-grain
1 small white onion, chopped
2 garlic cloves, peeled and finely chopped
3 cups loosely packed sliced stemmed spinach leaves (start
    with about 4 ounces and slice the leaves 1/4 inch thick)
1 1/2 cups coarsely crumbled Mexican queso fresco
    (or firm goat cheese or feta)

CONTEMPORARY

1. ROASTING THE CHILE. Roast the chiles directly over a gas flame or on a baking sheet 4 inches below a very hot broiler, turning regularly, until the skin has blistered and blackened on all sides, about 5 minutes for an open flame, about 10 minutes for the broiler. Be careful not to char the flesh, only the skin. Cover with a kitchen towel and let stand for 5 minutes. Rub off the blackened skin, then pull out the stems and seed pods. Rinse briefly to remove any stray seeds and bits of skin. Chop into 1/4-inch pieces.

2. HEATING THE LIQUID. In a small saucepan or in a microwave oven, heat the broth or water until steaming; stir in about 3/4 teaspoon salt if using salted broth, 1 1/2 teaspoons if using unsalted broth or water. Cover and keep warm.

3. FRYING THE RICE. In a medium (3-quart) saucepan (one that's about 8 inches in diameter is perfect for even cooking) with a tight-fitting lid, heat the oil over medium. When hot, add the raw rice and onion and stir regularly until the grains have turned from translucent to milky-white, 4 to 5 minutes. Add the garlic and stir for a few seconds, until fragrant. For beautiful white rice, the grains should not brown.

4. **SIMMERING THE RICE.** Add the warm liquid and chopped roasted chile, stir thoroughly and scrape down any grains that are clinging to the side of the pan. Cover and cook over the lowest heat for 15 minutes—the temperature should be low enough that only the slightest hint of steam escapes from the lid.

5. **FINISHING THE RICE.** Remove the pan from the heat; uncover the pan and quickly distribute the spinach over the rice. Re-cover and let stand for 5 minutes. Uncover and test a grain of rice: If it's still a little hard, re-cover and set over low heat for about 5 minutes; if the rice has absorbed all the liquid (and is completely dry), sprinkle on 2 tablespoons of water before returning it to the heat.

   Uncover the rice, sprinkle the cheese over the top and fluff everything together with a fork. Spoon into a warm serving bowl and head for the table.

WORKING AHEAD: The rice can be successfully made ahead through Step 4; turn it out onto a baking sheet in a shallow layer to cool, then cover and refrigerate for up to 3 days. When ready to serve, reheat with the spinach in a microwave oven or a steamer. Or reheat on a baking sheet, covered with foil, in a 325°F oven until heated through, about 15 minutes. Toss in the cheese and serve.

Behind the scenes,
Neptuno restaurant

Questions and Answers from Our Testing

WHAT'S THE BEST TYPE OF RICE TO USE FOR THESE RECIPES? When I got to Mexico, my eyes were opened to a delicious world of rice flavors and textures. To help explain what I found, let me delve for a moment into basic rice classifications (long-, medium- and short-grain) and the differences between them. There are two kinds of starch in rice, amylose and amylopectin. At the long-grain end of the rice-length continuum, rice contains a high proportion of amylose starch, which translates into grains that stay firm and separate as they cook and have a dryish, almost mealy texture. At the short-grain end of the continuum, rice contains a high proportion of amylopectin, giving it a more substantial (some would say meatier/waxier) texture—definitely not mealy.

In Mexico, each region seems to have its preference—certain ones toward the meatier medium-grain rice, others toward the mealier long-grain rice. (I haven't seen short-grain rice used in Mexico.) You'll have to determine your own preference by trying different rices. We tested everything with American-grown long-grain and medium-grain rices (Riceland and La Preferida brands) and know these recipes work with either.

DOES THE PAN SIZE MATTER IN RICE COOKING? Yes. A pan that's too small or large for the quantity of rice you're cooking will adversely affect the texture of the rice, causing it to cook irregularly.

SHOULD THE RAW RICE FIRST BE SOAKED, AS SO MANY COOKS DO IN MEXICO? In the United States, we're warned not to wash and soak raw rice because doing so removes sprayed-on nutrients (ones that are intended to replace those lost during milling). In fact, our testing revealed that American milled rice doesn't cook particularly well if soaked before cooking. On the flip side, our experience is that rice imported from Mexico comes out best when soaked. When you look at rice from Mexico, it's clear that the grains aren't as thoroughly milled (you see bits of dark bran still on the grains), which, I surmise, is the reason for the difference in performance.

DO YOU HAVE TO FRY THE RAW RICE IN A LOT OF OIL, AS MOST COOKS DO IN MEXICO? Soaked rice needs a good depth of frying oil to fry evenly. Unsoaked rice (which is what these recipes call for) can be very successfully fried in a very small amount of oil. You need to stir it almost constantly to ensure even cooking.

DOES IT MATTER HOW LONG YOU FRY THE RICE IN THE HOT OIL? If you are using medium-grain rice, simply coating the rice with the oil (or even letting it fry for a couple of minutes in the oil) will turn out fairly sticky, very waxy-textured rice. Letting it cook until all of the grains have turned from translucent to milky-white, 4 to 5 minutes, ensures beautifully fluffy rice with separate grains. Letting the rice cook until it is browned gives it a very nutty taste and the lightest texture, though you may have quite a few broken grains in the finished pot.

SHOULD THE RICE BE COOKED UNCOVERED, AS SO MANY COOKS DO IN MEXICO? In Mexico, the traditional pot for cooking rice is an uncovered earthenware *cazuela*. But cooking rice this way can be tricky. A more foolproof method is to simmer the rice in a covered pot over low heat until the liquid is absorbed, then remove the pot from the heat and let it stand, covered, for the rice to finish cooking. If you are interested in cooking rice in an uncovered pot, refer to Mexican Rice Cooked the Mexican Way (page 178).

WHAT IS THE RIGHT HEAT FOR RICE COOKING? We found that low heat was essential for perfectly cooked grains. When the heat was too high, the water boiled away quickly resulting in unevenly cooked and splayed grains.

HOW MUCH BROTH OR WATER SHOULD YOU USE? You may be surprised by the liquid quantities we've given in these recipes, since they are below those given on most rice packages. I find that following the package recommendations yields mushy rice. Also, the type of rice and its freshness may affect liquid quantities a little, so it is always necessary to test the rice to be sure it is completely cooked.

CAN YOU DOUBLE OR TRIPLE THESE RECIPES? Yes. Simply double or triple all ingredients in either the Red Tomato Rice or the Classic Mexican White Rice *except* the broth or water. (Some cooks prefer less than double or triple the amount of salt.) Following are broth or water quantities:

Double recipe tomato rice	2 ¾ cups broth or water
Triple recipe tomato rice	4 ¼ cups broth or water
Double recipe white rice	4 cups broth or water
Triple recipe white rice	6 cups broth or water

For the most even cooking of these large batches, I bake the rice in a covered pan at 350°F for 25 minutes. When doubling the recipes, use an ovenproof 9- to 10-inch pan with a tight-fitting lid; when tripling, use an ovenproof 11- to 12-inch pan. After 25 minutes in the oven, test the rice and, if done, fluff it thoroughly to stop the cooking. Or, if making ahead, turn the rice out onto a baking sheet to cool.

CAN BROWN RICE BE SUBSTITUTED FOR WHITE RICE: To make red tomato rice with long-grain brown rice (the type I suggest for this recipe), simply increase the broth or water to 2 ½ cups, the simmering time to 40 minutes and the standing time (off the heat) to 15 minutes.

Beans

 I've eaten beans from my first mouthfuls—initially a few mashed barbecue beans from my folk's restaurant to start, then a spoonful of pintos simmered with ham hocks at my grandmother's table. Though she would never admit it to anyone but family, one of Grandma Potter's favorite meals was a bowl of steaming beans, hot buttermilk corn bread and pickled peppers. Meager beginnings and a tour through the Great Depression of the early '30s had taught her the stick-to-your-ribs value of an inexpensive pound of beans. But also she knew their honest, enticing savor.

The aroma of beans' earthy sweetness has suffused every kitchen I've had, welcoming all with a comforting embrace. Mingling with it, typically, is the scent of corn, be it Grandma's corn bread or fresh-baked corn tortillas.

And there is genius in our propensity for a beans-and-corn combination. Eating them together, researchers tell us, supplies all the amino acids necessary for our bodies to take advantage of the protein packed into each one. Alone they're not as effective. Together they're a nutritional powerhouse that is relied on the world around, especially where animal protein is scarce or looked on coolly.

Somewhere along the way, however, most of us in America learned to dismiss beans as inferior nutrition, as poor people's food. Meat is what builds strong bodies, we were told, along with Wonder Bread (or *Pan Bimbo* in Mexico). That's why my grandmother never willingly admitted her yearning for beans beyond the family borders. But things are different now. We are turning back to beans, a healthy complex carbohydrate that can provide our bodies with structure as well as steady energy for the long haul.

Mexicans had little animal protein before the Spaniards arrived, so they were in good part nourished by beans. To this day, especially in rural areas with few resources, a bowl of *frijoles de la olla* (whole beans from the simmering pot), a big stack of tortillas and some salsa make a meal. In big Mexican cities, beans have a strong hold too. Kids who haven't been totally won over by packaged processed fluff will grab a bowl of *frijoles de la olla* after school. A midmorning *almuerzo*'s eggs or *chilaquiles* would seem incomplete without a spoonful of creamy, rich fried beans (*frijoles refritos*) alongside. A fancy restaurant's grilled beef offering (*carne asada*) inevitably sports a helping of beans. Even the formal midday meal (*comida*) holds a place for the basic bean, after the main course and before the dessert. That's when beans are politely offered for anyone still hungry.

The way we Americans cook beans in many upscale restaurants illustrates, I think, how little we understand their potential. "Cook them in lots of water, till they're barely tender—*al dente*," I've been told by well-known, well-meaning chefs. The beans are pretty, for sure, but also indigestible and mealy. Beans need a long, slow coddling to reach their full flavor and smooth meaty texture

Our traditional recipe for *frijoles de la olla* lays the groundwork for richer, more complex preparations like *frijoles refritos*. For that classic, boiled beans are transformed with browned onions, garlic and fresh pork lard much the same way boiled potatoes north of the border are mashed with enriching butter and milk. Coarse or smooth, they're *refritos*—not fried *again*, as you might assume, but "well fried" or "intensely fried," as that *re* translates from Spanish. Our last recipe is a lesson in style and substance. Smoky Chipotle Beans with Wilted Spinach and *Masa* "Gnocchi" may sound thoroughly upscale-contemporary, but the words describe a tradition of beans and greens that runs deep in Mexico's culinary culture.

TRADITIONAL BENCHMARK: Eating a bowl of slow-simmered beans can be a transcendent experience if the beans are thoroughly creamy-tender and full of unique varietal flavor. There are many favorite styles of fried beans, from unctuous and smooth to lean and rustic. For everyday eating, I consider coarsely mashed beans rich with sweet bits of onion and garlic—and a small amount of fat—the perfect ones. For the complete Mexican bean experience, you need roasty-tasting pork lard and freshly herbal *epazote*.

WHEN TO THINK OF THESE RECIPES: A bowl of beans with corn tortillas and a simple, leafy salad is one of my favorite lunches. I wouldn't think of serving enchiladas or some of the simple soft tacos without a helping of beans on the side. They complete a spicy brunch, crispy tostada or steak cookout. Chipotle beans with spinach is a satisfying one-dish meal.

ADVICE FOR AMERICAN COOKS: A variety of beans is available practically everywhere, but buy them where there is good turnover. Really good lard is the kind you make yourself (see page 77) or buy from a Mexican or German butcher. Look for *epazote* at a well-stocked Mexican grocery or grow it.

Mexican Beans—from the pot or the skillet

FRIJOLES MEXICANOS—DE LA OLLA O REFRITOS

Makes 7 to 8 cups whole brothy beans or
5 cups fried beans, serving 8 to 10

FOR THE BROTHY BEANS:

1 pound (about 2 ½ cups) dried beans (any color you wish, from
   black to red, tan, white or speckled)
2 tablespoons rich-tasting pork lard (or even bacon drippings or
   fat rendered from chorizo sausage) or vegetable oil
1 medium white onion, chopped
1 large sprig fresh epazote (optional but delicious—especially
   with black beans)
Salt

FOR TURNING BROTHY BEANS INTO REFRITOS:

¼ cup vegetable oil or rich-tasting pork lard (or one of the
   other options listed above)
1 medium white onion, chopped
4 large garlic cloves, peeled and finely chopped
About ¾ cup (3 ounces) crumbled Mexican queso fresco or
   other crumbly fresh cheese, such as salted pressed farmer's
   cheese or feta, for garnish
A big handful of tortilla chips, for garnish (optional)

TRADITIONAL

I. PREPARING SIMPLE BOILED BEANS—*FRIJOLES DE LA OLLA*. Though beans in the United States are sold very clean, it's always a good idea to pour them out onto a baking sheet and sort through them, removing any little stones or debris you encounter; scoop the beans into a colander and rinse.

Pour the beans into a deep medium-large (4- to 6-quart) pot (preferably a heavy Dutch oven or Mexican earthenware *olla*). Measure in 2 ½ quarts water, then remove any beans that float (they're ones that are not fully formed). Add the fat or oil, onion and the optional *epazote*. Bring to a strong rolling boil, then reduce the heat (low to medium-low on most stoves) to keep the liquid at a very gentle simmer—any more than a slight rolling movement will cause the beans to break up some during cooking. Set a cover slightly askew (no need to cover the narrow-mouthed Mexican *olla*—its design takes care of maintaining even heat and controlling evaporation) and gently simmer, adding water as needed to keep the liquid level roughly the same, until the beans are thoroughly tender, about 2 hours.

Stir in 1½ teaspoons salt and simmer for 15 minutes longer to allow the salt to be absorbed, then taste and season with additional salt if you think necessary. The beans are now ready to serve in small bowls or to mash and fry.

2. FROM BOILED BEANS TO GREAT FRIED BEANS—*FRIJOLES REFRITOS*. Pour the beans into a colander set over a large bowl; discard the *epazote* if you used it. In a large (12-inch) heavy skillet (preferably nonstick), heat the oil or other fat over medium. Add the onion and cook, stirring regularly, until deeply golden brown, 7 to 8 minutes. Add the garlic and cook until very fragrant, about 1 minute. Now, begin adding the beans to the skillet a couple of large spoonfuls at a time, mashing them to a coarse puree with a wooden bean masher, an old-fashioned potato masher or the back of a large spoon. When all the beans have been added, stir in enough bean broth to give the mixture the consistency of soft mashed potatoes—this not-so-rich-version of *frijoles refritos* will thicken as it continues cooking and especially as it cools at the table.

Taste the beans and season with additional salt if necessary. Scoop onto a serving platter or spoon onto individual plates, sprinkle with the crumbled cheese and stud with the optional tortilla chips. You're ready to serve.

WORKING AHEAD: Beans, whether simply boiled or fried luxuriously in lard, will keep for 4 or 5 days in the refrigerator, tightly covered. The texture and flavor of the boiled beans' broth will improve after a day or so.

Smoky Chipotle Beans with Wilted Spinach and *Masa* "Gnocchi"

FRIJOLES ENCHIPOTLADOS CON ESPINACAS Y
CHOCHOYOTITOS

Serves 6 as a main dish

1 pound (about 2 1/2 cups) dried beans (black beans are great here,
　　as are red beans)

3 tablespoons olive oil, preferably extra-virgin

1 large onion, preferably a red one, chopped

6 garlic cloves, peeled and roughly chopped

12 ounces (2 medium-small round or 4 to 6 plum) ripe tomatoes
　　OR one 15-ounce can good-quality whole tomatoes in juice

3 to 4 canned chipotle chiles en adobo, roughly chopped

Salt

1 cup dried masa harina mixed with 1/2 cup plus 2 tablespoons
　　hot tap water
　　OR 1/2 pound fresh smooth-ground corn masa for tortillas

1/8 teaspoon baking powder

8 to 10 ounces spinach, stemmed and sliced 1/2 inch thick
　　(baby spinach is great here and needs neither stemming
　　nor slicing)

1. SIMMERING THE BEANS. Sort through the beans, removing any little stones or debris you encounter; scoop the beans into a colander and rinse.

Pour the beans into a medium-large (5- to 6-quart) pot (preferably a heavy Dutch oven). Measure in 2 1/2 quarts water, then remove any beans that float. Add *2 tablespoons* of the oil, the onion and garlic. Bring to a strong rolling boil, then reduce the heat (low to medium-low on most stoves) to keep the liquid at a very gentle simmer—any more than a slight rolling movement will cause the beans to break up some during cooking. Set a cover slightly askew and simmer, adding water as needed to keep the liquid level roughly the same, until the beans are thoroughly tender, 2 hours or longer.

2. SEASONING THE BEANS. *For fresh tomatoes:* Roast them on a baking sheet 4 inches below a very hot broiler until they're darkly roasted (they'll be blackened in spots), about 6 minutes. Flip them over and roast on the other side—5 or 6 minutes more will give you splotchy-black and blistered tomatoes that are soft and cooked through. Cool. Working over your baking sheet, pull off and discard the blackened skins and, for round tomatoes, cut out the hard cores. Transfer to a food processor or blender, along with all the juices on the baking sheet. *For canned tomatoes:* drain them and place in a food processor or blender.

    Add the chipotles to the tomatoes, then process to a smooth puree. Add the puree to the beans along with 1½ teaspoons salt. Partially cover and simmer, stirring frequently for 15 minutes. Taste and season with additional salt if necessary.

3. THE *MASA* DUMPLINGS. In a medium bowl, mix the *masa* (reconstituted or fresh) with the remaining *1 tablespoon* oil, the baking powder and ½ teaspoon salt. Roll into balls the size of marbles (you'll get about 30), pressing a dimple (a belly button, as they say in Mexico) into each one with your finger; place them on a plate as you go.

    Bring a large saucepan of water to a boil; reduce the heat to a gentle simmer and season the water with about 2 teaspoons salt. Add half of the *masa* dumplings and simmer gently until all have risen to the surface and are cooked through, about 3 minutes (remove one and test it by cutting in half—it should be soft but not doughy). Remove with a slotted spoon to a plate. Repeat with the remaining dumplings. Cover with plastic wrap if not using right away.

4. FINISHING THE DISH. Stir the spinach into the simmering beans, then lay the *masa* dumplings on top. Set the cover in place and remove the pot from the heat. Let stand for 5 to 10 minutes, until everything is heated through.

    With a large spoon, serve up hearty bowls of the bean "stew," gingerly mixing in the dumplings but being careful not to break them up.

WORKING AHEAD: This dish can be successfully made through Step 3—in fact, it's a little better after a day. Store the beans and dumplings in the refrigerator, covered. Finish Step 4 just before serving.

SMOKY CHIPOTLE BEANS WITH WILTED SPINACH
AND *MASA* "GNOCCHI" (PAGE 188)

Questions and Answers from Our Testing

What's the best bean? That's a matter of personal preference and, in Mexico, regional affiliation. Pinto is the standard of northern Mexico. Light-skinned *peruano*, purplish *flor de mayo* and tan *bayo* are everyday choices in west-central Mexico. Moving down through the country, at about Mexico City's latitude you cross an invisible bean belt, south of which most people eat black beans daily. Everyday choices aside, beans of every color (including the large runner beans called *ayocotes*) are found in practically all markets.

Each bean has its own special flavor. The most full flavored are red beans and black beans, red having a sweet edge and black a distinctively earthy one. White beans (navy, Great Northern) are the boneless, skinless chicken breasts of the bean world (rather bland, little texture), except for *peruanos*. *Peruanos'* color is more creamy than white and their flavor is rich, complex and quite vegetable-like, reminiscent of potato skins. Pintos and *bayos* offer a nice hint of earthiness, but not a lot of distinctive flavor.

Should beans be soaked before cooking? It depends on your motives. If you choose to soak beans to speed their cooking or because you're convinced that the beans will arrive at doneness more intact, you're on the right track. If you soak beans to make them more digestible, most researchers now say you're misguided: Several years ago, researchers declared that the complex sugars in beans can be hard for some people to digest, that those sugars are somewhat water soluble and that soaking beans *and discarding the soaking liquid* would make the beans more digestible. Now we know, however, that very little of those complex sugars actually soak out. Besides, when you discover that throwing out the soaking liquid translates into blander, colorless beans with watery cooking liquid, there's even less motivation for soaking beans.

What specialists do understand, however, is that in cultures where beans are consumed regularly, digestibility is not much of an issue. Everyone's body has become accustomed to processing those sugars.

Are there good alternatives to the Mexican bean-cooking pot (*olla*)? Truthfully, practically any American cooking pot will work for cooking beans. In Mexico, the most commonly used traditional pot is a bulbous earthenware vessel with a fairly narrow mouth. It offers three things: very gentle, evenly distributed heat; the perfect shape to control evaporation and a distinctive flavor (some of the earthiness of the earthenware actually perfumes the food). A heavy pot with a lid set askew is the best substitute, though it won't offer the flavor of earthenware. If you're concerned about the potential health hazards of lead-glazed Mexican earthenware, please read my comments on page 116.

IS PORK LARD ESSENTIAL IN MAKING TRADITIONAL MEXICAN BEANS? No, it's not essential, but I think it makes beans with the most satisfying flavor. If you're looking for a filling dish that's low in fat, eat beans brothy, not fried. If you want to use vegetable oil, increase the onions and garlic a little (and brown them well) to compensate for the loss of the roasty flavor of good pork lard.

HOW MUCH WATER DO YOU NEED FOR SIMMERING BEANS? If beans don't have enough water to float freely, they will cook unevenly. I suggest that you start a pound of beans in 2 1/2 quarts of water—which will look like a lot, but you will rarely need to add more during cooking.

AT WHAT TEMPERATURE SHOULD YOU SIMMER BEANS? Temperature is critical in bean cooking, because beans can absorb liquid only through the little "eye" on the side of each one. Water can't penetrate the skin of a dried bean. Maintaining the beans at a very gentle simmer (barely any movement in the pot—205° to 210°F on a thermometer) keeps absorption and softening moving along evenly. A full rolling boil creates stresses inside the slowly rehydrating beans, causing skins to break and the beans to cook irregularly. That explains why slow-cookers turn out creamy whole beans and pressure cookers broken ones.

HOW LONG SHOULD YOU SIMMER BEANS? If beans are not creamy inside, they're not done. And achieving creaminess takes time, usually 2 hours or more at a gentle simmer. We tasted a pot of pintos at regular intervals over 5 hours and here are our notes: chalky/gritty at 1 hour; softer but with bits of grittiness at 1 1/2 hours; done at 2 hours but not creamy; buttery-tender at 3 hours. After 3 hours, the beans got a little softer—the way I like them for soup—though even at 5 hours you wouldn't have called them overcooked. Too little simmering, rather than too much, is the mistake most American cooks make.

All that said, keep in mind that each bean type cooks at a different rate: Small white beans typically cook the most quickly and black beans the most slowly. Also, fresher dried beans cook faster than old ones.

SHOULD YOU SALT BEANS DURING OR AFTER COOKING? Our testing taught us that salt can be added at the beginning or the end with little noticeable difference. Acidic ingredients like tomatoes and vinegar, however, do cause bean skins to toughen, so add them only once the beans are cooked through.

Entrees

Chiles Rellenos

 My first bite of *chile relleno*—I was probably nine or ten before I got the courage to order one at El Chico in Oklahoma City, where I grew up—was heavily battered with so many fluffy eggs that it resembled an omelet. It was a typical Southwestern-style "relleno," as I was taught to call it, and it bore almost no resemblance to what I got when a friend invited me to help make dinner in Mexico City during my teenage years. The chiles she used were the larger, darker, very flavorful poblanos (we only knew the long light green Anaheims in OKC) and she stuffed them with chopped pork *picadillo* seasoned with cinnamon, cloves, almonds and raisins. Each chile was dipped into the lightest batter imaginable before being coaxed toward golden as it bobbed in the hot oil.

Stuffed peppers (that's literally what *chiles rellenos* means) spell out Special Occasion in Mexico, since stuffing anything typically heightens the enthusiasm in direct proportion to the amount of time a cook has to invest. Whole boned chicken gets stuffed into a French *galantine*, whole duck becomes Chinese eight-jeweled duck and *chiles*, as we know, find a *relleno*.

But not all chiles or *rellenos* are created equal. Regional variations abound. The poblano chile is well known and well loved practically everywhere in Mexico. But in Oaxaca, they prefer to stuff the smaller, hotter fresh *chile de agua* or the reconstituted dried *chile pasilla oaxaqueño*. In Veracruz, home of the jalapeño, that's the chile of choice. Some versions of *chiles rellenos*, like the stuffed *chile de agua* or the jalapeño, may be served sauceless, but the most common *chile relleno* is battered and fried, then served with a tomato broth in most Mexican households.

Since I don't want all the battering and frying of traditional *chiles rellenos* to dissuade you from tasting the magical mix of chiles and pork *picadillo,* I've also included a simple version of stuffed chiles baked with rustic tomato sauce and thick cream. *Chiles rellenos* welcome many approaches.

TRADITIONAL BENCHMARK: The Ideal *Chile Relleno*, if I can borrow a concept from Plato here, champions a heavenly whipped-egg softness, giving way to a roasted pepper juiciness, encasing rich pork mincemeat bejeweled with nuts and dried fruit. One bite and all distractions cease. While most Americans think "fried" equates to "crunchy," that's not part of the picture here—classic *chile relleno* batter is a soufflé batter, tender and comforting. And, to underscore that texture, the most classic preparation calls for dousing the chile with tangy tomato broth, which soaks into the golden envelope and gives it an even more voluptuous texture.

WHEN TO THINK OF THESE RECIPES: Classic *chiles rellenos* are impressive and a little time-consuming. So make them when you're putting your efforts into an exceptional dinner. Start your meal, perhaps, with Smoked Salmon–Black Bean Tostaditas (page 66), then serve a simple green salad in a mustardy vinaigrette with or after the *chiles rellenos* and, at the end, set out a homemade fruit ice and cookies. The baked *chiles rellenos* make a great buffet dish as well as a casual wintry main course for family or friends.

ADVICE FOR AMERICAN COOKS: If you can get nice-looking fresh poblano chiles, you've jumped the only ingredient hurdle. Then it's on to mastering the techniques of preparing the chiles for stuffing, preparing the soufflé batter, battering the chiles and frying them. All the techniques are manageable, though you'll notice increasingly better results the more times you make them.

Left: Dried guajillo chiles
Right: On the street in Oaxaca

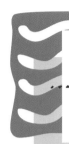

Classic Pork *Picadillo*–Stuffed Chiles in Tomato Broth

CHILES RELLENOS DE PICADILLO EN CALDILLO DE JITOMATE

Serves 8 as a moderate-sized main dish,
fewer if you have hefty eaters

3 tablespoons rich-tasting pork lard or vegetable oil

2 medium white onions, chopped into $1/4$-inch pieces

Two 28-ounce cans good-quality whole tomatoes in juice, undrained
OR 3 pounds (about 6 medium-large round or 20 plum) ripe
tomatoes, cored and cut into large pieces

1 teaspoon cinnamon, preferably freshly ground Mexican canela

1 teaspoon black pepper, preferably freshly ground

2 cups chicken or beef broth

$1/2$ cup slivered almonds

$1^1/2$ pounds coarsely ground pork shoulder (look for "chili grind" in
the grocery store, special order it from your butcher or see the note
in Questions and Answers on grinding it yourself)

$1/2$ cup raisins

1 tablespoon cider vinegar

Salt

Vegetable oil to a depth of 1 inch for frying

8 medium (about $1^1/2$ pounds total) fresh poblano chiles, not
twisted or deeply indented, preferably with long stems

Eight 6-inch wooden skewers or 16 toothpicks

6 large eggs, cold

2 tablespoons all-purpose flour, plus about 1 cup for dredging
the chiles

Sprigs of fresh cilantro, watercress or flat-leaf parsley for garnish

TRADITIONAL

1. THE BROTH BASE AND FILLING. In a medium-large (4-quart) saucepan, heat
the lard or oil over medium. Add the onions and cook, stirring regularly, until

they are very well browned, about 10 minutes. While the onions are cooking, puree the undrained canned tomatoes, or, if using fresh tomatoes, puree them with ⅔ cup water, using a blender or food processor and working in two batches if necessary.

When the onions are well browned, raise the heat to medium-high and add the pureed tomatoes, cinnamon and pepper. Stir regularly as the mixture boils briskly, reducing until it becomes the consistency of thick tomato sauce, about 25 minutes.

2. THE TOMATO BROTH. Remove 2 cups of the tomato mixture and set aside. Stir the broth into the mixture that remains. Partially cover and simmer over low heat for 45 minutes or so, while you're preparing the filling and chiles.

3. THE PORK *PICADILLO* FILLING. Set a large (12-inch) skillet (preferably nonstick) over medium-high heat. Add the almonds and stir around until they color to a deep golden, about 2 minutes. Remove.

Crumble the pork into the skillet and fry, stirring often, until thoroughly cooked (some of the edges should be browned and crispy), 10 to 15 minutes. If the pork has rendered a lot of fat, drain it off. Stir in the reserved 2 cups tomato mixture, the raisins and vinegar. Cook over medium heat, stirring regularly, until the mixture is very thick and homogeneous, about 20 minutes. Stir in the almonds, then taste and season with salt, usually about 1 teaspoon. Cool.

4. PREPARING THE CHILES. While the *picadillo* is cooking, pour 1 inch of oil into a deep heavy skillet or pot—the pot should be 12 inches wide and 3 to 4 inches deep for easiest maneuvering of the chiles—and set over medium to medium-high to heat to 350°F. (Using a thermometer is the most accurate way to assure the proper heat, but there are other reliable clues: The oil releases that "hot oil" aroma and its surface begins shimmering. When you think the oil is hot, test the edge of a chile—it should sizzle vigorously. Remember—smoking oil is dangerously overheated and will give the chiles a bad taste.) In two batches, fry the chiles, turning them continually, for about 1 minute, until they are evenly blistered (they'll look uniformly light green, having lightened as they blister). Drain on paper towels. Remove the oil from the heat.

When the chiles are cool enough to handle, rub off the blistered skins, then cut an incision in the side of each one, starting ½ inch below the stem end and continuing to within ½ inch of the tip. One by one, work your index finger inside each chile and dislodge all the seeds clustered just below the stem. Quickly rinse the seeds from inside the chiles, being careful not to rip or tear the opening any wider; rinse off any stray bits of skin. Drain cut side down on paper towels.

5. STUFFING THE CHILES. Stuff each well-drained chile with about ¹/₂ cup of the cooled pork filling, then slightly overlap the two sides of the incision and pin them back together with a skewer or 2 toothpicks. For the greatest ease in battering and frying, flatten the chiles slightly, place on a parchment-lined baking sheet and freeze for about 1 hour to firm. (For notes on working with thoroughly frozen chiles, please see Working Ahead below.)

6. BATTERING AND FRYING THE CHILES. Reheat the oil to 350°F; set up a tray lined with several layers of paper towels. Separate the eggs: whites into the bowl of an electric mixer, the yolks into a small bowl. Add ¹/₂ teaspoon salt to the whites and begin beating them on medium speed. When they are beginning to look dry and hold a stiff peak but are not at all rigid, beat in the yolks two at a time until well incorporated. Lastly, beat in the *2 tablespoons* flour. Spread the *1 cup* flour on a plate.

    One at a time, batter the first four chiles: Roll in the flour, shake off the excess, pick up by the stem, dip into the batter and quickly pull straight up out of the batter, then lay into the hot oil. (If your kitchen is very warm, it's best to hold the remaining batter for the second round in the refrigerator.) Once the first four chiles are in the oil, begin gently, gently basting them with spoonfuls of hot oil (this will help set the uncooked batter on top). When they're richly golden on the bottom, about 4 minutes, use one small metal spatula underneath and another one (or a spoon) on top to gently turn the chiles over. Fry until the other side is richly golden, another 3 to 4 minutes. Using the metal spatula, remove the chiles to the paper towels to drain. Repeat with the remaining chiles.

7. SERVING THE CHILES. Heat the oven to 400°F. Once all the fried chiles have cooled for at least 5 minutes, pick them up by carefully rolling each one onto one hand, then transfer to a baking sheet (lined with parchment if you wish, for extra ease at serving time). Pull out the skewers by twisting them gently. Bake for 15 minutes to heat thoroughly, to render some of the absorbed oil and to crisp slightly.

    Meanwhile, bring the tomato broth to a boil and check the consistency: It should be similar to a brothy tomato soup. If it's too thick, thin with a little water or broth; if too thin, boil rapidly until thickened slightly. Season it with salt, usually about ¹/₂ teaspoon.

    Ladle about ¹/₂ cup of the broth into each of eight deep serving bowls (large soup bowls or pasta bowls are perfect here). Nestle in one of the chiles, garnish with herb sprigs and get ready for a taste of real Mexico.

WORKING AHEAD: The beauty of this dish is the way so many steps can be done in advance. The brothy sauce and filling (Steps 1 through 3) can be made several days in advance and stored in the refrigerator, covered. The chiles can be blistered, peeled and seeded (Step 4) a day in advance, though if I were that far ahead, I'd stuff (Step 5) and freeze them too, just for ease in the frying. Battered and fried chiles will hold for an hour or two at room temperature before reheating them in the 400°F oven (Step 7). (If you freeze the chiles until frozen solid, be sure to complete the frying (Step 6) a full half hour in advance of oven reheating to allow for full defrosting.) While oven heating the chiles, warm the broth, and you're ready to serve.

VARIATION: *Cheese Chiles Rellenos:* Coarsely shred 1 pound melting cheese, such as Mexican Chihuahua, Monterey Jack, brick or mild cheddar. Divide the cheese into 8 portions and form each into a football shape. Stuff the cheese into the chiles, then batter, fry, oven heat and serve as directed.

Oaxacan-style chile relleno

Chicken-and-Mushroom-Stuffed Chiles with tomatoes and cream

CHILES RELLENOS DE POLLO Y HONGOS A LA CREMA

Serves 8 as a moderate-sized main dish, fewer if you have hefty eaters

4 1/2 tablespoons olive oil, preferably extra-virgin, or vegetable oil

2 medium white onions, chopped into 1/4-inch pieces

Two 28-ounce cans good-quality whole tomatoes in juice, undrained
    OR 3 pounds (about 6 medium-large round or 20 plum) ripe
    tomatoes, cored and cut into large pieces

1 teaspoon cinnamon, preferably freshly ground Mexican canela

1 teaspoon black pepper, preferably freshly ground

2 cups (about 4 ounces) sliced stemmed flavorful mushrooms,
    such as shiitakes

Kernels cut from 2 ears corn (about 1 1/2 cups)

2 teaspoons cider vinegar

3 cups coarsely shredded cooked chicken (consider a rotisserie or
    smoked chicken here)

1 packed cup thinly sliced spinach
    OR 1/3 cup chopped fresh cilantro

Salt

1 cup chicken or beef broth

8 medium (about 1 1/2 pounds total) fresh poblano chiles, not twisted
    or deeply indented, preferably with long stems

3/4 cup homemade crema (page 133), crème fraîche or heavy
    (whipping) cream

CONTEMPORARY

1. **THE SAUCE AND FILLING BASE.** In a medium-large (4-quart) saucepan, heat *3 tablespoons* of the oil over medium. Add the onions and cook, stirring regularly, until well browned, about 10 minutes. While the onions are cooking, puree the undrained canned tomatoes, or, if using fresh tomatoes, puree them with 2/3 cup water, in a blender or food processor, working in two batches if necessary.

   When the onions are well browned, raise the heat to medium-high and add the tomato puree, cinnamon and pepper. Stir regularly as the mixture boils briskly, reducing to the consistency of thick tomato sauce, about 25 minutes. Remove from heat.

2.   THE FILLING. In a large (10- to 12-inch) skillet (preferably nonstick), heat the remaining 1 1/2 *tablespoons* oil over medium-high. Add the mushrooms and cook, stirring often, until the edges turn golden, about 5 minutes.

Stir in half of the tomato mixture, the corn and vinegar and continue to cook over medium heat, stirring regularly, until the mixture is thick enough to hold its shape in a spoon, about 15 minutes. Stir in the chicken and spinach or cilantro. Taste and season with salt, usually about 1 teaspoon.

3.   THE TOMATO SAUCE. Stir the broth into the remaining tomato mixture. Partially cover and simmer over low heat for 45 minutes or so, while you're preparing the chiles.

4.   PREPARING THE CHILES. Roast the chiles directly over a gas flame or on a baking sheet 4 inches below a very hot broiler, turning regularly, until the skins have blistered and blackened on all sides, about 5 minutes for an open flame, about 10 minutes for the broiler. Be careful not to char the flesh, only the skin. Cover with a kitchen towel and let stand for 5 minutes. Rub off the blackened skin, then cut an incision in the side of each one, starting 1/2 inch below the stem end and continuing to within 1/2 inch of the tip. One by one, work your index finger inside each chile and dislodge all the seeds clustered just below the stem. Quickly rinse the seeds from inside the chiles, being careful not to rip the opening any wider; rinse off any stray bits of skin. Drain cut side down on paper towels.

5.   STUFFING AND BAKING THE CHILES. Heat the oven to 375°F. Fill each chile with about 1/2 cup of the chicken mixture and re-form it into its original shape, then lay seam side down in a 13 x 9-inch baking dish. Check the consistency of the tomato sauce: It should be medium-thick. If it is too thick, stir in a little water; if too thin, simmer briskly until thickened. Taste and season with salt, usually about 1/2 teaspoon.

Pour the sauce over the chiles, covering them, then drizzle with the *crema, crème fraîche* or cream. Bake until the sauce is bubbling vigorously and the cream is beginning to brown, about 20 minutes. Carry the bubbling beauty straight to your waiting guests.

WORKING AHEAD: Every part of this dish can be prepared a day or two ahead. Refrigerate the sauce, filling and chiles separately, well wrapped. Stuff the chiles and sauce and bake them just before you're ready to serve. If all the components are cold, bake at 350°F for 30 to 40 minutes.

CLASSIC PORK PICADILLO—STUFFED CHILES RELLENOS
(PAGE 196) IN PROGRESS

QUESTIONS AND ANSWERS FROM OUR TESTING

WHAT'S THE BEST WAY TO ACHIEVE GREAT-TEXTURED, PERFECTLY PEELED CHILES FOR STUFFING? For all-around ease in handling, choose medium (4- to 5-inch) chiles (large ones are a little unwieldy) that have no deep crevices (it's hard to blister and peel the skin inside crevices). After trying open-flame roasting, broiler roasting and oil blistering of the chiles, we can say that oil blistering is the easiest chile-skinning method for this dish because the hot oil blisters *all* the skin evenly without softening the flesh too much. (The softer flesh that results from the other methods makes cleaning and stuffing a bit more difficult.) In the traditional recipe, we recommend the oil-blistering method and then use the same oil for frying the battered chiles. It's efficient on all levels.

HOW DO YOU MAKE THE SIMPLEST, BEST-FLAVORED, BEST-TEXTURED PORK *PICA-DILLO*? The grind of pork is important—a coarser grind gives a better texture. Typical supermarket ground pork is so fine that the *picadillo* comes out mushy. You can partially freeze cubes of boneless pork shoulder and grind them yourself in small batches in a food processor, or ask for coarsely ground pork at the butcher. Browning the pork is essential, as is the texture and flavor it takes on from the cooked-down tomato mixture.

WHAT'S THE BEST WAY TO ACCOMPLISH A LIGHT, EVEN BATTER COATING THAT COMES OUT AS GREASELESS AS POSSIBLE? Far and away the most common batter for chiles in Mexico is a simple soufflé batter made from beaten egg whites into which egg yolks are folded. This batter deflates fairly quickly, but adding a little flour makes it more stable (albeit a little less airy, which is why some cooks don't do it) and creates a less greasy coating. Since adding flour buys you enough time to allow for frying both rounds of chiles, I say do it. Cold eggs, we discovered, produce a better-textured batter (the opposite of what most soufflé recipes tell you). And freezing the chiles to firm them makes the process of battering and frying the most manageable (a technique we figured out in our restaurant years ago). Even if you allow the chiles to freeze thoroughly, the end result is very, very good. As *chiles rellenos* fry, it's important to keep the oil as close to 350°F as possible. Too low, and the chiles come out greasy, too hot, and they brown before the batter is set.

IS THERE ANY WAY TO FINISH *CHILES RELLENOS* IN ADVANCE? Though most cooks in Mexico tell you to serve the chiles the second they come from the oil, I've known for years that they actually benefit from being completed ahead and then heated in a hot oven. This heating renders out some of the oil they absorb during frying.

Turkey with Red Mole

 Red *mole* is Mexico's national dish, which may surprise you if the breadth of your Mexican culinary experience is tacos and burritos. Come to think of it, the word "dish" isn't exactly accurate, since *mole* is a sauce, the National Sauce, and I've seen it served with everything from poultry and meat to vegetables and seafood.

When I first let a spoonful of classic Mexican red *mole* bathe my tongue, it was an experience comparable to taking in the vista from the rim of the Grand Canyon—singular, breathtaking, saturating my senses—because *mole* involves so many senses, and in such a complex and thrilling way.

Sure, the list of ingredients for any classic red *mole* is long (though the version I've worked out here is the simplest way to honest traditional flavor), and so is the cooking time. But that's what it takes to create a unique beauty of these proportions, one that fires all the taste buds simultaneously by weaving together sweetness from fruits and dried chiles (which offer a dancing tingle, a shadow of bitterness and an aromatic earthiness), tanginess from tomatillos and velvety richness from ground nuts. When you finally, triumphantly set the finished platter on the table, filled with lustrous red-brown sauce, your sense of achievement explodes. You celebrate.

And *mole* is celebration. This dish—the pride of all Mexico—holds the same place as our Thanksgiving turkey, though it's certainly made more often. It truly might be more important, since in most homes *mole* is the culinary offering made to the ancestors (*and* to the living) during Days of the Dead in November.

So much in Mexico is part of the culture of *mole*. The word itself shows deep roots, harkening back to ancient Aztec times, when *molli* simply meant "sauce." Huge arms-wide earthenware *cazuelas* are always sold as "perfect for *mole*." Cooks set out on special *mole* shopping trips, searching out the supplest dried chiles, the freshest nuts and seeds, the nicest-looking spices for the culinary dance that follows.

Families are chauvinistic about ingredients and cooking methods. And staunch traditionalists sniff disapprovingly at the thought of buying one of the prepared *mole* bases available in Mexican markets. Some wouldn't even consider grinding all the ingredients with the help of an electric blender. Only the *metate* (the lava-rock grinding stone), they say, truly releases all the flavor and gives the most velvety texture. And they have a point. Blender blades chop the ingredients very fine, whereas stone-crushing smoothes everything into an aromatic mass. Which isn't to say a blenderized *mole* is second-rate. It's wonderful— and *doable* for most of us.

So try these recipes, either the traditional one with turkey breast or the contemporary version of roasted Cornish hens with a *mole* of dried apricots, pine nuts and the sweetness of ancho chile. I think both will help you to understand *mole*'s mythic mystique as well as its earthy sensuality. Neither, though, has much to do with the American tourist's understanding of the dish as "chicken (or whatever) in chocolate sauce." Chocolate isn't what *mole* is about. The celebratory rhythm of dark-skinned elegance *is*.

TRADITIONAL BENCHMARK: At its heart, red *mole* is a red chile sauce (usually combining several chiles for a rounder, more complete flavor) that's thickened and enriched by nuts and seeds and trimmed out with an array of spices. So the best classic red *mole*—no matter whose "perfect" recipe you make—is a thrill to taste. It's balanced so well that no one flavor stands out or dominates.

WHEN TO THINK OF THESE RECIPES: When it's time to impress. Don't clutter the menu with too many other things or you'll detract from the *mole*. *Mole* is rich and complex, so start with a brothy soup like Tortilla Soup (page 152), and accompany the main attraction with white rice (page 176) and steamy corn tortillas. No one will forget your accomplishment.

ADVICE FOR AMERICAN COOKS: Think of it this way: If you want to make *mole*, you're in the mood for cooking. And real cooking always involves good ingredients and some time. The only ingredients you may have to search out are the dried chiles (available in Mexican groceries and by mail-order). We've streamlined the steps—well, streamlined them compared to many *mole* recipes. Just keep your eye on the prize. The satisfaction will be palpable when you spoon that sauce onto the plate. So get cooking.

Classic Red *Mole* with Turkey

MOLE ROJO CLÁSICO DE GUAJOLOTE

Serves 8, with welcome leftovers of sauce (with the turkey, you'll probably serve about half of the 7 cups *mole* you make)

5 ounces (3 medium) tomatillos, husked and rinsed

¹/₂ cup (about 2 ¹/₂ ounces) sesame seeds

¹/₂ cup rich-tasting pork lard or vegetable oil, plus a little more if necessary

6 medium (about 3 ounces total) dried mulato chiles, stemmed and seeded

3 medium (about 1¹/₂ ounces total) dried ancho chiles, stemmed and seeded

5 medium (about 1¹/₂ ounces total) dried pasilla chiles, stemmed and seeded

4 garlic cloves, peeled

A scant ¹/₂ cup (about 2 ounces) unskinned almonds

¹/₂ cup (about 2 ounces) raisins

1 whole (about 4 pounds) boneless turkey breast with skin on, the two halves cut apart and any netting removed (some brands sell individual turkey breasts as 2-pound roasts— you'll need two of them)

Salt

¹/₂ teaspoon cinnamon, preferably freshly ground Mexican canela

¹/₄ teaspoon black pepper, preferably freshly ground

¹/₄ teaspoon anise, preferably freshly ground (optional)

A scant ¹/₈ teaspoon cloves, preferably freshly ground

1 slice firm white bread, darkly toasted and broken into several pieces

1 ounce (about one-third of a 3.3-ounce tablet) Mexican chocolate, roughly chopped

4 to 5 tablespoons sugar

Sprigs of watercress or fresh flat-leaf parsley for garnish

TRADITIONAL

1. GETTING STARTED. To ensure success and to streamline this rather complex preparation, first set out all the ingredients, completing basic preparations as described: Husk and rinse the tomatillos, stem and seed the dried chiles, peel the garlic, grind the spices if you're using whole, toast the bread, chop the chocolate.

   Spread the tomatillos on a baking sheet and roast them 4 inches below a very hot broiler until darkly roasted, even blackened in spots, about 5 minutes. Flip them over and roast on the other side, 4 or 5 minutes, until splotchy-black, blistered and soft.

   Set out two large bowls and scrape the tomatillos, juice and all, into one of them. Set out a pair of tongs and a slotted spoon.

2. INITIAL TOASTING AND BROWNING. In an ungreased small skillet set over medium heat, toast the sesame seeds, stirring constantly, until golden, about 5 minutes. Scrape two-thirds of them in with the tomatillos; set the rest aside for garnish.

   Set a large (8- to 9-quart) pot (preferably a Dutch oven or Mexican *cazuela*) over medium heat. Measure the lard or oil into the pot. Turn on an exhaust fan or open a window or door. Tear the chiles into flat pieces, and, when the lard or oil is hot, fry the chiles, three or four pieces at a time, flipping them nearly continually with the tongs, until their interior side has changed to a lighter color, about 20 to 30 seconds total frying time. Don't toast them so darkly that they begin to smoke—that would make the *mole* bitter. As they're done, remove them to the empty bowl, being careful to drain as much fat as possible back into the pot. Cover the toasted chiles with hot tap water and place a small plate on them to keep them submerged. Let stand for about 30 minutes.

   Meanwhile, remove any stray chile seeds left in the fat. With the pot still over medium heat, fry the garlic and almonds, stirring regularly, until browned (the garlic should be soft, the almonds browned through), about 5 minutes. With the slotted spoon, remove to the tomatillo bowl, draining as much fat as possible back into the pot.

   Now add the raisins to the hot pot. Stir with your slotted spoon for 20 to 30 seconds, until they've puffed and browned slightly. Scoop them out, draining as much fat as possible back into the pot, and add to the tomatillos.

   Raise the temperature under the pot to medium-high. Sprinkle all sides of the turkey breast halves with salt, then lay one in the pot. Thoroughly brown it on all sides, about 10 minutes total. Remove to a clean plate; brown the other half in the same way. (Cover and refrigerate if not completing Steps 3 and 4 within an hour or so.) Set the pot aside.

3. BLENDING AND STRAINING. Use tongs to transfer the rehydrated chiles to a blender, leaving the soaking liquid behind. Taste the soaking liquid, and, if it is not bitter, measure 2 ½ cups into the blender. If it is, throw it away and measure in 2 ½ cups water. Blend the chiles to a smooth puree, adding a little extra water if necessary to keep the mixture moving through the blades. Press the chile mixture through a medium-mesh strainer back into the empty chile-soaking bowl.

   Without washing the blender jar, scrape the tomatillo mixture into it. Add 1 cup water along with the cinnamon, pepper, optional anise, cloves, bread and chocolate. Blend to a smooth puree, adding a little extra water if necessary to keep the mixture moving. Press through the strainer back into the tomatillo bowl.

4. SEARING AND SIMMERING. Check the fat in the pot: If there's more than a light coating over the bottom, pour off the excess; if the pot's pretty dry, film the bottom with a little more lard or oil. Set over medium-high heat. When quite hot, scrape in the chile puree and stir nearly constantly until the mixture has darkened considerably and thickened to the consistency of tomato paste, 10 to 15 minutes. Add the tomatillo puree and continue stirring until once again the mixture has thickened to the consistency of tomato paste, another 5 to 10 minutes.

   Add 6 cups water to the pot and stir to combine thoroughly. Partially cover, reduce the heat to medium-low and simmer gently, stirring occasionally, for 45 minutes. Check the consistency: The *mole* should be thick enough to coat a spoon, but not too thickly. If it's too thin, simmer it briskly over medium to medium-high heat until a little thicker; if too thick, stir in a little water.

   Taste and season with salt, usually about 1 ¾ teaspoons, and the sugar (if you're new to seasoning *mole*, keep in mind that it's a delicate balance of salty, sweet and spicy; it's best to start with the minimum quantities I've suggested, then refine the seasoning just before serving).

5. BRAISING AND SERVING THE TURKEY. Heat the oven to 325°F. Lay the turkey in the *mole*, cover (use foil if you're working in a *cazuela*) and place in the oven. Cook until an instant-read thermometer placed in the center of the turkey breast registers 150°F (there should be only the slightest hint of pink if you cut into it), about 40 minutes. (If the turkey breast was refrigerated before going into the hot pot of *mole*, allow an additional 10 to 15 minutes cooking time.)

Remove the turkey from the *mole* and place on a cutting board. Cover with foil and let it stand at room temperature for 10 minutes.

Slice the turkey ½ inch thick, then arrange the slices slightly overlapping on a warm large deep serving platter. If the *mole* has thickened beyond the consistency of a medium cream soup, thin it with a little water. Taste and season with a little more salt or sugar if you think necessary. Ladle a generous amount (3 to 4 cups) of *mole* over or around the turkey slices and sprinkle with the reserved sesame seeds. Decorate the platter with sprigs of watercress or parsley, and you're ready for a party.

WORKING AHEAD: *Mole* can be successfully made ahead—even getting better with 2 or 3 days residence, well covered, in the refrigerator. Though braising the turkey can be done a day ahead (cover and refrigerate it separately from the *mole*), that approach is not my first choice, because it is difficult to reheat cooked turkey and not have it dry out. Instead, complete the *mole* through the simmering (Step 4); cool, cover and refrigerate the *mole* and the browned but uncooked turkey breast separately for up to 3 days. Just before serving, warm the *mole* in the pot, nestle in the turkey breast, braise and serve as described in Step 5. The turkey breast will be much juicier.

Prepared mole base *in Mexico City market*

Classic Red *Mole* with Turkey (page 206)

Roasted Cornish Hens with Apricot– Pine Nut *Mole*

POLLITOS EN MOLE DE CHABACANO Y PIÑON

Serves 4, with welcome leftovers of sauce
(with the hens, you'll serve less than half
of the 7 cups *mole* you make)

5 ounces (3 medium) tomatillos, husked and rinsed

¹/₂ cup (about 2 ¹/₂ ounces) sesame seeds

¹/₂ cup rich-tasting pork lard or vegetable oil, plus a
     little more if necessary

12 medium (6 ounces total) dried ancho chiles, stemmed and seeded

4 garlic cloves, peeled

²/₃ cup (about 3 ounces) pine nuts

²/₃ cup (about 4 ounces) dried apricots, coarsely chopped

7 cups chicken broth, plus a little more if needed, store-bought or
     homemade (page 148)

¹/₂ teaspoon cinnamon, preferably freshly ground
     Mexican canela

¹/₄ teaspoon black pepper, preferably freshly ground

A scant ¹/₈ teaspoon cloves, preferably freshly ground

1 ounce (about one-third of a 3.3-ounce tablet)
     Mexican chocolate, roughly chopped

1 slice firm white bread, darkly toasted and broken
     into several pieces

Salt

4 to 5 tablespoons sugar

4 Cornish game hens (each about 1 ¹/₄ pounds)

A little vegetable oil for the hens

Sprigs of watercress or fresh flat-leaf parsley for garnish

I. GETTING STARTED. To ensure success and to make this rather complex preparation as simple as possible, first set out all the ingredients, completing basic
preparations as described: Husk and rinse the tomatillos, stem and seed the dried

chiles, peel the garlic, grind the spices if you're using whole, toast the bread, chop the chocolate.

Spread the tomatillos on a baking sheet and roast them 4 inches below a very hot broiler until darkly roasted, even blackened in spots, about 5 minutes. Flip them over and roast on the other side for 4 or 5 minutes, until splotchy-black, blistered and soft.

Set out two large bowls and scrape the tomatillos, juice and all, into one of them. Set out a pair of tongs and a slotted spoon.

2. INITIAL TOASTING AND FRYING. In an ungreased small skillet over medium heat, toast the sesame seeds, stirring constantly, until golden, about 5 minutes. Scrape *two-thirds* of them in with the tomatillos; set the rest aside for garnish.

Measure the lard or oil into a large (8- to 9-quart) pot (preferably a Dutch oven or Mexican *cazuela*) and set over medium heat. Turn on an exhaust fan or open a window or door. Tear the chiles into flat pieces, and, when the lard or oil is hot, fry the chiles, three or four pieces at a time, flipping them nearly continually with the tongs, until their interior side has changed to a lighter color, about 20 to 30 seconds total frying time. Don't toast so darkly that they begin to smoke—that would make the *mole* bitter. As they're done, remove them to the empty bowl, being careful to drain as much fat as possible back into the pot. Cover the toasted chiles with hot tap water and place a small plate on them to keep them submerged. Let stand for about 30 minutes.

Meanwhile, remove any stray chile seeds left in the fat. With the pot still over medium heat, fry the garlic, stirring regularly, until browned and soft, about 5 minutes. With the slotted spoon, remove to the tomatillo bowl, draining as much fat as possible back into the pot. Add the pine nuts to the pot and stir until they're lightly toasted, 1 to 2 minutes. Remove with the slotted spoon, letting as much fat as possible drain back into the pot, and add to the tomatillo bowl. Add the apricots as well.

3. BLENDING AND STRAINING. Use tongs to transfer the rehydrated chiles to a blender, leaving the soaking liquid behind. Taste the soaking liquid, and, if it is not bitter, measure 2 ½ cups into the blender. If it is, throw it away and measure in 2 ½ cups water. Blend the chiles to a smooth puree, adding a little extra water if necessary to keep the mixture moving through the blades. Press the chile mixture through a medium-mesh strainer back into the empty chile-soaking bowl.

Without washing the blender jar, scrape the tomatillo mixture into it. Add

1 cup of the broth along with the cinnamon, pepper, cloves, chocolate and bread. Blend to a smooth puree, adding a little extra broth if necessary to keep the mixture moving. Press through the strainer back into the tomatillo bowl.

4. SEARING AND SIMMERING. Check the fat in the pot: If there's more than a light coating over the bottom, pour off the excess; if the pot's pretty dry, film the bottom with a little more lard or oil. Set over medium-high heat. When quite hot, scrape in the chile puree and stir nearly constantly until the mixture has darkened considerably and thickened to the consistency of tomato paste, 10 to 15 minutes. Add the tomatillo puree and continue stirring until once again the mixture has thickened to the consistency of tomato paste, another 5 to 10 minutes.

Add the remaining *6 cups* broth to the pot and stir to combine thoroughly. Partially cover, reduce the heat to medium-low and simmer gently, stirring occasionally, for 45 minutes. Check the consistency: The *mole* should be thick enough to coat a spoon, but not too thickly. If it's too thin, simmer it briskly over medium to medium-high heat until a little thicker; if too thick, stir in a little water.

Taste and season with salt, usually about 1 teaspoon, and the sugar (if you're new to seasoning *mole*, keep in mind that it's a delicate balance of salty, sweet and spicy; it's best to start with the minimum quantities I've suggested, then refine the seasoning just before serving). Keep warm, over very low heat, partially covered, while you roast the hens.

5. ROASTING AND SERVING THE CORNISH HENS. Heat the oven to 450°F. Rinse the hens and pat dry. Tie the legs together and twist the last joint of the wings up over the breast and then down behind the "shoulders," tucking them in firmly to keep them in place. Lightly oil a large roasting pan and place the birds in it, breast side up and legs facing out. Brush or spray the hens with a little oil and sprinkle them generously with salt. Roast for about 35 minutes, until the juices run clear when the thighs are pierced with a knife.

Ladle a generous amount of *mole* onto each of four warm dinner plates. Set the hens into the sauce, sprinkle liberally with the reserved sesame seeds and decorate with watercress or parsley. Your very special dinner is ready.

WORKING AHEAD: *Mole* can be successfully made ahead—even getting better after 2 or 3 days in the refrigerator; cover well. Just before serving, roast the hens and warm the *mole.*

Questions and Answers from Our Testing

What are the essential ingredients necessary for creating complex classic red *mole* flavor? Having eaten hundreds of *moles* over a period of more than thirty years, I've finally developed a sort of *mole* sense. Now I walk into a kitchen and say, "Wow, it smells like *mole* is cooking here." Or I taste a sauce called *"mole"* and I know someone's using the word pretty loosely. In our testing, we discovered that essential *mole* ingredients fall into several groups: the chiles, the thickeners, the fruits and vegetables and the seasonings. *Dried chiles:* Though you can make a simple red *mole* from one dried chile, the classic three chiles—mulato, pasilla and ancho—provide the full flavor most Mexicans expect from *mole*. Mulato chile contributes depth with a hint of bitterness (think coffee flavor). Pasilla chile brings in robustness and a nice amount of heat (think spicy bitter chocolate). And ancho chile adds a hint of sweetness or dried-fruit fruitiness (think the sweetest sun-dried tomatoes you've tasted). *Thickeners:* Sesame seeds are such an essential thickener/flavoring to *mole* that in Mexico it's not uncommon to hear one adoring lover say to the other, "You're the sesame of my *mole*." Almonds, though, add richness in a way that sesame can't. *Fruits and vegetables:* Raisins (or other dried fruit) underscore the natural fruitiness of the chiles. And tomatillos focus flavors with their brightness. *Seasonings:* Only a certain few spices make *mole* into *mole*—and several of those are spices we North Americans associate with sweets: cinnamon, cloves and chocolate. Yes, chocolate. Here it's used as a spice, and in a well-made *mole*, the chocolate will gently underscore the natural bitter chocolate flavors present in the pasilla chiles. Anise is not found in all red *moles*, and its use is up to your discretion. I love it.

What are the essential techniques necessary for creating that total *mole* flavor? *Basic toasting and browning:* Practically all ingredients in *mole* are browned to bring out their sweetness and add depth. Skipping this step is a little like not toasting a bun over the coals when you're grilling hamburgers—why wouldn't you take that obvious step when the flavor is so much better? Though some cooks dry-toast chiles for *mole*, our comparative testing proved that oil-toasting gives the sauce even more flavor because the toasting is more thorough. *Blending and straining:* I've seen traditional cooks reduce bowlfuls of reconstituted chiles or nut-studded mixtures to absolutely smooth purees on a *metate* (lava-rock grinding stone). I've seen super-duper blenders turn chunkiness into velvety smoothness. But lacking those two options, most of us will simply use an average blender to its best advantage (which won't make everything totally smooth) and then strain out any unground bits. A food processor, while good for many Mexican sauces, won't handle the sesame seeds and some chile skins, both of which are particularly difficult to grind. A medium-mesh (rather than fine-mesh) wire strainer is adequate and efficient for straining here. *Searing the sauce base:* For most American cooks, this is the most unfamiliar technique—but it's one of the most critical. In searing the chile puree into a thick paste, you're smoothing out the rough edges, heightening the sweetness and intensifying and unifying the flavors. If your finished *mole* tastes rough and disjointed, you probably should have cooked the chile puree longer. The more thoroughly you cook that puree, the more unified the flavors. A deep pot and a spatter screen will help make this step less of a cleanup ordeal; the thick paste tends to send little emissaries from the gurgling pot as the mixture concentrates and thickens. *Simmering the sauce:* Don't skimp here. As with most long-simmered dishes, simmering time is in direct proportion to the final harmony. And keep in mind that the flavors are even more unified the day after the sauce is finished.

WHAT IS THE ROLE OF LARD IN TRADITIONAL *MOLE* FLAVOR? There are some dishes that need a certain fat to taste right to me: butter in puff pastry, bacon fat in country gravy, olive oil in pesto . . . and lard in *mole* and tamales. (It's fresh roasty-flavored pork lard I'm talking about here, not the hydrogenated white lard with no flavor.) You can make a perfectly good *mole* with vegetable oil—not butter or olive oil, both of which taste of *something else.* Just remember, too much fat is too much fat. Drain all the fried ingredients carefully, or you'll end up with a rich dish that's over the top.

WHAT IS THE PERFECT BALANCE OF SEASONING, ESPECIALLY SALT AND SUGAR? If this is your first time making *mole,* I encourage you to add my suggested quantities of salt and sugar, then taste what you have. The quantities I call for may seem large, but remember, you are making *a lot* of sauce here. And anything thickened with nuts and seeds will not taste right until you add the proper amount of salt. Also, dried chiles are technically dried fruits—with a slightly bitter edge. Adding enough sugar to bring out their natural fruitiness, but not enough to make the sauce taste sweet, buffers bitterness.

WHAT HAPPENS TO THE LEFTOVER SAUCE? Unexpected wonders. I never make *mole* in a small quantity. It doesn't take any more time to make a large batch than it does a small one, it keeps well in the refrigerator, it freezes well (it may look a little "broken" when defrosted, but will return to a velvety state when reblended) and it goes with all kinds of things. Let leftover sauce become a special spur-of-the-moment meal on chicken enchiladas (a very common use of *mole* in Mexico), on roasted vegetables or on grilled pork tenderloin or chicken breasts. One of my favorite private "leftovers" meals is black beans (sometimes mashed potatoes) with *mole* and warm corn tortillas.

Chicken with Green Pipián
(Pumpkin Seed Sauce)

 To my eyes, green *pipián* is one of the most elegant, herbal green colors. It wakes me up with a little bite from green chiles, the tang of tomatillos and the frank verdancy of *epazote* and cilantro. But I'd never call it rowdy or rough, for it's always caressing with the luxuriant texture of smoothly ground pumpkin seeds, toasted for maximum body and earthy nuttiness.

Green *pipián* is a sauce of ancient standing in Mexico—native tomatillos, green chiles and herbs ground smooth with native pumpkin seeds—and that makes its name a puzzle. *Pipián,* you see, is the Spanish name—not the ancient Aztec one—for a nut- or seed-thickened sauce, a type of sauce the Spaniards knew well. But why, for a sauce so thoroughly indigenous to Mexico, did the borrowed *"pipián"* become its given name? Why not the Aztec-rooted word *"mole"*?

Well, in some regions of Mexico this same sauce *is* known as *mole*—*mole verde*, green *mole*. And folks who call it that understand perfectly that *mole* is a category of sauces that embraces more than the famous red-brown *moles*. They're using the word *"mole"* more as the Aztecs did, to mean sauce, albeit a special one. Perhaps in other regions the name *pipián* stuck because this sauce celebrates pumpkin seeds (*pepitas* in Spanish) above everything else.

Pumpkin seeds have long been a cherished part of the nutritional trinity (The Three Sisters to indigenous peoples)—the corn, beans and squash that have nourished the Americas for aeons. And while most of us think of squash as tender zucchini or crookneck, it's the large, hard native squashes (including a host of pumpkins) that were prized mostly for their protein-and-vitamin-rich seeds. Rather than roasting those seeds for a snack, cooks used them to thicken and enrich sauces. And to those sauces they added some vegetables, a little meat and some herbs, like the recipe that follows for *Pipián Verde de Pollo*. It's a dish that's at home in a market stall, but one that also can be dressed up: Replace the pumpkin seeds with simpler, richer-tasting almonds, fiddle with the herbs a little and serve it with seared shrimp. It's an elegant showstopper.

TRADITIONAL BENCHMARK: To the uninitiated green *pipián* may sound exotic—nutty-toasty pumpkin seeds, herbs, tomatillos. Yet think of it this way: A perfect green *pipián* has a nutty richness (like satay sauce in an Asian restaurant) but, rather than veering toward sweet, it offers the perfect balance of tomatillo tanginess and an herbal-green chile freshness. When it comes to texture, not everyone agrees about what constitutes perfection. Some like a coarser texture that says, "I'm thickened with ground pumpkin seeds"; others, like me, are looking for a velvety smoothness that makes you think "light-bodied cream sauce."

WHEN TO THINK OF THESE RECIPES: When you're looking for a rather simple dish to make for those smitten with wanderlust—dreamed or realized. Green *pipián* will take you into markets redolent with strong herbs. Into comfortable eateries far from home, where the drama is from a bougainvillea outside and the aromas wafting up from the plate. Serve a brothy soup to start, simple white rice with the *pipián* and a tropical fruit ice for dessert. And, of course, to make the trip complete, some old Augustín Lara ballads on the stereo.

ADVICE FOR AMERICAN COOKS: For the traditional recipe, pumpkin seeds are a must, but they're widely available (called *pepitas* in Spanish) in Mexican markets, well stocked grocery stores and health food stores. If untoasted pumpkin seeds are hard to locate, look in the grocery store's snack aisle for toasted salted ones; they'll work (skip the toasting step, of course), though they may not taste as fresh. If *epazote* isn't on your horizon (it shows up at quite a few Mexican grocers in the United States these days, but not usually in regular supermarkets), add more cilantro. Avoid dried *epazote*—it's only used in Mexico for medicinal purposes. And if chayote isn't available, double the zucchini or choose yellow crooknecks or pattypans instead.

Chicken in Easy Green Pumpkin Seed Sauce

PIPIÁN VERDE DE POLLO

Serves 6 (there will be about 4 cups *pipián*)

6 (about 3 3/4 pounds total) bone-in chicken breast halves
1 small white onion, sliced
4 garlic cloves, peeled and halved
1/2 teaspoon EACH dried marjoram and thyme
3 bay leaves
Salt
1 1/4 cups (about 6 ounces) hulled untoasted pumpkin seeds (pepitas)
8 ounces (5 to 6 medium) tomatillos, husked, rinsed and
    roughly chopped
2 large romaine lettuce leaves, torn into large pieces
Fresh hot green chiles to taste (roughly 2 serranos or
    1 jalapeño), stemmed and roughly chopped
Leaves from a small sprig of fresh epazote, plus an
    additional sprig for garnish
1/2 cup loosely packed chopped fresh cilantro, plus
    a few sprigs for garnish
1 1/2 tablespoons vegetable oil or olive oil
2 medium (about 12 ounces total) chayote, peeled if you wish,
    pitted and cut into 1/2-inch cubes
2 medium (10 ounces total) zucchini, ends trimmed and
    cut into 1/2-inch cubes

TRADITIONAL

1. POACHING THE CHICKEN. If the chicken breast halves still have their wings attached, cut the final two joints off each wing (this makes for a nicer-looking presentation). Measure 2 1/2 quarts of water into a large (6- to 8-quart) pot. Add *half* of the onion, *half* of the garlic, the marjoram and thyme, bay and 1 1/2 teaspoons salt. Bring to a boil, then add the chicken breasts and simmer, uncovered, over medium heat for 10 minutes. Cover the pot and let stand *off the heat* for 10 minutes. Remove the chicken from the pot and set aside. Strain the broth and skim off any fat that rises to the top.

2. THE SAUCE. In a heavy medium (4-quart) pot (preferably a Dutch oven or Mexican *cazuela*), dry-toast the pumpkin seeds: Set the pot over medium heat, add the pumpkin seeds and, after the first one pops, stir constantly until all have popped from flat to round, about 5 minutes. Don't let them darken past golden or the sauce will be brownish and slightly bitter. Cool the pumpkin seeds. Set aside 3 tablespoons for garnish and transfer the rest to a blender.

   Add the remaining onion and garlic to the blender along with the tomatillos, lettuce, chiles, *epazote* and cilantro. Pour in 1 cup of the strained broth and blend to a smooth puree.

   In the pumpkin seed–toasting pot, heat the oil over medium-high. When hot enough to make a drop of the puree sizzle sharply, add it all at once. Stir as the mixture darkens slightly and thickens considerably, about 10 minutes. Stir in 2 cups of the broth, reduce the heat to medium-low and simmer for about 20 minutes for the flavors to mellow and the sauce to thicken to a medium consistency.

3. FINISHING THE DISH. While the sauce is simmering, steam the chayote in a vegetable steamer for 3 minutes. Add the zucchini and steam for 2 to 3 minutes more, stirring everything several times to ensure even cooking. (If you find it easier, you can blanch the vegetables in boiling salted water—cook the chayote for 3 minutes, then add the zucchini for a final minute of boiling.) Drain the vegetables and spread out on a plate to stop the cooking.

   When the sauce has simmered for 20 minutes, it will likely look coarse; I prefer to smooth it to a velvety texture by blending it again in small batches (loosely covered or center of blender lid removed to avoid blender explosions). Return the sauce to the pot, taste it and season with salt, usually about 3/4 teaspoon. If the sauce has thickened beyond a light-cream-sauce consistency, thin with broth.

   Slip the cooked chicken breasts into the sauce, then add the cooked vegetables. Simmer over medium heat just long enough to heat everything through, about 5 minutes, then spoon the chicken, vegetables and sauce out onto a warm serving platter. Sprinkle with the reserved pumpkin seeds and decorate with herb sprigs, and you're ready to offer a unique experience to your guests.

WORKING AHEAD: The chicken can be poached and the sauce made a day ahead; store them separately, covered, in the refrigerator. Let the chicken warm to room temperature before heating it in the sauce. The vegetables are best cooked shortly before you serve them.

Shrimp in Simple Green Almond Sauce

CAMARONES EN PIPIÁN DE ALMENDRA

Serves 6 generously (there will be about 4 cups *pipián*)

1 cup (about 5 ounces) blanched almonds

1/4 cup olive oil, preferably extra-virgin, plus a little more if needed

1/2 small white onion, sliced

1 garlic clove, peeled and halved

Fresh hot green chiles to taste (roughly 2 serranos or
    1 jalapeño), stemmed and roughly chopped

9 ounces (5 to 6 medium) tomatillos, husked, rinsed
    and roughly chopped

8 radish leaves

3/4 cup loosely packed chopped fresh cilantro

1/2 cup loosely packed fresh flat-leaf parsley leaves, plus
    a few sprigs for garnish

3 cups fish or chicken broth

Salt

2 pounds (about 48) medium-large shrimp, peeled
    (leaving the last joint and tail intact if you wish)

CONTEMPORARY

I.   THE SAUCE. Heat the oven to 350°F. Spread the almonds out on a baking sheet and toast them in the oven until golden (but not browned) and fragrant, about 10 minutes. Cool and set aside a scant 1/4 cup for garnish.

In a heavy medium (4-quart) pot (preferably a Dutch oven or Mexican *cazuela*), heat 1 1/2 *tablespoons* of the oil over medium, then add the onion, garlic and chiles. Cook, stirring regularly, until tender but not brown, about 3 minutes. Use a slotted spoon to remove the vegetables to a blender. Set the pot aside.

Add the almonds, tomatillos, radish leaves, 1/2 *cup* of the cilantro and all the parsley to the blender. Pour in 1 *cup* of the broth and blend to a smooth puree. (This will take a little time because almonds are quite hard.) A drop of sauce rubbed between your fingers shouldn't feel gritty.

Heat *1 tablespoon* of the oil in the pot over medium-high. When hot enough to make a drop of the puree sizzle sharply, add it all at once. Stir as the mixture darkens slightly and thickens considerably, about 10 minutes. Stir in the remaining *2 cups* broth, reduce the heat to medium-low and simmer for about 20 minutes for the flavors to mellow and the sauce to thicken to a medium consistency (it should coat a spoon nicely). I prefer to smooth it to a velvety texture by blending the sauce again in small batches (loosely covered to avoid blender explosions). Return the sauce to the pan, taste it and season with salt, usually about ¹/₂ teaspoon, depending on the saltiness of the broth.

2. THE SHRIMP. While the sauce is cooking, devein the shrimp if you wish: One by one, lay each shrimp on your work surface, make a shallow incision by running a small sharp knife down the back—head to tail—about ¹/₈ inch deep. This will expose the dark (usually) intestinal tract; pull or scrape it out and discard. Cover and refrigerate if you're not finishing the dish right away.

3. FINISHING THE DISH. When you're ready to serve, turn the oven onto the lowest setting. Sprinkle the shrimp generously with salt, tossing them to coat evenly. In a large heavy skillet (or wok), heat *1¹/₂ tablespoons* of the oil over medium-high (or high for a wok). When hot, lay in *half* of the shrimp in a single uncrowded layer (or just plunk them into the wok and start stir-frying). When they've curled and turned milky white underneath, about 1¹/₂ minutes, use a pair of tongs to turn them over and cook the other side, about 1 minute more (stir-fry for a couple of minutes total in the wok). Sprinkle with *half* the remaining ¹/₄ *cup* cilantro and toss well. Be careful not to overcook the shrimp—stop when there's still a hint of translucence in the middle. Transfer the shrimp to a plate and keep warm in the oven while you cook the rest, using more oil if you need it.

Roughly chop the reserved almonds. Ladle a portion of the sauce onto each of six warm dinner plates. Arrange the shrimp over the sauce and decorate with a few leaves of parsley and a sprinkling of almonds, and your beautiful dinner's ready.

WORKING AHEAD: The sauce can be made ahead and stored covered in the refrigerator for several days. Warm it just before cooking the shrimp. It is my opinion that shrimp should always be cooked just before they're eaten.

CHICKEN IN EASY GREEN PUMPKIN SEED SAUCE (PAGE 218)

QUESTIONS AND ANSWERS FROM OUR TESTING

ARE HULLED OR UNHULLED PUMPKIN SEEDS BEST FOR TRADITIONAL *PIPIÁN*? Except as salty Halloween snacks, unhulled pumpkin seeds rarely show up in our supermarkets. In Mexico (and Mexican groceries in the States), however, you'll find different varieties of unhulled seeds, and cooks in different parts of Mexico have their favorites. Unhulled seeds make a sauce that is less rich (there's a smaller proportion of the oily, protein-rich kernel), a little woodsier and just a little starchier. If you want to use unhulled seeds, measure out the same volume of seeds (1¼ cups), which will weigh half as much (3 ounces). Both blendings will take a little longer because of the toughness of the hulls; use a high-powered blender (like a Vita-Mix) for the smoothest results. My personal preference is for the silky rich, smooth sauce you get from using hulled seeds.

SHOULD THE SEEDS BE TOASTED OR UNTOASTED? The seeds need to be lightly toasted to give them a texture that will blend smoothly and bring out their flavor.

WHAT'S THE RIGHT AMOUNT OF TOMATILLO FOR THE PERFECT BALANCE? While you might think, as we did in our initial testing, that a greater proportion of tomatillos would give a brighter, lighter flavor, tomatillos are actually better as an undercurrent to the rich seeds. Too many tomatillos can overwhelm the pumpkin seeds.

WHAT PIECE OF EQUIPMENT PRODUCES THE BEST-TEXTURED *PIPIÁN*? If you want the best-textured and best-flavored *pipián*, use a blender (unless, of course, you feel comfortable using the volcanic rock *metate* and *mano* to grind everything to a smooth paste—that *truly* gives the best texture and flavor). But not all blenders are created equal—some multispeed plastic models don't have near the pureeing capabilities of, say, a commercial-quality Waring blender or the oh-so-powerful Vita-Mix. An immersion (stick) blender does an admirable job of the second—not the first—blending. A food processor won't produce a smooth enough texture.

REFINEMENTS: *Chicken cooking:* I chose to poach our American chicken gently because a gentle 10-minute simmer followed by a 10-minute steep—off the heat—yields meat that's moist enough to stand up to reheating in the sauce. The poaching broth is light enough to underscore, but not interfere with, the other flavors. (For the almond *pipián,* be sure to use a *light* chicken broth—not a reduced stock—or the flavors will be out of balance.) *Seasoning: Pipián,* like bean dishes, can taste oddly out of whack until you season it properly with salt. I've offered guidelines, but I suggest you add salt a little at a time, tasting along the way. *Quantity of sauce:* The sauce quantity is generous (²⁄₃ cup per serving), because sauce is what the dish is all about.

Chicken Adobado
(with Red Chile Marinade)

 Adobar, adobado, adobo—they're words that swirl freely through a Spanish-speaker's gastronomic conversations, with references that range from general to quirky to country-specific. If you don't speak Spanish, though, their subtle differences may not be apparent. So let's start at ground zero—with the verb *adobar*. It means "to marinate," and every Spanish-speaking country seems to have its favorite *adobo* (marinade). When something is *adobado,* it is marinated. And, in Mexico, there's one marinade that's embraced from border to border, a red chile marinade that's sassy, salty, savory and spicy, and a perfect way (at least to my taste buds) to flavor meat, poultry or fish destined for the grill, hot oven or frying pan. If our Spanish lesson stopped there, all would be easy. But there's a ringer: An *adobo* can also be a sauce that embodies all those same full red chile flavors, though with the volume turned down to "sauce" level.

Whether marinade or sauce, the preparation of an *adobo* starts with what I consider the quintessential Mexican flavor—dried ripe red chile flavor. It pierces far beyond the foreigner's stereotypical concept of Mexican food full of happy jalapeño salsas and crunchy chips. It pierces right to the very heart of Mexican seasoning.

When making an *adobo* marinade or sauce, some cooks prefer the sweetness of dried ancho chiles, others the bright spiciness of dried guajillo chiles. Some throw in a few smoldering chipotles or árbols or piquíns. But most agree on the supporting flavors: garlic, spices and vinegar (a good amount of vinegar for the marinade, a much smaller amount for the sauce).

A chicken marinated in red chile *adobo* and perfectly roasted (a traditional dish called *pollo adobado*) has all the magnetism of the best home cooking. You simply can't wait to cut through the flavorful, rustic-looking lacquer, fork up a mouthful of the juicy meat and spear one of the tender, crusty potatoes that have roasted alongside. One bite, and you'll understand the potential of Mexican marinade.

The same holds for my contemporary roast duck with red chile sauce, where part of the marinade is simmered with broth to become a tangy *adobo* sauce for the slow-roasted, mahogany-glazed duck. The sauce is a little tangier than you might use for stewing pork or chicken, but it works well with the richness of the duck. The flavors are honest and authentic, yet the presentation of carved duck in a pool of earthy red sauce with a scattering of crunchy jícama relish is as elegantly contemporary as you can get.

TRADITIONAL BENCHMARK: The best *adobo*—marinade or sauce—has a rich roundness to it, weaving together the full sweetness of the dried chiles (playing down their inherent bit of bitterness) with aromatic garlic, a smattering of herbs and spices and just enough vinegar to give it a spark. When *adobo* is made as a marinade, it is right when the consistency is that of steak sauce; it'll be punchy, lively and just a little demanding. When *adobo* is made as a sauce, the flavors are fused during simmering into a gentler, less edgy beauty.

WHEN TO THINK OF THESE RECIPES: Though I'd make Red Chile–Marinated Chicken for a family dinner, it's a dish that's plenty dressy for company. For family, I'd put together a salad of balsamic-dressed romaine and lots of radishes to serve with the chicken. For company, I'd make some guacamole (page 4) to start, serve the salad and end the meal with fresh, simple flavors like a fruit ice or just ripe fruit. The duck, on the other hand, is definitely special-occasion fare, taking longer to prepare (though it's not hard) and offering more dazzle. It's rich enough to welcome a spoonful of white rice (page 176) and rather simple flavors both to start and end the meal, unless of course a birthday cake is in order. That would be a real feast.

ADVICE FOR AMERICAN COOKS: I chose an all-ancho *adobo* because anchos are widely available in grocery stores and by mail-order. Should dried guajillos or New Mexico chiles be easier for you to get or more to your taste, either can be substituted for or combined with the anchos (use 3 ounces of chile total). Understanding dried chile flavor takes some experience; it's more complex than fresh chile flavor.

Red Chile–Marinated Chicken Roasted with Potatoes

POLLO ADOBADO CON PAPAS

Serves 4

3 tablespoons vegetable oil, plus a little for the potatoes
6 medium (about 3 ounces total) dried ancho chiles,
     stemmed, seeded and torn into flat pieces
3 garlic cloves, peeled
1 teaspoon dried oregano, preferably Mexican
$^1/_2$ teaspoon black pepper, preferably freshly ground
$^1/_4$ teaspoon cumin, preferably freshly ground
$^1/_8$ teaspoon cloves, preferably freshly ground
1 teaspoon sugar
Salt
$^1/_3$ cup plus 1 tablespoon cider vinegar
One 3$^1/_2$-pound chicken
10 small (about 1$^1/_4$ pounds total) red-skin potatoes,
     scrubbed and halved
1 medium white onion, thinly sliced
Sprigs of watercress for garnish

TRADITIONAL

1.   THE *ADOBO* MARINADE. Measure *3 tablespoons* of the oil into a medium skillet and set over medium heat. When hot, oil-toast the chiles 1 or 2 pieces at a time until very toasty smelling and blistered, only a few seconds per side. Transfer the chiles to a bowl. Measure in 2 cups hot tap water; a small plate on the top will keep the chiles submerged. Let rehydrate for about 20 minutes.

Place the garlic, oregano, pepper, cumin, cloves, sugar, 2 teaspoons salt and $^1/_3$ *cup* of the vinegar in a blender or food processor. Pour in the rehydrated chiles, liquid and all. Process the mixture to a smooth puree. Press through a medium-mesh strainer set over a bowl. Taste the *adobo*: It should be a little "bitey" from the chiles, tangy from the vinegar, spicy from the herbs and spices and a little salty. The consistency should be a little runnier than you might think—thinnish but with nice body, like steak sauce. If it's too thick, the sauce will look gloppy on the bird (rather than covering the bird evenly) and brown irregularly.

2. FLATTENING AND MARINATING THE CHICKEN. Rinse the chicken and pat dry with paper towels. Twist the last joint of the wings up over the breast and then down behind the "shoulders," tucking them in firmly to keep them in place during roasting. Flip the chicken onto its breast. Using poultry shears, cut down through the backbone from tail to neck, staying as near as possible to the center of the bone (to keep the skin attached). If you don't have shears, lay the bird on its back, insert a long heavy knife into the body cavity and press down hard with a rocking motion to cut through the length of the backbone.

   Open the bird out onto your work surface, breast side up. Make sure that the legs are turned inward. Using your fist or a mallet, wallop the bird on the breast—hard enough to dislodge the center bones and flatten out the breast. To keep the drumsticks in place during cooking, make a small slit in the skin on each side of the bird between the thigh and the breast, then push the end of each leg through. Transfer to a large bowl. Smear half of the *adobo* all over the chicken. Refrigerate, covered, for at least 1 hour or as long as overnight. (Refrigerate or freeze the remaining *adobo* for another use—such as smearing on fish or pork or lamb chops before grilling or broiling them.)

3. ROASTING THE CHICKEN. Heat the oven to 375°F. Remove the chicken from the marinade and place in a large roasting pan (at least 18 x 13 inches) breast side up; reserve the marinade that's left behind. Pour 1/3 cup water around the chicken. Toss the potatoes lightly with oil, strew them around the chicken and sprinkle them with salt. Cover the pan with foil and slide into the oven.

   Roast, stirring the potatoes every 15 minutes, until the potatoes are tender and the chicken juices run clear when the thigh is pierced deeply with a fork (an instant-read thermometer should register about 160°F when inserted at the thickest part of the thigh), about 1 1/4 hours.

   Spoon the reserved marinade over the chicken and potatoes, smearing it around to coat everything evenly. Return the chicken to the oven and roast uncovered to give a beautiful glazed look to the chicken, about 10 minutes longer.

4. THE ONIONS. While the chicken is roasting, mix together the sliced onion and remaining *1 tablespoon* vinegar in a small bowl.

5. CARVING THE CHICKEN AND SERVING. With the help of a large fork and a spat-

ula, transfer the chicken to a cutting board. If time permits, tent with foil and let rest for 5 to 10 minutes to avoid losing too much of its juice during carving.

With a sharp knife (preferably a large chef's knife), split the bird in two down the breast, cutting gently through the skin. Because you broke some bones when flattening the bird, you will meet with little resistance. To remove the legs, cut between the thighs and breast, using the curved creases as guidelines.

Arrange the chicken pieces in the center of a large warm serving platter. Use a slotted spoon to transfer the potatoes to the platter, surrounding the chicken. Sprinkle the chicken with the onions. Decorate with sprigs of watercress, and you've got a beautiful meal ready for your guests.

WORKING AHEAD: The *adobo* marinade keeps for a week in the refrigerator; it freezes well for a month or two. The chicken and potatoes are best roasted shortly before serving, though they'll hold in a very low oven for a half hour or so.

FOR THE ADVENTURER

Conejo en Adobo (Red Chile—Roasted Rabbit)

For 4 to 6 people, cut up 2 rabbits: Cut off the hindquarters (they're like the leg/thighs of chicken) and the forequarters (they're small, but resemble the hindquarters) by using a large sharp knife to cut through the joints that attach them to the body. Now, cut the back in half at the point where the loin ends and the rib cage begins. Discard the rib portion (it has almost no meat on it). Cut off the flap on the opposite end of the loin portion, then cut the loin in half (across the backbone, as you did when you separated ribs from loin), creating 2 smaller serving pieces. Transfer to a large bowl. Make the *adobo* (Step 1 in the chicken recipe) and spoon about half of it over the rabbit pieces. Refrigerate, covered, for at least 1 hour or as long as overnight. Arrange the rabbit pieces in a large roasting pan in a single layer. Then add the potatoes and water as directed in Step 3, cover the pan with foil or a lid and roast in a 375°F oven for 1 hour. Uncover, baste the rabbit with the *adobo* juices in the pan and return it to the oven for about 10 minutes, until the rabbit is tender (it'll come free from the bone easily) and beautifully glazed.

ROAST DUCK WITH RED CHILE *ADOBO* SAUCE
AND JÍCAMA RELISH (PAGE 230)

Roast Duck with Red Chile *Adobo* Sauce and jícama relish

PATO EN ADOBO CON SALSA DE JÍCAMA

Serves 4

3 tablespoons vegetable oil

6 medium (about 3 ounces total) dried ancho chiles, stemmed, seeded and torn into flat pieces

3 garlic cloves, peeled

1 teaspoon dried oregano, preferably Mexican

$^1/_2$ teaspoon black pepper, preferably freshly ground

$^1/_4$ teaspoon cumin, preferably freshly ground

$^1/_8$ teaspoon cloves, preferably freshly ground

Salt

4 teaspoons sugar, or more to taste

$^1/_3$ cup plus 1 $^1/_2$ tablespoons cider vinegar

Two 4-pound ducks, thawed if frozen

2 cups chicken broth, plus a bit more if needed

1 small red onion, finely diced

$^3/_4$ cup finely diced peeled jícama

$^1/_4$ cup chopped dried cranberries

3 tablespoons coarsely chopped fresh cilantro

CONTEMPORARY

1. THE *ADOBO* MARINADE. Measure the oil into a medium skillet and set over medium heat. When hot, oil-toast the chiles, 1 or 2 pieces at a time, until very toasty smelling and blistered, only a few seconds per side. Transfer the chiles to a bowl. Pour off all but a generous film of oil from the skillet and set aside. Measure 2 cups hot tap water into the bowl with the chiles; a small plate on top will keep the chiles submerged. Let rehydrate for about 20 minutes.

    Place the garlic, oregano, pepper, cumin, cloves, 1 $^1/_2$ teaspoons salt, *1 teaspoon* of the sugar and $^1/_3$ *cup* of the vinegar in a blender or food processor. Pour in the rehydrated chiles, liquid and all. Process the mixture to a smooth puree. Press through a medium-mesh strainer set over a bowl.

2. MARINATING THE DUCK. For ease in carving, use a thin-bladed knife to cut out the wishbone at the neck end of the ducks (lift up the flap of neck skin and cut out the upside-down V-shaped bone that outlines the small cavity). Trim off all but 1 inch of the excess skin at the neck. With a small sharp knife, make a shallow slit under each wing and at the point where the thighs join the back (this will let rendering fat escape easily). Turn the birds over and, with the tines of a fork, prick the skin all over at 3/4-inch intervals (try not to go in as far as the meat). Rinse the ducks, pat dry with paper towels and place in a nonaluminum baking dish. Smear one-third of the *adobo* over the ducks, coating them well. Refrigerate for at least 8 hours or overnight (this long marinating helps the skin to crisp and color beautifully during roasting).

3. FROM MARINADE TO *ADOBO* SAUCE. Set the chile-frying skillet over medium heat. When quite hot, add the remaining *adobo* and stir until reduced to the thickness of tomato paste, about 10 minutes. Stir in the broth, reduce the heat to medium-low and simmer for 30 minutes or so. The finished sauce should be quite light in texture—not watery, but only one stage thicker. Season with the remaining *1 tablespoon* sugar. Taste and add more sugar and salt if you think necessary—it should be a little sweet-sour with a hint of saltiness. Cool, cover and refrigerate.

4. ROASTING THE DUCK. Heat the oven to 325°F. Remove the ducks from the marinade and set on an oiled rack at least 1 inch above the bottom of a large roasting pan. (Discard any remaining marinade.) Add 1 cup water to the roasting pan (this ensures that the rendered fat will create the least amount of smoke in the kitchen). Roast for about 2 hours, checking every 30 minutes to make sure that the water hasn't evaporated—add more if it has. Once or twice during roasting, grasp each duck with a pair of tongs and tip it up to drain accumulated fat and juices from the cavity into the pan.

   The ducks are done when you can twist a leg (use a couple of paper towels as padding to avoid getting burned) and it gives at the joint. Another test for doneness is to insert an instant-read thermometer into the thickest part of the thigh—it should read 180°F.

5. THE JÍCAMA RELISH. While the ducks are roasting, combine the diced onion, jícama, dried cranberries, and the remaining *1 1/2 tablespoons* vinegar in a small bowl. Taste and season with a little salt. Stir in the cilantro.

6. CARVING AND SERVING THE DUCK. In a small pan or in the microwave, warm the *adobo* sauce. You may find it necessary to thin the sauce with a little water or broth to give it the appropriate cream-sauce consistency.

With the help of a large fork and a spatula, transfer one of the ducks to a cutting board and position it with its tail toward you. With a sharp knife (preferably a large chef's knife), remove the leg-thigh quarters by cutting through the skin that holds them to the body, then continuing straight down through the joint that attaches them to the back. (After you've cut through the skin, pry the leg-thigh down and away from the body and you'll see the whiteness of the joint—remember that duck joints are tighter than chicken joints.) In the same manner, cut through the joints that attach the wings to the body.

To carve the breast, you have two options: Either cut out the backbone using a pair of kitchen shears, then use your large knife to cut right down through the breast, splitting it in two (because there's a cavity in the center, it'll feel like you're squashing the breast a little before the knife really begins to cut through). Or use a thin-bladed boning knife to carve the breast meat off the bone, starting at the top of the breast on one side of the breastbone and cutting below the meat along the contour of the bones. (First you'll cut straight down for a ¹/₂ inch or so at the breastbone, then you'll flatten out and proceed around the ribs.) Slice the boneless duck breast into 3 or 4 pieces for a beautiful presentation if you like. Repeat to carve the second duck.

Arrange the duck pieces on individual plates or on a large warm serving platter. Spoon the warm *adobo* sauce over or around the duck, then spoon a little jícama relish onto each piece. Now you're ready for a real treat.

WORKING AHEAD: This dish is much better if you marinate the duck a day ahead (or at least early in the day you'll serve it). The marinade and finished sauce will keep for days if refrigerated, well covered. The jícama relish is best made within a couple of hours of dinner. The roasted duck will hold perfectly in a very low oven for an hour, so don't hesitate to cook it before guests arrive. It's best carved just before serving.

VARIATION: *Charcoal-Grilled Ducks:* Prepare a charcoal fire and bank the coals to the sides of the grill for indirect cooking. Set a heatproof pan between the coals. Pour 1 ¹/₂ inches of water into the pan, set the cooking grate in place, and set the ducks on the grate over the drip pan. Cover the grill. Cook until the ducks are a deep, beautiful bronze color, about 2 hours (325°F is ideal). To maintain an even temperature, add more charcoal regularly.

QUESTIONS AND ANSWERS FROM OUR TESTING

DO THE CHILES NEED TO BE TOASTED—AND HOW? An *adobo* sauce or marinade made with untoasted chiles is one-dimensional, allowing any bitterness in the chiles to step front and center. Dry-toasting the chiles on a griddle or skillet gives a light complexity, but, as we discovered in our testing, it offers nothing like the full roasty richness that comes from oil-toasting (the process is really like quick-frying). Also, chiles that have been oil-toasted give a silkier texture to the finished marinade or sauce.

WILL BOTH THE BLENDER AND FOOD PROCESSOR PRODUCE A GOOD-TEXTURED MARINADE/SAUCE? The ancient traditional piece of equipment for reducing rehydrated dried chiles to a puree is the three-legged sloping lava-rock grinding stone, the *metate,* with its flattened rolling pin–like *mano* to do the back-and-forth grinding. The electric blender has replaced the *metate* in many (really *most*) Mexican home kitchens, but it purees by finely chopping with high-speed blades, rather than by crushing. That difference doesn't mean much in a preparation like this one; it's more striking with nut- and seed-thickened sauces like *moles* and *pipianes*. Truth is, a food processor, though not a common piece of equipment in Mexico, can produce an *adobo* marinade or sauce with a texture that matches the blender version. Whether using the *metate,* blender or food processor, you'll want to strain out the bits of tough chile skin and any stray seeds that remain in the puree. You don't need anything fancy: A simple medium-mesh strainer from the grocery store is perfectly adequate. By the way, this is not overrefinement of a typically rustic cuisine. For centuries, cooks in Mexico have strained out those unattractive little bits.

WHAT IS THE BEST APPROACH TO MARINATING AND ROASTING THE CHICKEN? An overnight marinade yields the most flavorful chicken; we were nearly as happy when we tried a 2-hour approach. How to handle the chicken was not so straightforward, however. An untrussed bird (our first experiment) looked a little too . . . haphazard for us, and the breast was dry by the time the thighs were cooked. Trussing the bird made it look prettier, but it needed an extra 15 minutes to cook, further drying out the breast and causing the marinade to darken so much that it tasted bitter. So we decided to cut through the backbone and flatten the chicken into a uniform thickness (a technique I learned back in the 1970s from Richard Olney's *Simple French Food*). That was the answer: The light and dark meat cooked through in the same amount of time. As an added bonus, the chicken is very easy to carve. During our final round of testing, we decided to cover the chicken and potatoes with foil for most of the roasting time to ensure that everything cooked uniformly and the *adobo* didn't brown too much and become bitter.

WHAT IS THE BEST WAY TO BALANCE THE FLAVORS OF RED CHILE SAUCES? Red chile sauces need a fair amount of salt to bring out their full flavor. But they need a little sugar, in my opinion, to balance that touch of inherent bitterness red chiles typically have. Not enough to make the sauce taste sweet, just mellow. Sugar, by the way, also balances heat; so if your sauce is a little spicy, sugar can tame it a touch.

VARIATION: *Lamb chops:* Brush 1-inch-thick loin or rib lamb chops with *adobo* marinade and grill them until as done as you like (it'll take 8 to 10 minutes for medium rare).

Bundles of red
radishes

Fish a la Veracruzana
(with Tomatoes, Capers, Olives and Herbs)

Some folks say they don't like Mexican food, but I think that's because they haven't really gotten to know it. It played out that way with Frances Calderón de la Barca, the Scottish-born wife of Spain's first minister to Mexico. When her boat landed in the port town of Veracruz in 1839, after a stormy voyage from New York via Cuba, she wrote to her sister (the letter was collected in her memoir, *Life in Mexico*) that she was more than underwhelmed by the culinary offerings of her temporary homeland:

> 18 December 1839. *We had a plentiful supper—fish, meat, wine, and chocolate, fruit and sweetmeats; the cookery, Spanish Vera-Crucified. A taste of the style was enough for me, garlic and oil enveloping meat, fish and fowl, with pimentos and plantains, and all kinds of curious fruit, which I cannot yet endure.*

But, like many folks, Frances saw things differently once she'd had the opportunity to luxuriate a little in the vibrant sophistication of True Mexican Cooking. So much so that at the end of her two-year Mexican sojourn, she confided:

> 6 January 1842. *Vera Cruz cookery, which two years ago I thought detestable, now appears to me delicious! What excellent fish! . . . Well, this is a trifle; but after all, in trifles as in matter of moment, how necessary for a traveller to compare his judgments at different periods, and to correct them!*

Now, the Veracruz-style fish cooking Mrs. Calderón de la Barca was won by has more Spanish influence than the cooking of, say, central or southern Mexico. Just a single bite of the region's namesake dish—whole fish baked in a briny, chunky tomato sauce—and you're transported to the sunny coast . . . of the Mediterranean.

Though tomatoes are one of the prize indigenous ingredients of the New World, they've come to mean Mediterranean to most of us. You see, the Spaniards carried tomatoes back to Europe, where the Europeans bred them larger and sweeter than the New World original and they became naturalized European citizens.

There have been numerous waves of immigration—human *and* botanical—over the centuries from Spain to Mexico's "Mediterranean," Veracruz. So European capers and olives and herbs like flat-leaf parsley have become commonplace on the tables of that region. But Veracruz cooking isn't just Mediterranean cooking. It's more multidimensional than that—less skittish about flavor, more energetic. The pickled jalapeños in this otherwise European-seeming recipe prove that point in a pretty obvious way.

But let's fast-forward "fish *a la veracruzana*" into Twenty-First-Century America on a warm afternoon: For me, it comes out as a cool rustic fresh tomato sauce nestling a few grilled salmon steaks, the whole affair perfumed with lemon zest and fresh thyme and punctuated with briny capers, olives and spicy chiles. I think that dresses the time-honored original in very up-to-date clothing.

TRADITIONAL BENCHMARK: For me, the sauce on the perfect fish *a la veracruzana* is a little chunky with diced tomatoes, capers and olives; a little juicy (never thick or pasty); and a little rich from olive oil. It has the perfect flavor when the tomatoes are ripe, balanced with a little tang and spice (chiles, olives, capers) and perfumed with herbs. The best fish to be prepared *a la veracruzana* is a meaty-textured fresh one.

WHEN TO THINK OF THESE RECIPES: If you don't live near an ocean, cooking the classic whole snapper *a la veracruzana* may not readily cross your mind. But if it does, I'll bet the occasion is a special one—one that might otherwise call for a crown roast of pork or prime rib of beef. For a complete, dazzle-them dinner, I'd start out with a spirited soup like Tortilla Soup (page 152) and serve the fish with a spoonful of classic white rice (page 176), then set out a perfect flan (page 308) for dessert. The contemporary grilled salmon or the not-so-adventurous traditional version made with fillets can be dressy or casual; *veracruzana* sauce is easy, versatile and delicious warm or cool.

ADVICE FOR AMERICAN COOKS: I've spelled out very carefully how to pull off this whole-fish classic with relative ease and composure. That doesn't mean, however, that some cooks won't find themselves whole fish–challenged when pursuing: (1) a big fresh fish, (2) a pan big enough to cook the fish in, (3) a platter the right size to serve it on and (4) the courage to carve it. For those who simply don't want to scale the wall, replace the single whole fish with fish fillets (see For the Not-So-Adventurous, page 241).

SALMON READY FOR THE GRILL, WITH LEMON-AND-THYME-
SCENTED *SALSA VERACRUZANA* (PAGE 242)

Whole Fish Veracruz-Style with Tomatoes, Capers, Olives and Herbs

PESCADO A LA VERACRUZANA

Serves 4 to 6

One 4-pound cleaned and scaled snapper, grouper or other firm
    meaty fish, such as striped bass, black bass or pompano (ask
    the fishmonger to cut out the red gills and trim off the fins
    at the top, bottom and alongside the gills)

Juice of 2 limes

Salt

1/4 cup olive oil, preferably extra-virgin

1 medium white onion, thinly sliced

4 large garlic cloves, peeled and finely chopped

3 pounds (6 medium-large round) ripe tomatoes,
    peeled (if you wish), cored and chopped into 1/2-inch
    pieces (about 7 cups)

3 to 4 bay leaves

1 1/2 teaspoons dried oregano, preferably Mexican

3 tablespoons roughly chopped fresh flat-leaf parsley, plus
    a few sprigs for garnish

1 cup pitted, roughly sliced green olives, preferably
    manzanillo olives

1/4 cup capers, drained and rinsed

3 pickled jalapeño chiles, stemmed, seeded and thinly sliced,
    store-bought or homemade (page 244)
    OR 6 whole pickled güero/largo chiles

TRADITIONAL

I. MARINATING THE FISH. Cut two parallel slashes across each side of the fish, cutting down through the flesh to the backbone (see illustration, page 240). Put the fish into a large baking dish. Drizzle both sides with the lime juice and sprinkle liberally with salt, about 1 1/2 teaspoons per side. Cover and refrigerate for an hour or so (but no more than 4 hours).

2. PREPARING THE SAUCE. In a medium (4- or 5-quart) pot (preferably a Dutch oven or Mexican *cazuela*), heat the oil over medium. Add the onion and cook, stirring regularly, until just beginning to brown, about 5 minutes. Add the garlic and cook 1 minute more, stirring several times. Raise the heat to medium-high and add the tomatoes, bay leaves, oregano, parsley and *half* of the olives, capers and chiles. Simmer briskly, stirring frequently, for about 5 minutes to evaporate some of the liquid. Reduce the heat to medium-low, stir in 1 cup of water and simmer for 15 minutes. Taste and season with salt, usually about 1 teaspoon. Remove from the heat.

3. BAKING THE FISH. Heat the oven to 350°F. Lightly oil a roasting pan large enough to hold the fish comfortably. Remove the fish from the lime mixture and lay it in the pan. (If the tail sticks out of the pan, crimp a piece of oiled aluminum foil around it to prevent burning.) Cover the fish with the steaming tomato sauce. Bake in the center of the oven until the flesh flakes when gently but firmly pressed at the point where the body meets the head, just above the gills (this is the thickest part), 50 to 55 minutes.

   Using two sturdy metal spatulas, and a lot of composure, carefully transfer the fish to a large serving platter. Tip up the baking pan to collect the sauce and spoon it over the fish. Sprinkle with the remaining olives, capers and chiles and decorate with sprigs of parsley.

4. SERVING. Carry your bounteous platter to the table for all to behold—this is dramatic stuff. Now to the serving, which is not as hard as you might think. First, set out a sharp knife (a boning or filleting knife works best here) and the two spatulas. Next, scrape the tomato sauce away from the body of the fish so you can see where you are cutting. Use the knife to cut an outline of the meatiest part: Starting where the head meets the flesh (and following the head shape), cut from the top of the fish down to the gill area, cutting all the way down to the bone. At the gill area (just past the center of the fish), turn the knife 90 degrees and cut straight down the length of the fish to the tail. Turn the platter so that you're facing the top of the fish. Now, holding the knife blade horizontally, slice into the meat just above the backbone, starting where the head meets the flesh and continuing all the way to the tail. Keep cutting farther and farther in until you reach the cut you made down the length of the fish. The top fillet is now free. Cut the fillet into 3 pieces (you can use the slashes you made before cooking as part of the cuts), then use a spatula to transfer the pieces to dinner plates (see illustration

below). Generously spoon sauce over each piece. (The lower belly part you're leaving behind has some meat—mostly bony meat—that's great to pick at later.) Lift off the now-exposed skeletal structure, starting at the tail and holding down the bottom fillet with the spatula, and discard it. The second fillet is now ready to cut into thirds and serve with the sauce. If you're inclined to remove the fish's cheeks, you'll discover why they're a delicacy.

WORKING AHEAD: The sauce keeps well for a day or two in the refrigerator, well covered. I don't really recommend rewarming fish or holding it warm for very long. But I have turned leftovers into a magnificent picnic dish by pulling all the cooked fish off the bones (discard all skin and bones) and layering it with the tomato sauce in a serving dish. Refrigerate the assembly until you are ready to set out.

VARIATIONS: *Small whole fish:* Choose four 1- to 1¼-pound whole fish and reduce the baking time to about 20 minutes. *Chicken:* Use two quartered chickens and bake them for 35 minutes in the sauce.

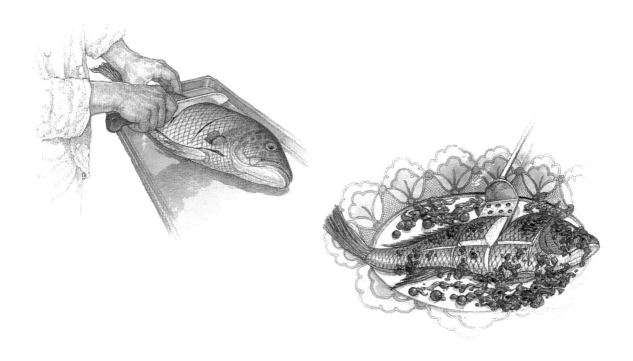

Filetes de Pescado a la Veracruzana (Fish Fillets Braised with Tomatoes, Capers, Olives and Herbs)

This is a no fuss, no muss dish that's lower on the drama scale, but still high in flavor. To feed 6, simply marinate six 5- to 6-ounce boneless, skinless fish fillets (striped bass, snapper or the like) in the juice of 2 limes with about $1/2$ teaspoon salt in the refrigerator for up to 1 hour—no more. Prepare the sauce as described in Step 2 of the recipe. Remove the fish from the marinade and lay in a single layer in an oiled 13 x 9-inch baking dish. Spoon about 5 cups of the hot tomato sauce over the fish (save the remaining sauce for another use) and bake at 350°F until the fish flakes under firm but gentle pressure, about 10 minutes. Use a spatula to transfer each fillet to a dinner plate, spoon on the sauce from the pan, sprinkle with the reserved capers, olives and chiles, decorate with the parsley and serve.

Bacalao a la Veracruzana (Veracruz-Style Salt Cod)

This is a very traditional dish for Christmas Eve. I've had it two ways, one a rather dryish "hash" of the cod and sauce, the other a moister mixture of cod chunks in a bit of sauce. My favorite is sort of in between the two, and here's how to make it: To feed 4 to 6, soak 1 pound boneless, skinless salt cod in a generous amount of cold water for 24 hours, changing the water 3 times. Bring the cod to a gentle simmer in fresh water to cover; cook for 15 to 20 minutes, until the meat flakes easily. Drain and flake into $1/2$-inch chunks. Cut 12 ounces boiling potatoes (such as red-skins) into $1/2$-inch pieces and simmer in salted water until tender, about 15 minutes. Prepare $1/2$ recipe of the sauce (Step 2 in the whole fish recipe), using the full $1/4$ cup olive oil and adding the olives, capers and chiles all at once. Once the sauce has simmered its 15 minutes, add the cooked cod and potatoes and simmer briskly over medium heat until the sauce is no longer juicy, about 15 minutes. Taste and season with salt if necessary—though it's doubtful any will be needed.

Grilled Salmon with Lemon-and-Thyme-Scented Salsa Veracruzana

SALMÓN ASADO A LA VERACRUZANA CON LIMÓN
AMARILLO Y TOMILLO

Serves 6

$^1/_4$ cup olive oil, preferably extra-virgin, plus a little for
    oiling the salmon
1 medium white onion, thinly sliced
4 garlic cloves, peeled and finely chopped
3 pounds (6 medium-large round or 18 to 24 plum)
    ripe tomatoes (you might want to use a mixture of
    yellow and red tomatoes), cored and chopped into
    $^1/_2$-inch pieces (about 7 cups)
2 tablespoons chopped fresh thyme (lemon thyme is wonderful
    here, if that's an option), plus a few sprigs for garnish
2 teaspoons finely chopped lemon zest (colored rind only—
    no white pith)
1 cup pitted, roughly sliced green olives, preferably
    manzanillo olives
$^1/_4$ cup capers, drained and rinsed
3 pickled jalapeño chiles, store-bought or homemade
    (page 244), stemmed, seeded and thinly sliced
Salt
Six 7- to 8-ounce salmon steaks, about 1 inch thick

CONTEMPORARY

I. PREPARING THE SAUCE. In a medium (4- or 5-quart) pot (preferably a Dutch oven or Mexican *cazuela*), heat the olive oil over medium. Add the onion and cook, stirring regularly, until just beginning to brown, about 5 minutes. Add the garlic and cook 1 minute more, stirring several times. Raise the heat to medium-high and add the tomatoes, thyme, lemon zest and *half* of the olives, capers and chiles. Simmer briskly, stirring frequently, for about 5 minutes to evaporate some of the liquid. Reduce the heat to medium-low, stir in 1 cup of water and simmer for 15 minutes. Taste and season with salt, usually about 1 teaspoon. Remove from the heat to cool.

2. GRILLING THE FISH. Heat a gas grill to medium-high or light a charcoal fire and let it burn just until the coals are covered with gray ash and very hot. Reduce the heat on one side of the gas grill to medium-low or set up the charcoal grill for indirect cooking by banking all the coals to one side, leaving the other half of the grill empty. Set the cooking grate in place, cover the grill and let the grate heat up, 5 minutes or so.

   If desired, use a wooden pick to skewer the ends of each salmon steak together so they don't tear off during the grilling. Brush or spray both sides of the salmon steaks with oil and sprinkle with salt. Lay the salmon steaks over the hottest part of the fire and cook for about 4 minutes, until nicely browned underneath. Using a spatula, carefully flip the fish over onto the cooler side of the grill for 2 to 4 minutes to get the salmon to that medium-rare, still-slightly-translucent-in-the-center stage that I love. (Or judge your own preference for doneness accordingly.)

3. COOLING THE FISH IN THE SAUCE. Spoon the sauce into a deep platter and nestle the fish in it. Let stand at room temperature for about an hour to bring together the flavors of fish and sauce.

4. SERVING. Sprinkle the fish with the remaining olives, capers and chiles and decorate with thyme sprigs, and you're ready to serve.

WORKING AHEAD: Everything about this dish says "make ahead." The sauce will keep for several days in the refrigerator, well covered. In fact, the whole dish can be made a day ahead without much compromise in quality—simply wrap it and refrigerate. Let the fish and sauce warm to room temperature before serving. If you make the dish early on the day you're serving, don't let it stand at room temperature any longer than 2 hours without refrigeration.

JALAPEÑOS EN ESCABECHE

• PICKLED JALAPEÑOS

Though the chiles are the stars here, there are other goodies in the pot—carrots, garlic, onions and herbs—all working together to create a wonderful, thoroughly invigorating experience. Like waistlines in modern America, the size of jalapeños has been increasing, so I suggest you buy 12 ounces or measure out 3 cups. The number of chiles isn't very reliable. These pickled jalapeños are much better if allowed to stand for at least a day after they're made.

Makes about 5 cups

¹/₃ cup vegetable oil
10 garlic cloves, peeled
2 medium carrots, peeled and sliced (a diagonal slice looks very nice)
12 ounces (about 20) fresh jalapeño chiles (about 3 cups)
1 large white onion, sliced
1¹/₂ cups cider vinegar
4 bay leaves
2 large sprigs EACH fresh thyme and marjoram
    OR ¹/₂ teaspoon EACH dried thyme and marjoram
Salt

In a large skillet, heat the oil over medium. Add the garlic and cook, stirring frequently, until beginning to brown, about 3 minutes. Add the carrots, chiles and onion and continue cooking and stirring until the onion is translucent, about 5 minutes. Stir in the vinegar, bay leaves, herbs, a generous teaspoon of salt and 1¹/₂ cups water, bring to a simmer, partially cover and cook until the carrots are just tender, about 10 minutes. (The chiles will have begun their inevitable fade toward olive green.) Cool.

Pour the mixture into a nonaluminum container, cover and refrigerate a day before eating or using in a dish. There should be enough pickling juice to completely cover the chiles; if there isn't, mix up what you need to add using half vinegar, half water and season it with a little salt. Stored in the refrigerator, these chiles will keep easily for more than a month.

Questions and Answers from Our Testing

What kind of tomatoes work well in this preparation, and should they be peeled? This one is simple: Round tomatoes produce a juicy, elegantly textured sauce, while plum tomatoes produce a much thicker sauce that can look a little stand-offish. The ripeness (or not) of the tomatoes is remarkably apparent in this sauce, so if you can't get really ripe fresh tomatoes, use three 28-ounce cans whole round tomatoes packed in juice. Drain them and chop them into ½-inch pieces—just be aware that the flavor won't be as full as that of ripe fresh tomatoes.

To peel or not to peel? That's your choice. Taking the time to give the tomatoes a 15-second dunk in boiling water so as to be able to strip off their skins *does* make a sauce that's a little more refined, texturally speaking. But then, the sauce by definition is rustic-textured with chunky olives and capers. I don't think peeling necessarily improves this dish.

What kind of fish works well in this preparation? In testing a variety of fish, we all agreed that freshness was more important than variety, but that meatier, large-flake fish like snapper, grouper, striped (and other) bass and halibut are most harmonious with the chunky sauce. Delicately textured fish like sole seem soft (almost mushy) up against the sauce. If you're adventurous enough to cook a whole fish, then you'll probably be up for some of the less common, underused species such as porgy, tilefish or corvina. Choosing one of those helps to take the pressure off the few species everyone always asks for, many of which are being found in dwindling numbers these days. Choosing underused species makes good ecological sense.

What's the best way to go about finding and storing a large fish? Unless you live in a fishing area with a thriving market, you'll need to order a large fish well in advance of serving. I've even had good luck ordering a large fish through a chain grocery store's fish counter, though I'd suggest you search out a good fish store for the best and freshest. Make sure your fish has been thoroughly scaled, the gills removed and the fins snipped. Rinse it well when you get home, then refrigerate; if you're not using it that day, wrap it in a well-sealed heavy plastic bag and refrigerate it packed in ice in a roasting pan (or in the refrigerator's meat bin). If you change the ice daily, a fresh fish will stay fresh for a couple of days. Ditto fish fillets.

Are there any tricks to cooking a large fish? It's common in Mexico to make diagonal slashes across both sides of the fish before cooking. The reason: to allow the heat (and flavor) to penetrate the fish evenly, preventing thinner parts from overcooking before thicker ones are done.

Refinements: *Olives:* Satisfying both tradition and good taste, green olives are the ticket. While the cheap pitted green olives on grocery store shelves are manzanillos, they have less taste and texture than imported Spanish manzanillos with the pits still in. If you can find high-quality cracked Spanish green olives, your pitting job will be easier. *Pickled chiles:* Choose only Mexican-style pickled jalapeños. Some popular American brands are crunchy and slightly sweet—more like spicy bread-and-butter pickles. The pickled güero chiles (available canned or bottled in Mexican markets) have a lighter, fruitier flavor than jalapeños, more like the flavor in Italian *giardiniera*.

Right: Rick and Lanie enjoying classic seafood dishes
Left: Chopping onions for escabeche

Fish in Escabeche
(Brothy Vinaigrette with Herbs and Vegetables)

You've probably seen the word *"escabeche"* on a can of spicy, puckery pickled jalapeños from Mexico, the ones that have the slightly oily texture, the herbs and garlic and the slices of onion and carrot. More than simple pickled peppers, the *jalapeños en escabeche* are almost a side dish, with all those vegetables and seasonings.

Now, while it's true that pickled jalapeños are the most common *escabeche* preparation Mexico knows, it's not the only one. Nor is Mexico the only country that makes an *escabeche*. In fact, such preparations are so commonly associated with many European countries that I've heard well-meaning visitors in Mexico—folks with a good knowledge of Spanish—pronounce the word "es-cah-BESH," rather than the typical "es-cah-BAY-chay." They're using French pronunciation and perhaps even expecting the French *escabèche* preparation—pan-seared fish with a saucy vinaigrette made from wine vinegar, wine, olive oil, stock, herbs, onions and garlic.

The concept of *escabeche* has migrated throughout a good part of the world. And everywhere it's taken up residence, it dresses in different clothes, does its hair differently, gets more (or less) of a suntan. Many researchers think that the *escabeche* journey started with a fish dish in the medieval Arab world that was carried through Spain, France and Italy, across the Atlantic to Central and South America and then all the way over to the Philippines. Probably other countries have their *escabeches;* I just haven't stumbled onto them yet.

It'll come as no surprise that Mexican *escabeche* is my favorite. When not exclusively featuring chiles, it's most frequently that all-around-the-world fish dish (except in Yucatán, where it's usually made with chicken). But in Mexico, the richer, heavier flavors (like European wine and stock) are replaced by fruit vinegar and the clean, clear, unobtrusive flavor of water. Herbs are a part of the Mexican version, as they are in many places, but often there's a little cinnamon, clove and black pepper too. And, of course, in Mexico the dish wouldn't be complete without the insistent chiles—and, in some versions, other vegetables like green beans, mushrooms, tomatoes and so forth. It's simply a lighter, brighter, more complexly perfumed dish than its European counterpart.

Taste my contemporary exotic Quail in Red Onion *Escabeche,* and you'll sense how easily this dish shows its likely Arab roots. The sweet spices scent the little birds (they're *so* good cooked over a charcoal fire), and the *escabeche* tastes as if it was just made for the addition of olives and currants.

TRADITIONAL BENCHMARK: To me, whether served warm or cool, the perfect *escabeche* offers the flavor of summer—less bracing, say, than a penetrating *ceviche,* but still tangy, light, vegetably and flavorful (with a hint of mystery). For the fullest, sweetest flavors, the vegetables in an *escabeche* are fully cooked, but not too soft. Oil gives the *escabeche* a little lusciousness, and vinegar brightens everything. The perfect *escabeche* has enough liquid to give each diner a nice pool (three or four tablespoons) of brothy vinaigrette to spoon up, offering the complete savor of the herbs and spices. And the fish? If it's fresh (or the best-quality frozen), practically any fish can be part of a great *escabeche.*

WHEN TO THINK OF THESE RECIPES: Though this is one of my all-time favorite picnic dishes, it also makes a wonderful warm-weather main dish (or dressy first course) at a nicely set table. And it's great in winter, especially after (or during) the largesse of the holidays, when something light but flavorfully satisfying is right. *Escabeche* is a great showcase for other vegetables—farmers' market baby zucchini or green beans in the summer, beets and specialty mushrooms in the fall and winter. Use them to replace some of the onions and carrots.

ADVICE FOR AMERICAN COOKS: If you don't have a reliable source for fish, make the dish with salmon fillets or peeled shrimp, since good-quality selections of both are more widely available (the shrimp will take a little less time to cook than fish fillets).

Seared Fish Fillets in *Escabeche*

FILETES DE PESCADO EN ESCABECHE

Serves 6

¹/₂ cup olive oil, preferably extra-virgin

Six 5- to 6-ounce boneless, skinless fish fillets, about ³/₄ inch thick
   (my favorites are snapper or halibut, but this preparation is also
   wonderful with mahimahi, grouper, salmon or practically any
   moderately firm textured, large-flake fish)

2 medium white onions, sliced ¹/₄ inch thick

3 medium carrots, peeled and cut into ¹/₄-inch cubes

6 garlic cloves, peeled and quartered

3 bay leaves

Leaves from 6 sprigs fresh thyme, roughly chopped,
   plus some whole sprigs for garnish
   OR ¹/₂ teaspoon dried thyme

Leaves from 6 sprigs fresh marjoram, roughly chopped,
   plus some whole sprigs for garnish
   OR ¹/₂ teaspoon dried marjoram

3 whole cloves

¹/₄ teaspoon black pepper, preferably freshly ground

A 2-inch piece of cinnamon stick, preferably Mexican
   canela

¹/₄ cup cider vinegar

1 cup water or light fish or chicken broth

Salt

3 to 4 large fresh or pickled jalapeño chiles, store-bought or
   homemade (page 244), stemmed, seeded and
   cut lengthwise into thin strips

TRADITIONAL

1. BROWNING THE FISH. In a large (12-inch) heavy skillet (preferably well-seasoned cast iron or nonstick), heat the olive oil over medium-high. Pat the fish fillets dry with paper towels, then lay them in a single uncrowded layer in the hot oil (you may need to do this in batches, depending on the size of your pan and the fillets). Brown richly on one side, 3 to 4 minutes, then flip the fillets over and brown the other side, letting the fish cook until it flakes under firm pressure, 2 to 3 minutes more. Remove the fillets to a plate and set aside.

2. THE *ESCABECHE*. Reduce the heat under the pan to medium and add the onions, carrots and garlic. Stir regularly until the onions are translucent and the carrots almost soft, about 5 minutes. Add the bay leaves, thyme, marjoram, cloves, black pepper, cinnamon, vinegar and water or broth. Cover and simmer over medium-low heat for 15 minutes to bring the flavors together. Taste and season with salt, usually about ¾ teaspoon, then stir in the jalapeño strips.

3. SERVING. If you want to serve the dish warm, simply lay the fillets over the simmering *escabeche,* cover and gently heat for 4 to 5 minutes. It's easiest to serve the warm dish by placing a piece of fish on each of six dinner plates, then spooning a portion of the brothy *escabeche* over each one, arranging sprigs of herbs decoratively on top. To serve the dish cool, simply arrange the fish on a deep serving platter and spoon the *escabeche* over it all. As it cools, the fish and vegetables will absorb much of the liquid, making this an ideal warm-weather main dish.

WORKING AHEAD: If serving the dish warm, you can brown the fish and simmer the *escabeche* several hours in advance. Refrigerate. Rewarm the fish and *escabeche* just before serving. If serving the dish cool, it's best the day it's made, but it will keep for a day or two in the refrigerator; allow it to come to room temperature before serving.

FOR THE ADVENTURER

Pulpo y Nopales en Escabeche (Octopus and Cactus Paddles in Escabeche)

Clean 3 pounds octopus (usually 2 medium): Cut off the eyes if still attached, cut open the head and wash thoroughly and cut out the beak—the hard mouth area where the tentacles come together; if they are still attached, cut off the straggly last 1½ inches of each tentacle. Simmer slowly in generously salted water to cover until completely tender (cut off a piece and taste it to check the tenderness), 1½ to 2 hours. Let cool in the broth.

Drain (strain and reserve the flavorful broth for another use, such as the seafood stew on page 159), then clean the octopus under cold water, rubbing off the skin (most will come off very easily—don't worry about the rest) and little "suction cups" that run down each tentacle. Cut into 1-inch pieces.

Trim off the spines from 1 pound (about 8 medium) cactus paddles, then cut them into ¾-inch squares. Toss with a little oil, spread on a baking sheet, sprinkle with salt and bake at 375°F for about 20 minutes, until tender and all the liquid they've exuded has evaporated. Cool and combine with the octopus.

Make the *escabeche* as described in Step 2 of the traditional recipe and add it to the octopus-cactus mixture. Taste and season with salt. Serve cool or barely warm.

Calabacitas *for sale*

Grilled Quail in Red Onion *Escabeche*

CODORNICES ASADOS EN ESCABECHE DE CEBOLLA ROJA

Serves 6

12 semi-boneless quail (see Questions and Answers, page 255)
  (about 5 ounces each), thawed if frozen
3 whole cloves
$^1/_2$ teaspoon whole black peppercorns
A 1-inch piece of cinnamon stick, preferably Mexican canela
Salt
$^1/_3$ cup olive oil, preferably extra-virgin, plus
  a little extra for grilling the quail
2 medium red onions, sliced $^1/_4$ inch thick
6 garlic cloves, peeled and quartered
3 bay leaves
Leaves from 6 sprigs fresh thyme, roughly chopped,
  plus some whole sprigs for garnish
  OR $^1/_2$ teaspoon dried thyme
Leaves from 6 sprigs fresh marjoram, roughly chopped, plus
  some whole sprigs for garnish
  OR $^1/_2$ teaspoon dried marjoram
$^2/_3$ cup green olives, preferably manzanillos, pitted and halved
$^1/_2$ cup dried currants
$1^1/_2$ cups water or light chicken broth
$^1/_2$ cup manzanilla or fino sherry, white wine or water
3 tablespoons sherry vinegar
3 large pickled jalapeño chiles, store-bought or homemade (page 244),
  stemmed, seeded and cut lengthwise into thin strips

CONTEMPORARY

I. MARINATING THE QUAIL. With kitchen string, tie each quail's legs together at the bottom. To hold the wings in place during grilling, twist the last joint of the wings up over the breast and then down behind the "shoulders," tucking them in firmly.

In a mortar or spice grinder, pulverize the cloves, black pepper and cinnamon. Set about $^1/_4$ teaspoon of the mixture aside. Use the remainder to dust both sides of the quail, then sprinkle them generously with salt. Cover the quail and refrigerate for at least an hour (or as long as overnight).

2. THE ESCABECHE. In a large (12-inch) heavy skillet (preferably well-seasoned cast iron or nonstick), heat the olive oil over medium. When hot, add the onions and garlic. Stir regularly until the onions are translucent, 5 to 6 minutes. Scoop out half of the onions and set aside. Add the $1/4$ teaspoon reserved ground spices along with the bay leaves, thyme, marjoram, olives, currants, water or broth, sherry (or its substitutes) and vinegar to the onions remaining in the pan. Cover and simmer over medium-low heat for 15 minutes to bring the flavors together. Taste and season with salt, usually about $1/4$ teaspoon, depending on the saltiness of the broth, then stir in the jalapeño strips and remove from the heat. Cool, then stir in the reserved onions (these add a nice crunch to the finished dish).

3. GRILLING THE QUAIL. Heat a gas grill to medium-high or light a charcoal fire and let it burn just until the coals are covered with gray ash and very hot. Reduce the burner(s) in the center of the gas grill to low or set up the charcoal grill for indirect cooking by banking all the coals to one side, leaving the other half of the grill empty. Set the cooking grate in place, cover the grill and let the grate heat up, 5 minutes or so. Either brush or spray the quail on both sides with a little olive oil, then lay them breast side down on the grill with the legs toward the hottest area of the grill. Cover and cook until richly browned, about 3 minutes. Flip the quail and move to the cooler portion of the grill, still with the legs toward the hot area (quail finished over a cooler fire always seems juicier). Cover and continue grilling for 3 to 5 minutes more. They're fully cooked when a fork can easily pull the meat from the leg bone; it's normal for fully cooked quail meat to remain a little pink at the bone. Remove the quail to a plate.

4. SERVING. To serve the quail warm, individual servings are easiest: Place 2 quail, slightly overlapping, on each of six dinner plates, then spoon a portion of *escabeche* over each one, arranging the sprigs of herbs decoratively on top. To serve the dish cool, simply arrange the grilled quail on a deep serving platter and pour the *escabeche* over it all. As it cools, the quail and vegetables will absorb much of the liquid, making it easy to pass.

WORKING AHEAD: The finished dish keeps beautifully, well covered in the refrigerator, for a couple of days. Remove from the refrigerator about 1 hour before serving so it comes to room temperature.

Questions and Answers from Our Testing

Is olive oil essential to create a traditional-tasting dish? You can eat *escabeches* in seaside restaurants all over Mexico and find nary a one made with olive oil. Olive oil can be in short supply and prohibitively expensive in Mexico. Cookbooks in Mexico, tomes compiled by the country's most influential cooks, however, nearly always specify the stuff. And there's a reason. In such a simple preparation, it adds substantially to the fullness of flavor in the final dish. I encourage you to use it, choosing the style (light, heavy, fruity, nutty) that you like best.

What's the right vinegar to use? The type of vinegar you use really affects the flavor of the finished dish. In Mexico, cooks often use a very mildly tangy fruit-based vinegar (typically made from overripe pineapples or bananas; some even use a light sweet-sour *pulque* vinegar from the fermented sap of the agave). The closest we can come to achieving that authentic flavor (without making our own fruit vinegar) is to choose our commercial apple cider vinegar. It is stronger (both in flavor and acidity), though, than fruit vinegar in Mexico. So, in these recipes, we've reduced the amount of vinegar from the Mexican original. Wine vinegar has a very different flavor. Not bad, just different—heavier, mellower, not so lively. I don't really recommend it here.

Is broth necessary for a complete flavor? Having been brought up to put European cooking on a pedestal (I've since reformed), for years I thought that the ultimate goal of all but the pastry kitchen was to get the concentrated flavor of meat, fish or poultry into as many preparations as possible through the addition of rich stocks. Those rich, meaty flavors can be wonderful, but when all is said and done, they're pretty domineering. All that just to say: Broth or stock isn't necessary in this light, bright dish.

What's the best fish to use here? Though practically any very fresh fish will work in this preparation, my preference is for large-flaked fish like snapper, grouper, mahimahi, wahoo, halibut, striped bass and the like. The chunkiness of the sauce works better with their meatier texture. If you can get *really fresh* mackerel, kingfish or bluefish (difficult unless you live near the source), this tangy preparation offers the perfect balance to their robust flavors.

Is the dish best served warm or cool? Personally, I prefer room temperature for both the fish and quail dishes. As everything cools together, the flavors mingle in a really beautiful way. And the sauce is brightly seasoned enough to serve at room temperature without tasting the slightest bit dull. That's not to say I don't also enjoy warm *escabeche*.

REFINEMENTS: *Quail:* Though for even, easy grill-cooking I highly recommend semi-boneless quail (those with the backbone, breastbone and ribs removed—wings and legs left bone-in), they're sometimes hard to find. If you can only get whole bone-in quail, use a pair of kitchen shears to cut each quail in half, cutting alongside the backbone and then right down through the breastbone.

VARIATION: *Chicken:* You can substitute chicken (anything from the fast-cooking boneless, skinless chicken breasts to the succulent bone-in thighs) for the fish in the traditional recipe. Each part of the chicken will cook in its own time: Small boneless breasts cook just about as fast as fish fillets; thighs take about 25 minutes.

Ajo criollo
(native garlic)

Seafood in Mojo de Ajo
(Toasty, Slow-Cooked Garlic)

 What is it about garlic that attracts eaters on every continent? The voluptuous curves of each cluster of cloves? The delicate perfume that explodes into pure olfactory sensation when one of the crescents is crushed? The way its full aroma tickles our deep insides as it roasts or sautés—like the musk of white truffles or the sultry sway of a dance partner on a warm summer night?

Garlic, that most outgoing member of the onion family, is for those who love living life to the fullest. That's not to say it's just for daredevils, though. Sure, it can be the Stone Cold Steve Austin of the flavor world, but if you know how to coax it along, you'll have the simple, elegant strength of Pierce Brosnan.

Elegance is what *slow-cooked* garlic gives you. Barely bubbling in warm olive oil for long enough to take on the color of brown sugar, garlic changes from brash to seductive. Its flavor transforms from sharp and bitey to mellow and nutty. But never does it turn timid.

That's why *mojo de ajo,* that "bath of [slow-cooked] garlic," as it's called in Spanish, is one of Mexico's favorite dressings for seafood. A mess of sautéed shrimp or a crusty pan-seared fillet of *robalo* (Mexico's ubiquitous white-fleshed snook) and spoonfuls of glistening, aromatic garlic make a perfect pair. Neither seafood nor garlic is irresolute, but they sing together joyously. Courageously simple and luxurious.

Though there is a wild leek—a ramp, to use its right name—that is native to the New World, garlic as we know it (and used in the proportions we're talking about here) was brought to the Americas with the Europeans, perhaps originally because of its long-known health benefits. (Food and health in those Spanish colonial days were inextricably linked in a wise way that we're finally getting back to.) Garlic is one of the greatest health-promoting foods, packed with antibacterial, antifungal and antithrombotic properties. Besides, its flavor lifts the spirit, which does wonders in promoting well-being.

When you're making something as garlicky as *mojo de ajo* in Mexico, you want to choose the best garlic—which isn't always the kind with the largest, easy-to-peel cloves. In fact, the garlic most cooks love in Mexico is a small-cloved, red-tinged *ajo criollo* ("native garlic" that's been around so long it's a naturalized Mexican) with a dynamic flavor that puts other garlic to shame.

Aromatic *mojo de ajo* over sweet shrimp is thrilling, though I'll admit that it's a dish that tips the scales in the richness category. Definitely special-occasion stuff, though not as special as my contemporary broiled lobster tails with a crusty, creamy cap of *mojo* mayonnaise. That's a beauty that'll make you dream with the angels, as they say in Mexico.

TRADITIONAL BENCHMARK: The garlic in a perfect *mojo de ajo* is meltingly soft, having been prepared with enough good oil to cook the garlic evenly and to pool luxuriously at the bottom of the plate. It's golden in color, sweet and nutty in flavor and almost a touch gooey in texture. Since this is Mexican *mojo* (as opposed to Cuban *mojo criollo,* say), lime juice balances the garlic-oil richness and a touch of red chile adds a little awe. Perfect seafood in *mojo de ajo* means perfectly *fresh* seafood, full of flavor and texture (no place for mild, wimpy, fine-flaked fish, in my opinion).

WHEN TO THINK OF THESE RECIPES: When it's time to make just the right dish for that spirited someone—without spending all day doing it. Anything *mojo de ajo* is rich, so it's best to keep the accompaniments simple: White rice is standard on *mojo de ajo* plates in Mexico; crusty bread is another popular accompaniment, but my choice is hot corn tortillas. Start with a tangy *ceviche* or even a vegetable (like asparagus) vinaigrette salad. Finish with fresh poached fruit or a simple free-form fruit tart. You could serve the shrimp or the lobster on a buffet too, warm or at room temperature. But don't forget a good bottle of white wine. Viognier is my favorite here, but a not-too-oaky Chardonnay is good too.

ADVICE FOR AMERICAN COOKS: As with other simple dishes, the quality of each ingredient is the cook's biggest challenge—each one is important. Thankfully, all ingredients for these dishes are easily accessible in the United States, except, perhaps, the chipotle chiles. Though I love their spicy smokiness in the *mojo,* you could simply skip them (or substitute thinly sliced dried guajillo chiles) and still have a perfectly delectable dish to offer your guests.

Quick-Fried Shrimp with Sweet Toasty Garlic

CAMARONES AL MOJO DE AJO

TRADITIONAL

Serves 6 generously

3/4 cup peeled garlic cloves (about 2 large heads)
1 cup good-quality oil, preferably extra-virgin olive oil
Salt
Juice of 1 lime
2 canned chipotle chiles en adobo, seeded and cut
    into thin strips
2 limes, cut into wedges
2 pounds (about 48) medium-large shrimp, peeled (leaving
    the last joint and tail intact if you wish)
3 tablespoons chopped fresh cilantro or flat-leaf parsley (optional)

1. **PREPARING THE** *MOJO DE AJO.* Either chop the garlic with a sharp knife into ⅛-inch bits or drop the cloves through the feed tube of a food processor with the motor running and process until the pieces are roughly ⅛ inch in size. You should have about ½ cup chopped garlic. Scoop into a small (1-quart) saucepan, measure in the oil (you need it all for even cooking) and ½ teaspoon salt and set over medium-low heat. Stir occasionally as the mixture comes *barely* to a simmer (there should be just a hint of movement on the surface of the oil). Adjust the heat to the very lowest possible setting to keep the mixture at that very gentle simmer (bubbles will rise in the pot like sparkling mineral water) and cook, stirring occasionally, until the garlic is a *soft,* pale golden (the color of light brown sugar), about 30 minutes. The slower the cooking, the sweeter the garlic.

   Add the lime juice to the pan and simmer until most of the juice has evaporated or been absorbed into the garlic, about 5 minutes. Stir in the chiles, then taste the *mojo de ajo* and add a little more salt if you think it needs it. Keep the pan over low heat, so the garlic will be warm when the shrimp are ready. Scoop the lime wedges into a serving bowl and set on the table.

2. **THE SHRIMP.** Devein the shrimp if you wish: One by one, lay the shrimp on your work surface, make a shallow incision down the back and pull or scrape out the dark (usually) intestinal tract.

Set a large (12-inch) heavy skillet (preferably nonstick) over medium-high heat and spoon in 1 ½ tablespoons of the oil (but not any garlic) from the *mojo*. Add *half* of the shrimp to the skillet, sprinkle generously with salt and stir gently and continuously until the shrimp are just cooked through, 3 to 4 minutes. Stir in *half* the cilantro or parsley, if you're using it. Scoop the shrimp onto a deep serving platter. Repeat with another 1 ½ tablespoons of the garlicky oil and the remaining shrimp.

When all of the shrimp are cooked, use a slotted spoon to scoop out the warm bits of garlic and chiles from the *mojo* pan, and scatter them over the shrimp. (You may have as much as ⅓ cup of the oil left over, for which you'll be grateful—it's wonderful for sautéing practically anything.) If you're a garlic lover, you're about to have the treat of your life, served with the lime wedges to add sparkle.

Working Ahead: The *mojo de ajo* keeps for a couple of weeks in the refrigerator (the oil will become solid but will liquify again at room temperature), so I never recommend making a small amount. *Mojo* in the refrigerator represents great potential for a quick wonderful meal. Warm cold *mojo* slowly before using. For the best texture, cook the shrimp immediately before serving. Or cook them an hour or so ahead, douse them with the garlic *mojo* and serve it all at room temperature.

Roasted Lobster Tails with *Mojo* Mayonnaise

COLAS DE LANGOSTA ASADAS CON MAYONESA AL AJO

Serves 6

³/₄ cup peeled garlic cloves (about 2 large heads)
1 ¹/₄ cups good-quality vegetable oil (I like expeller-pressed
    canola oil here), plus a little extra for the lobster
2 large egg yolks
3 tablespoons fresh lime juice, plus a little for the watercress
2 canned chipotle chiles en adobo, *seeded and finely chopped*
Salt
Six 6-ounce uncooked lobster tails in the shell
3 bunches watercress, large stems removed

1. PREPARING THE *MOJO DE AJO*. Either chop the garlic with a sharp knife into ¹/₈-inch bits or drop the cloves through the feed tube of a food processor with the motor running and process until the pieces are roughly ¹/₈ inch in size. You should have about ¹/₂ cup chopped garlic. Scoop into a small (1-quart) saucepan, measure in the oil (you need it all for even cooking) and set over medium-low heat. Stir occasionally as the mixture comes *barely* to a simmer (there should be just a hint of movement on the surface of the oil). Adjust the heat to the very lowest possible setting to keep the mixture at that very gentle simmer (bubbles will rise in the pot like sparkling mineral water) and cook, stirring occasionally, until the garlic is a soft, pale golden (the color of light brown sugar), about 30 minutes. The slower the cooking, the sweeter the garlic. Cool to room temperature and transfer to a small pitcher or measuring cup with a pour spout.

2. THE *MOJO* MAYONNAISE. In a food processor or blender, combine the egg yolks and lime juice. Pulse to combine, then, with the machine running, *slowly* dribble in the oil from the *mojo,* not worrying if stray bits of garlic go in as well. As you dribble in the oil, the mixture will thicken into a mayonnaise. When all the oil is in and the mayonnaise is thick, spoon in the garlic and process only long enough to combine (there should still be plenty of discernible pieces of garlic). Scrape into a bowl, stir in the chopped chipotles and taste and season with salt, usually about ³/₄ teaspoon. Refrigerate, covered.

3. **PREPARING THE LOBSTER.** If the lobster tails are frozen, defrost them slowly in the refrigerator (this will take about 24 hours) or in a tightly sealed plastic bag under *cold* running water (allow about 45 minutes). Using a pair of sharp kitchen shears, cut through the shell of each lobster tail down the center of the back, stopping when you reach the fan tail. Pry apart the cut shell and run your finger underneath to ensure the meat is loose all the way to the fan tail. Then, holding the shell apart with one hand, lift the uncooked tail meat through the opening, leaving it connected only at the fan tail end. Push the shell back together and let the lobster meat rest on top of the shell (see illustration, page 259). The thin membrane-like covering over the meat will likely have been split when you cut the shell; if it's not, snip it apart completely. The meat will look like a giant butterflied shrimp. Cover and refrigerate if not cooking right away.

4. **ROASTING THE LOBSTER.** Heat the broiler. Lay the prepared lobster tails on a baking sheet, spreading out the fan tails. Brush or spray the lobster meat with oil. Place about 8 inches below the broiler. Broil for 5 minutes. Remove from the broiler and check one of the tails for doneness by cutting off about ½ inch of the meat at the front: It should be just about tender but still have a hint of translucency in the center. If it is still quite far from done, return the lobster to the broiler for about another minute or so.

   Smear the meat (including the sides) evenly with an ⅛-inch layer of *mojo* mayonnaise and return to the broiler. Broil until the mayonnaise is golden brown, about 1 minute more.

5. **SERVING.** Transfer the lobster to a serving platter. Toss the watercress with a little lime juice and salt and arrange it around the tails. Serve your lucky guests, passing the remaining mayonnaise separately.

WORKING AHEAD: *Mojo de ajo* keeps for a couple of weeks in the refrigerator. Let it come to room temperature before using it to make the mayonnaise in Step 2. Homemade mayonnaise is quite perishable—up to 2 days tightly covered in the refrigerator is just about the maximum. Fresh or defrosted lobster tails will keep about 1 day if you refrigerate them on a bed of ice. Broil the lobster tails when you're ready to serve them.

VARIATION: For a simpler approach, split the lobster (shell and all) down the length of the tail. Broil as directed (including the slathering with mayonnaise) cut side up.

Langosta Entera Asada con Mayonesa al Ajo (Roasted Whole Lobster with *Mojo* Mayonnaise)

For most cooks, limited broiler space makes it difficult to roast more than 2 whole 1 ½-pound lobsters—enough to serve 4 people—so plan to cook this lobster for more intimate occasions. First make the *mojo* mayonnaise. Second, kill and cut up the live lobsters: Holding one of the lively lobsters firmly, head toward you on a cutting board, place the tip of a large knife or cleaver at the center of the cross-shaped mark at the back of the head (where the head meets the body). With force, cut right down through the head toward you, splitting it in half. Wait a couple of minutes for any movement to cease. Turn the lobster around and split the tail in a similar fashion; cut the two lobster halves in half where the head section meets the tail. Pull out and discard the grayish sac from the two head section halves, then look for the dark (usually) intestinal tract that runs down the length of the tail; pull it out. Twist off the "legs," then twist off the arm (often referred to as the "knuckle") and claw from each half. Twist or cut off the claws from the arms. Use the back of your knife to crack the claws. Twist or cut off and discard the antenna. At this point you should have a split front half (head), a split tail, 2 arms and 2 claws. Cut up the second lobster in the same way.

Turn on the broiler. Heat a large (12-inch) heavy skillet, with an ovenproof handle, over medium-high heat. When it's really hot, film it with oil, then lay in the lobster pieces in a single layer, shell side down. After about 2 minutes, when the shells have mostly turned bright red, use tongs to turn the pieces over. Set the pan 6 inches below the broiler and cook for about 2 minutes. Test a piece of the tail: It should be fully tender at the place where the tail is connected to the body. Turn the head and tail pieces shell side down, laying them as flat as possible. Spread the meat liberally with the mayonnaise. Return to the broiler until golden, about 1 minute more. Pile the lobster pieces onto a serving platter and drizzle with the pan juices. Garnish with parsley sprigs and serve with additional mayonnaise.

QUICK-FRIED SHRIMP WITH SWEET TOASTY GARLIC
(PAGE 258)

QUESTIONS AND ANSWERS FROM OUR TESTING

WHICH GARLIC VARIETIES MAKE THE BEST *MOJO DE AJO*? We found after numerous tests that the standard-issue large-clove, soft-neck (braidable), white Italian garlic—the one most of us find easily available and easy to use—makes a very good *mojo de ajo*. But the very best *mojo de ajo* is made from the more aromatic, more complex heirloom varieties, like the tiny-clove, hard-neck red Mexican garlic. So search for it or other heirloom varieties at your farmers' market, if that interests you. But stay away from elephant garlic. Yes, the peeling will go faster, but the *mojo* will have much less flavor and the pieces of garlic will get sticky and clump together in the oil.

WHAT'S THE BEST WAY TO PEEL AND CHOP THE GARLIC? There are a couple of garlic-peeling devices on the market—a flexible tube offers quite an interesting tactile experience as you massage the peels off the cloves inside—that you might find helpful. Personally, I don't find any frustration in peeling the cloves individually with a small knife, either as is or after a gentle flattening against the countertop with the side of a large knife (this loosens the papery skin). My preference is not to buy peeled garlic; much of it is peeled with an acid solution and it never tastes very fresh to me. In Mexico, some cooks simply leave the thin papery skins on the small cloves of red *criollo* garlic. It's not the most refined way to make *mojo de ajo,* but it's not bad.

If you want the most even texture and most beautiful dish, hand chop the garlic into very tiny dice (what chefs would call a small *brunoise*). For expediency, use a food processor—I think you'll find the end result quite acceptable.

WHAT'S THE BEST OIL TO USE FOR THIS PREPARATION? Of all the tests we did, I liked *mojo de ajo* best when it was made with a good fruity olive oil. That, however, is not the most commonly used oil in Mexico. There, they typically opt for a neutral vegetable oil, olive oil being less available and much more expensive. Of the vegetable oils we tried, I recommend expeller-pressed canola oil (one that says it can take high heat). Truthfully, all oils except olive oil tasted pretty much the same—and a lot like garlic—when the cooking was finished. Corn oil was the least attractive, because it caused the garlic to clump together and it has a heavier, mouth-coating quality.

WHAT'S THE BEST WAY TO COOK *MOJO DE AJO*? In order to cook the garlic evenly (without risking overcooking on the edges), the garlic needs to float freely in the oil—for this quantity of garlic, there needs to be at least 1 inch of oil. In order to ensure that depth, you'll need a pan that's about 6 inches in diameter (a 1-quart saucepan is perfect). And for the garlic to cook evenly, the pan needs to be heavy—no hot spots. An All-Clad stainless steel saucepan is my favorite for cooking *mojo de ajo*. I can't emphasize enough how important it is to regulate the temperature so that the garlic isn't cooking too quickly (you may even need a "flame-tamer" under the pan to get the temperature low enough). We thought the steady heat of a low oven might be the ticket, but it was less reliable, and we had to be checking and stirring every few minutes.

REFINEMENTS: *Shrimp-cooking methods:* I've outlined a big-skillet way to cook the shrimp, a pound at a time. If you're comfortable with a wok and a very hot burner, stir-fry the shrimp in a little of the garlic oil in 2 or 3 batches; their texture will be crisper than that of the skillet-cooked ones. *Amount of oil:* Though you need all the oil for slowly cooking the garlic, you won't use it all for serving—what you'll actually use is about 2 tablespoons per serving. Leftover garlic oil is a treasure that you can keep in the refrigerator for several weeks to use for sautéing fish or chicken, for kneading into bread dough or for wonderful salad dressings (especially Caesar dressing).

VARIATION: *Fish fillets in* mojo de ajo: If fish fillets are more to your liking than shrimp, sear them in a hot pan in a little garlicky oil from the *mojo de ajo.* About 8 minutes per inch of thickness (half the time on each side) is typical timing for most fish; 5 to 6 minutes for medium-rare (with fresh tuna, for example).

Typical seafood restaurant offering

Pork in Salsa Verde
(Tomatillo Sauce)

 Tomatillos are remarkable. They're sold appropriately ripe (none of those tomato-ripening problems) and they hold well for weeks, even a month or more, in the refrigerator without losing anything. They have a bright, fresh flavor—a little citrusy and herbal. Their high pectin content naturally thickens a sauce in a way I can only describe as lilting. And they're relatively inexpensive.

So why, with such dynamic attributes, have tomatillos never had their turn as the darlings of the food aficionados? Why have they not become this year's Dijon mustard, ginger, balsamic vinegar or chipotle pepper? Who knows? But I can't say I feel bad for them, since there's no predicting what contortions such popularity might have subjected them to. I'm glad the tomatillo has stayed firmly rooted in Mexican soil and seasonings.

You may first encounter tomatillos in an herby fresh green tomatillo *salsa,* enticingly knit together with onion, green chiles and cilantro. Whether all the ingredients are raw and blender-chopped into a slushy salsa or the tomatillos are cooked first to give the stuff a more spoonable consistency, Mexico's lively tomatillo salsa is a world-class condiment for tacos or other snacks.

On the other hand, Mexico's slow-simmered tomatillo *sauce* (also called *salsa* in Spanish—a fact that confuses many who don't speak Spanish) is made from the same ingredients but cooked with enriching broth or browned meat. It is more mature, perhaps even a bit motherly. Think of this warm sauce as the Mexican equivalent of an Italian grandma's tomato sauce—basic and satisfying. In fact, some researchers think that sauces made from tomatillos were the Original Mexican Sauces, tomato sauces playing a less important role in pre-Columbian times.

Tomatillo sauces sure spell Mexico to me. A homey tomatillo-braised pork loin, releasing its captivating aroma, warms up any cool evening. My contemporary crispy-crusted fish set in a lovely verdant tomatillo pool dresses up the heretofore-humble tomatillo sauce for an elegant night on the town.

TRADITIONAL BENCHMARK: To me, the perfect tomatillo-braised pork balances the natural tanginess of roasted tomatillos with the sweetness of slow-cooked onions and garlic and the richness of browned pork. A few potatoes add just the right simple earthy contrast. And perfect pork? Cooked slowly in a moist environment for just the right amount of time, it's tender and juicy.

WHEN TO THINK OF THESE RECIPES: Say you want to make something flavorful for the family or a few friends, but it just has to be casual. Tomatillo-braised pork will draw them straight to the kitchen when you take the lid off the pot, announcing that you've made something pretty special. The corn flake–crusted fish fillets, however, are another matter entirely. They make a dressy dish for times when you want to let your guests know there's no reason to go out to a restaurant.

ADVICE FOR AMERICAN COOKS: Make sure to use *fresh* (not canned) tomatillos; they are available practically everywhere these days, from chain groceries to farmers' markets. Canned tomatillos are not my favorite, and I don't recommend making these dishes with them—they will taste overly acrid.

Left: Simple market altar
Right: Cazuelas, ollas and chocolate pots

Tomatillo-Braised Pork Loin

LOMO DE PUERCO EN SALSA VERDE

Serves 6

TRADITIONAL

1 ½ tablespoons rich-tasting pork lard or olive or vegetable oil
One 2-pound boneless pork loin roast, untied if in two pieces
1 pound (10 to 12 medium) tomatillos, husked and rinsed
Fresh hot green chiles to taste (roughly 3 serranos or
 1 jalapeño), stemmed
1 medium white onion, sliced
3 large garlic cloves, peeled and finely chopped
1 to 2 large sprigs fresh epazote, plus extra sprigs for garnish
 OR ⅓ cup chopped fresh cilantro, plus a few sprigs for garnish
Salt
10 small (about 1 ¼ pounds total) red-skin potatoes,
 scrubbed and quartered

1. **BROWNING THE PORK.** In a medium (4- to 5-quart) Dutch oven or other heavy pot with a tight-fitting lid, heat the lard or oil over medium. When quite hot, lay in the pork loin (if it is in two pieces, don't crowd them, or they'll stew rather than brown). Brown well on one side, about 5 minutes, then turn over and brown the other side. Remove the pot from the heat and transfer the pork to a plate; set the Dutch oven or pot aside to use for the sauce.

2. **THE SAUCE.** Roast the tomatillos and chiles on a baking sheet 4 inches below a very hot broiler until darkly roasted, even blackened in spots, about 5 minutes. Flip them over and roast on the other side—4 to 5 minutes more will give you splotchy-black and blistered tomatillos and chiles that are soft and cooked through. Cool, then transfer everything to a food processor or blender, being careful to scrape up all the delicious juice that has run out onto the baking sheet. Process until smoothly pureed.

 Set the pork-browning pot over medium heat. When hot, add the onion and cook, stirring regularly, until golden, about 7 minutes. Stir in the garlic and cook a minute longer. Raise the heat to medium-high, and, when the oil is really sizzling, add the tomatillo puree all at once. Stir until noticeably darker and very thick, 3 to 4 minutes. Add 1 ½ cups of water and the *epazote* or cilantro. Taste and season with salt, usually 1 teaspoon. Stir everything thoroughly.

3. BRAISING THE PORK. Heat the oven to 325°F. Nestle the browned pork into the warm sauce, cover the pot and set in the oven. Cook for 30 minutes.

While the meat is cooking, simmer the potatoes in heavily salted water to cover until tender, about 10 minutes. Drain and set aside.

When the pork has cooked for 30 minutes, nestle the cooked potatoes into the sauce around the meat, re-cover and cook until the pork registers about 145°F on a meat or instant-read thermometer, 5 to 10 minutes longer. The meat will feel rather firm (not hard) to the touch and cutting into the center will reveal only the slightest hint of pink.

4. SERVING THE DISH. With a pair of tongs and a spatula, transfer the pork to a cutting board. Let it rest for 3 or 4 minutes while you finish the sauce: Spoon off any fat on the top of the sauce, taste the sauce and season it with additional salt if you think necessary. Spoon the sauce and potatoes onto a warm deep serving platter.

Cut the pork into ¼-inch slices and arrange them over the sauce. Decorate the platter with *epazote* or cilantro sprigs and you're ready for a great meal.

WORKING AHEAD: The pork can be browned and the sauce made a day ahead; refrigerate separately, well covered, until a couple of hours before you're ready to braise the pork. The meat will have the best texture if braised just before serving, though it will hold fine in a very *low* oven (uncover the pot) for about a half hour if you slightly undercook the pork—it'll finish cooking as it sits.

CORN FLAKE—CRUSTED FISH FILLETS WITH ROASTED
TOMATILLO SAUCE AND FRIED CORN (PAGE 271)

Corn Flake–Crusted Fish Fillets with Roasted Tomatillo Sauce and Fried Corn

PESCADO "ENCORNFLECADO" EN SALSA VERDE CON
ESQUITES FRITOS

Serves 6

¹/₂ cup all-purpose flour

Salt

2 large eggs

One 7-ounce box corn flakes

Six 5- to 6-ounce skinless fish fillets (choose snapper, grouper, halibut,
striped bass, mahimahi or other medium-flake light-flavored
fish), about ³/₄ inch thick

1 pound (10 to 12 medium) tomatillos, husked and rinsed

Fresh hot green chiles to taste (roughly 3 serranos or 1 jalapeño),
stemmed

2 tablespoons olive oil

1 medium white onion, sliced

3 large garlic cloves, peeled and finely chopped

2 cups light fish or chicken broth

²/₃ cup loosely packed chopped fresh cilantro, plus a few sprigs
for garnish

2 cups fresh corn kernels (you'll need about 3 ears of sweet corn
or, for the most traditional Mexican flavor, 2 ears of field
corn at the "milk" stage—what we called roasting ears
when I was a kid)

Vegetable oil to a depth of ¹/₄ inch for panfrying

CONTEMPORARY

1. **"BREADING" THE FISH.** Spread the flour on a deep plate (or pie plate), then stir
   in ¹/₂ teaspoon salt. Break the eggs onto another deep plate and add 3 tablespoons
   water and ¹/₂ teaspoon salt. Beat with a fork until completely liquid. Spread the
   corn flakes on a third plate, then use the back of a measuring cup to gently break
   them into ¹/₄-inch pieces.

Dredge all sides of 1 fish fillet in the flour, then lay it in the egg mixture. Use a large fork to flip it over, then carefully transfer the drippy piece of fish to the plate of corn flakes. Sprinkle flakes from the dish over the top of the fish and press them in firmly; the fish should be thoroughly coated with flakes. Transfer to another plate or baking sheet, then "bread" the remaining fillets. Refrigerate uncovered for at least 1 hour, or up to 6 hours.

2. THE SAUCE. Roast the tomatillos and chiles on a baking sheet 4 inches below a very hot broiler until darkly roasted, even blackened in spots, about 5 minutes. Flip them over and roast on the other side—4 to 5 minutes more will give you splotchy-black and blistered tomatillos and chiles that are soft and cooked through. Cool, then transfer everything to a food processor or blender, being careful to scrape up all the delicious juice that has run out onto the baking sheet. Process until smoothly pureed.

Set a heavy medium (4-quart) saucepan over medium heat and measure in *1 tablespoon* of the olive oil. When hot, add the onion and cook, stirring regularly, until richly golden, about 7 minutes. Stir in the garlic and cook for a minute longer. Raise the heat to medium-high, and, when the oil is really sizzling, add the tomatillo puree all at once. Stir until noticeably darker and very thick, 3 to 4 minutes. Add the broth and *1/3 cup* of the cilantro. Stir everything thoroughly. Simmer, stirring often, over medium-low heat until the flavors mellow and the consistency thickens enough to coat a spoon (but not too heavily), about 30 minutes. Taste and season with salt, usually about 3/4 teaspoon. Keep warm over low heat.

3. FINISHING THE DISH. In a medium skillet, heat the remaining *1 tablespoon* olive oil over medium. When hot, add the corn and stir frequently until nicely browned, 5 to 10 minutes. Sweet corn will be a little chewy, field corn will be quite chewy, meaning you may want to dribble a little water in the pan to steam the kernels to a bit more tenderness. Set aside in the pan.

Turn on the oven to the lowest setting. Heat 1/4 inch of vegetable oil in a large heavy skillet over medium to medium-high. When the oil is hot enough to make an edge of a "breaded" fillet really sizzle, fry the fillets in two batches. (They shouldn't be crowded in the pan, or they won't crust and brown nicely.) They'll need to cook about 2 minutes per side to brown and be done enough to flake under firm pressure—it takes a little practice to check this without breaking the crust very much. Carefully transfer the first batch of cooked fillets to a paper towel–lined baking sheet and keep warm in the oven while you're frying the second batch.

Spoon the warm sauce (thin it with a little water if it has thickened) onto a deep warm platter and arrange the crusty fish fillets slightly overlapping down the center. Sprinkle the whole affair with the corn (reheat it if it has cooled off) and the remaining *⅓ cup* cilantro. Garnish with the cilantro sprigs and you're ready to make your triumphant entrance to the dining room.

WORKING AHEAD: Though this restauranty dish may be more than you want to tackle just before your guests sit down, you can easily do it in stages. Make the sauce and the corn a day ahead (store them separately, covered, in the refrigerator), then rewarm both just before serving. Bread the fish up to 6 hours ahead, then fry it just before you're ready to serve.

QUESTIONS AND ANSWERS FROM OUR TESTING

WHICH TASTES BEST: A SAUCE MADE FROM RAW, BOILED OR ROASTED TOMATILLOS? We tried all three versions and this is what we found: A sauce made from *raw* tomatillos (chopped as fine as possible in a food processor with the chiles) simmered with the sautéed onion and garlic had an overly coarse texture and the most aggressively acidic, in-your-face tomatillo flavor—nothing mellow about it. A sauce made from *boiled* tomatillos had an attractive medium-bodied consistency, and the flavor was pleasantly tangy—not too aggressive, not too intense. But the sauce made with *roasted* tomatillos was the prettiest (a luxurious thickishness with attractive dark flecks) and the tastiest (more sweet notes to balance the tomatillos' natural tanginess, robust but mellow).

IS THE TRADITIONAL SEARING OF THE SAUCE BASE NECESSARY? Searing the tomatillo puree in a hot pan filmed with oil, then stirring it until thickened and darkened to the consistency of tomato paste offers another round of concentrating, fusing and sweetening of the flavors, making the most well-balanced and sophisticated-tasting sauce—still tangy, yet mellow.

WHAT CUT OF PORK IS BEST FOR MAKING THE BRAISED PORK DISH? That depends on how you want to serve the finished dish. Using 1-inch cubes of pork shoulder, browned and gently simmered in the sauce (this can be done on the stove top instead of in the oven), produces the typical homey stew you frequently find in Mexico. Braising pork loin in the sauce, then slicing it, offers prettier presentation options and a texture many of us consider very attractive—making the dish appropriate for a special dinner. With pork bred so lean in the United States these days, you need to be careful not to overcook the pork loin; using an instant-read thermometer is the most reliable way to judge doneness.

REFINEMENTS: *Seasoning the sauce:* Some cooks confuse the tomatillo's natural acidity with saltiness and proclaim the dish to be seasoned when it's not. Seasoning with the right amount of salt balances acidity, so do it carefully. *Water v. broth in the sauce:* When we tried making the braised pork dish with broth instead of water, it tasted overly rich to us, its meat flavor masking the tomatillo flavor. Simply braising the pork in the sauce gives the sauce plenty of meat flavor. Of course, in the contemporary fish dish, the sauce never sees the fish until they meet on the plate, so we use broth in the sauce to add the necessary mellow note.

VARIATIONS: *Chicken:* Chicken can easily replace pork in the braised dish. For juiciness and flavor, I'd choose to cook chicken on the bone, and to ensure that it's all done at the same time, I'd choose either dark or light meat—1 to 2 chicken thighs per person (depending on their size) or 6 half chicken breasts. Brown and braise as directed, 30 to 35 minutes for thighs, 20 to 25 minutes for breasts. *Tomatillos and dairy:* A little homemade *crema* (page 133), *crème fraîche* or heavy (whipping) cream does wonders to mellow tomatillo sauce. *Purslane* (verdolagas): Though tomatillo sauce welcomes practically any kind of leafy green, it is traditionally made in Mexico with the vitamin-packed, citrus-flavored purslane. Look for it in farmers' markets in the summer or in some Mexican groceries year-round. Cut off the thick stems at the base, then cut the rest into 1½-inch segments, stems and all. Add the greens to the pork along with the potatoes in Step 3.

At the carnicería y tocinería
(meat and bacon stall)

Beef a la Mexicana
(with Roasted Tomatoes and Green Chiles)

 Okay, I guess it's true: Everything they eat in Mexico is prepared *a la mexicana*—well, with the exception of the food, say, in French restaurants and sushi bars. But some dishes strike such a special chord that they need to be singled out. They're dishes that cause mouths to water and chests to swell with nationalistic pride. They're the dishes that are christened, heart-and-soul, *a la mexicana.*

Now, *mole* is undoubtedly Mexico's national dish, but no one would call it *mole a la mexicana*. That would indulge the faint possibility of a *mole a la francesa* or *mole a la italiana,* which of course would be unthinkable. So dishes labeled *a la mexicana* have to start with a more universal base (a piece of beef, say, or a skillet of eggs), then smack it with a Mexican flavor stamp.

There are no flavors more proudly heralded as Mexican than juicy, sweet-tart, red-ripe tomatoes and thrilling fresh chile peppers. And in Mexico, the kitchen artisans know how to get the absolute best out of them. They know how to work with big, dark green chiles like poblanos (compact, complex, not-too-spicy flavor), roasting them to add a smoky edge. And they know how to let tomatoes (usually the tangy varieties) stay on the vine long enough to come to full flavor, then cook them intensely to concentrate their sweet richness. Buoy up those two fruits (yes, they're *both* botanically fruits, though we use them as vegetables) with the pure bright flavor of white onion (some add aromatic heirloom garlic), and you've got an experience *a la mexicana* that ignites the senses.

Red, white and green—joyous, vibrant colors on the national flag of Mexico. Red tomato, white onion and green chile—awesome, amicable flavors on the plates of Mexico.

Beef tips *a la mexicana* (pan-seared or braised meat with tomato and roasted green chile) are as common in Mexico as steak and potatoes are north of the border. But short ribs braised with those same flavors, as in the recipe that follows, are even homier, more luscious than the ubiquitous tips. When you turn the tomato-chile-onion trio into a roasty salsa, then use it both as marinade and condiment for broiled or grilled flank steak, you add a contemporary patina to a satisfying combination that has stood the test of time. These two approaches just scratch the surface of real cooking *a la mexicana.*

TRADITIONAL BENCHMARK: It's hard to describe a benchmark for dishes in a class as broad, as amorphous as those tagged *a la mexicana*. The best of them, though, have that comfortable savor of Grandma's table—if your grandma is Mexican and a great cook. She would choose the best, ripest produce, but nothing fancy. And she'd cook it in an easy-going way, knowing just how long to linger on the roasting of the chiles or how long to cook the meat. And everything would be just right, all done without a chef's self-conscious flair.

To my taste, the braised short ribs are best when the tomatoes in the sauce are rich, but not overly concentrated or pasty; the flavor of the poblano permeates each bite, but doesn't wrestle with the sweetness of the tomato; and the browned meat adds a beautiful complexity, but one that's kept in check by the sauce. It's that Grandma thing: simple food done right.

WHEN TO THINK OF THESE RECIPES: The braised short ribs come to my mind in cool weather, the flank steak when it's time for a T-shirt and shorts. Both are casual and go well with mashed potatoes (skins on, kind of lumpy) or classic white rice (page 176). I'd add grilled green vegetables (zucchini, chayote, green beans) or steamed ones (sugar snap peas, even broccoli). This is easygoing fare, so you should be too.

ADVICE FOR AMERICAN COOKS: These recipes offer a good place to begin exploring Mexican main dishes. The flavors are easy to love and *so* typically "Mexican home cooking." If poblano chiles aren't in your market, substitute long green Anaheim chiles, another large chile (chilaca, banana/wax, even Cubanelle) or a couple of jalapeños (no need to roast them). Or think about moving: These dishes are so rewarding, you just have to make them.

Beef Short Ribs with Tomatoes, Roasted Poblanos and Herbs

COSTILLAS DE RES A LA MEXICANA

Serves 4

5 medium (about 1 pound total) fresh poblano chiles

2 tablespoons rich-tasting pork lard or vegetable oil

A generous 2 pounds bone-in beef short ribs, trimmed of excess fat

1 large white onion, sliced

6 garlic cloves, peeled and finely chopped

1 1/2 pounds (3 medium-large round or 9 to 12 plum) ripe
tomatoes, cored and chopped into 1/2-inch pieces
OR one 28-ounce can good-quality tomatoes packed
in juice, drained and chopped into 1/2-inch pieces

Salt

1 large sprig fresh epazote, plus an additional sprig
(optional) for garnish
OR 1 1/2 teaspoons chopped fresh thyme and/or marjoram,
plus a sprig or two (optional) for garnish

TRADITIONAL

1. ROASTING THE POBLANOS. Roast the poblanos directly over a gas flame or on a baking sheet 4 inches below a very hot broiler, turning regularly until the skin has blistered and blackened on all sides, about 5 minutes for an open flame, about 10 minutes for the broiler. Be careful not to char the flesh, only the skin. Cover with a kitchen towel and let stand for 5 minutes. Rub off the blackened skin, then pull out the stems and seed pods. Tear the chiles open and rinse briefly to remove any stray seeds and bits of skin. Slice into 1/4-inch strips.

2. SEARING THE MEAT. Heat the oven to 325°F. In a medium-large (4- to 6-quart) pot (preferably a Dutch oven or Mexican *cazuela*), heat the lard or oil over medium-high. Lay in the short ribs in a single, uncrowded layer, working in batches if necessary. When richly browned on one side, about 5 minutes, turn them over and brown the other side, 3 to 5 minutes more. Remove to a plate and tip off all but a generous coating of oil on the bottom of the pot.

3. THE FLAVORINGS. Set the pot back on the stove and reduce the heat to medium. Add the onion and cook, stirring frequently, until golden, about 7 minutes. Add the garlic and stir for another minute, then add the tomatoes. Stir occasionally until the tomatoes have softened and lost their juicy look (about 3 minutes for fresh tomatoes, 3 to 5 minutes for canned). Stir in the poblano strips, 1 teaspoon salt and the herb(s).

4. BRAISING THE MEAT. Nestle the browned meat into the tomato mixture, spooning some of it over the top. Cover the pot (a piece of foil works for the *cazuela*) and set in the oven. After 1 ½ hours, check the meat: it should be fork-tender. If not, re-cover and braise for an extra 15 minutes or so.

5. SERVING THE DISH. Using a spatula, remove the meat to a warm serving platter. Tip the pot to collect the chunky sauce at one side and spoon off the fat that rises to the top. Taste the sauce and season with additional salt if you think it needs it. Spoon the sauce around the meat. This homey dish doesn't actually need a garnish, but if you have a sprig of *epazote,* thyme or marjoram, it'll look beautiful here.

WORKING AHEAD: There's a warm hominess to this dish if it's made a day or two ahead and stored in the refrigerator until you are ready to reheat it (this may be done in a covered pot on the stove or in a 325°F oven; first discard any solidified fat from the surface). For a just-braised texture (and to ensure that your guests' mouths water from the aromas), you can prepare the dish through Step 3 and cover and refrigerate the two parts separately, then continue within a couple of hours of serving. The finished dish will hold well for an hour or so in a very low oven.

Broiled Flank Steak with Tomato-Poblano Salsa

CARNE ASADA A LA MEXICANA

Serves 6

4 medium (about 12 ounces total) fresh poblano chiles

1 1/2 pounds ripe tomatoes, preferably plum—you'll need 9 to 12

1 small white onion, sliced crosswise

4 garlic cloves, peeled

1 teaspoon chopped fresh thyme

    OR 2 to 3 tablespoons chopped fresh cilantro

Salt

2 tablespoons olive oil, preferably extra-virgin

1 tablespoon vinegar, preferably balsamic

2 teaspoons sugar

1 1/2 pounds (up to 2 pounds, if you like) flank steak,

    about 1 inch thick

A large bunch of watercress for garnish

CONTEMPORARY

1. ROASTING THE POBLANOS, TOMATOES, ONION AND GARLIC. Roast the poblanos and tomatoes on a baking sheet 4 inches below a very hot broiler until they're darkly roasted (they'll be blackened in spots), about 5 minutes. Flip them over and roast on the other side—4 to 6 minutes more will give you splotchy-black and blistered tomatoes and chiles that are soft and cooked through. The poblanos may be completely blistered and blackened before the tomatoes are—remove them as soon as they are done.

Turn the oven down to 425°F. Separate the onion into rings. Mix together the onion and whole garlic cloves on another baking sheet. Roast, stirring every few minutes, until the onions are richly browned (they'll look soft, even have a touch of char on some of the edges) and the garlic feels soft and is browned in spots, about 20 minutes total. Cool.

Pull off the skin from the tomatoes and cut out the cores, working over your baking sheet to collect the juices. Pull the blackened skins off the chiles, then pull out the stems and seed pods. Tear the poblanos open, rinse briefly to remove any stray seeds and bits of skin and chop into 1/4-inch pieces. Place in a large bowl.

2. FINISHING THE SALSA. Combine the onions and garlic in a food processor or blender and pulse to chop into small bits. Add the tomatoes (and all of their juice) and continue pulsing until the whole thing looks like a very coarse puree. Stir this course puree into the poblanos along with the thyme or cilantro. Scoop $1/2$ cup of the mixture back into the food processor or blender and set aside. Add enough water to the remaining mixture to give it an easily spoonable consistency (you'll usually need about $1/3$ cup). Taste and season with salt, usually about $1/2$ teaspoon.

3. BROILING AND SERVING THE MEAT. Heat the broiler. To the blender or food processor with the salsa base add the oil, vinegar, sugar and $1/2$ teaspoon salt and process to a smooth puree.

Lay the flank steak on a broiler pan or on a rack set on a baking sheet. Baste evenly with half of the salsa puree and set the steak 4 inches under the broiler. Broil until richly browned on one side, about 4 minutes, then flip the meat over, baste with the remaining salsa puree and broil the other side. With a good hot broiler, total broiling time for medium-rare meat is about 8 to 10 minutes. Transfer the meat to a cutting board. It's best to let the meat rest, covered loosely with foil, for 3 or 4 minutes before slicing.

With a sharp knife (preferably a long slicing knife), thinly slice the meat on a diagonal (this will give you lovely slices cut across the grain for maximum tenderness). Arrange the slices on a warm serving platter and garnish with the watercress. Serve the salsa in a decorative bowl, for each of your guests to spoon on *al gusto*.

WORKING AHEAD: Though the salsa will keep well in the refrigerator for several days, its flavors are the brightest shortly after it's made. The meat, of course, should be cooked just before serving—unless you want to serve it at room temperature (a good idea for a picnic).

GRILLING VARIATION: Heat a gas grill to medium-high or light a charcoal fire and let it burn until the coals are covered with gray ash and very hot. Set the cooking grate (use a cast-iron one if you have it) in place and allow it to get hot, about 5 minutes. Brush one side of the steak with vegetable oil, then lay oiled side down on the grate. Baste with half the salsa puree, cover the grill and cook for 4 minutes. Flip the meat over, baste with the remaining salsa puree, cover and let the other side cook. With a hot grill, the total time will be about 8 minutes for medium-rare.

QUESTIONS AND ANSWERS FROM OUR TESTING

WHAT'S THE RIGHT TOMATO FOR THE DISH? Thinking "fresh is best," we started our testing with a duel: plum tomatoes v. round tomatoes. What we found was that ripeness is more important than tomato variety—the riper, the better in this dish. But if you have a choice between ripe plum tomatoes and ripe round ones, choose round for the traditional recipe. They make a juicy braising sauce, whereas plum tomatoes yield a denser, thicker sauce that looks as if it would feel more at home on pasta or pizza. In one blind tasting, when our fresh tomatoes weren't ripe, we all gravitated toward the canned tomato version.

From a guy who loves *roasted* tomatoes: In this dish, since the meat is well-browned, we could tell no difference between roasted and unroasted fresh tomatoes.

WHAT CHILE MAKES THE MOST TRADITIONAL-TASTING DISH? Poblano. It gives the fullest, richest flavor with just the right amount of heat (though be aware that heat levels vary in poblanos). Though it's impractical for most cooks, roasting the poblanos over a wood or charcoal fire lifts this dish to a new level. When roasting chiles, be sure to char only the skin, not the flesh.

IS THE MEXICAN FRESH HERB *EPAZOTE* ESSENTIAL IN THE TRADITIONAL DISH, OR ARE THERE SUBSTITUTES? *Epazote* gives this dish a very delectable, very Mexican flavor. But it is not always easy to find, even in Mexican groceries. Fortunately, it grows like a weed (which is what many gardeners think of it), so start planning now for the full experience of *Costillas de Res a la Mexicana* next summer. Not possible? Then try a little marjoram and/or thyme (fresh is much better than dried here)—Mediterranean herbs that are used widely in Mexico.

WHAT'S THE BEST MEAT FOR THE BRAISED DISH, AND WHAT'S THE BEST WAY TO COOK IT? Though you can make a delicious braised beef a la mexicana with chuck roast, bottom rump roast, brisket or even shanks, there's a reason we fell in love with short ribs. As they slowly braise in the sauce, they enrich that tomatoey beauty with remarkable body from their connective tissues and with flavor from the meat and bone. To minimize excess richness, trim off the short ribs' external fat and brown them well to render some of the internal fat. But browning does more than just render fat: It makes this dish taste heavenly.

IS USING LARD IN THE TRADITIONAL DISH IMPORTANT? Though not as crucial here as it is in tamales or *mole*, fresh lard produces the most well rounded flavor.

VARIATION: *Other meats:* A very tasty dish can be made from pork country-style ribs (they take about 1½ hours to cook) or chicken thighs (give them 30 to 35 minutes).

Carne Asada
(Mexican-Style Grilled Steak)

Smoky fire is a definitive part of Mexico's culinary gene pool—the smoky fire used for grilling and roasting meat, for passing its heat into an earthenware bean-simmering pot or through a griddle for roasting chiles, onions, garlic, tomatoes and tomatillos. If your experience of "Mexican food" is enchiladas or tacos at your local chain eatery, smoky fire may come as an unexpected player in True Mexican Flavor.

Years ago, in the northern Mexican state of Sonora, I drove out into the countryside to eat at a famous *restaurante campestre,* a relaxed and rustic open-air restaurant. Smoke and the sizzling smell of cooking meat enveloped everyone in a cloud of festivity and music and noise. On a heavy metal grate supported above the live fire, steaks were finding their perfect degree of doneness. *Sonoran* steaks, the beefy pride of Mexico.

In Guadalajara, the *restaurantes campestres* go beyond steaks to spit-roasted lamb, quail, chicken, chorizo and pork or beef ribs. A place like El Canelo comes to mind, its fire pit the size of a Honda Civic. Around the fiercely radiating fire of oak and mesquite, the grill masters thrust vertical spits of meat into the hot earth, then slowly turn them.

Mexico's most famous *carne asada, carne asada a la tampiqueña,* was originally prepared on a griddle (though *asada* can be translated as "grilled," its full meaning is broader, embracing all cooking with dry heat—practically anything except boiling, steaming and frying). Invented by José Luís Loredo at the Tampico Club in Mexico City back in the early 1940s, *carne asada a la tampiqueña* started with thin-cut beef tenderloin that was lightly marinated, then seared on a hot griddle and served with a tasty sampling of guacamole, beans, green-sauced enchiladas and fried fresh cheese.

Indeed, for steak to become Mexican Steak, it needs to keep company with the right dinner partners. My classic *carne asada* recipe spells out how to pull off the whole full-flavored feast quite manageably—guacamole, beans, salsa, even a grilled cactus salad for a truly authentic touch. I suggest you get all your guests involved in the preparations, making cooking part of the afternoon's or evening's fun. For a less involved endeavor, trade grilled beef for grilled fish and serve it simply with a salsa that welcomes all kinds of tomatoes. Look for the great-tasting heirloom varieties for the most memorable experience.

TRADITIONAL BENCHMARK: The perfect *carne asada,* in my opinion, is perfect because of the meat's role in the larger context of the perfect Mexican cookout meal. The grilled meat punctuates mouthfuls of tender beans, tangy-crunchy cactus salad, luxuriant guacamole and spicy fresh tomato salsa. And to me, the meat fits into all this perfection if it's cooked over live fire, tastes beefy and has the right amount of chew—a judgment that's as personal as the right amount of spiciness.

WHEN TO THINK OF THESE RECIPES: When you want to splurge on friends or family to celebrate summer—or the thought of summer (I've grilled steaks in the fireplace in winter when I've found good vine-ripe tomatoes at the grocery). The full steak cookout I've outlined is complete and filling, begging only for a few spicy nuts to munch on before dinner and homemade fruit ice or ice cream for dessert. The contemporary grilled fish is a lighter meal—but still very special. I'd serve the fish and salsa with rustic mashed potatoes and a leafy green salad.

ADVICE FOR AMERICAN COOKS: If you don't have a good butcher nearby, a natural foods grocery can supply you with naturally raised beef, and many top-flight grocery stores carry premium beef like Certified Angus Beef. Make the effort to look for cactus in a Mexican or well-stocked grocery store, because it's tasty and has such an intriguing texture. But if you can't find it, make a green bean salad instead (see the variation on page 292). And of course, since tomatoes are essential in most of the side dishes, the most memorable party will be one held during local tomato season.

The Complete Mexican Steak Cookout, with cactus salad, guacamole, salsa and beans

CARNE ASADA—LA CAMPESTRE COMPLETA
PARA TODOS

Serves 8

1 pound dried beans (pinto, black, pink or, truthfully, anything
   that catches your fancy)
3 tablespoons rich-tasting pork lard
   OR 4 thick slices smoky bacon, cut into ¹/₂-inch pieces
1 large white onion, finely chopped
12 large garlic cloves, peeled and finely chopped
4 large limes
Salt
Eight 6- to 10-ounce beef steaks (my preference is for bone-in rib
   steaks or strip steaks, but rib-eyes, boneless strip steaks, tenderloin,
   chuck steaks and sirloin steaks are all good)
8 medium (about 1 pound total) cactus paddles
1 pound (2 medium-large round or 6 to 8 plum) ripe tomatoes
Fresh hot green chiles to taste (roughly 3 serranos or
   1 jalapeño), stemmed
²/₃ cup chopped fresh cilantro, plus a few sprigs for garnish
4 large ripe avocados
Olive oil or vegetable oil for coating the cactus and steaks
A few nice-looking lettuce leaves for serving
2 to 3 tablespoons grated Mexican queso añejo or
   other dry grating cheese, such as Romano or Parmesan

TRADITIONAL

1. THE BEANS. Rinse the beans, then place them in a medium (4- to 5-quart) heavy pot (preferably an earthenware Mexican *olla*) and measure in 2 ¹/₂ quarts water. Remove any beans that float, then add the pork lard or bacon, *half* of the onion and *one-quarter* of the garlic. Set over medium-high heat and bring to a strong, rolling boil. Reduce the heat to about medium-low (just enough to keep the beans

at a bare simmer), partially cover the pot and cook until the beans are thoroughly tender (no chalkiness left), about 2 hours, depending on the type and freshness of the beans. Stir the beans every 15 minutes or so, to make sure that none are sticking and that the water still covers the beans, allowing them to more or less float freely. Add additional water as necessary.

2. MARINATING THE STEAKS. Meanwhile, squeeze the juice of 2 of the limes into a large nonaluminum dish. Mix in another $1/4$ of the garlic and 1 teaspoon salt. Dip both sides of each steak in the mixture, smearing the salty marinade over all sides. Cover and refrigerate for 1 to 2 hours (no more).

3. CLEANING THE CACTUS. One by one, clean the cactus paddles: Holding each paddle gingerly between the nodes of the prickly spines, trim off the edge that outlines the paddle, including the blunt end where the paddle was severed from the plant, then slice or scrape off the spiny nodes from both sides. Set aside until you're ready to grill.

4. MAKING THE SALSA. Chop the tomatoes into small ($1/8$-inch) dice and scoop into a bowl. Finely chop the chiles, seeds and all, and scrape in with the tomatoes. Scoop the remaining chopped onion into a strainer and rinse under cold water; shake off the excess moisture and add to the bowl. Stir in *half* of the remaining garlic, the juice of 1 of the limes and *half* of the chopped cilantro. Taste and season with salt, usually about $3/4$ teaspoon. Scoop two-thirds of the mixture into a salsa dish; leave the rest in the bowl. Cover both and refrigerate.

5. FINISHING THE BEANS. When the beans are completely tender, season them with salt, usually 1 to 1 $1/2$ teaspoons. Let simmer for an additional 10 to 15 minutes for the beans to absorb the salt, then taste and add more salt if you think necessary. The beans should have just enough broth to cover them. If too soupy, simmer briskly until the broth is reduced, being careful to stir them regularly so none stick; if not brothy enough, stir in a little water. Keep warm over very low heat.

6. PUTTING TOGETHER THE GUACAMOLE. Halve and pit the avocados, then scoop their flesh into a large bowl. Add the remaining garlic, the juice of the remaining lime and the remaining cilantro. Using the back of a large spoon or an old-fashioned potato masher, coarsely mash the avocados, mixing in the flavorings. Taste and season with salt, usually about 1 $1/4$ teaspoons. Scrape into a serving bowl. Cover with plastic wrap placed directly on the surface of the guacamole and refrigerate.

7. GRILLING, GRILLING. Heat a gas grill to medium-high or light a charcoal fire and let it burn until the coals are covered with gray ash and very hot (the fire feels almost intolerably hot to most cooks when they hold their hand 4 or 5 inches above the grill grate for 5 seconds). Set the cooking grate in place, cover the grill and let the grate heat up, 5 minutes or so.

Brush or spray the cactus paddles on both sides with oil and sprinkle with salt. Lay on the grill grate, cover the grill and cook for about 5 minutes, until browned in places. Flip the paddles over, cover and grill until they're browned on the other side, darkened to an olive green color and softened enough to look limp when picked up with a pair of tongs (this indicates they're cooked through). Lay out the cactus in a single layer on a rack and cool completely.

When it is cool, cut the cactus into squares a little smaller than ½ inch. Mix with the reserved salsa that's still in the mixing bowl. Taste and season with salt if needed. Line a serving bowl with lettuce leaves, scoop in the cactus salad and set on the table, along with the bowl of salsa. Uncover the guacamole, sprinkle with the cheese, decorate it with cilantro sprigs and set on the table.

Remove the steaks from the marinade, brush or spray with oil, lay them on the hot grill and cook, turning once, until done to your liking: For medium-rare, a ½-inch-thick steak will need about 2½ minutes on each side over medium-high heat. Move the steaks to the edge of the grill while you spread out eight dinner plates (warm ones will preserve the heat of the steaks).

8. SERVING THE FEAST. Ladle a helping of the beans into each of eight small bowls or cups and set them on the plates along with the steaks, then carry them to your lucky guests. Pass the cactus salad, salsa and guacamole along with some warm tortillas, if you like.

WORKING AHEAD: The beans can be completely made ahead (refrigerate the cooled beans, well covered, then warm them shortly before serving, adjusting the consistency and seasoning as necessary). The cactus can be grilled ahead too, but that means heating the grill twice. The steaks really shouldn't marinate for more than 2 hours (especially thinish ones), or they'll become too limy and lose their color. The salsa and guacamole won't hold much longer than 2 hours either. Grilled steaks, of course, are at their peak hot off the grate.

Spicy Grilled Tuna (or other fish) with Heirloom Tomato Salsa

ATÚN ASADO CON SALSA MEXICANA A LA ANTIGUA

Serves 6

8 large garlic cloves, unpeeled

Fresh hot green chiles to taste (roughly 2 serranos or
    4 jalapeños), stemmed

$^1/_3$ cup fresh lime juice

Salt

Six 5- to 6-ounce fresh tuna steaks or skinless meaty fish fillets,
    such as snapper, grouper, wahoo, marlin or salmon,
    about $^3/_4$ inch thick

3 cups chopped ($^1/_4$-inch dice) heirloom tomatoes—use what you
    can find, but think about a variety of colors and flavors, from
    Black Prince to Green Zebra to Sun Gold to Brandywine
    (you'll need about 1 $^1/_2$ pounds)

1 small red onion, finely chopped

2 to 4 tablespoons chopped fresh herbs—the intensity of the
    herb(s) you choose will dictate quantity (cilantro is predictably
    delicious, a touch of mint is springy, a little lemon
    thyme or lemon balm or lemon verbena adds sunshine
    and basil, well, who doesn't like basil?), plus a few sprigs
    for garnish

Olive oil or vegetable oil for brushing or spraying the fish

CONTEMPORARY

I. THE MARINADE/FLAVORING. In a small dry skillet, roast the unpeeled garlic and the chiles over medium heat, turning occasionally, until soft (the skins of both will have blackened in spots, which is okay as long as the flesh doesn't burn), 5 to 10 minutes for the chiles, 15 minutes for the garlic. Cool, then peel the garlic.

   Place both garlic and chiles in a food processor or blender along with the lime juice. Run the machine until the mixture is as smoothly pureed as possible. Season highly with salt, usually about $^3/_4$ teaspoon.

2. MARINATING THE TUNA. Scoop two-thirds of the marinade into a large nonaluminum baking dish. Lay the fish in the marinade and smear the mixture on all sides of each piece. Cover and refrigerate while you prepare the salsa.

3. THE SALSA. Scrape the remaining marinade into a medium bowl. Mix in the chopped tomatoes. Scoop the onion into a small strainer, rinse under cold water and shake off the excess; add to the tomatoes. Stir in the herbs. Taste and season with additional salt, usually about $1/2$ teaspoon.

4. GRILLING THE FISH. Heat a gas grill to medium-high or light a charcoal fire and let it burn until the coals are covered with gray ash and very hot (the fire feels almost intolerably hot to most cooks when they hold their hand 4 or 5 inches above the grill grate for 5 seconds). Set the cooking grate in place, cover the grill and let the grate heat up, 5 minutes or so.

Remove the fish from the marinade, brush or spray with a generous coating of oil and lay on the hot grill. Cover the grill and cook for 3 minutes. Uncover, flip the fish over, cover once again and cook until the fish is as done as you like—1 to 2 minutes more is all that's needed for medium-rare tuna (my preference).

Transfer the fish to dinner plates, spoon on the beautiful salsa and decorate with herb sprigs—you're ready to eat.

WORKING AHEAD: There is little in this recipe that can be done in advance—except the marinade, which will hold for a day or so in the refrigerator if well covered. If the fish spends more than 3 or 4 hours in that limy marinade, it will get pickled. Beautiful tomatoes with salt and lime on them also begin to wilt after an hour or two.

THE COMPLETE MEXICAN STEAK COOKOUT, WITH CACTUS
SALAD, GUACAMOLE, SALSA, BEANS (PAGE 285) AND TORTILLAS

Questions and Answers from Our Testing

What's the best cut of steak for *carne asada*? That all depends on what you're looking for: authenticity, tenderness and/or flavor. For absolute authenticity, I'd choose a relatively thin steak that's not too tender . . . odd as that may sound. You see, Mexican beef—even the best—isn't usually as tender as really good American beef. And historically (for health reasons), most beef has been cooked well-done in that country. I've eaten a lot of thin-cut round or bone-in rib steaks in street stalls and inexpensive eateries, and they're delicious for their charred meaty flavor and satisfying chew. But Mexico has nice steak houses, too, and they offer thick tender steaks in a wide variety of cuts, either purchased from the best ranches in Mexico or imported.

For tenderness and flavor, you need to understand a little bovine anatomy. As you progress along the steer, from forequarter (front legs) to hindquarter (back legs), you progress from the tougher meat of the front-side chuck to the tenderness of rib, short loin and sirloin and then back again to the tougher meat (the hind-side rump). Anything that's vigorously exercised (like legs) is tougher, but also beefier in flavor. So the tenderest steaks typically come from the center, from the rib (rib steaks, rib-eyes, Delmonicos) or the short loin (New York/Kansas City strip steaks). Tenderloin is the most tender, being thoroughly protected beneath the rib and short loin. And T-bones and porterhouse steaks have a little short loin and a little tenderloin, offering a variety of textures.

To my taste, the much-lauded tenderloin (a.k.a. filet mignon, châteaubriand) is a little *too* tender and *too* light in beef flavor. All of the sirloin steaks combine light flavor with quite a bit of chewiness. The strip steaks are flavorful and tender, but I prefer a less fine-grained texture. So what's my favorite? If times are flush, I buy the very flavorful, nicely tender rib steak, preferably one with the bone still on to ensure absolute maximum flavor. If times are lean, I choose a chuck steak—great beefy flavor, okay tenderness (I don't mind actually having to chew steak) and terrific price.

What's the best traditional marinade, and how long should the steak be in it? In Mexico, meat for *carne asada* isn't heavily marinated. A little salt in some places, a squeeze of fresh lime juice in others, a little garlic in a few. We tested those three (plus an ill-fated attempt to add beer to the mix), liking them best together—just enough to add a flavorful freshness. Less than an hour with the marinade doesn't give much flavor; more than 2 hours makes the meat taste acidic and look discolored.

What's the best way to cook cactus? Though the average home cook in Mexico says to boil cactus, I take the Mexican grill cook's lead: I use the dry heat of a grill. Even an oven or a griddle will give similar results, playing down cactus's habit of exuding a gooey, okra-like liquid. When paddles are grilled whole, you never see that liquid. And, if they're cooked thoroughly, the cactus paddles will show scarcely any stickiness when they're cut into squares.

ARE STEAKS BEST WHEN COOKED ON A GAS OR CHARCOAL GRILL? As a person with both a gas and a charcoal grill, I can say I understand the attraction of gas. I turn to it regularly, because it's fast and convenient, and it does produce a tasty result. But when you compare that result with what you get from a charcoal or wood fire, it's clear which wins. Only cooking over live coals offers that full, enticing, thrilling flavor. Plus, I like the ritual of starting the fire, judging its temperature and maintaining that temperature throughout the cooking period. There's a craft to live-fire cooking that I'm proud to think I've nearly mastered. And isn't craftsmanship an aspect of cooking that most of us are attracted to?

WHAT IS THE BEST KIND OF CHARCOAL? A good many charcoal briquets are made of ground charcoal mixed with fillers (and sometimes petroleum products, which can give an off flavor to food). They're designed to burn consistently and not too hot. Lump hardwood charcoal, on the other hand, is wood that has been made into charcoal. Hardwood charcoal is very clean burning and hot—but be warned that it burns at a rather unpredictable rate, sometimes going from very hot to cool more quickly than you might expect. Also, make sure the hardwood charcoal you buy is from a company connected to sustainable-growth forests rather than those that are wreaking havoc on the land.

VARIATION: *Green Bean Salad:* Steam 1 pound cleaned green beans until crisp-tender, toss them with oil and salt, and then grill them over the highest heat, turning them repeatedly, for a couple of minutes until they begin to brown (you may want to invest in one of those perforated heavy metal vegetable-grilling pans so you don't lose the beans through the grates). Dice the cooled beans and mix them with the chopped tomato salsa instead of the cactus.

Barbacoa *(Slow-Cooked Meats, Pit-Style)*

 There's an earthy element to so much of Mexico's food: the brickish hues of dried chiles and all the *moles* made from them; the muted yellow, red or blue native corn that releases an elemental perfume as it's stone-ground into dough for tortillas; the primally scented beans simmering in an earthenware *olla.*

But the food that offers the most thoroughly enveloping, earthy experience is, without question, *barbacoa,* because it draws you right into a pit dug from earth, heated with rocks set aglow by a roaring bonfire. Meat wrapped in gathered leaves is lowered in (whole animals are preferred by *barbacoa* masters), then all is sealed tightly. In the smoky, steamy heat of this underground oven, the flavors of *terroir* fuse with those of fragrant leaves, smoky embers and roasting meat. Hours later, when the guests have assembled, the unearthing of the pit-cooked meat becomes a drawn-out moment, the culmination of shared festal anticipation that's woven into the flow of Mexican life, Mexican history.

If the *barbacoa* you sit down to is in central Mexico, it's a good bet that the meat will be lamb and the leaves that cover it the fleshy *pencas* of the agave plant. In northern Mexico, it'll probably be the succulent meat from cow's head; if there are leaves, they'll usually be agave; and the earthbound oven will likely have been traded in for an above-the-ground apparatus that replicates the original pit's steamy slow cooking. That above-the-ground oven is also typical in west-central Mexico, around Guadalajara, where goat or lamb *birria* is made with a red chile marinade. Goat or lamb in red chile marinade is the hallmark of southern-style *barbacoa* too, cooked with anisey avocado leaves. And in the Yucatan, pork is marinated in tangy, garlicky *achiote* seasoning and wrapped in banana leaves to make pit-cooked *cochinita pibil* (literally "little pig in a pit").

Besides being sealed in the ground with the aromatic leaves, Mexican *barbacoa* differs from American barbecue in another way: Mexican *barbacoa* is more about steam-roasting than smoke-roasting. You see, in many *barbacoa* styles, a soup pot is the first thing lowered into the hot pit. It's filled with a watery mix of vegetables, herbs and chiles. A grate goes on top and the leaf-wrapped meat on that, then the whole assembly is sealed in, leaving the soup's steam to tenderize the meat while the meat juices flavor the soup.

So what's the chance of digging a pit in your backyard? Slim for most of us, I bet. Even in Mexico these days, most folks plan for *barbacoa* at a restaurant, typically an outdoorsy country one called a *restaurante campestre*.

You can make *barbacoa* in your gas or electric oven, but the experience doesn't send me. If you make *barbacoa* in a closed-top kettle grill, though, complete with soup and aromatic leaves—that will leave a lasting impression.

TRADITIONAL BENCHMARK: Though in Mexico there are market stalls, shops and restaurants that sell hot *barbacoa* and *cochinita pibil* by the kilo for assemble-at-home quick tacos, the perfect version of either of these two dishes, in my opinion, has to be the centerpiece of a fiesta. The meat is fall-off-the-bone tender, subtly smoky, succulent and gently infused with the flavor of the marinade and leaf wrappers.

WHEN TO THINK OF THESE RECIPES: Though I get a hankering every winter to make a big barbecue in the snow (to remind myself about the upcoming pleasures of warm weather), I make dishes like *barbacoa* and *cochinita pibil* most in warm-weather months when I want relaxed time with friends or family in the backyard. Both recipes in this section serve a fairly large group, they're easy to get right and most steps can be done ahead. The *barbacoa* recipe creates its own brothy soup for a first course; the meat needs only salsa and warm corn tortillas (plus a plate of fried black beans, page 186, and a big vinaigrette-dressed romaine salad, if you wish). *Cochinita pibil* needs a first course—like dressy *ceviche* (page 14) or casual guacamole (page 6).

ADVICE FOR AMERICAN COOKS: You need four things: a kettle-style charcoal grill (or a large gas grill), courage to use it in new ways, patience and time. This is celebratory food, albeit very casual, that needs your care for several hours—like the best barbecue. If you want to cook goat, look for it in Mexican or Middle Eastern groceries. If guajillos are not available in your area, dried ancho chiles make a good substitute. The spice *achiote* (a.k.a. annatto), that rusty red seed, is readily available in Mexican and Caribbean groceries; it's essential to *cochinita pibil,* but it can be replaced with the seasoned, ready-to-use *achiote* paste found in Mexican groceries. The paste, called *recado rojo* or *adobo de achiote,* contains all the marinade ingredients except sour orange. Avocado and banana leaves are in some Mexican and many Asian groceries. Without the leaves, the dishes are still good, just not as complex or Mexican-tasting. Simply cover the pan with foil, then poke some holes in it to ensure proper cooking.

Red Chile Lamb, Goat or Chicken, Pit-Style— with braising-juice soup

BARBACOA DE BORREGO, CHIVO O POLLO

Serves 6 to 8 (you'll have about
8 generous cups of soup)

8 medium (about 2 ounces total) dried guajillo chiles, stemmed,
    seeded and torn into flat pieces
4 garlic cloves, peeled and roughly chopped
1 teaspoon dried oregano, preferably Mexican
A generous $^1/_2$ teaspoon black pepper, preferably freshly ground
A pinch of cloves, preferably freshly ground
Salt
6 pounds bone-in lamb shoulder roast, cut into 2-inch-thick slabs
    OR 6 pounds bone-in young goat (shoulder pieces of similar
    size if possible)
    OR two 3-pound chickens, cut into quarters
2 medium carrots, peeled and cut into $^1/_2$-inch cubes
1 small white onion, thinly sliced
5 small (about 10 ounces total) boiling potatoes (such as
    red-skins), scrubbed and halved
1 cup cooked (or canned) garbanzo beans
1 sprig fresh epazote, if available
2 to 3 dried chipotle chiles (optional)
About 30 dried Mexican avocado leaves, plus a few for garnish
    (see Questions and Answers, page 303)
Salsa, such as Red Chile–Tomatillo Salsa (page 35), for serving

TRADITIONAL

I. THE CHILE MARINADE. Toast the chile pieces a few at a time on a dry heavy skillet or griddle heated over medium, pressing them flat against the hot surface with a metal spatula until they are aromatic—about 10 seconds per side. (If the heat is right, you'll hear a slight crackle when you press down the chiles, but you shouldn't see more than the slightest wisp of smoke; when appropriately toasted, the inside surface of the chile will look noticeably lighter than before toasting.) Place in a bowl, add hot tap water to cover, set a small plate on top to keep the chiles submerged and let soak for 20 minutes. Use a pair of tongs to transfer the rehydrated chiles to a food processor or blender.

Add the garlic, oregano, black pepper and cloves to the processor or blender. Taste the soaking liquid and, if it is not bitter, add ²/₃ cup to the processor or blender; if it's bitter, add ²/₃ cup water. Blend to a smooth puree, then press through a medium-mesh strainer into a bowl or nonaluminum roasting pan large enough to hold the meat or chicken. Taste and season highly with salt, about 1 ½ teaspoons. Put the meat or chicken into the bowl or pan and coat it evenly and generously with the marinade. (Though the dried chiles boast a lingering color, I suggest you use your hands for this task.) Set aside while you prepare the grill.

2. SETTING UP THE GRILL AND COOKING POT. Heat a gas grill to medium-high or light a charcoal fire and let it burn just until the coals are covered with gray ash and very hot.

Choose a 12-quart pot about 8 inches deep and 10 to 12 inches across (you're going to be nestling this in the grill, so don't pick your prettiest one). Rub the bottom of the pot with some liquid dish soap (an old scouting trick to make cleaning the pot easier after cooking). Measure in 8 cups of water, then add the carrots, onion, potatoes, garbanzos, *epazote* (if you have it), optional chipotle chiles, *2 or 3* of the avocado leaves and 2 teaspoons salt. Nestle three upside-down custard cups or coffee cups in the liquid around the edge (they should to be ½ inch higher than the liquid) and set a wire grate or rack on them (a small round cooling rack or collapsible vegetable steamer works well here). Cover the grate or rack with about *half* of the remaining avocado leaves, then lay on half the meat or chicken. Cover with the remaining avocado leaves and the remaining meat or chicken.

3. COOKING THE *BARBACOA*. When the grill is ready, either turn the burner(s) in the center to medium-low or bank the coals to the sides for indirect cooking. Do not replace the cooking grate if using charcoal. Set the pot in the center of the gas grill or carefully nestle it in the middle of the coals. Be careful to keep the pot level. Set the grill's cover in place and let it all cook slowly until the meat or chicken is fall-off-the-bone tender—5 to 6 hours for lamb or goat, about 1 ½ hours for chicken. If your grill has a thermometer, aim to keep the temperature at between 300° and 350°F. To maintain an even temperature with charcoal, add more charcoal regularly (usually a few pieces every hour or so).

4. SERVING THE *BARBACOA*. When the meat or chicken is done, carefully remove the pot from the grill. Remove the meat or chicken and pull or cut it off the bone in large, appetizing-looking shreds. Since this is casual fiesta food, I suggest that you line a platter with avocado leaves (you can rinse off those used for cooking or start with new ones), pile the meat or chicken on top and sprinkle with some salt. Next, remove the grate or rack from the pot and take out its supports. Ladle off any fat floating on the surface of the broth, then taste and season the broth with additional salt if you think necessary. Discard the avocado leaves in the broth.

Serve the broth in small cups. I highly recommend serving warm corn tortillas so each guest can make soft tacos of tender meat splashed with salsa. Savoring spoonfuls of the luscious broth (*consomé* as it is called in Mexico) punctuated with bites of soft, sassy *barbacoa* tacos is about as close as you'll get to heaven on earth.

WORKING AHEAD: The chile marinade will keep in the refrigerator for a day or so. The meat or chicken can be coated with the seasoning a day in advance of cooking and refrigerated. Finished *barbacoa* and the *consomé* reheat beautifully, though I always like my guests to see the "unearthing."

Mezcal in reed shot-glasses with typical accompaniments

Slow-Roasted *Achiote* Pork in Banana Leaves

COCHINITA PIBIL

TRADITIONAL

Serves 12 to 15

5 tablespoons (about 2 ounces) achiote *seeds*

1¹/₂ tablespoons dried oregano, preferably Mexican

1¹/₂ tablespoons black pepper, preferably peppercorns

1¹/₄ teaspoons cumin, preferably seeds

¹/₂ teaspoon cloves, preferably whole

6 inches of ¹/₂-inch-diameter Mexican cinnamon (canela)
  sticks or 1¹/₂ tablespoons ground cinnamon

Salt

14 large garlic cloves, peeled and roughly chopped

1¹/₂ cups fresh sour orange juice
  OR 1 cup fresh lime juice plus ¹/₂ cup fresh orange juice

2 bone-in pork shoulder (Boston butt) roasts (about 12 pounds total),
  cut into 3-inch-wide cross sections (unless you have a meat saw,
  you'll need to get the butcher to do this for you)

One 1-pound package banana leaves, defrosted

PICKLED RED ONIONS:

3 large (about 1¹/₂ pounds total) red onions, sliced ¹/₈ inch thick

2 cups fresh sour orange juice
  OR 1¹/₃ cups fresh lime juice plus ²/₃ cup fresh orange juice

Roasted Habanero Salsa (page 302) for serving (optional)

I. THE *ACHIOTE* MARINADE. Measure the *achiote* seeds and oregano into a spice
    grinder, adding the black pepper, cumin, cloves and cinnamon, and run the
    grinder until everything's as powdery as you can get it (you may need to work in
    batches).

    In a blender, combine the ground mixture with 1 tablespoon salt, the garlic
    and sour orange juice (or lime juice plus orange juice). Blend until smooth—
    there should be very little grittiness when a little is rubbed between your fingers.

If you're working ahead, pour the mixture into a nonaluminum container, cover and refrigerate for 6 hours or longer. Before using, blend the mixture again to give it an even smoother texture. (The long steeping and second blending aren't absolutely essential, though without it, the marinade may be a little gritty.)

2. MARINATING THE MEAT. In a large bowl or large heavy plastic food bag, combine the meat and marinade, turning the meat to coat it evenly. (Though *achiote* has tenacious coloring properties, I suggest you do this quickly with your hands.) For the greatest penetration of flavor, let the meat marinate refrigerated (covered if in a bowl) for several hours, or even overnight.

3. SLOW-GRILLING THE PORK. Heat a gas grill to medium-high or light a charcoal fire and let it burn just until the coals are covered with gray ash and very hot. Using scissors, cut off the hard edge you'll find on most banana leaves (where the leaf attached to the central rib). Cut 3 sections of banana leaf, each about 1 foot longer than the length of a large roasting pan. Line the bottom and sides of the roasting pan with the leaves, overlapping them generously and letting them hang over the edges of the pan. Lay the meat in the pan and drizzle with all the marinade. Fold the banana leaf edges over the meat. Cut 3 more sections of banana leaf slightly longer than the pan. Lay them over the top of the meat, again generously overlapping; tuck them in around the sides.

When the grill is ready, either turn the burner(s) in the center to medium-low or bank the coals to the sides for indirect cooking. For the charcoal grill, set the grill grate in place. Set the pan on the grill grate and close the grill cover. Grill until the meat is thoroughly tender (work a fork in near a bone—the meat should easily come free), usually about 4 hours. If your grill has a thermometer, aim to keep the temperature between 300° and 350°F. To maintain an even temperature with charcoal, add more charcoal regularly (usually a few pieces every hour or so).

4. SIMPLE PICKLED ONIONS. While the meat is cooking, prepare the onions. Scoop the onions into a nonaluminum bowl. Pour boiling water over them and wait 10 seconds, then pour the onions into a strainer. Return the drained onions to the bowl, pour on the sour orange juice (or the lime-orange combo) and stir in 1 1/2 teaspoons salt. Cover and set aside until serving time.

5. SERVING. Remove the top banana leaves. Tip the pan to accumulate the juices in one end and spoon off the fat. Season with more salt if necessary.

You may want to remove the bones and cut the large pieces of meat into manageable serving sizes, but I suggest you leave everything right in the roasting pan for serving. Set out your *cochinita pibil* with a large fork and spoon (for spooning up all those juices). Drain the red onions and set out in a serving bowl to top each portion, along with the salsa to cautiously dab on each portion.

WORKING AHEAD: If you're the plan-ahead type, make the marinade on Day 1, reblend it and marinate the meat on Day 2 and then slow-roast the meat for serving on Day 3. The marinade will hold for a week or more in the refrigerator. Once the pork has been marinated, cook it within 24 hours. The finished dish will keep for a couple of days, covered and refrigerated (meat and juice only—no banana leaves), though the texture of the meat won't be quite as nice as fresh-from-the-oven. Warm refrigerated cooked meat slowly (a 300°F oven) in the juice, covered. The pickled onions will keep for a week or so in the refrigerator, well covered.

VARIATION: The pork can be baked in a 325°F oven instead of on the grill; cover the meat rather loosely with foil before baking.

Left: Serving the barbacoa broth
Right: Retrieving lamb barbacoa from the pit

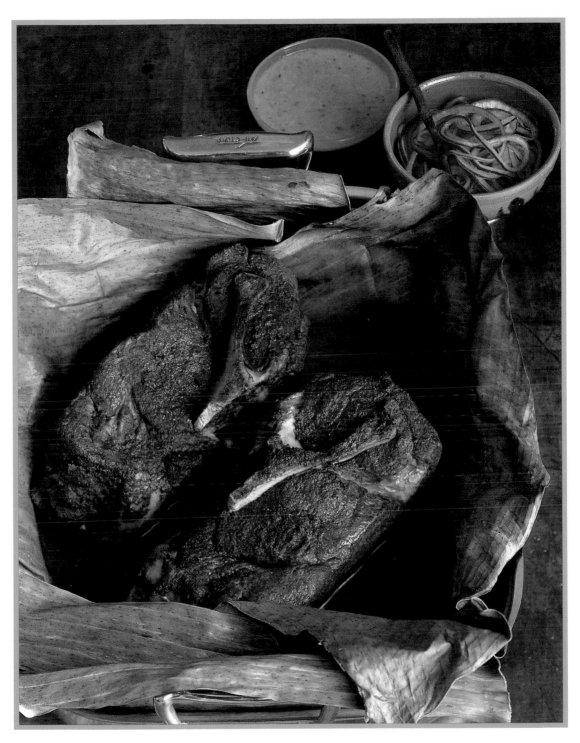

SLOW-ROASTED *ACHIOTE* PORK IN BANANA LEAVES (PAGE 298)

SALSA DE CHILE HABANERO ASADO

● ROASTED HABANERO SALSA

This is the most aromatic salsa—and the hottest. While roasting the main ingredients adds a balancing sweetness and lime juice provides enough muscle to wrestle those fiery pods, just a few drops of this flavorful concoction are enough to wake any food from slumber. You'll get the best texture and flavor with a mortar, though, lacking one, you can grind everything (with the water) in a blender or small food processor. No habaneros? It's wonderful made with an equivalent weight of serrano chiles.

Makes about ⅓ cup

8 medium (about 3 ounces total) fresh
    habanero chiles, stemmed
2 large garlic cloves, unpeeled
2 tablespoons fresh lime juice
Salt

In an ungreased skillet over medium heat, roast the chiles and garlic, turning regularly, until they're soft and darkened in spots, 5 to 10 minutes for the chiles, 15 minutes for the garlic. Cool and slip the skins off the garlic.

In a mortar, crush together the garlic and roasted chiles to a coarse puree. Stir in the lime juice and enough water to give it a spoonable consistency, usually 2 to 4 tablespoons. Taste (gingerly) and season with salt, usually about ½ teaspoon.

WORKING AHEAD: Refrigerated, this salsa will keep for several days.

QUESTIONS AND ANSWERS FROM OUR TESTING

WHAT IS THE BEST WAY TO CREATE PIT-COOKED FLAVOR AND TEXTURE? Real pit cooking in Mexico is quite involved—it's not just digging a hole, but building an in-ground oven. However, not all modern-day *barbacoa* and *cochinita pibil* are made in pits in Mexico. The span of what is used includes everything from an ordinary home oven to a steamer to a wood-burning beehive oven, with all kinds of custom-made contraptions along the way. They all have one thing in common: the ability to capture gentle steam around the meat. But the best cooks have figured out a way to use their apparatus-of-choice to also create a roasty edge on that steamy succulence, to ensure depth of flavor. That's what I'm offering with the grill—especially the charcoal-fired closed kettle grill.

WHAT ROLE DO THE LEAVES PLAY? The leaves used in making *barbacoa* and *cochinita pibil* add flavor (as wrapping in herbs would), and they protect the meat from drying out as it cooks. While leaves from any avocado tree will offer protection, only the leaves from the wild (nonhybridized) Mexican avocado add real flavor. When you find Mexican avocado leaves in the United States, they'll be dried. They look like huge bay leaves, revealing their family ties to that herb. If you live where *fresh* banana leaves are available in Hispanic or Asian markets, you'll need about 1½ pounds of the fresh leaves, because you'll have to trim off the heavy central stalks.

WHAT ARE THE BEST CUTS OF MEAT FOR THESE PREPARATIONS? The juiciest, most flavorful, easiest cut of meat to work with for this preparation is bone-in shoulder. It works for lamb, goat and pork. In our testing, we discovered that loin can turn out dry and leg can be lean and stringy. Chicken is an easy meat option for any cook; it's become so everyday, though, that I found it hard to think of chicken *barbacoa* as worthy of this special occasion. However, it *is* really delicious in this preparation.

WHAT CHILES MAKE THE BEST RED CHILE MARINADE FOR *BARBACOA*? I like dried guajillo chiles because of their bright flavor and medium heat, and because they combine so beautifully with garlic. Some cooks like to include anchos for richness and a hint of sweetness. We found that toasting the chiles added an important level of complexity, and, because of the long, mellowing cooking time, we liked the slightly bitter flavor that the soaking liquid added.

WHAT'S THE BEST *achiote* MARINADE FOR *COCHINITA PIBIL*? In the Yucatán, you can buy great fresh-ground *achiote* marinade paste (it will include the garlic, herbs, spices and some vinegar). Though in the United States you can also buy a box of the finished paste in a Mexican grocery, its flavor can be unpredictable—fresh-made is definitely the best. Yes, it takes a few minutes to prepare, but you can double the recipe and keep it in a well-sealed jar in the freezer for several months, ready to be used as a quick, very tasty marinade. Sour oranges, which are very common in the Yucatán (*naranja agria,* they're called there; Seville oranges or bitter oranges, they're often called here) are as sour as a lemon with a faint hint of orange flavor. If they aren't carried by your local Caribbean, Mexican, or European grocery stores (Europeans like to make marmalade from their aromatic rinds), a simple mixture of lime and orange juices is a very good replacement.

Open-air restaurante Campestre

Desserts
and Drinks

Flan

Turning out a flan is one bit of kitchen wizardry that always makes me smile. In making it, you first pour a liquid custard mixture into a mold tightly clad with hardened caramelized sugar. You bake it until it's no more set than a trembling Jell-O. Then, when serving time comes, you loosen it a little around the edge, turn it upside down on a plate and—*thwop*—hear it drop wonderously onto the plate, a beautifully set custard dripping in limpid, golden caramel syrup.

Kitchen recreation aside, flan's primary appeal lies for me in its satiny texture, rather than its beckoning ingredients: The combination of milk, eggs and sugar—all ingredients brought to Mexico by the Spaniards—describes basic desserts in many cuisines. So why has flan become The Mexican Dessert, available in practically every Mexican eatery on both sides of the border?

I think it's because most Mexicans cook from the heart, turning out dishes designed to nurture loved ones. And flan caresses like a tender, loving hand, making you feel relaxed, content right where you are. No matter what's come before—fiery, tangy, pungent, earthy—there's nothing more dreamy than a lingering mouthful of cool, creamy custard. It's an uncomplicated truth known the world around.

Now, flan wasn't always The Mexican Dessert. In fact, in pulling antique Mexican cookbooks off my shelf, I find that none of them before the middle of the nineteenth century even mentions flan. But after Mexico's midcentury encounter with the Hapsburg Empire (Maximilian and Carlota ruled Mexico for a few short years), a considerable amount of French influence took hold. Including flan, or *flaon,* as I find it first listed—a custard set with eggs.

Up to this point, Mexican desserts had largely been a wide array of fritters and thick, slow-simmered sweet fruit purees, both revealing Spain's interconnectedness with the Arab world. But apparently in the latter half of the nineteenth century, a time of change, elegant light-flavored flan stepped in to lead the culinary way. It was an "uptown" dessert that was easily doable in the typically oven-less Mexican home (it was originally baked in a closed hot water bath on an open burner, before ovens were common).

To make a perfect flan, though, is not exactly child's play. Which is why, I suspect, that it's mostly eaten out—everywhere from market *fondas,* street vendors' carts and *taquerías* to formal restaurants. But if you are lucky enough to have a grandma who makes a good flan, you can be sure she's very particular about one thing: texture. In our research, we encountered such strong predilections about what constitutes perfect flan texture, we settled on offering three alternatives. You can decide whether to make a flan that's clean-cutting and light-textured (it's almost glassy and very easy to unmold); one that's soft, creamy and rich; or one that's very creamy, concentrated and a little sweeter.

TRADITIONAL BENCHMARK: A perfect flan, in my opinion, has a softly sensuous, seductive texture—never any Swiss cheese–like holes that signal an overcooked, curdy texture. There's a beguiling sweetness that's tempered by an intriguing hint of bitterness from caramelized sugar. As a bite of perfect flan melts on the tongue, the perfume of vanilla—or cinnamon or another aromatic—drifts up, making the whole experience, well, pretty darn sexy.

WHEN TO THINK OF THIS RECIPE: Since everyone thinks of flan with Mexican food, you'd imagine that it fits in everywhere. Its sweet, caramely velvetiness is certainly welcome after a rustic, full-flavored meal, but some versions may be too rich for certain dishes. If your heart is set on a breathtaking flan to follow your spectacular, rich *mole,* choose the light-textured version and serve a brothy soup to start. A meal of simple soft tacos, beans and salsa, on the other hand, can handle the creamy or rich-and-commanding version of flan. Since flan is such a please-everyone (including the kids) dessert—and since it's *best* when made ahead—I think of it when I've invited folks over for dessert and coffee. Simple little sugar cookies (like classic Mexican *polvorones*) are a wonderful accompaniment.

ADVICE FOR AMERICAN COOKS: Once you're comfortable with the straightforward steps of caramelizing the sugar and slow-baking the custard to the right degree of doneness, flan making poses no challenges. And if you do have trouble with your caramel, just start again—all you will have wasted is a little sugar.

Classic Vanilla Flan—three choices

FLAN CLÁSICO DE VAINILLA

Below are three different lists of flan ingredients. Choose the one that makes a flan to suit your taste. The method is the same for all three versions.

Makes 6 individual flans in 6-ounce molds,
or 4 flans in 8-ounce molds

FOR CARAMELIZING THE MOLDS:

3/4 cup sugar

INGREDIENTS FOR LIGHT-TEXTURED FLAN

3/4 cup sugar
1 1/3 cups milk
1 1/3 cups half-and-half
Four 2 x 1/2-inch strips lime zest (colored rind only) (optional)
5 large eggs
1 1/2 teaspoons pure vanilla extract, preferably Mexican

INGREDIENTS FOR CREAMY FLAN:

3/4 cup sugar
1 1/3 cups milk
1 1/3 cups half-and-half
Four 2 x 1/2-inch strips lime zest (colored rind only) (optional)
3 large eggs
5 large egg yolks
1 1/2 teaspoons pure vanilla extract, preferably Mexican

INGREDIENTS FOR RICH-AND-COMMANDING FLAN:

1/4 cup sugar
1 1/2 cups milk
One 14-ounce can sweetened condensed milk
Four 2 x 1/2-inch strips lime zest (colored rind only) (optional)
3 large eggs
4 large egg yolks
1 1/2 teaspoons pure vanilla extract, preferably Mexican

TRADITIONAL

1. CARAMELIZING THE MOLDS. Choose six 6-ounce or four 8-ounce molds—custard cups, coffee cups or individual soufflé dishes. Set them in a baking pan at least 2 inches deep and large enough to give the molds at least 1/2 inch clearance all around.

   Measure the sugar into a small (1- to 1 1/2-quart) saucepan. Dribble 1/3 cup water around and over the sugar, evenly moistening it, then set over medium-high heat. When the mixture comes to a full boil, wash down the sides of the pan with a brush dipped in water (this dissolves any clinging sugar crystals). Reduce the heat to medium and boil without stirring until the syrup begins to turn golden, 3 to 5 minutes. Now, carefully start gently swirling the pan over the heat until the syrup is a deep straw color. Remove from the heat and continue swirling until the color is a rich amber. Quickly pour a portion of caramel into each of the molds. Immediately tilt the molds to evenly cover the bottom with caramel. (To clean the saucepan, fill it with water and set over medium heat to dissolve the stuck-on caramel.)

2. THE CUSTARD MIXTURE. Heat the oven to 325°F and position an oven rack in the middle. Bring a kettle of water to a simmer, and choose which style of flan you are going to make. In a medium (2 1/2- to 3-quart) saucepan, combine the sugar called for in the flan version of your choice, the milk and the half-and-half or condensed milk (whichever you're using). Set over medium heat, add the lime zest if you're using it and stir as the mixture comes to a simmer. Remove from the heat. If you're using lime zest, cover and let steep 10 minutes.

   In a large bowl, whisk the eggs (or egg and yolk combination) until liquid, then slowly whisk in the warm milk mixture. Stir in the vanilla and strain through a fine-mesh strainer into a pitcher or bowl. Pour or ladle one portion of the custard mixture into each of the molds.

3. BAKING THE CUSTARDS. Pull out the oven rack and set the pan holding the filled molds onto it. Carefully pour simmering water into the baking pan, letting it come two-thirds of the way up the sides of the molds. Carefully slide the rack back into the oven, close the door and bake until the custards are barely set in the middle, 50 to 60 minutes for small molds, 60 to 70 minutes for larger ones. Since most ovens don't offer completely even heat, I recommend turning the pan around about halfway through baking, even though it's a rather tricky maneuver.

   Let the custards cool in the hot water bath, which will take about an hour, so they slowly set completely.

4. SERVING THE FLANS. Though eating a barely warm flan can be an experience in lusciousness, I think it's best to refrigerate them for at least 2 hours before serv-

ing: They're easier to successfully unmold, their texture will have firmed in a way most folks find quite agreeable and more of the caramelized sugar will have dissolved into a wonderful caramel syrup. To serve, run a small knife around the top edge of each flan, penetrating about ½ inch below the surface. Quickly turn each mold over onto a serving plate. One by one, grasp plate and mold firmly and shake up and down and back and forth, until you hear the flan drop onto the plate. Remove the mold and scrape out sticky dissolving caramel from the inside, letting it drizzle down on the flan. Dessert's ready.

(Putting the empty molds to soak in very hot water will help remove any undissolved caramel.)

WORKING AHEAD: Covered and refrigerated, flans will keep very well for 4 to 5 days.

OTHER AROMAS TO PERFUME FLAN

Vanilla is a classic flan fragrance, but cinnamon pleases some traditional cooks. It's easy, however, to let your imagination wander, which is how we came up with these delicious variations on the original.

In Step 2, instead of the lime zest, steep one of the following in the milk mixture for 20 minutes (rather than 10 minutes, as called for in the recipe):

Fresh Mint Flan: five 3-inch sprigs fresh mint (peppermint, or spearmint, *hierba buena,* the most popular mint in Mexico); use mint sprigs as a garnish, for something fresh and aromatic.

Fresh Ginger Flan: 10 to 12 slices fresh ginger (each about the size of a quarter); use chopped crystallized ginger as a garnish, for an additional burst of flavor.

Coffee Flan: ⅓ to ½ cup ground coffee (I like dark-roasted coffee here, not too finely ground); use chopped candied orange peel or twisted strips of orange zest as a garnish, if you wish.

Lemon Verbena Flan: 15 to 20 leaves lemon verbena (this bushy herb is one of my favorites for herb tea and infusing dessert sauces; it's not readily available in grocery stores, but it's easy to grow); stand a verbena leaf in each flan, pushing the end of it into the custard to keep it upright, as a garnish.

CLASSIC CREAMY VANILLA FLAN (PAGE 308)

Questions and Answers from Our Testing

What's the best way to make caramelized sugar? Many cooks are afraid of making caramel because: (1) they may have had it turn chunky and crystalline during cooking (rather than remaining smooth and liquid); (2) caramel continues to cook and darken off the heat, making it difficult to know just when to remove it from the heat; and (3) the amber liquid is sticky and extremely hot. All those concerns can be addressed by carefully following the procedure outlined in the recipe. To ensure that the caramel is the right color, cook it in a lightweight pan (one that won't hold too much heat) and take it off the heat just before it's a rich golden brown. Caramel that never darkens past a light straw color is bland and nearly clear on a finished flan; darker is generally better. To ensure personal safety, have the molds set up beside the stove so that you can pour easily from the caramel-cooking pan.

What's the best mold to use? Individual straight-sided molds (like soufflé dishes—the small ones typically hold 8 ounces) make dramatic-looking flans, though they're not essential. Classic heatproof glass custard cups (usually 6-ounce capacity; available at most grocery stores) or coffee cups are perfectly usable. The thicker the mold, the longer the cooking time. Many cooks like to make one large flan and cut it like a cake. While that approach is doable, it's tricky to cook, unmold in one piece and cut. The first few times, use small molds, then you can graduate to a large mold if you wish.

Is a light-textured flan better than a dense one? That depends entirely on personal preference . . . or what is served before dessert. The primary difference between the three flan textures we outline is the quantity of egg yolks—more yolks mean a creamier richness. The last version also contains sweetened condensed milk (very popular in Mexico) in place of the half-and-half, giving it all the tantalizing lushness of that century-old canned product. Though half-and-half isn't common in Mexico, the local fresh farmers' milk can be richer and more flavorful than our milk. Combining milk and half-and-half is my way of approximating my favorite Mexican milk.

Is Mexican vanilla worth searching out? Mexico is the birthplace of vanilla—both the orchid plant that produces the vanilla pod and the process of turning those pods into one of the most enticing fragrances in the world. But vanilla, like coffee, offers a different experience when grown in different locations. Sniffed alongside vanillas of other origins, Mexican-grown vanilla is flowery and spicy (think cinnamon), while Madagascar Bourbon vanilla has a rich and dark aroma, Tahitian vanilla is robust and aggressive and Indonesian vanilla lacks distinction. Making the best vanilla extract is very labor intensive . . . which is reflected in the price. (If you find inexpensive Mexican vanilla, it most likely is made from coumarin and little or no real vanilla; avoid it.) See Sources (page 362) for how to obtain the best Mexican vanilla.

WHAT'S THE BEST WAY TO COOK FLAN? Old recipes direct the cook to set the flan mold(s) in a pan filled with hot water, cover the pan and simmer the assembly gently on top of the stove until the custard is set. Now we set the same assembly in the oven, where the heat is more even. Having baked nearly a hundred thousand flans at our restaurants, we are convinced that low, even heat (325°F) is essential. A low oven means longer cooking—and a more even texture.

HOW CAN YOU TELL WHEN FLAN IS DONE? Overbaking is the most common pitfall in flan making. While some folks have confided that they actually prefer "well-done" flan (shot through with holes, curdy, sweet-scrambled-egg flavor), I don't. So I cook flan only to the point that it wiggles like Jell-O when shaken gently—not still liquidy, but certainly not firmly set, browned or puffed. Letting the flan cool in the hot water bath allows it to slowly set completely.

ARE THERE ANY TRICKS TO UNMOLDING FLAN? It's easier than you may think. As flan cooks, the hard caramelized sugar begins to melt, creating a liquid layer on the bottom. Once you've run a knife around the side of a flan and turned it over onto a serving dish, a dislodging jiggle is all the custard needs to present itself, sauce and all.

REFINEMENTS: *Warming the milk:* This step has two functions: It extracts flavor from the lime zest, and it helps ensure a silken-textured flan by slowly warming the eggs.

VARIATION: *Making a large flan:* You'll need a 2-quart mold (such as a soufflé dish), preferably one that has a 7-inch diameter and is about 3 inches deep. Reduce the oven temperature to 300°F and cook it for about 1¼ hours; cover lightly with foil if the top starts to brown.

Rice Pudding

 Mexico is a humble country that's been kept together, in great part, by rice pudding. Tight webs of family ties have held the country together through regimes and revolutions, over impassable mountain ranges and impenetrable jungles. And rice pudding, I notice, is everywhere, acting like a catalyst for life-affirming domestic interludes that can start with fare as simple as a plastic plateful of soft tacos or as elegant as a china bowlful of squash blossom soup. Rice pudding is one of the human race's great comfort foods and, modest though it is, one that's welcome practically anywhere.

In Mexico, rice pudding is the creamy stove-top variety, rather than the custardy baked one. As the pudding simmers over low heat, the rice and milk create a beautiful sauce (especially if you've chosen the right kind of rice), one that's perfumed with *canela,* the flowery Mexican cinnamon.

TRADITIONAL BENCHMARK: The best Mexican rice pudding I can remember was in an old-fashioned restaurant in Mexico City. The grains had a tender but firm texture (like the best risotto), and they were enrobed in a rich milky creaminess. Dark raisins added interesting texture to the comforting creaminess and a counterpoint to the pudding's gentle sweetness.

WHEN TO THINK OF THIS RECIPE: Rice pudding is so simple and so delicious when served warm from the pot that I often take the quick steps to get it started as I begin preparing dinner. Rice pudding isn't dressy like flan, so I rarely plan it as part of a special meal—unless I know that at least one of my guests is wild about it. If that's the case, I'll make a little *piloncillo* syrup to drizzle over the pudding, replace the raisins with dried cherries, strawberries or cranberries (just to make it different) and serve it topped with pomegranate seeds or raspberries. Or I'll stir in some fresh mango while it's warm. Or I'll make the pudding into crispy little croquettes to serve with ice cream. Rice pudding certainly adapts itself to fancier presentations, though no version honestly surpasses the warm classic enjoyed at the kitchen table with family.

ADVICE FOR AMERICAN COOKS: Make double—you never have enough.

Mexican Rice Pudding with cinnamon and dried fruit

ARROZ CON LECHE CLÁSICO

Makes about 5½ cups, serving 6 generously

TRADITIONAL

A 2-inch piece of cinnamon stick, preferably Mexican canela,
   plus (optional) a little ground cinnamon for serving
*Two 2-inch strips orange zest (colored rind only), taken off
   the orange with a vegetable peeler*
Salt
1 cup rice, preferably medium-grain
4 cups milk (use whole milk for a creamier texture)
³/₄ cup sugar
*½ cup raisins (or other chopped dried fruit—such as cherries,
   mangoes, cranberries or apricots)*
About ³/₄ cup Mexican Raw Sugar Syrup (page 317) (optional)

1. **PRELIMINARY RICE COOKING.** Measure 1 ³/₄ cups water into a medium (3-quart) saucepan. Add the cinnamon stick, orange zest and ½ teaspoon salt. Bring to a boil, cover and simmer over low heat for 5 minutes. Stir in the rice, cover and cook until tender, about 20 minutes. Remove the cinnamon and orange zest.

2. **FROM COOKED RICE TO PUDDING.** Add the milk and sugar to the pan. Set over medium to medium-low heat and simmer until the mixture *just begins to thicken* (it should look no thicker than heavy cream), 15 to 20 minutes. Stir in the raisins (or other dried fruit). The pudding will thicken considerably as it cools.

3. **SERVING THE RICE PUDDING.** I think rice pudding is at its most delectable when it is slightly warm. I suggest you either serve it freshly made and still warm from the pan or reheat it in the microwave or on the stove top, stirring gently to avoid breaking the grains. Spoon the rice pudding into a serving dish or individual bowls, dust with cinnamon or drizzle with the sugar syrup and carry to the table. A wonderful, warm treat awaits.

WORKING AHEAD: The pudding can be made a day or two ahead through Step 2. Cover and refrigerate. Cold pudding thickens, so stir in enough milk to soften it.

HORCHATA DE ALMENDRA
● ALMOND-RICE COOLER

Though it may sound a touch odd to North Americans, this milky-looking cool drink is ubiquitous in Mexico. It's refreshing while offering the comforting flavors of rice pudding. But since it's made from soaked *raw* rice, there's no thickishness to make it heavy or cloying. I am, however, offering a recipe enriched with almonds (patterned after my all-time favorite version at Casilda in the old downtown Oaxaca market); most cooks use only rice. And, for those interested in a seductive experience, make *horchata* with milk rather than water.

Makes 6 cups, serving 8

²/₃ cup (5 ounces) rice—medium- or long-grain rice is fine
1¼ cups (6 ounces) blanched almonds
A 3-inch piece cinnamon stick, preferably Mexican canela
4½ cups water (or 2½ cups water and 2 cups milk)
1 cup sugar, plus a little more if desired

In a large bowl, combine the rice, almonds, cinnamon stick and *2½ cups* of the water—here it should be hot tap water. Cool, cover and refrigerate overnight.

Pour the mixture into the blender, add the sugar and blend on high for several minutes, until the mixture is as smooth as possible—they'll still be a hint of grittiness when you rub a drop between your fingers. Strain through a fine sieve (if yours isn't very fine, line it with cheesecloth), pressing on the solids until only a dryish pulp remains. Pour into a pitcher, add the remaining *2 cups* (cold) water (or the milk), taste and sweeten with a little more sugar if you wish. Serve over ice. In Oaxaca, they swirl a little pureed red cactus fruit (*tuna* or *jiotilla*) into each glass, turning the *horchata* rosy, then top the drink with cubed cantaloupe and broken pecans.

MIEL DE PILONCILLO
- MEXICAN RAW SUGAR SYRUP

The traditional sugar of Mexico—*piloncillo*—is in every market, poised to add its rich, complex, dark flavors to classic dishes. You'll see baskets of the solid cones (the name *piloncillo* translates as "little pylon," describing the cone's shape), varying in color from honey-golden to molasses-black. The darker the color, the more robust the flavor. Cone sizes vary greatly, from as little as ¾ ounce to more than 9 ounces. Melting the sugar into a syrup is classic on crispy, thin *buñuelo* fritters at Christmas, but its uses are limitless.

Makes about ¾ cup

1 large (8- to 9-ounce) cone piloncillo *(Mexican raw sugar)*
One 2-inch strip orange zest (colored rind only),
   taken off the orange with a vegetable peeler
⅛ teaspoon anise seed

In a small saucepan, combine the *piloncillo* with 2 cups water, the orange zest and anise seed. Set over medium heat and bring to a gentle boil. Stir regularly until the sugar cone melts completely, then maintain that gentle boil until the mixture has reduced to a syrupy consistency, 20 to 30 minutes. Cool, then strain into a jar. The syrup will keep for several weeks in the refrigerator.

Mexican rice pudding at an open-air restaurant

QUESTIONS AND ANSWERS FROM OUR TESTING

WHAT'S THE BEST RICE FOR RICE PUDDING? After testing several different types of rice, our unanimous preference was for medium-grain rice, because it yields the firmest grains and the creamiest texture. (In fact, medium-grain rice is sometimes called "pudding rice" in England.) Long-grain rice makes a very respectable pudding, though one with a slightly softer grain and a milkier, less silken texture.

IS MILK THE BEST LIQUID TO USE FOR RICE PUDDING? We tried rice pudding with milk, cream, half-and-half and evaporated milk—the latter chosen in hopes that it would give us a rich-tasting, yet lean dessert. The winner, I think, depends on the role of rice pudding in your meal. For a little something sweet, universally appealing and relatively wholesome at the end of an everyday meal, rice pudding made with whole milk tops my list. For a richer dessert to finish a special-occasion meal, I'd replace up to half the milk with half-and-half or up to a quarter of it with heavy cream. (I included another luxurious version, thickened with egg yolks, in my first book, *Authentic Mexican*.) Much to my disappointment, evaporated milk gave the pudding a dingy hue and a taste I can only describe as odd. Rather than cook the rice first in water, you can do all the cooking in milk; start with 6 cups milk and simmer it all the way to pudding. The result will be quite rich and creamy, with grains that are a bit firmer.

ARE THERE ANY TRICKS TO COOKING RICE PUDDING? For me, the only trick to making a perfect rice pudding is knowing when to take the pot from the heat. Overcooking results in a thick mass that'll take a considerable amount of milk to thin to the appropriately creamy consistency.

VARIATION: *Arroz con Leche y Mango* (Mango Rice Pudding): Stir 2 cups diced peeled ripe mango into the pudding in place of the raisins or dried fruit. A tablespoon or so of dark rum underscores the wonderfully exotic perfume.

A CONTEMPORARY TWIST: *Croquetas de Arroz con Leche* (Crispy Rice Pudding Croquettes): Make the rice pudding without raisins, simmering it in Step 2 until thick enough for a spoon to stand up in it. Remove from the heat and stir in 4 beaten egg yolks. Return to the heat and cook, stirring, for 2 minutes. Turn off the heat. Let stand until lukewarm, then, with a *small* ice cream scoop or a soupspoon, scoop out rounds of the mixture (each one about 1 rounded tablespoon), lining them up on a buttered baking sheet about 2 inches apart. Using the back of a spoon, flatten them into disks ½ inch thick and about 2 inches across. Chill thoroughly. Brush with melted butter, then bake until browned underneath (about 13 minutes) in a 425°F oven. Serve 4 of the crusty, creamy-centered rounds, browned side up, to each guest, with a spoonful of ice cream or thick cream and a bit of sweetened crushed raspberries laced with lime juice. Dust with powdered sugar.

Cajeta *(Goat's Milk Caramel Sauce)*

 Cajeta is more than caramel sauce. I'll certainly admit that it *looks* like caramel sauce, all golden brown and glossy. But *cajeta's* flavor is fuller and more complex because of the goat's milk that gives it substance and the fact that it simmers slowly, reducing in volume and concentrating as it takes on that beautiful muted amber color. The result trades the clamorous solo flavor of caramelized sugar, on which our typical caramel sauce is built, for a quieter ensemble of browned richness that hints at butterscotch—and childhood. Most everyone is wild about *cajeta*. You may have fallen in love with something similar already in the now-popular *dulce de leche* ice cream.

I was smitten from the first time I stood in a Mexican friend's kitchen, spooning some *cajeta* out of a jar (grocery-store stuff, not even very good) and spreading it on one of those plain, crisp Maria cookies that seem to have been created in Mexico for just this purpose. Though "caramel sauce on cookies" may sound odd or messy to us, it doesn't to Mexicans, because they think of *cajeta* as a spread as well as a sauce.

For years, I've collected old Mexican cookbooks dating back to the beginning of the nineteenth century. And when I peruse the collection of sweets recipes those books contain, I find whole sections of *cajetas,* confections that one book describes as thick mixtures that can be spooned into small wooden boxes, which can be put away and preserved for a long time without spoiling. . . . Sounds like a sweet spread to me, like a marmalade. Following the definition, the author gives six dozen recipes, ranging from peach, pineapple and guava to jícama, fava bean, chayote and rice (all sweet). Only a few of them contain milk, but all the recipes do have three things in common: (1) sufficient sugar to preserve the main ingredient(s), (2) a thick consistency (what Mexican cookbook authors still today describe as the *punto de cajeta,* the point when a mixture has boiled long enough that you can see swipes of the pot's bottom as you stir) and (3) the *cajeta's* final resting place in a *cajita*—the little balsa-wood box that gives the mixture its name.

Now, all that may seem a far cry from a jar of caramel sauce. But somewhere along the way, a plain and simple milk-based *cajeta* was born, *cajeta de leche,* as it's described in a 1947 cookbook, the main specialty of Celaya, Guanajuato. Today that version is practically the only *cajeta* you can find.

In Mexico, I get a hankering for the caramely richness of *cajeta* when I come across a stand proffering golden fried plantains (cooking bananas) in a street fair. Drizzled with *cajeta* and, perhaps, thick cream, they're a thrill. Or I look for *cajeta* in the ice cream stores, swirled into vanilla creaminess. Or in a fancy restaurant, dousing crepes and baked till bubbly in the oven. *Cajeta* is comfortable everywhere, including practically any modern creation you might dream up.

I've dreamed up rustic little apple tarts—*cajeta* infusing the fruit and pooling on the plate. A tangy berry salsa gives just the right counterpoint to the sweetness.

TRADITIONAL BENCHMARK: Perfect *cajeta* is like perfect wine: silky-smooth, balanced and complex. Though it's a sweet, syrupy sauce, the best *cajeta* is light-bodied, not cloying. It's made with goat's milk, providing a full flavor and a sweet-balancing tang. And it's simmered slowly, developing full depth-of-flavor and a rich golden-brown color.

WHEN TO THINK OF THESE RECIPES: You'll probably make your first batch of *cajeta* when a special dessert is in order—be it *cajeta*-drizzled fresh fruit or ice cream, or the stunning (but more involved) *cajeta* apple tarts. After the first go-round, you'll probably think about doing a batch periodically, to have on hand for quick desserts or late-night "tastings" at the refrigerator door.

ADVICE FOR AMERICAN COOKS: Though the best *cajeta* is made with goat's milk and Mexican cinnamon (*canela*), a respectable version can be created from cow's milk and American cinnamon.

Bakery window

Goat's Milk Caramel Sauce

CAJETA

Makes about 3 cups

2 quarts goat's milk or a combination of goat's milk
    and cow's milk—or even all cow's milk
    (use whole milk in all cases)
2 cups sugar
A 2-inch piece of cinnamon stick, preferably
    Mexican canela
1/2 teaspoon baking soda, dissolved in
    1 tablespoon water

TRADITIONAL

1. SIMMERING THE *CAJETA*. In a medium-large (6-quart) pot (preferably a Dutch oven or Mexican copper *cazo*), combine the milk, sugar and cinnamon stick and set over medium heat. Stir regularly until the milk comes to a simmer (all the sugar should have dissolved by this point). Remove the pot from the heat and stir in the dissolved baking soda—it'll foam up if the goat's milk is acidic. When the bubbles subside, return the pot to the heat.

   Adjust the heat to maintain the mixture at a brisk simmer (too high, and the mixture will boil over; too low, and the cooking time will seem interminable). Cook, stirring regularly, until the mixture turns pale golden, more or less 1 hour.

   Now, begin stirring frequently as the mixture colors to caramel-brown and thickens to the consistency of maple syrup—you'll notice the bubbles becoming larger and glassier. Stir regularly so nothing sticks to the bottom of the pot. Test a couple of drops on a cold plate: When cool, the *cajeta* should be the consistency of a medium-thick caramel sauce. If the cooled *cajeta* is thicker (almost like caramel candy), stir in a tablespoon or so of water and remove from the heat; if too runny, keep cooking.

2. FINISHING THE *CAJETA*. Pour the *cajeta* through a fine-mesh strainer set over a bowl or wide-mouthed storage jar. When cool, cover and refrigerate until you're ready to serve. Warming the *cajeta* before serving (a microwave oven is efficient here) makes it extra delicious.

WORKING AHEAD: *Cajeta* keeps for a month or more in the refrigerator. Keep it tightly covered to keep it from absorbing other flavors.

VARIATION: *Cajeta Inspirations: Cajeta* makes a memorable sundae topping drizzled over butter pecan or chocolate ice cream. Crepes rolled around sweetened cream cheese and baked under a blanket of cajeta are a showstopper (if you wish, top them with toasted nuts or sweet fried plantains). *Cajeta* is a natural over cheesecake or berries (add a spoonful of sour cream and a little shaved chocolate for pizzazz).

FRIED PLANTAINS • PLÁTANOS MACHOS FRITOS

Makes enough for a single batch of white rice or to serve 2 to 4 as a side dish or dessert

Plantains are cooking bananas that are used both green, as a potato-like vegetable, and ripe. As the fruit ripens, its sweetness increases dramatically, while it maintains a wonderful tanginess. Cooking dissipates mouth-drying tannins, which explains why plantains are rarely eaten raw. Ripe, plantains are quite soft (but not mushy) and nearly black. As a dessert, fried plantains are often served with *crema* (page 133) and occasionally with goat's milk caramel sauce (*cajeta*, page 321).

¹/₄ cup vegetable oil or butter
2 large black-ripe plantains, peeled (you may need a knife to
    get through the tough skin) and sliced on a diagonal
    about ¹/₄ inch thick

In a large (12-inch) skillet (preferably nonstick or well-seasoned cast iron), heat the oil or butter over medium. In two batches, lay in the plantain slices and cook until browned, about 3 minutes per side. Remove to a serving plate or arrange over the top of warm white rice.

RUSTIC *CAJETA* APPLE TARTS WITH BERRY "SALSA" (PAGE 324)

Rustic *Cajeta* Apple Tarts with Berry "Salsa"

TARTALETAS RÚSTICAS DE MANZANA CON CAJETA
Y SALSA DE MORAS

The easy, foolproof pastry for these rustic tarts was inspired by a recipe from Rose Levy Beranbaum's remarkable *The Pie and Pastry Bible*.

Makes 6 individual tarts

1 ⅓ cups (6 ounces) all-purpose flour
⅛ teaspoon baking powder
Salt
6 ounces (¾ cup) cold unsalted butter, cut into small pieces
One 3-ounce package cream cheese, chilled, cut into small pieces
1 ½ teaspoons cider vinegar
5 medium (about 2 pounds total) firm cooking apples (such as Gala
    or Granny Smith)
1 teaspoon finely chopped lime or lemon zest (colored rind only
    removed with a peeler or zester and finely chopped)
About 1 cup cajeta, store-bought or homemade (page 321)
2 cups berries (such as raspberries, blackberries, or hulled,
    sliced strawberries—even defrosted individually quick-frozen
    berries will work here)
1 to 2 tablespoons sugar, to taste
About ¾ cup homemade crema (page 133), crème fraîche
    or sour cream thinned with a little milk (optional)

CONTEMPORARY

I. THE DOUGH. In a food processor, combine the flour, baking powder and ⅛ teaspoon salt. Pulse to mix thoroughly. Add *4 ounces (½ cup)* of the butter and all the cream cheese, then pulse 5 or 6 times until the mixture looks like coarse crumbs. Drizzle the vinegar and 1 ½ tablespoons ice water over the dough and pulse 3 times to bring the mixture together into rough clumps. Turn out onto your work surface, divide into 6 parts and roll each into a ball. Place the balls on a plate, cover with plastic wrap and refrigerate for about 45 minutes.

2.   THE APPLE FILLING. Peel and core the apples, then cut them into ½-inch cubes; you should have about 6 cups. In a large (12-inch) heavy skillet (preferably nonstick), heat the remaining *2 ounces (¼ cup)* butter over medium-high. Add the apples and stir nearly constantly as they cook, first releasing their juice, then softening and browning as the juice evaporates, 8 to 10 minutes. When the apples are soft (if you've chosen firm cooking apples, they won't be falling apart) and browned, add ½ *teaspoon* of the lime or lemon zest and ¼ *cup* of the *cajeta*. Stir for a minute or two, then remove from the heat. Scoop the apple mixture onto a baking sheet to cool to room temperature, about 15 minutes.

3.   FORMING THE TARTS. While the apples are cooling, roll out each ball of dough into a 6-inch round on a lightly floured work surface. Transfer the pastry rounds to a parchment-covered or lightly oiled baking sheet, leaving about 2 inches between them. If the apples haven't cooled to room temperature by this point, cover the pastry rounds with plastic wrap and refrigerate.

Spoon ⅓ cup of the filling onto the center of each pastry round, leaving a 1½- inch border all around. Carefully fold the dough edges up over the filling toward the center, gently pleating the dough as necessary. If time allows, place the baking sheet in the freezer for about 20 minutes.

4.   BAKING AND SERVING THE TARTS. Heat the oven to 400°F. Bake the tarts until richly golden and crispy, about 20 to 25 minutes. Remove from the oven and drizzle a generous ½ *tablespoon* of the remaining *cajeta* into the center of each tart. Cool on a wire rack.

In a small bowl, mix the berries with the remaining ½ *teaspoon* lime or lemon zest and the sugar. Mash the mixture slightly to crush some of the berries. Let the mixture stand for a few minutes to meld the flavors.

Serve the tarts warm, with a spoonful or two of the optional *crema* or sour cream, the berry "salsa" and a little drizzle of the remaining *cajeta*.

WORKING AHEAD: Both the dough and filling can be made 3 days ahead if kept well covered and refrigerated. The formed tarts can be held for 6 hours or so in the refrigerator (skip the freezing step; instead, simply cover them with plastic wrap and refrigerate). I think these tarts are best served within 3 or 4 hours of their baking. Rewarming cooled tarts gives them renewed life.

QUESTIONS AND ANSWERS FROM OUR TESTING

IS GOAT'S MILK ESSENTIAL TO PRODUCING *CAJETA*? No, cow's milk will do the job. Goat's milk, however, makes the more complexly flavored *cajeta* that is so prized in Mexico. We made test batches with cow's milk, goat's milk, half-and-half and a combination of cow's and goat's milk. Our favorite was the combination—balancing the tang and complexity of goat's milk with sweetness from cow's milk, while at the same time being more economical. Half-and-half yields a very rich, pudding-like texture rather than a syrupy one.

DOES MEXICAN *CANELA* GIVE A DIFFERENT FLAVOR THAN AMERICAN CINNAMON? Yes, and once you spend some time with Mexican *canela*'s gentle, perfumey lilt, I think you'll be seduced. *Canela* is the "true cinnamon" from Vietnam and Ceylon. Though it's often referred to as Mexican cinnamon in the United States, it's actually grown in Southeast Asia; Mexico just happens to be the largest user of it in the world. American cinnamon (a.k.a. cassia) has a more aggressive flavor—think cinnamon oil (what's used to emblazen those kid-favorite cinnamon heart candies).

HOW DOES THE ADDITION OF BAKING SODA AFFECT *CAJETA*? We call *cajeta* caramel, even though it does not contain caramelized sugar. Sugar caramelizes at high temperatures (above 320°F), but this preparation never rises above boiling, 212°F. So how does it develop that caramely color and flavor? Making *cajeta* involves browning milk solids (like browning butter), which you have to do slowly to achieve a beautiful golden brown color. Adding baking soda neutralizes the acid and promotes the browning of those milk solids. In our testing, a batch of soda-free *cajeta* came out very, very pale. A batch made with soda-neutralized milk *but no sugar* turned to a beautiful golden brown, though it didn't have the glossy, syrupy consistency that the sugar gives.

WHAT IS THE RIGHT VESSEL FOR *CAJETA* MAKING? In Mexico, an unlined copper vessel called a *cazo* is traditional, because it gives the most gentle, even distribution of heat and its sides flare, helping control boil-overs. You can find *cazos* fairly regularly at Mexican markets on both sides of the border; when purchasing a *cazo* for cooking, choose a heavy one, not a shiny, flimsy decorative one. A copper *cazo* isn't necessary, however. Perfect *cajeta* can be made in any heavy pot (enameled cast iron works particularly well). For 2 quarts of milk, a 6-quart pot gives the right depth for slow evaporation. Smaller pots encourage boil-overs; larger pots allow the milk to reduce too quickly, yielding light-colored, light-flavored *cajeta*.

WHAT IS THE RIGHT TEMPERATURE FOR SIMMERING *CAJETA*? For the richest flavor, *cajeta* needs to simmer slowly as it reduces to about one-quarter its original volume.

Just enough heat to produce a very gentle roll across the surface of the milk mixture is the right choice to avoid boil-overs and control reduction.

REFINEMENTS: *Corn syrup and* cajeta: Many commercial *cajetas* contain a significant amount of corn syrup. It gives a glossier, more corn syrup–like consistency, as well as an increased yield (you don't have to boil down the milk as far to reach the desired thickness). The final flavor, however, is lighter, with overtones of corn syrup. *Large-batch* cajeta: *Cajeta* made in large batches is typically the best *cajeta*, since it takes longer to reduce, thus ensuring plenty of time to develop the best flavor and color. When doubling, tripling or quadrupling this recipe, simply multiply all ingredients and choose an appropriately sized pan.

VARIATIONS: Cajeta *Pudding:* There is a version of *cajeta* I used to eat in Mexico City that was less reduced and made into a pudding. To make it, simmer the milk mixture slowly until reduced to 4½ cups, then whisk in 3 tablespoons cornstarch dissolved in ¼ cup milk. Whisk until thickened and simmering. The flavor is less intense than regular *cajeta.*

Double-Caramel Cajeta: Another version of *cajeta* starts by mixing the sugar with ½ cup water and boiling the mixture without stirring until it caramelizes to the color of strong tea, then adding the milk(s) and cinnamon—there will be a very hot whoosh of steam that rises—and whisking over the heat until the caramel has dissolved. Continue to simmer until reduced to the typical *cajeta* consistency. There is no need for baking soda. Some call this darker, more strongly flavored version *cajeta quemada,* burnt *cajeta.*

Spirited Cajeta: Many versions of *cajeta* contain alcohol (grain alcohol, sherry, rum, brandy, etc.) and are called *cajetas envinadas,* spirited *cajetas.* For a single batch, add 2 tablespoons of your alcohol of choice when the *cajeta* is cool.

Mexican Chocolate

Just imagine a "Mexican Starbucks": earthenware pavers on the floor; vibrant splashes of color throughout the comfortable atmosphere; warming, frothy drinks; and the smell of fresh-ground beans. Chocolate beans.

Mexico, you see, has for millennia celebrated the native-born chocolate, not coffee, as the morning cup. The state of Tabasco, on Mexico's Gulf Coast, is chocolate's birthplace. And chocolate has been so treasured throughout the land that, in pre-Columbian times, the beans were used as currency as well as to nourish kings and courtesans.

But not in the form of bonbons or cake or hot fudge sauce. Those came later, outside Mexico and fueled by other nationalities' creative energies. In its homeland, "chocolate" was, and still is, a beverage—originally a bitter, coffee-like brew that was seasoned with herbs and spices (even chiles), then, after the Spanish conquest, a sweetened libation. In regions where it's a specialty, much pride is taken in its quality, flavorings and freshness.

In Mexico's southern state of Oaxaca, for instance, folks are crazy about homemade chocolate. The best cooks buy the market's best cacao beans (they look like unskinned almonds), toast them (again, like almonds) and rub off their skins, then grind them with sugar, cinnamon and sometimes almonds. The most exacting cooks hand-grind the chocolate on a stone *metate,* that lava-rock grinding stone that also grinds corn for tortillas. They warm the *metate* over a few live coals, then work the dark paste back and forth with a rock-grinding roller until it's a shiny, near-molten mass. With a clap, clap, clap, they mold it into disks.

Later, it's whipped into a creamy liquid offering for friends and family. To do that, the solid disk of chocolate is roughly chopped, mixed with hot water or milk and beaten to a froth. There's a special bulbous, narrow-mouthed pot (*olla para chocolate*) for holding the hot chocolaty liquid in Mexico, and a carved wooden beater (*molinillo*) for dissolving the bits and creating the beloved froth. (Long before the cappuccino craze, ancient Mexicans understood the foam on chocolate to be life-giving, nourishing the soul.)

If using water for hot chocolate seems an austerity measure, you've probably never tasted really great, fresh-ground, homemade Mexican chocolate. That specialty shows off its full richness when made with water, no muting milk to distract attention. You can order a good version of *chocolate de agua* (water-made chocolate) at many stalls in Oaxaca's 20 de

Noviembre market, one side of which is devoted to enticingly aromatic chocolate-grinding enterprises (customers choose their beans and add-ins, then watch as they're ground to a paste between electrically driven millstones). It's served in a deep wide bowl that resembles a French *café au lait* bowl, with anise-laced egg bread (*pan de yema*).

But churros—those addictive, crispy, ridged, cylindrical fritters—probably come to more Mexicans' minds than *pan de yema* when they think of hot chocolate. Mexico's chocolate and churros are like America's coffee and donuts.

And chocolate candy, chocolate truffles, chocolate for desserts—where do they fit into Mexico's culinary viewpoint? Primarily as a specialty, I'd say, since Mexican candy stores are filled mostly with fruit- and milk-based confections. To use chocolate for candy making and most desserts, it needs to be conched, a complex process that smooths the chocolate into minute particles, allowing the chocolate to melt into an oozy, flowing liquid. Mexican chocolate has never gotten that treatment, so it doesn't really melt. To use it in baking, as I've done in the Mexican Chocolate Streusel Cake, its robust, perfumey flavor must be woven in as you would cocoa powder.

TRADITIONAL BENCHMARK: A frothy cup of fresh-ground Mexican chocolate is my benchmark—not too sweet, enriched with almonds and perfumed with cinnamon. Because it's so fresh, this chocolate sings loud and clear with dark, roasty, rustic chocolate fullness. My perfect Mexican chocolate shows a more artless side of the cocoa bean, not European chocolate's creamy subtlety. You might say it plays Celia Cruz to European chocolate's Maria Callas.

WHEN TO THINK OF THESE RECIPES: A cup of Mexican hot chocolate makes any breakfast (*desayuno*) special. It's a wonderful late-afternoon treat (*merienda*). And with a Mexican streusel-topped bun (*concha*), it's the perfect light supper (*cena*) or before-bed sweet. *Champurrado* (chocolate *atole*) is typically drunk with tamales; the combination is so satisfying that many folks think of it as a complete morning meal. Our contemporary Mexican chocolate cake would be my daughter's dream breakfast, but I think it's more appropriate as an after-school snack or casual dessert. It holds well, so it's perfect to contribute to a potluck or put out on a buffet.

ADVICE FOR AMERICAN COOKS: Look for Mexican chocolate in well-stocked grocery stores or Mexican groceries, or order it by mail. There is no substitute.

Mexican Hot Chocolate

CHOCOLATE MEXICANO

Makes about 3 cups, serving 4

TRADITIONAL

2 ¹/₂ cups milk or water
1 cup (about 5 ounces) chopped
     Mexican chocolate (no need to chop
     the chocolate fine)

1. In a medium-small (2-quart) saucepan, combine the milk or water and chocolate. Stir over medium heat until the mixture is steaming hot and the chocolate more or less dissolved (there will still be small pieces). Pour into a Mexican chocolate pot (*olla para chocolate*) or a blender.

   If using the Mexican pot, put a wooden *molinillo* in the pot and begin whipping the chocolate by rolling the handle quickly back and forth between your palms. The movement is a little like rubbing your palms against each other to warm them in cold weather—only here the *molinillo*'s wooden handle is between them. After about 2 minutes of vigorous beating, dip a spoon into the mixture to make sure the chocolate has dissolved (they'll always be a few bits of chocolate on the bottom) and the mixture is very foamy.

   If using a blender, loosely cover (or take out the lid's removable center cap—this eliminates dangerous pressure build-up when blending hot mixtures) and blend until the mixture is homogeneous and foamy, about 30 seconds. (Alternatively, use an immersion blender in a tall pitcher and blend until foamy.)

2. Pour into cups, dividing the foam equally, and they're ready to serve.

WORKING AHEAD: Frothy Mexican hot chocolate waits for no one.

MEXICAN
HOT CHOCOLATE
(PAGE 330)

CHURROS
(PAGE 332)

CHURROS • CRUNCHY FLUTED FRITTERS

These long, golden beauties are my weakness—but, thankfully, only when they're warm. Which isn't the way you always find them. So many places nowadays serve fancy new filled churros, like a Mexican version of a bismarck donut. The filling is there, I contend, to divert your attention from the fact that the churro is cold, perhaps even stale. Churros are really rewarding to make, because they're easy and everyone loves them. All you need is a cookie gun, sturdy pastry bag or *churrera* (churros press) to form them.

Makes twelve to fourteen 5-inch churros, or more, depending on the size of the tip

2 tablespoons vegetable oil

1 tablespoon sugar, plus ²/₃ cup to roll the churros in

Salt

1 cup (4¹/₂ ounces) all-purpose flour

Vegetable oil to a depth of 1 inch for frying

¹/₂ teaspoon cinnamon, preferably freshly ground
  Mexican canela *(optional)*

1. THE DOUGH. In a medium-small (2-quart) saucepan, combine the oil, *1 table-spoon* sugar and ¹/₂ teaspoon salt with 1 cup water. Set over high heat and bring to a boil, stirring occasionally. Remove from the heat and add the flour all at once, stirring vigorously until the mixture forms a thick, smooth-textured ball. Let cool in the pan.

2. FRYING THE CHURROS. Spread the ²/₃ *cup* sugar over the bottom of a baking pan and mix in the optional cinnamon. When you're ready to eat the churros, heat the oil in a large pan (my preference for ease and consistency of temperature is a heavy pan or cast-iron skillet that's about 9 inches across and 3 inches deep) over medium to medium-high to about 375°F (the oil will shimmer on the surface and give off that characteristic hot oil aroma).

   Scoop the dough into a *churrera*, a cookie press fitted with a ³/₈-inch fluted opening or a heavy-duty (canvas-type) pastry bag fitted with a ³/₈-inch star tip. Holding your pressing apparatus a few inches above the hot oil, press out a

5-inch length of dough (the end will dangle into the oil), then pull it free from the press with your fingertips. Cook this one churro, turning occasionally, until it is deep golden brown, about 2 to 3 minutes if the oil temperature is right. Remove it to drain on paper towels and let it cool a minute, then break it open to check for doneness—it should be just a little soft inside, but not doughy. Too low an oil temperature, and the churros will take a long time to color, usually bursting apart before they're brown; too high a temperature and they'll brown quickly but not cook through.

Adjust the oil temperature if necessary, then press out and fry the churros 4 or 5 at a time, draining each batch on paper towels. Roll the churros luxuriously in the sugar mixture while they're still warm. They're ready to enjoy.

WORKING AHEAD: The churro dough (Step 1) can be prepared up to several hours before frying; cover it and leave at room temperature. If you can't fry the churros just before eating, warm them for 3 or 4 minutes in a 350°F oven, but always serve them warm.

VARIATION: Add ¼ cup (1 ounce) finely ground pecans and ½ teaspoon very finely chopped lime zest (colored rind only) to the dough along with the flour.

Panaderías *specialize in breads, rolls, and cookies*

Mexican Chocolate Streusel Cake

PASTEL DE CHOCOLATE MEXICANO

Serves 12

One 18- or 19-ounce package Mexican chocolate, roughly chopped

FOR THE STREUSEL TOPPING:

1 large egg yolk
Salt (optional)
3 1/2 ounces (7 tablespoons) butter, at room temperature
1 cup (4 1/2 ounces) all-purpose flour

FOR THE CAKE:

1 3/4 cups (8 ounces) all-purpose flour
1 1/4 teaspoons baking powder
One 8 ounce package cream cheese, at room temperature
8 ounces (1 cup) unsalted butter, at room temperature
2/3 cup granulated sugar
4 large eggs, at room temperature

Powdered sugar for dusting the cake

1. THE STREUSEL TOPPING. In a food processor, pulse *half* of the Mexican chocolate until it is the consistency of coarse crumbs. Remove and set aside for the batter. Add the remaining chocolate to the processor and process it to the consistency of coarse crumbs. Mix the egg yolk and 1/2 teaspoon salt (if using salted butter, omit the salt) in a small bowl, stirring to dissolve the salt. Add to the processor along with the butter and the flour. Pulse just until everything is thoroughly combined—it should look crumbly, not be processed to a paste. Set aside.

2. THE CAKE. Heat the oven to 350°F. Butter and flour a 13 x 9-inch baking pan. Sift together the flour and baking powder.

    In the bowl of an electric mixer, beating on medium speed, combine the cream cheese, butter and granulated sugar. Beat until light and fluffy, 2 to 3 minutes. One at a time, add the eggs, beating until each one is thoroughly incorporated before adding the next. Add the sifted flour mixture, scrape down the sides of the bowl and beat for 1 minute, just until the flour is incorporated. Last, use a large spoon to stir the reserved chopped chocolate into the batter.

Scrape the batter into the prepared pan and smooth the top. Crumble the streusel topping evenly over the batter, making sure there are no large lumps—lumps may sink during baking. Bake in the center of the oven until springy (the edges will have just begun to pull away from the sides of the pan) and a toothpick inserted in the center comes out clean, 35 to 40 minutes.

Cool on a wire rack (in my opinion, this cake tastes best when still slightly warm), then cut into squares and serve dusted with powdered sugar. Vanilla, caramel or cinnamon-scented ice cream sure goes well with a bite of this *pastel*.

WORKING AHEAD: Tightly wrapped, the finished cake keeps beautifully for several days. You may want to rewarm pieces of the cake in a low oven before serving.

Left: Grinding Mexican cinnamon (canela) and cacao beans
Right: Freshly ground sweetened chocolate ready for sale

MEXICAN CHOCOLATE STREUSEL CAKE (PAGE 334)

Warm, Comforting Chocolaty *Masa*-Thickened Beverage

CHAMPURRADO (ATOLE DE CHOCOLATE)

Makes 8 cups, serving 10 to 12

1 cup (8 ounces) fresh smooth-ground corn masa
      for tortillas
      OR ²/₃ cup powdered masa harina *mixed*
      with ¹/₂ *cup warm water*
1 ¹/₄ cups (about 6 ounces) chopped
      Mexican chocolate
3 ¹/₂ cups milk, or a bit more if needed
²/₃ cup sugar

TRADITIONAL

1. In a blender, combine the fresh or reconstituted *masa* with the chocolate and 3 cups water. Blend until smooth.

    Strain into a medium (4-quart) saucepan, add the milk and sugar and set over medium heat. Stir (or whisk) constantly as the mixture thickens and comes to a simmer, about 10 minutes. *Atole* should be served about the consistency of heavy cream—no thicker. If yours is thicker, whisk in a little milk or water.

2. Ladle or pour into cups or mugs.

WORKING AHEAD: The warm beverage will hold in a thermal pot or over very low heat for an hour or more. If it thickens, thin with milk.

VARIATION: *Cinnamon* Atole: Omit the chocolate and, along with the milk, add a 3-inch piece of cinnamon stick (Mexican *canela* is definitive here). Simmer slowly for 20 minutes to bring out the best of the cinnamon.

QUESTIONS AND ANSWERS FROM OUR TESTING

ARE ALL MEXICAN CHOCOLATES EQUAL? I've tromped through the cacao-growing region of Tabasco in southern Mexico and tasted the freshly fermented chocolate there. Several times a year I have the opportunity to taste the freshly ground chocolate from several mills in Oaxaca (I'm always drawn back to El Mayordomo and La Soledad). I've sampled every brand of Mexican chocolate I can lay my hands on in the United States. And here are my comments: Freshly ground chocolate in Mexico is as superior to the packaged Mexican chocolate you find in American stores as freshly ground dark-roast coffee beans are to the preground grocery store variety. But, when I am far from Mexico, I reach for El Popular, because it's robust and not too sweet. El Caporal is good too, having a pronounced almond flavor. Ibarra and Abuelita (two easily available brands) are decent, though they are quite sweet, with strong cinnamon flavors.

FOR MEXICAN-STYLE HOT CHOCOLATE, WHAT'S THE RIGHT PROPORTION OF CHOCOLATE TO MILK OR WATER? That's a matter of taste, and my taste has actually changed. Since writing my first cookbook, I've developed a taste for a stronger cup. Now I recommend 5 ounces (if you're using Ibarra chocolate, that'll be about 1 ²/₃ disks) for 2 ½ cups milk or water. If using water, you may want a little more chocolate, especially if the chocolate you're using isn't terribly fresh.

ARE A MEXICAN CHOCOLATE POT (*OLLA*) AND BEATER (*MOLINILLO*) THE BEST PIECES OF EQUIPMENT FOR MAKING MEXICAN-STYLE HOT CHOCOLATE? The shape of a Mexican chocolate pot allows for the mixture to be beaten vigorously with the wooden chocolate beater without having anything splash out. Traditionalists say it's the only way to get well-blended chocolate with the best foam. But few of us have the traditional pot. And the wooden chocolate beater, while more common in the United States than the pot, is still in pretty short supply. So most of us will pour everything into a blender and turn out the liveliest of lively foams. An immersion blender in a deep saucepan will produce the same results.

REFINEMENTS: *Chopping chocolate for hot chocolate and streusel cake:* Mexican chocolate is hard, but cuttable, with a large knife. If you approach the task as more or less *shaving* the chocolate off the block, the procedure will actually go more easily and quickly. Though it's a lot to do by hand, I prefer hand-chopped (really hand-shaved) Mexican chocolate for the streusel cake, rather than processor-chopped, because it produces a cake with better texture.

The Quintessentially Tropical Mango

Mangoes smell outlandishly enticing—at least to me. More than any other widely available tropical fruit, they carry the fully intense aroma that inhabits markets of torrid climes. Some find that fragrance a little reckless, verging on improper. Others—like me—feel it has an affect similar to that of white truffles and saffron, creating a deep-down itch that's only scratched by consuming big mouthfuls of the perfumed fruit.

When you see the enormous mango tree heavy with fruit, you can't help but speculate that it was really the mango that was Eve's temptation in the Garden of Eden. The smooth ovals are extended on beckoning leads, as if to say, "Pick me. *Please,* pick me. I'm ready for you." And when snapped from the lifeline, the green-smelling fruit begins its final maturation to softness, juiciness and full, heady aroma. Some mangoes, like avocados, don't completely ripen on the tree. They do that best in a warm place, once picked.

When the fruit is soft (but not mushy) and aromatic, it's ready to eat. In Mexico, folks peel mangoes, slice the flesh from the pit, to which it clings tenaciously, and squeeze a little lime on top (perhaps salt and chile too, if that fits the mood). Street vendors carve mangoes like flowers with lime-squeezed "petals" of sweet flesh stuck fast to the pit, making the sometimes fibrous fruit manageable for the wanderer. Wedges of mango with cucumber and jícama—and salt, chile and lime—served in sno-cone cups are another simple street snack. And whirred in the blender, jazzed with lime, mellowed with sugar and made refreshingly sloshy with cold water, mango becomes a favorite street drink in Mexico.

Mango's mostly casual, you see, like a juicy fresh peach. On occasion, though, it's been known to show up amid a show-stopping blaze in dishes like Tequila-Flamed Mangoes. The mangoes' texture firms to a delectable chewiness during the long baking. Plus, their flavor concentrates, giving them all the vitality they need to stand up to the tequila.

THE BEST MANGO I'VE EVER EATEN: Since mangoes have been cultivated since at least 2000 B.C. (most think that first happened in India) and over fifteen hundred varieties have been catalogued, I can't say my experience is very extensive. That's not to say I haven't eaten a lot of mangoes and don't have some pretty clear opinions. My favorite mango is slippery, slithery, almost melt-in-your-mouth, with little of the stringiness that plagues certain varieties. A mouthful releases that characteristic burst of mango flavor, like the best peach you've ever eaten, but with a more compact flavor that's intensely redolent of spices and tropical muskiness. That pretty much describes the smallish, oval (almost kidney-shaped), flat, yellow-orange Manila mango from Mexico. Imagine mango flavor enriched with ripe, ripe banana, sweet spices and egg yolks (odd as that may sound). Manila mangoes are hard to find in the United States, but a hybrid version, Ataúlfo (often sold as honey sweet or honey Manila), is becoming more available, especially in Mexican groceries. The type of mango that's much more readily available is a large roundish mango with a greenish-orange skin with blushes of red—usually the Haden or Tommy Atkins varieties. These have a tropical flavor, but one that veers in the direction of coconut, rather than banana. Their flavor is less intense, though still quite delicious, and their flesh is stringier and less compact.

WHEN TO THINK OF THESE RECIPES: The mango cooler is fairly filling and typically served with spicy tacos and the like (its sweetness beautifully balances heat). Tequila-Flamed Mangoes are an easy dessert to do when you need something dramatic and special.

ADVICE FOR AMERICAN COOKS: Though many mangoes don't finish ripening until they're picked, they need to be fully developed before picking. And once picked, they don't like deep chilling (which would make them darken and ripen unevenly) or stacking (they bruise easily as they ripen). To ripen mangoes to aromatic softness, place them in a bowl in a warm part of your kitchen (some say that wrapping them in a paper bag helps trap the maturation-promoting ethylene gas that the fruit naturally emits). Once they are ripe, you can store them in the refrigerator, but cold will mute their flavor a little.

MANGO, JÍCAMA AND CUCUMBER STREET SNACK (PAGE 344)

Mango Cooler with Prickly Pear

AGUA DE MANGO CON TUNA

**Makes a little more than 3 quarts,
serving 12 to 16**

8 medium (about 6 pounds total) ripe mangoes
1 cup sugar, plus a little extra if needed
½ cup fresh lime juice, plus a little extra
    if needed
3 large red-fleshed (not green-fleshed)
    prickly pears
Slices (wheels) of lime for garnish

TRADITIONAL

1. **CUTTING AND PUREEING THE MANGOES.** Peel the mangoes with a sharp paring knife, then cut the flesh from the pits: A mango pit (to which the flesh clings tightly) is flattish and oval, more or less a smaller version of the mango's overall shape. To cut the flesh off the pit, stand the mango on one end and slice the flesh from one flat side of the pit. Turn the mango around and slice the flesh from the other side. You'll be able to get a couple thin slices of flesh off the pit on each end.

    In a blender or food processor, puree the mango flesh. Push the puree through a medium-mesh strainer into a large measuring cup (or bowl). You should have about 4 cups.

2. **THE MANGO DRINK.** Pour the puree into a large bowl, punch bowl or traditional Mexican glass barrel. Stir in 2 quarts water, the sugar and lime juice; stir until the sugar is completely dissolved. Taste and add additional sugar or lime if you think the mixture needs it.

3. **THE PRICKLY PEARS.** Peel the prickly pears by slicing off both ends, then making a shallow incision down the length of each fruit (wearing rubber gloves will avoid annoying contact with those almost microscopic stickers). Gingerly hold the fruit with the thumb and first finger of one hand and, with the thumb and first finger of the other hand, peel off the thickish exterior of each one. In the blender or food processor, reduce the nuggets of crimson prickly pear flesh to a puree by pulsing the machine (running it continually will chop up the black

seeds—not too pretty in the finished drink). Push through a medium-mesh strainer; you should have about ½ cup.

4. **FINISHING THE DRINK.** Stir the prickly pear puree into the mango mixture. Serve in tall glasses over ice, the rim of each glass garnished with lime.

WORKING AHEAD: The drink is best served the day it's made; refrigerate leftovers, well covered.

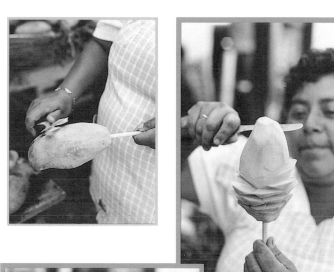

Clockwise from top left: Carving a mango "flower" and topping it with hot sauce for a street snack

ENSALADA DE MANGO, JÍCAMA Y PEPINO
● MANGO, JÍCAMA AND CUCUMBER STREET SNACK

These walk-around snacks or appetizers (or "salads," as they're called in Spanish) spell warm weather relaxation with friends in the backyard. If you have the spot, set up a cutting board with all the ingredients and make these beauties as the folks arrive. Better yet, press a guest into creative service.

Serves 6 to 8

2 medium (about 1 ½ pounds total) mangoes, peeled, flesh cut
    from the pits and sliced into 1/2-inch-wide "fingers" or wedges
1 medium (about 1 pound) jícama, peeled and cut into long
    ½-inch-wide "fingers" or wedges
1 long seedless "English" cucumber (or 2 regular cucumbers),
    cut into long ½-inch-wide "fingers" or wedges
About 1 teaspoon pure ground chile (buy pure guajillo or ancho
    chile in a Mexican grocery or substitute a little cayenne)
Salt
2 limes, each cut into 6 wedges

In pointed sno-cone cups (you'll need a sno-cone holder or a glass to support each cup) or in paper cups or glasses, combine a portion of mango, jícama and cucumber "fingers" or wedges (they will be standing in the cups). Mix the chile and ½ teaspoon salt; sprinkle over the "salads." Serve with lime wedges for the guests to squeeze over the pieces as they eat them.

VARIATION: *A Different Presentation:* Cut the mango, jícama and cucumber into cubes instead of "fingers" and mix together in a large bowl. Juice the limes (rather than cutting them into wedges) and drizzle over the mixture. Sprinkle with the salt and chile, and serve on a buffet or pass at the table.

Tequila-Flamed Mangoes

MANGOS FLAMEADOS

Serves 6

4 medium (about 3 pounds total) ripe mangoes
2 ounces (¹/₄ cup) butter
¹/₂ cup (packed) brown sugar
¹/₄ to ¹/₃ cup tequila (with all the other flavors, a simple
    blanco tequila is fine here)
3 tablespoons granulated sugar
About 1 cup homemade crema (page 133), crème fraîche
    or sour cream for serving
    OR 1¹/₂ to 2 cups ice cream (really good vanilla
    ice cream is my preference)

CONTEMPORARY

1. CUTTING THE MANGOES. Peel the mangoes with a sharp paring knife, then cut the flesh from the pits: A mango pit (to which the flesh clings tightly) is flattish and oval, more or less a smaller version of the mango's overall shape. To cut the flesh off the pit, stand the mango on one end and slice the flesh from one side of the pit. Turn the mango around and slice the flesh from the other side. You'll be able to get a couple thin slices of flesh off the pit on each end. Cut the large pieces into long ¹/₂-inch-wide "fingers" or wedges.

2. BAKING THE MANGOES. Heat the oven to 350°F. Place the butter in a 13 x 9-inch baking dish and set in the oven. When melted, about 5 minutes, remove from the oven and add the mango slices. Sprinkle with the brown sugar and stir gently to coat the mangoes completely, then spread out everything evenly in the dish. Bake, shaking the dish occasionally, for about 45 minutes—the mango juices will quickly seep out, then slowly simmer away, leaving you with toothsome mango slices that have a wonderfully concentrated flavor.

3. FLAMING AND SERVING. Just before serving, pour the tequila into a small saucepan and set over low heat—don't let the tequila get too hot, or it won't flame. Sprinkle the mangoes evenly with the granulated sugar, then lower the lights and get everyone's attention. Pour the tequila over the hot mangoes and immediately

light it. Holding the baking dish with a towel or pot holder, shake it back and forth (this is for effect—it'll give you more dramatic flames). When the flames subside, spoon a portion of mangoes onto each of six dessert plates. Serve with a dollop of *crema* or ice cream.

WORKING AHEAD: The dish can be made successfully through Step 2. It's best finished and served within a few hours, though it can be covered and refrigerated for a day. Rewarm made-ahead mangoes before flaming.

Fresh fruit ices at
Chagüita in Oaxaca

Tequila, Margaritas, Beer and Wine

Let's face it: Most Americans say they love Mexican food because of the crisp-fried tortillas, the melted cheese and . . . the margaritas. None of which—honestly—characterize food in Mexico. Most tortillas there are eaten steamy and soft. The cheese is typically a light dusting of crumbled fresh or aged garnishing cheese. And the margaritas, well, for most folks, they're not really margaritas at all—just a tall, skinny shot glass (*caballito*) or small snifter of tequila, with, perhaps, a side of lime, salt and (rather than the orange liqueur of a margarita) a spicy chaser of tomatoey *sangrita*. At a meal, a bright-flavored tequila (an unaged silver—*blanco* in Spanish—or less-than-a-year-old *reposado*) is served as an aperitif to open the palate and spirit; a wood-aged, more-than-a-year-old *añejo* is best appreciated at the end of a meal. In my opinion, tequila (solo or mixed up into margaritas) doesn't really have much of a place during a special meal. Beer and wine, however, do.

BEER: Beer's tongue-tingling effervescence, together with its flavors of slightly bitter, clean-tasting hops and rich, slightly sweet malt, make it a perfect accompaniment to a mouthful of casual, spicy enchiladas or *chilaquiles* or a steaming bowl of *pozole*. Mexico turns out a good array of beers, from the dependable medium-bodied, lightly hoppy Bohemia and Carta Blanca to the sweet and malty dark Negra Modelo (and, to a lesser extent, Dos Equis), the hoppy Dos Equis Lager and the light, dry Corona. These are mostly lager-style beers, which isn't surprising, considering that many breweries in Mexico have long been owned by the families of Germans, Austrians and Swiss immigrants. These were the people who brought their beer- and cheese-making traditions to Mexico back in the mid-nineteenth century, when the Hapsburg Emperor Maximilian was ruling Mexico.

And where did the tradition of lime in the beer come from? Well, it appears that the whole thing was a marketing gimmick dreamed up ages ago by a beer company with strong ties to a can manufacturer. Customers weren't thrilled with the taste of beer in a can. So the company got everyone excited about the cool new idea of beer with lime—*its* beer with lime—and, presto, no one could taste the can flavor anymore. I usually don't like lime in beer, though it can add a welcome refreshing zing on a hot day.

WINE: Now, wine at a Mexican meal may strike you as unexpected, even hoity-toity. I feel just the opposite. When I've crafted an impressive turkey in *mole* or fish *a la veracruzana,* wine seems the obvious choice of libation. Good wine, after all, offers a world of lush flavor possibilities—sophisticated, integrated and well balanced. Like a good *mole.* But the old "white with fish, red with meat" adage doesn't explain how I pair wine with Mexican food.

Here's a brief summary of how I do it: Rather than focus on the meat or fish, I think about the flavor range of the entire dish. With the brighter flavors of Mexican cooking (tomatillos, fresh chiles, cilantro, lime), I choose dry white wines, concentrating mostly on tangier wines like Sauvignon Blanc for zestier dishes; fuller-flavored, fruity-but-dry wines like dry Riesling or Viognier for less brightly flavored dishes. With the earthy, more concentrated flavors of Mexican cooking (dried chiles, tomatoes, *epazote*), I choose red wines, turning my attention mostly to dry wines with a good amount of complex fruitiness, like full-flavored Pinot Noir, Syrah and Grenache. With the world awash in Cabernet, Merlot and Chardonnay, the grape varietals I've mentioned here may not have appeared on your radar screen. They're quite readily available, wonderfully delicious and worth your attention. In general, dry wines with a good amount of fruit and a balancing tang weave their way beautifully through Mexican dishes. Those that are high in alcohol and mouth-drying tannins (red wine only) make spicy dishes taste spicier.

I also love exploring the wines of Spain and Italy with Mexican food; their honest Mediterranean flavors frequently harmonize with Mexican dishes as well as wines from California and France. The Mexican wine industry, though centuries old, is small but growing energetically. Most of Mexico's best wines come from Baja California.

MARGARITAS: But what about margaritas? Don't they have a place? Yes, they do. They've certainly developed a following on this side of the Rio Grande, and of late they're becoming pretty well known to the average guy in Mexico. I'm not convinced that we have the definitive story about this libation's creation (was it for tequila-inexperienced tourists at Mexican beach resorts or for a dainty lady who didn't want to suck on a lime?), but I'm sure the original was not a slushy concoction made with artificially flavored sweet-and-sour mix.

Of all the margaritas, my current favorite is the simplest: fresh lime juice, orange liqueur and tequila, shaken with ice and served "up" in a martini glass. Like all good culinary endeavors, simple approaches work best with good ingredients. That means fresh-squeezed lime juice, decent orange liqueur and good tequila.

TEQUILA: The best tequilas are those that say "100% agave" on the label. Tequila is made from agave (*maguey* in Spanish), a member of the lily family—*not* a cactus, as many people think. It's the roasted heart of this huge aloe look-alike that is fermented and distilled; Mexican tequila-making laws allow tequila makers to add up to 49 percent sugar—usually just regular granulated sugar—to the fermenting mash and still call their product "tequila." This practice produces tequila with a fairly undistinguished flavor, whereas tequilas made from 100 percent agave, naturally, have the full agave flavor.

The same tequila-making laws regulate the aging of tequila, but age has a different effect on this distillate than it does, say, on brandy. Brandy is made from grapes, and grapes produce one crop each year. When they are distilled to clear brandy (that's what brandy looks like when it comes from the still), the stuff is pretty tasteless and hard to swallow. It needs a long time in wood casks to mellow and pick up enriching flavors. The agave plant, on the other hand, takes eight to twelve years to come to full maturity. And when it is distilled to clear tequila, its flavor is rich and full. Though tequila may benefit from a few months of age to mellow that fiery, just-distilled edge, it doesn't necessarily improve with a lot of wood aging. In fact, a long wood aging can mask tequila's unique, enticing flavor, making it taste like an odd brandy.

To serve really good tequila "neat," pour it into snifters (or shot glasses—though these don't allow you to appreciate the aroma). It's common in Mexico to have coarse salt and a bowl of cut limes on the table, for those who want to lick a little salt off the back of the hand (it gets sprinkled into that little indention between thumb and first finger), drink the tequila (usually done in a single gulp with this ritual) and then suck on a piece of lime. It may be an amusing practice when done by immoderate young men, but it's not beneficial to good tequila or long-term good health. With a predinner, bright-tasting *blanco* or *reposado,* another snifter or shot glass full of the tangy *sangrita* chaser is appropriate, offering a sort of deconstructed bloody Mary. When serving an *añejo,* my recommendation is to simply pour it into a snifter—nothing else is necessary.

Pure-and-Simple Shaken Margarita— the Classic

MARGARITA CLÁSICA

This is my favorite margarita—a strong, tangy, bright-flavored wonder that's been shaken to iciness. Though it's best served in old-fashioned 4-ounce martini glasses, those are scarce in this bigger-is-better world. So I wrote this version for today's 6-ounce glass. Just remember: They're strong.

Makes 4 generous drinks

1 cup tequila, preferably a young silver or reposado 100 percent
    agave tequila—look for widely distributed ones like
    El Tesoro, Cuervo Tradicional or Herradura, or
    search out distinctive small-production tequilas
    like Chamucos or Suave Patria
¹/₂ cup Cointreau or other orange liqueur
    (see Questions and Answers, page 351)
¹/₃ cup fresh lime juice, plus a little extra for moistening
    the rims of the glasses
A little sugar if necessary
About ¹/₃ cup coarse (kosher) salt for crusting the
    rims of the glasses
About 3 cups medium ice cubes

TRADITIONAL

In a small pitcher, combine the tequila, orange liqueur and lime juice. Taste and add more lime or a touch of sugar if desired (keep in mind that it will taste a little tangier once it's been shaken).

Spread out the salt on a small plate. Moisten the rims of four 6-ounce martini glasses with a little lime juice (if you have a cut lime, even an already-squeezed one, just moisten the rims by running it around them). Dip the rim of each glass in the salt, creating a thin, even crust all around the rim.

Pour half of the margarita mixture into a cocktail shaker, add *half* of the ice cubes and shake vigorously for about 15 seconds (this is important to achieve the perfect strength—some of the ice needs to melt into the margarita—and the right degree of frostiness). Strain into two of the prepared glasses, then repeat with the remaining margarita mixture. Relax and enjoy.

QUESTIONS AND ANSWERS FROM OUR TESTING

WHICH TEQUILAS AND ORANGE LIQUEURS ARE BEST? Tequilas that are not 100 percent agave (such as Cuervo Gold) make perfectly tasty margaritas—just ones that are not as bright and distinctly agave flavored. Though those tequilas are much more economical, 100 percent agave tequila so shines here that it's worth the investment. For orange liqueur, I rely on Cointreau for this margarita recipe because of its elegant, full flavor. The orange liqueur called Triple-Sec is much less expensive, but it has a different, brasher, less elegantly powerful flavor. *To make the classic margarita recipe with Cuervo Gold tequila and Triple Sec,* increase the lime juice to ½ cup. The additional tartness brightens these two distillates; if the result is too tart, add 1 teaspoon sugar.

CAN MARGARITAS MADE USING THIS RECIPE SIMPLY BE SERVED ON THE ROCKS? If you're without a shaker or prefer margaritas on the rocks, fill four salt-rimmed 8-ounce rocks glasses comfortably with ice, stir ½ cup water into the margarita mix and then pour over the ice. Whole ice cubes melt slowly, so it's necessary to add the ½ cup water so the mixture doesn't taste unbearably strong—think of it as compensating for all the ice that's forced to melt into the mixture as it's shaken.

CAN MARGARITAS MADE FROM THIS RECIPE BE SERVED FROZEN? Though frozen margaritas aren't my favorite, you can make the slushy version using the Cuervo Gold–Triple Sec recipe above, *omitting the water.* In batches, blend with ice.

CAN THE MARGARITA RECIPE BE MADE LESS STRONG, LESS EXPENSIVELY? A classic margarita *is* strong, perhaps stronger (and more expensive) than what you might like to offer. If that is your concern, make the classic margarita recipe with Cuervo Gold tequila and Triple Sec, increasing the lime juice to ½ cup, adding 1 tablespoon sugar and ½ cup water. This recipe doubles, triples, quadruples easily, and with the additional lime and water, you'll get an extra drink out of each batch. Note that making this version with great tequila and Cointreau yields a disappointing, watery drink.

MEXICAN CULINARY GLOSSARY

(NOTE: UNLESS OTHERWISE SPECIFIED, "MEXICAN GROCERIES"
ALWAYS REFERS TO THOSE IN THE UNITED STATES)

• • • • • • • • • • • • • • •

Achiote

USES: This orange-red seed with a hard-to-describe earthy flavor is a primary spice in the Yucatan section of Mexico, especially for pork and chicken, but in many other savory dishes as well.

FINDING: Mexican, Caribbean and other Latin American groceries, well-stocked groceries and by mail (see Sources, page 361).

CHOOSING: Intensely colored seeds have more flavor than pale ones.

STORING: Dark, cool, dry place for up to a year.

OTHER NAME: Anatto

Avocados (Aguacates)

FINDING: Most groceries, though Mexican groceries frequently offer avocados ripe and in the greatest variety.

CHOOSING: The pebbly, dark-skinned Hass avocado has a very buttery texture and doesn't discolor quickly when cut. Smooth, green-skinned Fuertes are a good option for similar reasons. Large, shiny, smooth, green-skinned Florida avocados have a much less creamy texture. Never choose avocados with soft spots, and ones that are so ripe that the pit shakes around inside. For mashing, choose avocados that give under gentle pressure; for chopping or slices, choose ones that are a little firmer.

RIPENING AND STORING: Ripen avocados in a paper bag on the counter top, until the flesh gives. Once ripe, store in the refrigerator, unwrapped, for 3 to 7 days, depending on variety (Hass may be stored longer than other varieties).

Avocado Leaves (Hojas de Aguacate)

USES: To season dishes as bay leaves would (though with a more anisey flavor), especially bean dishes; they are also steamed with meat in making certain regional barbacoas.

FINDING: Some Mexican grocery stores and by mail (see Sources, page 361).

CHOOSING: In Mexico, fresh as well as dried leaves are available, though, as with bay leaves, dried ones have excellent flavor. Dried leaves with a vibrantly olive-green color have more flavor than pale ones. Unbroken leaves are typically a sign of careful handling and higher quality. Only leaves

from the native wild Mexican avocado have a strong flavor.

STORING: Dark, cool, dry place, preferably in a sealed container, for up to a year.

Banana Leaves (Hojas de Plátano)

USES: To wrap and gently flavor foods, especially tamales and meats, for cooking.

FINDING: Mexican (and other Latin American) groceries, some Asian ones and by mail (see Sources, page 361).

CHOOSING: Frozen banana leaves are more readily available than fresh, and frozen ones add excellent flavor. Fresh or frozen, the leaves should be soft, intact and not yellow. The packages of frozen ones should not contain ice crystals, indicating repeated thawing and freezing.

STORING: Fresh ones in the refrigerator, loosely wrapped, for a week or more, frozen ones in the freezer (in the original package) for up to 3 months; defrosted, in the refrigerator for a week or more.

Beans, Dried (Frijoles)

FINDING: Most groceries, though Mexican groceries frequently have the greatest variety.

CHOOSING: Unblemished beans with the most vibrant color are typically the highest quality. Most beans in the United States are well cleaned, though ones bought from bulk bins (here or in Mexico) need to be checked for pebbles and other debris.

STORING: Dark, cool, dry place, preferably in the sealed container, for up to a year.

Cactus Paddles (Nopales)

USES: Cleaned and cooked to eat as a vegetable, frequently welcomed in relish-like salads because of its tangy crunchiness.

FINDING: Most Mexican groceries as well as some well-stocked general groceries.

CHOOSING: Vibrantly colored, firm paddles have better taste and texture than dull, limp ones. Smaller ones are more tender and have a less sticky texture than large ones.

STORING: In the refrigerator, loosely wrapped, for up to two weeks.

Achiote

Mexican Cinnamon

Epazote

Aromatic Herbs

Piloncillo

Mexican Oregano

Mexican Fresh Cheese

Mexican Chocolate

Hulled Pumpkin Seeds

Avocado Leaves

Mexican Aged Cheese

Cilantro

MEXICAN FLAVORINGS

Unhulled Pumpkin Seeds

Cazuelas and Ollas (Earthenware Cooking Pots)

FINDING: Some Mexican groceries in the United States, nearly all markets in Mexico.

CHOOSING: If they are intended for cooking rather than serving or decoration, cazuelas and ollas will not be glazed on the bottom. The glaze should cover the inside completely and there should be no cracks or chips.

USING: The glazes of most Mexican cazuelas and ollas contain lead, so, for health reasons, the pots should not be used for long cooking (2 hours or more) or storing of acidic dishes. Earthenware can crack over extremely high heat.

CURING: To cure a new cazuela or olla, rub the unglazed exterior with a cut clove of garlic, fill the pot half full with water, set over medium heat and let come to a boil (because of the slow heat conductivity, this will take at least half an hour). Boil for 30 minutes, then empty and use.

Chayote

USES: Steamed or boiled, most typically as a stew vegetable, though occasionally cooked and used in salads.

FINDING: Most well-stocked groceries; nearly all Mexican groceries.

CHOOSING: Chayotes with unblemished skin that shows no sign of shriveling are ones of highest quality. Some Mexican cooks prefer the dark-green spiny chayotes, saying their flesh is sweeter and less watery.

STORING: In the refrigerator, loosely wrapped, for a week or more.

Cheese, Fresh and Aged Mexican (Queso Fresco y Queso Añejo)

USES: These non-melting cheese varieties are typically sprinkled over beans and corn-masa snacks (antojitos such as tacos and enchiladas), as we would sprinkle Parmesan on pasta. The fresh variety is occasionally served as an appetizer (it can be marinated or flavored), and in some regions it is pan-fried and served with a sauce or salsa.

FINDING: Most Mexican groceries, some well-stocked general groceries and by mail (see Sources, page 361).

OTHER NAMES: queso ranchero, queso de metate, queso panela

CHOOSING: Fresh Mexican cheese (queso fresco) has a lighter, tangier, milkier flavor and crumbles coarsely; aged Mexican cheese has a stronger, nuttier, saltier flavor and crumbles finely. In most dishes, they can be interchanged, though cooks and diners have strong preferences. Most domestically made, fresh and aged Mexican cheeses are blander than their Mexican counterparts. Some

Mexican markets in the United States carry imported aged Mexican cheese, usually labeled by its origin, the city of Cotija.

STORING: Fresh Mexican cheese: in the refrigerator, well wrapped, for a week or so; aged Mexican cheese: in the refrigerator (or cool, dark, dry place), well wrapped, for several months.

Chiles, Fresh (Chiles Frescos)

FINDING: Most groceries, though Mexican groceries frequently have the greatest variety.

CHOOSING: Unblemished chiles that are not shriveled are the highest-quality ones.

STORING: In the refrigerator, loosely wrapped for 2 weeks or more.

Chiles, Dried (Chiles Secos)

FINDING: Most Mexican groceries, some well-stocked general groceries and by mail (see Sources, page 361).

CHOOSING: Unbroken, unblemished, pliable chiles with vibrant color typically have much better flavor than mangled-looking, pale or unevenly colored ones.

STORING: In a dark, cool, dry place, preferably in a sealed container, for up to 6 months; for longer storage, freeze in a sealed container for up to a year.

Chocolate, Mexican

FINDING: Most Mexican groceries, some well-stocked general groceries and by mail (see Sources, page 361).

CHOOSING: Each of the commercially available brands of this coarsely ground, cinnamon-infused chocolate has its followers, Ibarra apparently being the most popular (at least most widely distributed). All are quite sweet and without the full rich flavor of Mexico's best regional examples. When traveling to a region of Mexico specializing in Mexican chocolate (e.g. Oaxaca, Michoacan or Puebla), it is worth bringing some home. Chocolate is allowed through customs.

STORING: Dark, cool, dry place, well wrapped, for up to a year.

Chorizo Sausage

FINDING: Most Mexican groceries and some well-stocked general groceries.

CHOOSING: Locally made versions of this fresh sausage (it's very different from Spanish pepperoni-like chorizo) are typically better than mass-produced, widely distributed ones. The best ones have distinctive texture (not mushy), balanced spices and enough vinegar to brighten and focus the sausage's pronounced chile flavor. It should not be excessively picante.

STORING: In the refrigerator, well wrapped, for up to a week; frozen for 3 months.

Cilantro
FINDING: Most groceries.
CHOOSING: Look for bundles of this very aromatic herb with unblemished leaves that are not wilted.
STORING: In the refrigerator, in a glass with water, as you would cut flowers, loosely covered with a plastic bag; or in the refrigerator, rolled in a very lightly dampened towel, in a plastic bag.

Corn, *Nixtamal* (Half-Cooked Hominy)
USES: For stone-grinding into a paste *(masa)* for corn tortillas, tamales and other dishes; for boiling into fully cooked hominy for *pozole* (pork and hominy soup).
FINDING: Tortilla factories and the refrigerator or freezer cases of some Mexican groceries.
CHOOSING: The hull that turns yellow orange during the corn's brief cooking with calcium hydroxide should be washed off, leaving a white, pale yellow or gray-blue kernel, depending on the kernel color to begin with. If it is not, rinse the nixtamal well.
STORING: In the refrigerator, well covered, for 3 days; in the freezer for 3 months.

Corn *Masa*, Fresh
USES: To make tortillas, tamales and the base of other snacks.
FINDING: Tortilla factories and some Mexican groceries (especially on weekends).
CHOOSING: Fresh corn *masa* typically comes in two grinds, smooth and coarse. Smooth-ground *masa* is used for tortillas and practically all other dishes, except certain tamales, for which coarse-ground *masa* is preferred.
STORING: Smooth-ground *masa* makes the best tortillas when freshly ground, kept at room temperature, well covered, and used within 12 hours. Though the tortillas will be a little heavier, the *masa* may be refrigerated, well covered, for a day or two. For all other uses, it may be refrigerated for 3 days. Coarse-ground *masa* may be refrigerated, well covered, for 3 days; it may also be frozen for up to 3 months.

Corn *Masa Harina*
USES: As a substitute for fresh ground corn *masa* in making tortillas, tamales and the base of other snacks.
FINDING: Most Mexican groceries, many general groceries and by mail (see Sources, page 361).
CHOOSING: Most agree that Maseca is the brand that has the best taste and texture. Maseca also makes a coarser *masa harina* for tamales.
STORING: A cool, dry place, preferably in a sealed container, for 3 months; in the freezer for up to a year.

Corn Husks (*Hojas de Maíz, Hojas para Tamal*)
USES: Mostly for wrapping tamales, though occasionally for wrapping and gentle flavoring for meat or fish during cooking.
FINDING: Most Mexican groceries, many general groceries and by mail (see Sources, page 361).
CHOOSING: Large, unbroken, unblemished corn husks are the easiest ones to work with.
STORING: Cool, dark, dry place, preferably in a sealed container, for up to a year.

Cream, Thick (*Crema Mexicana*)
FINDING: Most Mexican groceries, well-stocked general groceries (look for *crème fraîche*), and by mail (see Sources, page 361).
CHOOSING: Read the ingredient list on cream containers in Mexican groceries: some of these *"cremas"* are no different than stabilized sour cream (which relies on pectin, gum or carrigenan for thickeners rather than culture or butter fat), lacking the texture and cooking properties of real Mexican *crema* or *crème fraîche*.
STORING: In the refrigerator, well sealed, for up to 2 weeks.

Earthenware Cooking Vessels
(see *Cazuelas* and *Ollas*)

Epazote
USES: As a pungently flavored cooked herb, typically with black beans, but also with a wide variety of sauces in all but west-central and northern Mexico.
FINDING: In some Mexican groceries, growing wild in many places, cultivated in your own garden.
CHOOSING: In Mexican groceries, *epazote* can be rather wilted. It will still be good for cooking.
STORING: Once picked, in the refrigerator, in a glass with water, as you would cut flowers, loosely covered with a plastic bag; or in the refrigerator, rolled in a very lightly dampened towel, in a plastic bag.

Herbs, Aromatic (*Hierbas de Olor*)
USES: These bundles of drying marjoram, thyme and bay are the typical broth herbs in Mexico, though they can be used individually wherever you think appropriate.
FINDING: Bundles of *hierbas de olor* are available in many Mexican groceries, partially or fully dried.
CHOOSING: Herbs that are relatively unbroken and have a vibrant color are usually more full flavored than ones that have been force-dried in bleaching sunlight or poorly stored.

Ancho

Poblano

Jalapeño

Pasilla

Serrano

"meco"

Guajillo

Mulato

SAN MARCOS
CHIPOTLE
PEPPERS
in adobo sauce
NET WT. 7 oz. (198)

Habanero

"monta"

FRESH AND DRIED CHILES

"canned"

Chipotle

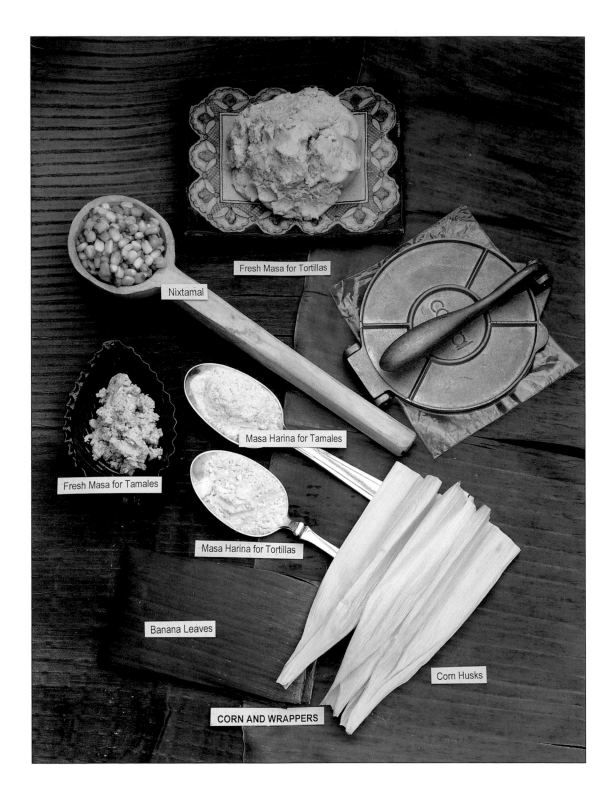

Fresh Masa for Tortillas

Nixtamal

Masa Harina for Tamales

Fresh Masa for Tamales

Masa Harina for Tortillas

Banana Leaves

Corn Husks

CORN AND WRAPPERS

STORING: In a cool, dark, dry place, preferably in a sealed container, for up 3 months.

Jícama

USES: This slightly sweet, crisp-and-crunchy root vegetable is typically peeled and eaten raw as a vegetable (usually with chile and lime, or in a salady preparation); rarely cooked.

FINDING: Most well-stocked general groceries and nearly all Mexican groceries.

CHOOSING: Smaller (no more than 1-pound) jícamas with thin, taut, unblemished skin are usually the sweetest and crispest.

STORING; In the refrigerator, unwrapped, for up to a month.

Lard, Fresh Pork (*Manteca de Puerco*)

FINDING: Meat counters in Mexican groceries; Mexican or German (or other Eastern European) butchers.

CHOOSING: Lard that is more tan than white typically has a fuller, roastier, rich pork flavor. By Mexican standards, the best-made will be solid (though a little soft) at room temperature.

STORING: In the refrigerator, well sealed, for up to 3 months; frozen for a year.

Masa (see Corn)

Masa Harina (see Corn)

Molcajete (see Mortar)

Mortar, Mexican (*Molcajete*)

FINDING: Some Mexican groceries in the United States, nearly all markets in Mexico.

CHOOSING: Dense-feeling *molcajetes* that are made of the darkest basalt, that feel extremely heavy for their size, and that have a deep, quart-size bowl (the inside of which is not too rough) are the most cherished ones in Mexico.

CURING: A new basalt *molcajete* needs to be cured by grinding dampened raw rice to a powder in the bowl several times, until the powdered rice no longer looks dirty.

Nixtamal (see Corn, *Nixtamal*)

Ollas (see *Cazuelas* and *Ollas*)

Orange, Sour (*Naranja Agria*)

USES: As a seasoning, much like lime juice, in salsas, marinades and soups.

OTHER NAMES: *Naranja* (without the *agria*) in Yucatan, Seville orange, bitter orange.

FINDING: Occasionally in Latin American, Mediterranean and some well-stocked groceries.

CHOOSING: A typically bumpy-skinned sour orange that is unblemished, not withered and feels heavy is the best-tasting, juiciest one.

STORING: In the refrigerator, loosely wrapped, for up to a month.

Oregano, Mexican

FINDING: In most Mexican groceries, in many general groceries with regular bottled herbs (the bottles may be labeled only "oregano;" fine print may reveal its Mexican origin), and by mail (see Sources, page 361).

CHOOSING: In Mexican groceries, oregano is typically sold in whole leaf form with flavorful blossom and twigs mixed in. Though its twigginess is a disadvantage, this oregano typically has the freshest, fullest flavor.

STORING: In a cool, dark, dry place, well sealed, for up to 3 months.

Piloncillo Sugar

USES: In rustic desserts, candies, syrups and beverages.

OTHER NAMES: *Panocha*.

FINDING: In most Mexican groceries and by mail (see Sources, page 361).

CHOOSING: Light-colored *piloncillo* has the lightest flavor; dark *piloncillo* has a stronger molasses tang. *Piloncillo* is always sold in a solid mass, usually in a cone, that varies in size from 3/4-ounce to over a kilo; a standard-size cone is 8 to 10 ounces.

STORING: In a cool, dark, dry place, well wrapped, for a year or more.

Plantain Bananas (*Plátanos Machos*)

USES: When green, plantains are fried for chips or cooked as a starchy stew vegetable. When ripe, they are cooked (usually fried) as a dessert or sweet ingredient in meat dishes or sauces.

FINDING: In many Mexican and well-stocked general groceries.

CHOOSING: To use plantains green, choose ones that are firm and have a green tinge to the yellow skin. To use ripe, choose plantains that are fully soft and are nearly completely black—much riper looking than regular bananas. If you buy green plantains, allow about a week for them to ripen.

STORING: At room temperature, uncovered, until ripe. Once ripe, in the refrigerator, uncovered for up to a week.

Prickly Pears (*Tunas*)

USES: This refreshing, light-flavored fruit (think strawberries and watermelon) serves as a flavoring for drinks, ices or sauces.

FINDING: In many Mexican and well-stocked general groceries.

Sour Orange

Jícama

Cactus Paddles

Ripe Plantain

Prickly Pears

Tomatillos

Squash Blossoms

Chayotes

Round Mango

Manila-type Mango

FRUITS AND VEGETABLES

CHOOSING: Prickly pears that have no blemishes and offer a little give (but are still firm) are usually the best ones. Red-fleshed and green-fleshed (usually called "white") prickly pears are the most commonly available. They look almost the same on the outside. Red prickly pears have a fuller flavor.

STORING: In the refrigerator, loosely covered, for up to a month. Prickly pears are typically harvested and sold ripe because they keep well for a long time.

Pumpkin Seeds (*Pepitas*)

FINDING: In most Mexican groceries, natural foods (bulk) stores and some well-stocked general groceries. Toasted ones are occasionally available in the snack aisle.

CHOOSING: Hulled seeds give a fuller flavor and richer texture to sauces. Unhulled seeds (usually only available in Mexican markets) give an earthier flavor. Seeds that are clean and intact, with a vibrant color, are typically the ones with the fullest, freshest flavor.

STORING: In a cool, dark, dry place, preferably in a sealed container, for up to a month; frozen for up to 6 months.

Sour Oranges (see Oranges)

Squash Blossoms (*Flores de Calabaza*)

USES: As a filling in quesadillas and other corn *masa* snack (*antojitos*), in soups and occasionally for stuffing or in sauces.

FINDING: In farmers' markets, in specialty produce stores and cultivated in your garden.

CHOOSING: Fresh-looking blossoms are the most gratifying to work with. Slightly withered ones work fine for most Mexican preparations since they are cooked.

STORING: In the refrigerator on a plate or tray, loosely covered with a plastic bag, for 3 days.

Tortilla Press (*Tortillera*)

FINDING: In many Mexican groceries, hardware stores in Mexican communities, well-stocked cookware stores and by mail (see Sources, page 361).

CHOOSING: Cast-iron presses are heavier than aluminum ones and stay put better during pressing. Ones that have at least an 8-inch diameter offer more flexibility than smaller ones. Though some traditional cooks prefer wooden presses, they can be bulky and cumbersome for occasional use.

USING: Corn tortillas are always pressed out between sheets of plastic. Tortilla presses cannot be used for flour tortillas.

Tomatillos (regionally *Tomates, Tomates Verdes, Fresadillas*)

FINDING: In nearly all Mexican groceries, in most well-stocked general groceries and in some farmer's markets.

CHOOSING: Unblemished, light lime-green tomatillos that are firm and completely fill the papery husk that covers them are the ones with the most characteristic tangy, citrusy flavor. Tomatillos are picked mature and green, so ripeness isn't an issue like it is with tomatoes.

STORING: In the refrigerator, loosely covered, for a month or more.

Tomatoes, Round and Plum (regionally *Tomates* or *Jitomates Redondos y Guajes*)

FINDING: In all groceries and in farmers' markets.

CHOOSING: Though tomatoes are available year-round in all groceries, they are rarely full of flavor unless you're buying tomatoes that have been ripened on the vine. True vine-ripe tomatoes are difficult to ship far distances, so they will typically be grown nearby or be very expensive. Plum tomatoes are meatier than round tomatoes and produce thicker cooked sauces. Round tomatoes are juicier than plum tomatoes and produce more appealing salsas. Ripeness is more important than variety, however, since plum and round tomatoes can be interchanged in recipes.

STORING: At room temperature until thoroughly ripe. If you cannot use tomatoes once they are ripe, they may be refrigerated, though cold dulls their flavor. In the refrigerator, a ripe tomato will hold for a week; because of textural changes, refrigerated tomatoes are best cooked.

Vanilla (*Vainilla*)

FINDING: Though pure vanilla extract is available widely in general groceries and specialty shops, Mexican vanilla extract is typically available only in Mexican groceries. What is sold there is often not pure and may contain coumarin, the consumption of which the FDA discourages. The best quality, coumarin-free pure Mexican vanilla extract (and Mexican vanilla beans) can be purchased in some specialty stores and by mail (see Sources, page 361).

CHOOSING: Because making an extract from vanilla beans is expensive, exacting work, vanilla extracts vary widely. Price is frequently an indicator of quality. The best extracts are remarkably different from average ones, as pure extracts are from imitation (or "doctored" pure) ones.

STORING: A cool, dark place for up to a year.

AN INTERNET GUIDE TO MAIL-ORDER SOURCES FOR MEXICAN COOKING

Besides our own site, Frontera Kitchens (www.fronterakitchens.com; (800) 509-4441), where you can find most of the ingredients and cooking equipment called for in this book, I recommend the following:

GOOD OVERALL SITE FOR MEXICAN PRODUCTS

• • • • • • • • • • • • • • • • •

The CMC Company (www.thecmccompany.com; (800) CMC-2780): Most ingredients for Mexican cooking, except fresh ones. All the dried chiles called for in this book, pure powdered chile, canned pickled chiles, *piloncillo*, Mexican chocolate, Mexican *canela* (cinnamon), Mexican oregano, Maseca brand *masa harina*, dried avocado leaves, pumpkin seeds, corn husks, achiote (annatto) seeds (look under Jamaican products), already-made (and seasoned) achiote paste, black beans, basalt mortars (*molcajetes*), griddles and tortilla presses.

OTHER GENERAL SITES

Latin Grocer (www.latingrocer.com; 877-477-2323): Among its list of general Mexican grocery items, this site has the harder-to-find Maseca brand *masa harina* for tamales, as well as Latin music and cigars.

Que Rico (www.querico.com; 800-523-1963): Not a very complete listing at present, but one that is growing.

Pacific Island Market International Grocery (www.asiamex.com; 877-274-2639): A good smattering of ingredients, including the very good El Popular brand Mexican chocolate.

THE BEST SINGLE-FOCUS SITES

Chile Today Hot Tamale (www.chiletoday.com; 800-HOT-PEPPER): Very good quality dried chiles, including all those we call for (also pure powdered chile in various flavors). Interesting web site with lots of good information.

Los Chileros de Nuevo Mexico (www.hotchilepepper.com; 505-471-6967): This somewhat cumbersome site has very good chiles to offer (keep in mind that they call pasilla chile "chile negro"); among a smattering of non-chile items, this is *the* place for southwestern dried *pozole* corn for making *pozole*.

Cheese Express (www.cheeseexpress.com; 888-530-0505): All the Mexican cheeses we call for in this book except Chihuahua.

The Mozzarella Company (www.mozzco.com; 800-798-2954): Order the *queso blanco* for a very nice, handmade *queso fresco*-type cheese; the one flavored with *epazote* and serranos is wonderful, as are all the other cheeses (including the cacciota, which is a wonderful substitute for Chihuahua).

Penzeys Spices (www.penzeys.com; 800-741-7787): This site offers some of the best spices available anywhere, including Mexican *canela* (Ceylon "true" cinnamon), achiote (annatto) seeds, Mexican oregano, and a smattering of dried chiles and powdered chiles.

King Arthur Flour (www.kingarthurflour.com; 800-827-6836): A very cool site offering Nielsen-Massey Mexican vanilla—the best of the best.

Frieda's Finest (www.friedas.com; 714-826-6100): Of the few vegetables-by-mail sites, this is the only one with special enough offerings to tempt me. But you pay dearly for those banana leaves, prickly pears (they call them cactus pears), tomatillos (including the tiny, intensely flavored *tomate milpero*), cactus paddles, jícama, plantains and chayote. They also have a good selection of fresh chiles (and a few dried ones), plus Mexican sugar (*piloncillo*).

Sur La Table (www.surlatable.com; 800-243-0852): Tortilla presses, griddles and lime squeezers help make the meal, but many harmonious serving pieces are offered as well.

A Smattering of Sites for Gardeners

Native Seeds/SEARCH (www.nativeseeds.org; 520-622-5561): This site will open your eyes to the little known varieties that have been traditionally eaten in the American southwest and Mexico for eons, ranging from from greens, chiles and herbs to corn, beans and squash; pay attention to the climate each seed it best suited for. They also proffer wonderfully sturdy and attractive Mexican tortilla baskets and wooden cooking implements.

Seeds of Change (www.seedsofchange.com; 888-762-7333): This is one of my favorite sites for organic seeds, offering a general listing. Do notice the magenta spreen lambs quarters (a relative of the popular Mexican all-green lambs quarters called *quelites*), purslane (*verdolagas*), *epazote*, tomatillos, tomatoes, chiles.

Johnny's (www.johnnyseeds.com; 207-437-9294): A good source for Mexican oregano and *epazote* seeds, as well as a wide variety of greens, tomatoes, tomatillos and squash (including the pale zucchini-like magda that's similar to what's grown in Mexico).

BIBLIOGRAPHY

MEXICO'S BEST COOKBOOKS: MY FAVORITE BAKER'S DOZEN

•·•·•·•·•·•··•···•·•·•·•··•··•··•·•··•·

Almazán, María Teresa de la Rosa de. *Gastronomía mexiquense*. México: Gobierno del Estado de México, 1987.

Caraza Campos, Laura B. de, and Georgina Luna Parra. *Guías gastronómicas méxico desconocido*. México, D.F.: Editorial Jilguero, S.A. de C.V., 1993-1995.

Carbia, María A. de. *México en la cocina de Marichú*. 3rd ed. México, D.F.: Editorial Época, S.A., 1969.

De'Angeli, Alicia Gironella and Jorge. *El gran libro de la cocina mexicana*. México, D.F.: Ediciones Larousse, 1980.

Fernández, Beatriz L., María Yani and Margarita Zafiro. *. . . y la comida se hizo . . . .* México, D.F.: ISSSTE/Trillas, 1984-1988.

Lara, Silvia Luz Carillo. *Cocina yucateca traditional*. México, D.F.: Editorial Diana, S.A. de C.V., 1994.

Muñoz Zurita, Ricardo. *Verde en la cocina mexicana*. México, D.F.: La Fundación Hérdez, AC, 1999.

Quintana, Patricia. *La cocina de los angeles*. Puebla: Promotores Voluntarios Del Hospital Para El Niño Poblano, A.C., 1992.

Ramos Espinosa, Virginia. *Los mejores platillos mexicanos*. México, D.F.: Editorial Diana, S.A. de C.V., 1976.

Stoopen, María, and Ana Laura Delgado. *La cocina veracruzana*. Veracruz: Gobierno del Estado de Veracruz, 1992.

Vásquez Colmenares, Ana María Guzmán de. *Tradiciones gastronómicas oaxaqueñas*. Oaxaca: Comité Organizador del CDL Aniversario, 1982.

Velázquez de León, Josefina. *Platillos regionales de la República Mexicana*. México, D.F.: Editorial de la Compañia Nacional de Subsistencias Populares, 1971.

Voluntariado Nacional. *Comida familiar en los estados de la República*. Mexico, D.F.: Banco Nacional de Crédito Rural, S.N.C., 1987-1988.

INDEX

•♦·•♦•♦♦•♦♦♦•

PAGE NUMBERS IN *ITALICS* REFER TO ILLUSTRATIONS OF RECIPES.

seafood:
  lime-marinated, 11–21
  in *mojo de ajo*, 256–65
  stew, Mexican, 157–63
seared:
  fish fillets in *escabeche*, 249–50
  steak tacos with blistered
    serranos and browned onions,
    98–99
  serranos, blistered, seared steak
    tacos with browned onions
    and, 98–99
short ribs, beef, with tomatoes,
  roasted poblanos and herbs,
  278–79
shredded beef, classic, *gorditas*
  (corn *masa* pockets) with,
  42–44, 45
shrimp:
  ceviche "cocktail," 13,16–17
  in Mexican seafood stew,
    159–60
  quick-fried, with sweet toasty
    garlic, 258–59, 263
  in simple green almond sauce,
    220–21
  stew, spicy grilled, 161–62
  skirt steak tacos, grilled, with roast-
    ed poblano *rajas*, 91, 92–93
slow-cooked meats, pit-style (*barbacoa*), 293–304
slow-roasted *achiote* pork in banana
  leaves, 298–300, 301
smoked salmon–black bean tostaditas, 66–67
smoky:
  chipotle beans with wilted
    spinach and *masa* "gnocchi,"
    188–89, 190
  chipotle chile, melted mozzarel-
    la casserole with mushrooms
    and, 28–29
  tomato-chile salsa, garlicky
    grilled portobello mushrooms
    with, 94–95
snack, street, cucumber, mango
  and jícama, 341, 344
sopa de tortilla:
  *con chile pasilla, queso fresco y
    aguacate*, 152–53
  *y hongos con chile chipotle y queso
    de cabra*, 154–55
sopes (corn *masa* boats), 31–39
  crispy potato, with salsa, goat
    cheese and herb salad, 36–37,
    45
  perfectly simple, 33–34

sopes:
  *de papa con salsa, queso de cabra
    y ensalada de hierbas*, 36–37
  sencillos, 33–34
soup, braising-juice, red chile
  lamb, goat or chicken, pit
  style—with, 295–97
soup, chicken, 140–49
  basic broth, 148
  meal-in-a-bowl ranch-style,
    142–43
  spicy grilled, with summer
    vegetables, 145, 146–47
  squash blossom, 144
soup, tortilla, 150–56
  mushroom-studded, with
    chipotle chiles and goat
    cheese, 154–55
  with pasilla chile, fresh cheese
    and avocado, 152–53
spicy:
  chipotle pork tacos with sun-
    dried tomato salsa, 102–3
  grilled chicken soup with sum-
    mer vegetables, 145, 146–47
  grilled fish with heirloom
    tomato salsa, 288–89
  grilled shrimp stew, 161–62
  grilled tuna with heirloom
    tomato salsa, 288–89
spinach:
  rice with roasted poblano, fresh
    cheese and, 180–81
  wilted, smoky chipotle beans
    with *masa* "gnocchi," 188–89,
    190
spirited *cajeta*, 327
squash blossom:
  chicken soup, 144
  quesadillas, griddle-baked, 53,
    56–57
squid, in Mexican seafood stew,
  159–60
steak:
  flank, broiled, with tomato-
    poblano salsa, 280–81
  flank, grilled, with tomato-
    poblano salsa, 281
  Mexican-style grilled (*carne
    asada*), 283–92
  seared, tacos with blistered ser-
    ranos and browned onions,
    98–99
  skirt, tacos grilled, with roasted
    poblano *rajas*, 91, 92–93
stew:
  Mexican seafood, 157–63

stew (*cont.*)
  pork and hominy (*posole*),
    164–71
  red pork and hominy, 166–68,
    169
  shrimp, spicy grilled, 161–62
street-style red chile enchiladas,
  122–23
streusel cake, Mexican chocolate,
  334–35, 336
sugar syrup, Mexican raw, 317
summer vegetables, spicy grilled
  chicken soup with, 145,
  146–47
sun-dried tomato salsa, spicy
  chipotle pork tacos with, 102–3
sweet tamales with pineapple and
  raisins, 82–84
syrup, Mexican raw sugar, 317

T
tacos:
  chipotle chicken salad, 114
  grilled skirt steak, with roasted
    poblano *rajas*, 91, 92–93
  guajillo-spiked pork-and-pota-
    toes, 112–13
  home-style, with casserole fill-
    ings, 108–17
  Mexican-style zucchini, 110–11
  potato-chorizo, with simple avo-
    cado salsa, 96–97
  seared steak, with blistered ser-
    ranos and browned onions,
    98–99
  spicy chipotle pork, with sun-
    dried tomato salsa, 102–3
  taquería, with grilled and
    griddled fillings, 89–107
tacos:
  de arrachera al carbón con rajas,
    91, 92–93
  de bistec con chiles torreados,
    98–99
  de calabacitas a la mexicana, 110–11
  de cazuela, 108–17
  *de papas con chorizo y salsa de
    aguacate*, 96–97
  de pollo en ensalada enchipotlada,
    114
  *de puerco enchipotlado con salsa
    de jitomate pasado*, 102–3
  de puerco y papas al guajillo,
    112–13
tamales, 71–88
  casserole-style zucchini, 85–86
  green chile chicken, 74–76